WOMEN'S WORK

WOMEN'S WORK

Development and the Division of Labor by Gender

Eleanor Leacock
Helen I. Safa
& Contributors

BERGIN & GARVEY PUBLISHERS, INC.
MASSACHUSETTS

First published in 1986 by
Bergin & Garvey Publishers, Inc.
670 Amherst Road
South Hadley, MA 01075

Earlier versions of the Introduction, chapters 2, 4, 5, 8, 9, 11, 13, and 14, and the Postscript, appeared in *Signs,* vol. 7, no. 2, Winter 1981. © 1981 by The University of Chicago. An earlier version of chapter 1 appeared in *Comparative Studies in Society and History,* vol. 20, no. 3, 1978.

PHOTO CREDITS: Cover photo (paperback edition), frontispiece, and p. xiv, Paul Doughty, University of Florida; p. viii, S. Shashahani; p. 72, Diane Bell; p. 136, OEF International.

6789   987654321

Library of Congress Cataloging-in-Publication Data

Main entry under title:

Women's work.

   Bibliography: p.
   Includes index.
   1. Sexual division of labor—Congresses.   2. Women—
Employment—Congresses.   3. Women in rural development—
Congresses.   I. Leacock, Eleanor Burke, 1922–
II. Safa, Helen Icken.
HD6060.6.W66   1986   305.4'3   85-26674
ISBN 0-89789-035-3
ISBN 0-89789-036-1 (pbk.)

Printed in the United States of America

Contents

PART I
The Gender Division of Labor and the Stages of Industrial Capitalism

Preface

This book is based on a conference on the Sexual Division of Labor, Development, and Women's Status, sponsored by the Wenner-Gren Foundation for Anthropological Research and held at Burg Wartenstein, Austria. After all the books that have focused on women during the past decade, one may well ask, Why yet another book dealing with the division of labor by gender? What can this topic contribute to the seemingly endless debate over the sources of gender inequality or to discussions of strategies for combating women's subordination? And what is the topic's relevance to pragmatic concerns such as equality in pay, adequate child care, and family nutrition, which have a compelling immediacy for women?

Since the division of labor by gender is a cultural universal, we saw a book on the topic as an opportunity to integrate what have been essentially separate discourses: the debate about the sources of gender inequality and the discussion of the impact of development on women's status. By bringing together scholars who have examined the origins of female subordination and the status of women in egalitarian societies and others who have raised issues dealing with women and development, this book, we felt, would yield new insights into important questions regarding development policies and women's status today. In order to compare the development process in Europe with that in contemporary Third-World countries, we also added to the discussion some of the important research now being done on changing forms of women's labor in Europe during the transition from an agrarian to an urban, industrial society.

We approached the Wenner-Gren Foundation for Anthropological Research about a symposium on development and the division of labor by gender, because it seemed that the small intimate setting of the Wenner-Gren conference center at Burg Wartenstein would be ideal for enabling a group of scholars to discuss at length three topics: (1) historical evolutionary changes in the structure of the gender division of labor; (2) the transition from peasant to industrial society, and the significance that the transformation from household to factory production had for the gender division of labor and women's

ix

status; and (3) changes in the gender division of labor in contemporary peasant and other nonindustrial societies brought about by their increasing incorporation into an international market economy.

The setting of Burg Wartenstein was indeed ideal. It was the first time that the Wenner-Gren Foundation had hosted an all-female symposium, a reflection of the fact that the leading contemporary research on the gender division of labor and development has been done by women. The fields of anthropology, economics, history, and sociology were all represented. Participants from Third-World countries in Asia, Africa, and Latin America, as well as from Australia, Europe, and the United States, spent a week in intensive discussion. The increasing number of prominent scholars in Third-World countries who are turning their attention to women's issues speaks to the growth and significance of the women's movement throughout the world.

All but three of the participants at Burg Wartenstein have contributed chapters to this book. A chapter by Carmen Diana Deere and Magdalena Leon de Leal on "Peasant Production, Proletarianization, and the Sexual Division of Labor in the Andes" has been published elsewhere (Benería 1983). We thank Verena Stolcke Martinez-Alier and Kate Young for their participation at the conference and regret that they were not able to find the time to prepare their papers for publication here. Wanda Minge was also too busy with other commitments to work on her chapter, but we have included an earlier work of hers on the important subject of peasant-to-worker transition in Europe.

In sum, the chapters in this book deal with the issue of gender inequality both at the family or household level and at the level of the community or society—or in what have been called the private and public domains. Much of the debate among feminists over whether patriarchy or capitalism is the primary contemporary basis for women's subordination has focused on which domain is more important. To a considerable extent, those who stress the domestic domain center on patriarchy, while those concerned with the public domain emphasize capitalism. Somewhat differing views were represented at the conference and the following chapters do not reflect complete agreement. However, all agreed on the inseparable link between the gender division of labor at the household level and such a division at the societal level, demonstrating that no strategy of change confined to one level alone can succeed in eradicating female subordination, even under socialism. It is also clear that capitalism builds upon and reinforces the sexual inequalities engendered by patriarchy in those preindustrial societies where private property and commodity production have already led to stratification and the formation of male-centered households.

An evolutionary perspective on the gender division of labor thus enables one to see that the relation between the domestic and public domains is not static but instead is highly responsive to—indeed, is a central part of—changes in the relations of production as a whole. As one moves from formerly egalitarian societies such as those of the Australian Aborigines to peasant societies, and finally to industrial societies based on wage labor, one sees a split between the two domains developing and sharpening, with women increasingly confined to the domestic sphere. However, the chapters in this volume also show that the incorporation of women into wage labor is no panacea if the gender division of labor at the household level remains the same, burdening women with the "double day." With rich ethnographic detail, the authors presented here make the point that the productive and reproductive roles of women cannot be separated, that the division into domestic and public domains is artificial, and that the debate about one domain over the other is futile.

Eight of the following chapters, as well as the Introduction and the Postscript, were published in a special issue of *Signs* (vol. 7, no. 2, 1981), although they all have been revised for the present book. We wish to thank *Signs* for permission to reprint this material, and to thank Barbara Gelpi and the other editors of *Signs* for their helpful editorial assistance.

We also wish to express our deep gratitude to Lita Osmundsen, Director of Research at the Wenner-Gren Foundation, and to her staff for their generous help in the planning of the conference and for their financial support in the preparation and publication of the results. Burg Wartenstein closed its doors as a scholarly retreat in 1980, but it remains an important landmark for all those who had the opportunity to enjoy its tradition of lively intellectual debate carried on in an atmosphere of warm hospitality. This book is one small tribute to the fruitful international scholarly exchange which the Wenner-Gren Foundation has sought to promote.

ELEANOR LEACOCK
Department of Anthropology
The City College
City University of New York

HELEN I. SAFA
Director, Center for Latin American Studies
University of Florida

WOMEN'S WORK

Introduction

MARÍA PATRICIA FERNÁNDEZ KELLY

More than a decade has elapsed since the celebration of International Women's Year in Mexico City in 1975, and it has been almost two centuries since Mary Wollstonecrafts's publication of *A Vindication of the Rights of Women* in London in 1792. The two events are connected by the persistence of interest on the part of feminists and social thinkers about the condition of women in capitalist societies. Contemporary feminism has added few new ideas to Wollstonecraft's vision of a just society where women would share equally the responsibilities and rewards of men. In the same vein, contemporary scholarship about women's economic and political participation has expounded upon but not altered the concerns that motivated the historic meeting in Mexico City. As researchers and social scientists we continue to try to understand the roots of gender inequality in a world made increasingly complex by the advent of business conglomerates, international capital investments, and advanced technology.

The contributions to this volume are at the forefront of this continuing effort. They include discussions and empirical data that are the result of systematic research underscoring gender as a variable with an analytical value similar to that of ethnicity and class. The main themes addressed are (1) the changing structure of the division of labor by gender in the context of social evolution, including the impact of economic development on women's work and status; and (2) the effects that the transition from peasant to industrial society—involving the passage from household to factory production—had upon both the sexual division of labor and women's social status.

Among the substantive questions that follow from these general topics are, What have been the major factors leading to changes in the division of labor throughout human history? How have autonomous historical processes been altered by the impact of capitalist development and the incorporation of subsistence economies into modern market economies? In what areas of socioeconomic organization has sexual stratification increased or diminished,

An earlier version of this chapter appeared in *Signs,* vol. 7, no. 2, Winter 1981. © 1981 by The University of Chicago.

and how does this key issue relate to the definition of "development"? What happens to the gender division of labor when households cease to function as productive units? Are women increasingly relegated to the domestic sphere in all cases? Do they achieve greater personal autonomy and authority through their participation in wage labor? How do women's situations vary with class, cultural context, and types of work performed?

The chapters in this volume suggest that a narrow definition of development confounds rather than elucidates women's role in society. Development cannot be defined in purely economic terms; it also has political, social, and ideological ramifications. Moreover, development interpreted broadly *should* include an expansion of choices, more equitable access to the resources that make life with dignity possible, and greater participation for all peoples—independently of gender, ethnicity, or race—in the decision-making processes that affect them.

Historically, industrialization and modernization have not been isolated forces. Rather, they have been, respectively, the objective and ideological counterparts of capitalist development. In peripheral and semiperipheral nations, capitalist investments have accentuated dependency on the highly industrialized core nations. In nineteenth century Europe (and later in other parts of the world) the transition from a subsistence to a market economy based on the use of wage labor caused a net loss of autonomy for kin-based groups and households. Individuals became more dependent on external political, economic, and ideological forces. A profound contradiction resulted from the increasing individuation of the labor force and the need to maintain collective mechanisms for the reproduction of the working class through preexisting but constantly evolving patterns of family, household, and kinship organization. In other words, the advance of capitalism created a dynamic opposition between productive and reproductive spheres.

Wanda Minge (ch. 1) illustrates this point from her work on the changes experienced by peasants as a result of industrialization in nineteenth-century and contemporary Europe. The commercialization of agriculture and the so-called enclosure movement brought about the pauperization of the English peasantry. The modern industrial family was born with the creation of a landless population that had no choice but to sell labor to the entrepreneurial class. Peasant families were forced to adopt survival strategies to maximize meager resources and access to income. Cottage industries manufacturing wool and cotton, for example, existed side by side with mills and factories. For a long time families competed with the new factories by relying on the labor provided by mothers and children.

During the early stages of industrialization this affected fertility rates. Families did not restrict the number of their offspring, as it was expected that every child would start working as early as the age of five or six. Once the delicate balance between increased family labor and access to subsistence income had been upset, increasing numbers of women and children left their homes to work in mills as apprentices and wage laborers. This had dramatic consequences. Mothers unable to care for their children were forced to leave them in the care of wet nurses or foundling hospitals. Infant mortality probably increased. An unprecedented level of exploitation of child labor set in. Gradually, households lost most of their directly productive functions, retaining only reproductive ones. A new ideology as to the purpose and rationale of family life emerged. New concepts of childhood and femininity were born. Over time, the demands of workers and protective legislation contributed to the confinement of women and children to the household.

The nineteenth century witnessed the final bifurcation of home and workplace as well as the systematic exclusion of women from public political activities. Some dimensions of this phenomenon are examined by Louise Tilly in a study of women's collective action during the process of proletarianization in nineteenth-century France. She notes that political history often ignores women (and men) who have no formal political roles. Thus, to remember that most women's political action has taken place outside the public sphere is to expand our definitions beyond the narrow terms of conventional wisdom.

In describing the participation of women in the economic struggles of nineteenth-century France, Tilly (ch. 2) draws intriguing parallels with the contemporary world. For example, the disparity in women's political rights restricted them to indirect and informal access to political influence. Women's "civil death," that is, the submersion of their juridical being under that of their father, husband, or other male relative, furthered dependence on the protection and support of men. Nevertheless, in reviewing the March on Versailles of October 1789, Tilly notes that women were represented in uncommon numbers. Why? Because women were frequently involved in food riots. It was they who had to make scarce income stretch to buy food when prices rose. Not surprisingly, food riots usually took place in the chief gathering place of women: the marketplace, where grain was moved and bread was sold. Thus, it was women who resorted to food riots, whereas men—who by the nineteenth century formed the majority of the industrial workers in France—expressed themselves politically through strikes. Food was the issue in both cases, but men's struggles over food were subsumed by struggles over wages. To the extent that women worked in households and could not express themselves through institutionalized channels such as strikes, their collective responses were aimed primarily at the lowering of food prices and at the achievement of a more equitable distribution rather than at higher wages alone.

The relationship between class and gender is taken up by Leith Mullings (ch. 3) in a study of nineteenth-century Afro-American families in the United States. She raises the question of the extent to which generalizations can be made about women without qualifications as to racial, ethnic, and class background. Access to wage employment may be considered a legitimate claim by Euro-American women confined to the drudgery of unpaid domestic labor, but for Afro-American women deprived of the choice to become home-makers, the same claim is trivial.

Slavery first, and afterwards segregation into menial, low-paying occupations, sharply limited the incorporation of Afro-American women into mainstream U.S. society. Nevertheless, the same factors did not reduce their attempts at restoring integrity to their fragmented personal and family lives. Throughout history Afro-American women have resorted to informal networks, reciprocity, and fictive kinship to cope with the demands of a society where gender inequality is compounded by class and race disparities. The uniqueness of their experience forces us to reconsider conventional definitions of femininity, family life, marriage, and motherhood.

The growing disparity between the developed and underdeveloped worlds, as well as the persistence of wage differentials between men and women, are the concerns underlying the chapter by Helen Safa (ch. 4). She describes the expansion during the last two decades of a new form of multinational enterprise, characterized primarily by the manufacture of exports in the less developed countries.

This phenomenon is based on the advantages afforded to capital by large international wage differentials. Multinational corporations involved in the production of electronics goods and apparel, as well as other light industries, have been at the forefront of this growing tendency in international capital investment. Relocation policies have affected the economies of highly developed countries like the United States and also those of developing countries.

In core countries the flight of industry has often resulted in growing unemployment among women and minorities employed in unskilled and semi-skilled assembly work. In developing countries, women's industrial employment of the kind described by Safa has been linked to high levels of unemployment and underemployment: it tends to reduce the bargaining capacity of the working class as a whole, maintain inadequate working conditions and low wages, and alter family composition and household structure.

Thus, while export processing may serve to integrate women into the development process by providing them with industrial employment, it also increases their vulnerability to exploitation. Here in a nutshell is the paradox confronted by many peripheral and semiperipheral nations. The wage levels, working conditions, stability, and possibilities for occupational mobility offered by this type of industrial employment could simply amount to a new kind of exploitation of Third-World women. Social-scientific research and a constant assessment of past experiences must lead to alternatives that produce new paths of development, not the well-worn ones created by the subordination of women and other vulnerable social groups.

The division of labor by gender has different meanings depending on its cultural and social contexts. The activities that women perform are variously defined in terms of both content and the social value attached to them. It cannot be said that women's labor is intrinsically inferior to that of men or that it is universally judged to be so. Diane Bell (ch. 5) provides a particularly dramatic example of the changes occurring in women's status after capitalist penetration. In her study of Aboriginal women's love rituals in central Australia, she notes that the sexual politics permeating Aboriginal societies call for a balance: male assertion of control and authority set against female independence and solidarity. In the constant creation of ritual and in the themes, imagery, symbolism, and structure of the love rituals themselves, women assert their separateness. The maintenance of strong cultural boundaries around their world reinforces their power base. As she explored women's mythologies, Bell found that Aboriginal women represent their world as self-contained, known, and secure. In implementing the responsibilties conferred upon them by the culture, women engage in work that is distinctively their own. In the past this ensured that they would be recognized as full members of their society. However, under the process of impoverishment and marginalization that has followed capitalist development in Australia, women's culture has lost much of its meaning; it has been trivialized by external forces. Although it is stubbornly maintained as a source of precarious identity, it no longer gives women status as full members of their society.

Turning to horticultural society, Annette Weiner's provocative findings (ch. 6) show the complexity of economic behavior among stateless groups. Building upon information obtained in Samoa and the Trobriand islands, she notes that the tendency on the part of Western scholars to interpret women's social status in terms of their participation in male-dominated activities has clouded the understanding of women's important role in horticultural societies.

Examining empirical evidence, Weiner notes that in the Trobriands wealth manufactured by women, in the form of banana bundles and fiber skirts, symbolizes the reproduction and regeneration of descent and kinship, fundamental tools for maintaining social stability and providing a base for the evolution of higher forms of political expression. The reproduction and regeneration of social relations requires constant affirmation and negotiation, and this is achieved through transactions involving the wealth created by women. The domains of male and female control and power remain separate. Yet these domains tend to complement rather than oppose each other. Although the male domain achieves levels of political prominence highly visible to Western observers and denied to women, in actual power relations it remains insecure and even fragmentary. It is women and their production (a combination of biological, economic, and symbolic functions) that provide the essential underpinnings for the regeneration and perpetuation of the male domain.

In looking at evidence collected among the sedentarized Mamasani pastoral nomads of Iran, Soheila Shashahani (ch. 7) concludes that the effects of development on the status of women have been negative. Therefore it is hazardous to condemn tradition and uphold the apparent freedom of choice espoused by Western and upper-class Iranian women. She argues that while certain traditional Iranian cultural traits have been used to prepare the ground for modernization, the political context in which questions relating to women have been posed should not be overlooked. For instance, the way in which the question of women was used by the recently deposed shah's regime cannot be used as a starting point for critical research about women without running the risk of falling prey to propaganda.

With respect to the Yoruba of Nigeria, Simi Afonja (ch. 8) maintains that preexisting forms of male domination were exacerbated by the penetration of capitalist development and Western mores. Paradoxically, these changes have afforded women some precarious advantages while at the same time creating many new dilemmas. Although the actual effect of Western economic patterns and mores upon developing nations remains a controversial issue, two points are clear. First, women's status and participation in economic and political affairs cannot be fully appreciated without consideration of the overall socio-economic reality of a nation or country. Second, to bolster their opposition to Western and imperialistic influences, nationalist struggles often make use of traditional ideologies that are deleterious to women's status. In short, where women are concerned, socioeconomic development frequently confronts irreconcilable alternatives.

Cultural norms sanctioning women's confinement to the household are more than ideological constructions. They express an objective reality in which domestic work is a mechanism subsidizing accumulation. Excluded from the realm of remunerated work, large groups of women have historically been transformed at various times into reserves of cheap labor. Paradoxically, women are subordinated, not because their work is socially inferior or unimportant, but precisely because of its importance. Women's labor both in production and in reproduction, is fundamental to the maintenance of economic and political systems.

Lourdes Benería and Gita Sen's analysis (ch. 9) of Ester Boserup's classic study, *Women's Role in Economic Development,* touches upon central questions in the ongoing debate over women's gains and losses under capitalism. While underscoring the merits of Boserup's pioneering work, the authors also point to its major limitations.

Boserup provided an insightful and provocative assortment of empirical and descriptive data regarding the gender division of labor. Although gender division is a feature of all known societies, the content of male and female social activities varies from case to case. With this perception, Boserup disproved the "dubious generalization" that attributes to men the provision of food in most communities, since women too have been and are food providers in many areas of the world. She also noted the impact that different agricultural methods characteristic of different geographical areas have upon the determination of gender-specific activities and spheres of social action. With this she made a significant departure from cultural and "naturalistic" explanations emphasizing instead the material circumstances confronted by men and women.

Boserup was less successful, however, when explaining the accentuation of women's economic and political subordination that can result from development. She correctly perceived the negative effects that colonialism and the penetration of capitalism into subsistence economies have often had on women. But she tacitly regarded them as anomalies that could be corrected through the implementation of specialized programs—programs presumably based on the kind of incisive research that she herself had carried out. This presupposition obviated the need for a profound modification of the productive system as a whole. As a consequence, Boserup's work expressed considerable hope that an emphasis on the education and training of women would enable them to prosper by attaining more equitable participation in development. In short, the historical legacy of colonialism could be reversed. Unfortunately, the experience of the last two decades has failed to validate this optimistic view. Recent writings point not only to an increase in the gap between men's and women's earnings throughout the world but also to a deterioration of women's educational status.

At the root of Boserup's limited perspective lies her unquestioning acceptance of a unique model of development: that of capitalist economies. Because Boserup did not distinguish between the internal logic of the productive system as a whole and the ideology of modernization, her work could only lead to reformist suggestions and somewhat simplistic explanations of women's social subordination. Benería and Sen suggest that a comprehensive analysis must incorporate Boserup's insights into an understanding of capital accumulation and expansion, including a study of gender and class. For example, Boserup's work cannot convincingly explain wage differentials between men and women, particularly when both sexes perform similar jobs. These can be understood only by setting aside neoclassical economic criteria and studying women's reproductive as well as their productive functions. In other words, to understand the dilemmas that development policies have brought about, one must assess the position of women both within the household and in the labor market.

The chapters that follow elaborate on a similar set of problems. Mona Hammam (ch. 10) provides case studies from the Islamic world. She notes that the extent to which Arab women are drawn into the wage-labor market cannot be considered a result of culture or a response to the seemingly inviolable laws and traditions of Islam. Rather, it reflects a varied interplay of social and economic forces, at the base of which lies the sexual division of labor within the household. In North Yemen, for example, it is estimated that in the average-sized family of six to eight persons the labor of two women is required to carry out the minimum household chores necessary for subsistence: fetching water, caring for livestock, gathering fuel, etc. In this case, the sexual division of labor within the household effectively bars women from access to regular wage employment, for only a household with three or four women can afford to release one for outside labor. Thus, cultural norms sanctioning women's confinement to the household are not idle ideological contructs. Rather, they express a reality in which unpaid domestic labor helps to subsidize production.

One of the consequences of the creation of a wage-labor market is that it undermines the preexisting division of labor within the household, which in subsistence economies allocates work to almost all family members. When the household is compelled to release one of its members to the wage-labor market, the family's productive relations must be reorganized, in terms of both task reallocation and labor time expended in each task. This affects migratory flows, the size of households, and the distribution of various chores on the basis of gender. Although culture undoubtedly has a measure of autonomy, it cannot alone explain the sexual division of labor.

Lourdes Arizpe and Josefina Aranda (ch. 11) focus on the strawberry agroindustry in Zamora and Jacona, Mexico, as an example of how gender divisions of labor are created. In seeking an explanation for the predominance of women in this industry they bypass notions of manual dexterity and other presumably feminine characteristics to conclude (1) that agroindustry in Zamora cannot compete with that of the United States in attracting migrant male labor; (2) that the region has a large population of young women who have very few alternatives for work and who at the same time are limited by strong cultural sanctions from migrating; and (3) that women will work for much less than the minimum wage and under conditions of constantly fluctuating schedules and work days. Culture intervenes by defining women's work as temporary and as a mechanism for supplementing family earnings. Agroindustrial capitalists use the social and cultural characteristics of the region (for example, high demographic growth, traditional cultural values that assign a subordinate role to women, the prevailing family structure, and local patterns of consumption) to lower production costs.

In her study of the gender division of labor in the Philippines, Elizabeth Eviota (ch. 12) provides a hard-hitting example of the extremes to which narrow development policies can lead. The expansion of a market economy and the integration of the Philippines into the international system of production have brought about a film of prosperity. At the same time the erosion of traditional forms of subsistence fishing and agriculture, and the movement of people through migration or forced relocation, have vastly increased inequalities of income and have lowered the majority vs. living standards. The state sanctioned and reinforced this process, by resorting to overt military rule and frequent repression. The Philippines provides an example of two realities, one captured by aggregate statistical data reflecting growth and one captured by first-hand studies of poverty-stricken populations showing the dismal effects of proletarianization and income maldistribution. Eviota concludes that the price of misguided development policies is an aggravation of class and gender inequalities.

Aline Wong (ch. 13) presents evidence on the impact of development on the sexual division of labor and women's status in Singapore. She notes that as a result of rapid industrialization based on the creation of a strong export platform, Singapore has achieved double-digit rates of growth, placing itself among middle-income countries by World Bank criteria. Industrialization and sustained economic growth have not only changed the structure of the economy and raised the living standard of the population, but have also produced very important consequences for the structure of the society. While some of these social and economic changes have benefited women, others' effects are questionable. Development in Singapore has minimally altered the sexual division of labor in the society. Even though women are now better educated and bear fewer children, they have not been fully integrated into the development process. Wong concludes that because of persistent sex inequalities and wage differentials, the earnings of working-class women are never sufficient to raise their families' status. The point is clear: industrial development of the kind studied by Wong tends to solidify rather than diminish social-class distinctions.

A book exploring the effects of capitalist development on women would not be complete without some examination of alternative economic and political strategies being carried out at present. Elisabeth Croll (ch. 14) does precisely that by evaluating the changes that have affected peasant women in four planned socialist economies—the Soviet Union, China, Cuba, and Tanzania. Although there are national variations, socialism has brought about improvements in the literacy and educational levels of women, and an awareness of the specific problems they confront as a result of their particular position in the productive and reproductive spheres.

Socialist governments have emphasized women's potential as legitimate participants in the remunerated labor force. Efforts have been made to increase women's educational and vocational levels and to provide them with information and services to regulate their fertility. In addition, socialist theory is concerned about the ways in which legal mechanisms can be developed that will enable women to gain access to land and other resources, as well as to achieve an equal standing with men in political decision making.

However, these purposes have met with limited success. In the four countries studied by Croll, male supremacy and the economic and political legacy of inequality have combined in various ways against women. Although they may have acquired greater representation as paid workers and perhaps have achieved consequent economic autonomy, women continue to shoulder the responsibilities of child rearing and household upkeep; the "double shift" persists.

In part this situation results from a common problem faced by socialist governments: accumulation and allocation of the capital needed to finance reproductive activities outside the home. Croll suggests that while there are ideological and cultural impediments to the achievement of this goal, the most important barriers are economic. The socialization of reproductive activities (a large portion of which are carried out in the household) is simply an enormously expensive task—one that is particularly difficult at the stage of development of the countries involved. Although the socialization of housework has not been achieved, it is clear that in planned economies the accumulation of capital for state expenditure may be in women's long-term interest.

In lieu of major radical reforms like the one just mentioned, emphasis in the four countries has been directed toward a more equitable distribution of household chores between men and women and toward the formation of separate women's organizations. The latter, although a matter of revolutionary expedience, are also signs of an inequality that may gradually disappear as these societies consolidate their economic and political position in the international context.

In sum, this book exemplifies the use of solid intellectual analysis to clarify the multifaceted participation of women in social development. The contributions are part of an ongoing effort to dispel serious misconceptions in orthodox social science. It is to be hoped that the valuable insights and knowledge they offer will be appreciated both by those who have made the study of gender their specialty and by mainstream social scientists. For too long the latter have preferred elegant abstractions to the simple but fundamental observation that societies are made of concrete human beings: women, as well as men.

PART I
The Gender Division of Labor and Stages of Industrial Capitalism

The chapters in this first section, on women and work in industrial capitalism, contradict two prevalent misconceptions about the relation of women to the development process in the West and about the nature of that process itself. In spite of much evidence to the contrary, it is still commonly assumed that development in the West followed simply and rationally from the application of scientific and technical knowledge to the production process, and that women have only recently become an important part of the public labor force. The fact is, however, that intensified exploitation was as basic to the development process as technological innovation, and a major form this took was the use of women as a special category of underpaid labor.

Wanda Minge's chapter outlines the changes brought about in family organization as the basis was being laid in Europe for women's "double day," and Leith Mullings describes the long hours of heavy labor forced upon slave women in the American South. Mullings's data point up the stark contrast between workday realities for Afro-American and poor white women in the early United States, and the ideology of "pure womanhood" being elaborated at the time. Thus the search for cheap female labor by multinational corporations, as analyzed here by Helen Safa, is only a new phase in a well-established pattern of using underpaid women in the work force. Louise Tilly's chapter on the protests of women factory workers in nineteenth-century France completes the outline of women in the work force in the capitalist West with an example of their organized struggles to better their conditions.

1

The Industrial Revolution and the European Family: "Childhood" as a Market for Family Labor

WANDA MINGE

The Industrial Revolution transferred both food production and home-based manufacture from the family to larger, nonkinship corporations.[1] But, contrary to what is said by historians of the family, industrialization has not brought about the demise of home-based family labor. Probably the most often cited premise in the study of the Western family is that "A fundamental characteristic of the world we have lost was the scene of labor, which was universally supposed to be the home" (Laslett 1971: 13). Those who study the transition of the family from a peasant type of production to wage-labor production unquestioningly accept this view of postpeasant family labor (for example, see Mendras 1970: 238).

The view that the family in Western society is not a labor group necessary to industrial production is perhaps based on an incomplete understanding of the effects of industrialization on family labor. What I shall try to show in this chapter is that while industrialization rendered the family noncompetitive with larger, mechanized production groups, it also created a new market for a new kind of family production.

In the early stages of industrialization in the late eighteenth century, human labor went onto the market as a raw commodity like land and capital. As child-labor legislation and compulsory education emerged during the nineteenth century, children were eventually rescued from factory and farm work so that they could be trained to meet the demand for increasingly specialized jobs.

It has been the family that pays most of the cost of reproducing the educated laborers necessary to industrial production. In the postpeasant stage of the family, children cost much more in family labor time and financial expenditures than they did in the peasant stage—a cost that has risen steadily since the beginning of the demand for educated laborers a century ago. Since transition, the family has not ceased to be a productive group, but its function has been transformed from a producer of food to primarily a reproducer of laborers for the highly educated labor market of Western industrial societies.

CHILD LABOR BEFORE THE INDUSTRIAL REVOLUTION

The history of the European peasant is one of small household economies based on the labor of all members of the resident nuclear family. From the earliest ethnography of the family (Arensberg 1937) to the more recent European ethnology, we have been reminded that the labor of the husband, the wife, and the children was necessary (Franklin 1969:15; see also Shanin 1971). In particular, child labor was customary throughout the history of family agriculture (van Bath 1963:184).

Where cottage industries (the putting-out system) were combined with agriculture, young children's labor was integral, as Herman Kellenbenz says of the seventeenth-century textile industry: "Whole families of peasants were involved: the children, often from four years of age onwards, turned the reeling machine, the women, and occasionally also men, wove the cloth" (1974:71). Children were employed in the spinning mills, hiring themselves out from about nine years of age. E. P. Thompson tells us that in the 1830s between one-third and one-half of the labor force in cotton mills was under twenty-one (1962:308). Louise Tilly's (1979) study of a French textile city shows that 38.9 percent of girls and 36.5 percent of boys aged ten to fourteen worked in the mills. And Mary Lynn McDougall refers to the "short childhood" of those in the working class: "Until the end of the nineteenth century, most working-class girls had short childhoods. Their play-filled days might end as early as the age of four if their parents worked at home and needed their assistance for such simple tasks as winding thread" (1977:271).

In his recent history of the English family from 1500 to 1800, Lawrence Stone says that children left home between the ages of seven and fourteen to begin work as domestic servants, laborers or apprentices in other families' homes:

> What one sees at these middle- and lower middle-class levels is a vast system of exchange by which parents sent their own children away from home—usually not very far—and the richer families took in the children of others as servants and laborers. As a result of this custom, some very

fragmentary census data suggest that from just before puberty until they married some ten years later, about two out of every three boys and three out of every four girls were living away from home. Nearly one-half of all husbandmen households and nearly one-quarter of craftsmen and trades-man households contained living-in servants or apprentices [Stone 1977:107].

Not only did children begin to work at an early age, but Stone suggests that many were treated with "indifference and neglect" (ibid:81). To a greater extent, Edward Shorter's study of three centuries of the family in Europe has conjured up a picture of "neglect" of children in peasant families. Document-ing reports from doctors and local officials, Shorter gives the impression that children were left alone for long stretches of time especially during harvest season and that this practice resulted in high infant mortality.

There are similar references to child neglect by families in the early factory system. E. P. Thompson says that the infants in wage-laboring families were left in the care of "old baby-farming crones, or children too small to find work at the mill" (1966:328; see also Stone 1977:662). Alternatively, children might be drugged with opiates, freeing the mother to leave them alone all day: "If [the mothers] worked outside the home, they left infants as young as ten days with paid nurses; they breast-fed infants as few as three times a day and weaned them as soon as possible; they and the nurses stifled infants' hungry cries with patent medicines laced with narcotics, one which bore the name Atkins Royal Infant Preservative!" (McDougall 1977:274; see also Marx 1964:398). McDougall says the infant mortality rate in these conditions was 68.8 percent.

From recent historical research there emerges the impression that sending young children away to wet nurses was a common practice: "Work on the practice of putting babies out to wet nurses and on the administration of foundling hospitals in the eighteenth and nineteenth centuries suggests that infants and young children were universally handled with the casualness appropriate to so many sacks of flour. Until after the mid-nineteenth century, town dwellers in France of virtually all social classes put their newborn infants in the care of wet nurses in the surrounding countryside for the first 10 to 24 months of their lives" (Reddy 1977:5; see also Shorter 1975:175). Reddy says that 25 percent of these children died before age one and 50 percent died before age five. Similarly, we are told that in England "the rich sent their children away to paid wet nurses, which resulted in a death rate double that of maternally fed babies" (Stone 1977:81). (In England this practice seems to have ended before it ended on the continent.)

Harvest season and factory work notwithstanding, Shorter states that "even when mothers were with their children . . . we note little of the affectionate concern, the playful efforts to help the infant develop as a person, that characterize the modern mother. Traditional babies were left pretty much to themselves" (1975:171). Stone suggests that it is the high infant and child mortality rates "which made it folly to invest too much emotional capital in such ephemeral beings" (1977:105). To what extent these accounts have an element of ethnocentric distortion about the treatment of children we cannot be certain, but they are consistent in suggesting that family life did not center around children and that there was an absence of parental investment as we know it in Western society today. The conclusion of each of these two recent histories of the modern Western family is, of course, that family emotions have changed over time. Stone ends his book by saying, "The only steady linear change over the last four hundred years seems to have been a growing concern for children" (1977:683).

The growing concern for children is reflected in literature. Phillippe Ariès's historical analysis of iconography reveals that the medieval world "did not know childhood or did not attempt to portray it" (1962:47). And Peter Coveney's study of the child in English literature tells us of the omission of the child until the late eighteenth century:

> Until the last decades of the eighteenth century the child did not exist as an important and continuous theme in English literature. Childhood as a major theme came with the generation of Blake and Wordsworth. There were of course children in English literature before the Romantics. . . . But in the Elizabethan drama, in the main body of Augustan verse, in the major eighteenth-century novel, the child is absent, or the occasion of a passing reference; at the most a subsidiary element in an adult world. . . . Within the course of a few decades the child emerges from comparative unimportance to become the focus of an unprecedented literary interest, and, in time, the central figure of an increasingly significant proportion of our literature [Coveney 1957:9].

In comparison to the family's treatment of children before the eighteenth century, Ariès says, "Our world is obsessed by the physical, moral, and sexual problems of childhood. This preoccupation was unknown to medieval civilization" (1962:411). He asks but, like others, does not answer, "How did we come from that ignorance of childhood to the centering of the family around the child in the nineteenth century?"

THE DEMAND FOR EDUCATION AND THE CONCEPT OF CHILDHOOD IN THE NINETEENTH CENTURY

I suggest that the differences in the treatment of children between preindustrial and industrial societies is more than a change in child-socialization mores or in family sentiment. It is a consequence of fundamental differences in the family's economic relation to preindustrial society on the one hand and to industrial society on the other.

The transfer of human labor from the kinship-based food-producing group to the larger, nonkin corporations of burgeoning industrial states is only a prerequisite for the development of a new need for *family* labor. Another necessary condition is the development of a demand for more educated laborers.

This demand was not an immediate result of the Industrial Revolution. In the early part of the revolution—the textile boom (1750–1830)—less skilled, mechanized laborers replaced skilled artisans (Kellenbenz 1974; Braun 1966). Hence it was feasible to employ child labor. It was the second stage of the revolution, the growth in manufacture of chemicals, iron, and steel, beginning about 1850, that created a demand for more skilled laborers. In his study of the effects on education of technical changes in the British and German iron and steel industries, 1860–1964, P. W. Musgrave concludes that specific inventions were landmarks in the development of a qualitatively different educational system: "Sudden particular change can be exemplified by the great nine-teenth-century inventions which ushered in the steel age, namely the Bessemer, the open hearth and the basic processes. In the twentieth century the continuous strip mill and the oxygen process are further examples. These innovations had considerable effect on the quantitative and qualitative demands made upon the educational system as mediated by the industry's labour force" (1967:2522).

The parallel development of universities and industries is shown in Michel Sanderson's history of British universities, 1850–1970. He says that "pressures arose in the nineteenth century which induced the universities and industry to turn toward each other. The fear of French and then German competition, the increasingly scientific nature of innovation, the emergence of the large firm and the rise of special skills like accountancy all created a need for the graduate in industry" (1972:389).

David Mitch says, however, that for the majority of the workers there was little increase in skills required and that the need for literacy during the nineteenth century resulted more from mechanization of agriculture—the sector of the economy that still employed the largest number of workers (1977:6–7).

Insofar as there was an increase in the demand for skilled labor in some sectors of production, it can only be seen as part of the motivation for the expansion of formal education. In a study of the development of education in nineteenth-century England and Wales, Patricia Quick says that the purpose of elementary education was not only to teach habits of industry, order, and obedience but also to diminish crime among working-class children (1974:79). William Lazonick's research on the relationship between the family and public education during industrialization in England suggests that a primary purpose for the development of a mass schooling system was ideological—to discipline the next generation for factory labor. School attendance became a requirement for children's unskilled factory work:

From the 1830's a state-supported, and eventually a state-run, mass schooling system was developed, the purpose of which was the moral preparation
of future workers for the world of wage labor. As working-class children
were excluded from the wage-labor force by the Factory Acts, they were
pushed into the school system. The education Act of 1870 which followed
fast on the heels of the wide-reaching Factory and Workshops Acts of
1867, gave local school boards the power to enforce the education of their
constituents up to age thirteen (the age up to which children could be
working at most "half time") [Lazonick 1978:26].

The shift to machine technology itself imposed a new discipline on labor,
well described by David Landes: "Now the work had to be done in a factory,
at a pace set by tireless, inanimate equipment, as part of a large team that had
to begin, pause, and stop in unison—all under the close eye of overseers,
enforcing assiduity by moral, pecuniary, occasionally even physical means of
compulsion" (1965:276). In an article entitled "Time, Work-Discipline, and
Industrial Capitalism," E. P. Thompson traces the diffusion of clocks and
watches at the "exact moment when the industrial revolution demanded a
greater synchronization of labor" (1966:69). "In all these ways—by the division of labour; the supervision of labour, fines; bells and clocks; money
incentives; preachings and schoolings; the suppression of fairs and sports—
new labour habits were formed, and a new time-discipline was immposed"
(ibid.:90). Hence, education was necessary as a means of uniform socialization, an institution to teach discipline[2] (cf. A. Field 1976).
    But more generally, in industrial society, life itself requires more education
than in preindustrial society. Harry Braverman's research on labor in the
twentieth century suggests that industrial society requires an increase in
education even more than it requires an increase in labor skills,[3] and that "the
average length of schooling is generally higher for urban populations, and the
shift of a population from farm to city brings with it, almost as an automatic
function, an increase in the term of education" (Braverman 1974:436).
    The concern with education affected different classes in different ways, but
what we see in the nineteenth century is a common response by all classes to
obtain education. Until the eighteenth century education involved only a small
part of society. The medieval Latin school instructed clerics of all ages. It was
not designed for children. The most common form of instruction for children
was the informal apprenticeship, or domestic services in other families'
homes. (Child exchanges had been common among European families since
the Middle Ages.) Beginning in the fifteenth century, landed aristocrats sub-
stituted schools for the apprenticeship; but until the eighteenth century,
education centered on upper-class families.
    The Industrial Revolution soon created a concern with education that
transformed society at all class levels. First, the middle-class industrialists saw
benefits to themselves in having a skilled labor force: "In the closing decades

of the eighteenth century a new interest in education arose among forward-looking industrialists and professional men in the chief manufacturing centres of the Midlands and northern England, most notably in Birmingham and Manchester. The projects advanced were primarily those of a class which was experiencing at firsthand the potentialities and effects of a now rapidly developing capitalist industry" (Simon 1960:17).

But soon the working class also wanted education—for self-protection. The physical atrocities committed against the workers during the first decades of the Industrial Revolution are too well known to require discussion here. Working conditions have been described in detail by E. P. Thompson (1966), J. L. Hammond and B. Hammond (1925), and Engels (1950), among others. In addition to the physical conditions in the factories, the impoverishment of the wage earners increased, reaching its cruelest periods around the turn of the century (during Speenhamland). The workers' pauperization was measured by the rising price of rye: "From 1726 to 1741 a farm laborer's family of five, of whom only the man of the house did paid work, had to spend 45% of the yearly wage on rye bread; in the period 1785–1789 the proportion had risen to 58% and in the critical year, 1789, it was 88%" (van Bath 1963:227).

Thus it is not suprising that the working class was quickly organized by political groups whose aim it was to educate them. Desperation and starvation moved the workers to a political fight which required literacy. Organized by the corresponding societies, groups of mechanics, artisans, and traders met weekly in one another's homes to read the work of writers such as Thomas Paine.

The nascent concern with education by all classes eventually rescued children from the factories and put them into schools. In the 1840s the middle class established the first boarding proprietary schools for their children. Although the working class could not afford these schools, they paid for their children's education, which in the beginning was little aided by the state:

> In Manchester, in 1834, 4,070 children were attending free or partially assisted schools; but another 13,108 were to be found in common day schools or in dame schools, which were entirely supported by fees ranging from 3d. to 9d. a week. About the same period, the working-class in Bristol, which had a population of 120,000, were paying over £15,000 a year for their children's education, a sum over half that reluctantly granted by Parliament in 1833 to aid the building of schools throughout England and Wales. This gives a glimpse of the extent to which the working class supported schools out of their own pockets [Simon 1960:254].

As education is a prerequisite for government in industrial states, England and other nations soon made elementary education mandatory—and at the same time emphasized the family's responsibility for the socialization of children. For example, when Gizot prepared the national law for primary education in France in 1833, he said: "Family feeling and duty is of great influence today; the politcal and legal bonds of the family have weakened; the natural and moral bonds have strengthened. . . . It is to this feeling of ambitious foresight in families that the Ministry of Education owes its popularity. Now a matter of great public interest has taken its place beside this powerful domestic interest. Necessary as it is for the family, the Ministry of Education, it is no less necessary for the State" (quoted in Thaubault 1971:56).

At the same time in the United States there was a parallel development by a "highly education-conscious labor movement" (Butts 1953:141). The Civil War was a triumph for industrial capitalism, which, by the turn of the century, overshadowed the agrarian way of life characterized by the South. In the decades following the Civil War a goal of private corporations and government alike was to extend practical education to all segments of the rapidly growing American society. This goal was realized in nineteenth-century America more than in Europe by means of the "single-track or ladder system of education, which began with elementary schools and was followed by secondary and high schools that led on to college and higher education" (ibid.:115).

By the end of the nineteenth century, national education systems, as they exist today, were formed in West Europe and the United States. During the last thirty years of the century, concern with education permeated even the rural areas of the industrialized countries. Roger Thaubault's (1971:159–63) description of the change wrought by a school system in one French village shows that between 1880 and 1900 both men and women began leaving the village either for wage labor for which their technical training had prepared them or for further education at teachers' colleges.

THE RISING COST OF REPRODUCTION SINCE 1850

As we have seen, education extended childhood beyond age five or seven. I am now concerned with showing the consequences to the family's labor of this extension of childhood by means of an expanding educational system in industrial societies. What started as a three-class movement was eventually intersected by state support, thus providing further impetus to all families to educate their children. The eventual consequence to the family is a steady and unremitting rise in the cost of reproducing children. In Europe "this new concern about education would gradually install itself in the heart of society and transform it from top to bottom. The family ceased to be simply an institution for the transmission of a name and an estate" (Ariés 1962:412). And in America, "despite the prevailing attitudes toward child nature that led to the treatment of the child as a sinful though miniature version of an adult person, there were signs that a change in outlook was in the making in the educational thought of the eighteenth century" (Butts 1953:71).

To understand that during transition from peasant society to industrial wage-labor society, the family underwent a qualitative change as a labor unit—

from one that produced food to one whose primary function was to socialize and educate laborers for an industrial labor market that increasingly depended on a different kind of labor—one must understand that the concept of childhood changed so radically that the cost to the family was not merely the money it paid for education per se. In fact, schooling is not the primary cost difference between children in peasant families and postpeasant families. What put a burden on the family in industrializing European countries and the United States was the extension of childhood from age five or six to age fifteen or sixteen for the middle class and to age twenty-two or twenty-three for those families who could send their children to a university. Whereas previously children worked when they became old enough to do so, now their parents found themselves supporting adolescents. Stone describes the gradual release of the child from more and more of its labor requirements: "The progressive postponement of the entry of children in the adult life of work, from seven when they started chores around the home, to fourteen when they became servants or apprentices in other households, to twenty-one when they finished their education, transformed the nature of childhood and created the problem of how to deal with large numbers of adolescent children with the drives and capacities of adults, but denied their responsibilities"(Stone 1977:684). The concept of adolescence, then, is a relatively recent phenomenon (Demos and Demos 1969).

To forego the labor of children for as long as a decade burdened parents as early as the 1870s in England. J. A. Banks has described the rapid expansion of public boarding schools for the middle class between 1840 and 1870 in England and says that "it is quite clear that the real problem of expense arose from the fact that they were keeping their sons at school for a longer period than necessary under a scheme of artisan apprenticeship. It was not the four guineas a year that the parents found embarrassing, but the cost involved in providing an adolescent with food and clothing when in an earlier generation he would have been helping to maintain himself"(1954:193).

Furthermore, one must realize that the cost of education extended beyond the direct cost of schooling. "Childhood" soon became a social institution in which parents were expected to invest money in the social life of adolescent dependents. Banks has estimated these extracurricular costs of education (1957:186) and says that as early as 1870 it was this indirect cost of education that determined how long the middle class could keep their children in school (ibid: 185–95).

Today direct education costs are still only part of the cost of children.[4] The International Labor Organization's *Household Income and Expenditure Statistics* indicates that direct educational costs of families in France, Germany, Denmark, Belgium, Austria, Greece, Ireland, Netherlands, Sweden, and the United States range between 0.5 percent and 4.8 percent of family income annually (ILO 1967).

Now, what proportion of family income is spent on children in West European countries? In 1950, the Statistical Office of the German government

TABLE 1.1

Percentage of Family Income Spent on a Child at Different Ages in Four-Person Households, Germany, 1950–51*

Household income (DM per year)	Age bracket of dependent child				
	1–6	6–10	10–14	14–19	Over 19
2,500–3,600	12.6	17.0	20.1	26.7	33.4
3,600–5,100	12.0	16.1	20.1	24.7	33.0
Over 5,100	12.0	15.2	19.6	23.8	31.6

*Germany, "Expenditure on Children within Families," *Wirtschaft und Statistik* (Sept. 1955).
SOURCE: Wynn (1972).

undertook a budget survey of 10,600 families in three income categories. Table 1.1 shows that the percentage allocation of expenditures to each child within these four-person households increases with the child's age and surpasses the expenditures on parents in the college-age years. Margaret Wynn (1974:156) cites a 1963–64 French family survey showing also that the expenditures per person on clothing for older children and adolescents is substantially higher than these expenditures by parents for themselves.

These figures tell us only about family income allocated to children. What about the family's cost in labor time? This is a cost to the family since the mother's time allocated to child care might, alternatively, be spent in wage labor. One way of looking at this cost is to figure the value of the possible alternative wage employment. Economists have recently computed the foregone wages of mothers in the United States to be an average of approximately $100,000 for each nonemployed mother. The range is between $75,000 for women with elementary school education to $155,000 for mothers who have education beyond a bachelor's degree (Reed and McIntosh 1972; Espenshade 1977).

Of course, another way to view the cost of children in a mother's labor time is to look at the amount of labor time she actually allocates to children— not the labor time she might have given in wage employment. I suggest that this latter approach reveals the "real" labor cost of children, since more time must be given to children than to a forty-hour-week wage job.

An extensive time-allocation study of urban and suburban families in ten European countries and the United States presents in detail thirty thousand person-days of time allocation to all types of daily activities in cities in France, German Democratic Republic, Federal Republic of Germany, Belgium, Czechoslovakia, Hungary, Bulgaria, Poland, Yugoslavia, Russia, and the United States. The study shows that unemployed married women spend an average of 7.2 hours a day in "household care" during a seven-day work week (Table 1.2). This is 25 percent more time than the average wage worker's week.

TABLE 1.2

Time Spent in Home-based Labor in Suburban Areas in Ten European Countries and the United States
(Hours per Day for Seven-Day week)

	Belgium	Bulgaria	Czechoslovakia	France	Fed. Rep. Germany (100 districts)	Fed. Rep. Germany (Osnabrück)	German Dem. Rep.	Hungary	Poland	U.S. (44 cities)	U.S. (Jackson, Miss.)	USSR	Yugoslavia (Kragujevac)	Yugoslavia (Mariabör)
Employed men, all days:	0.3	0.7	0.9	0.5	0.3	0.3	1.0	0.5	0.6	0.5	0.5	1.3	0.4	0.5
single	0.2	0.2	0.7	0.5	0.2	0.3	1.1	0.3	0.3	0.5	0.5	0.8	0.3	0.3
married	0.3	0.8	0.9	0.5	0.3	0.3	1.0	0.5	0.7	0.5	0.5	1.4	0.4	0.5
Employed women, all days:	3.0	3.2	4.5	3.5	4.1	3.5	4.7	4.2	3.6	3.3	3.3	3.7	3.8	4.6
single	1.9	2.5	3.6	2.7	2.5	2.2	4.0	2.7	2.5	2.7	2.7	2.8	2.5	3.4
married	3.7	3.4	3.8	4.0	5.1	4.5	4.8	4.7	4.1	3.7	3.6	4.0	4.3	5.0
no children	3.0	3.4	4.6	4.0	4.5	4.5	4.8	4.6	3.9	3.1	3.1	4.1	4.7	5.1
one child, under 4 yrs	3.6*	3.2	4.5	3.0	4.5*	4.9*	4.8	4.2	3.4	3.2†	2.7†	3.5	4.2	4.7
one child, over 4 yrs	3.9	3.3	4.2	4.3	5.4*	4.6*	4.5	4.4	4.4	4.0*	3.9*	4.3	4.5	
2–3 children, one under 4	3.6*	4.0	5.1	4.1	4.6*	4.2†	4.5	5.1*	4.3	4.5*	3.7†	4.8	4.1	5.2
2–3 children, one over 4	4.4	2.9	5.1	4.3	6.7*	4.8*	5.1	5.1	4.2	4.4	3.6	4.3	4.3	5.3
4+ children, one under 4	8.3†	—	—	3.4†	—	—	5.3	—	3.9†	5.3†	4.6†	5.3†	—	5.5†
4+ children, all over 4	4.6†	—	6.6*	4.2†	—	—	4.7	5.9†	4.6	4.6†	5.3†	5.2†	—	6.1*
Housewives, all days:	6.5	6.9	7.2	6.5	6.9	6.5	7.4	8.5	7.3	5.9	5.8	7.2	6.7	9.5
single	5.6	4.8*	5.9*	5.6*	5.8	5.8	—	7.8*	5.9	5.5*	—	6.7	5.6	8.5
married	6.6	7.4	7.3	6.9	7.0	6.5	7.4	8.6	7.4	5.9	5.8	7.4	6.8	9.6
no children	6.1	8.2*	7.3	6.9	6.8	6.5	7.7	8.4	7.2	6.0	5.4	6.8*	7.5	9.6
one child, under 4 yrs	5.6*	7.1*	6.3*	6.2	6.4	6.2*	6.8	8.3*	7.0	5.0*	5.3*	5.2†	6.6	9.7*
one child, over 4 yrs	6.8	7.0*	7.5*	6.7	7.2	6.5	7.8	8.7	8.1	6.1	5.5*	7.9*	6.5	9.8
2–3 children, one under	7.0	7.7†	7.6	5.8	6.8	6.1	7.0	7.6*	6.7	5.6	5.8	6.5†	6.3	8.6
2–3 children, all over 4	6.8	5.9*	7.3	6.6	7.9	6.7	7.5	9.0	7.6	6.0	6.1	9.1*	6.7	9.8
4+ children, one under 4	7.4*	—	8.0†	6.5	7.3*	6.5†	7.3	—	6.8†	6.4	6.8*	—	—	9.4*
4+ children, all over	7.5	—	8.0†	7.1	8.9†	8.3†	8.0	8.3†	7.9*	7.8*	6.5*	—	7.9*	9.2
All women, all days	4.9	3.7	5.1	5.0	5.8	5.1	5.5	5.7	4.7	4.7	4.7	3.9	5.3	6.4

*N between 10 and 29.
†N between 4 and 9.
——N less than 4.
SOURCE: Szala (1972: 126, Table 5).

In summary, these historical data bring into question the premise that "we have lost the world in which the scene of labor is the home."

In the middle of the nineteenth century the development of the need for educating wage-laborers created a previously unknown institution of "child-hood," which soon extended children's dependency into adolescence. The cost to the family soon became considerably greater than the foregone labor of children who no longer worked for the family. Since the beginning of the concern with education, children have subtly but rapidly developed into a labor-intensive, capital-intensive product of the family in industrial society.[5]

Now, how costly is the family's reproduction in Western industrial societies? It is not yet possible to give a definitive answer. We need to know many more facts about family time-allocation and financial expenditures in Europe today. At the moment, however, we can surmise that home-based family labor is a multimillion-dollar cottage industry on which industrial production is based.

Notes

1. I would like to thank Conrad Arensberg, Marvin Harris, David Mitch, Rayna Reiter, Jane Schneider and Eric Wolf. Robert Fogel, Tamara Hareven, Peter Laslett, Stanley Tambiah, William Lazonick, and Beatrice and John Whiting made helpful comments after this chapter had gone to press; I regret that the present version does not reflect all their suggestions. Support came from: a Wenner-Gren Foundation Library Fellowship (3233); a National Institute of Mental Health Fellowship (1 F31 MH 05097-01); a National Science Foundation grant (NSF BNS 75-22305); an Internship of the Population Council, and National Institute of Mental Health Grant (MH 14088).

2. A related reason for the development of education as a means to teach discipline was, of course, the expansion of military–industrial powers. Cipolla's statistics of eight occupation categories at the turn of the century in France show that Military recruits ranked third in literacy (1969:76, Table 7).

3. He points out, however, that frequently education is needed to get a job but is not needed for the job itself (Braverman 1975:438; see also Freeman 1975 and 1976).

4. To my knowledge, there does not exist an agglomerate study of the rising cost of education for West European countries since 1900. A recent attempt by the Carnegie Commission on Higher Education was abandoned due to the piecemeal nature of the results. Therefore, no comprehensive report was made from the study (Clark Kerr, personal communication).

5. The results of my own time-allocation study of families in a Swiss village during the peasant-to-worker transition show that as these families are being drawn into the modern Swiss wage-labor market, there is a correlation between the level of children's education and the domestic labor time of parents; there is an even stronger correlation with the mother's labor time (Minge-Kalman 1978).

The increasing cost of children parallels decreasing fertility rates. D. V. Glass tells us that in Britain, France, Germany, Belgium, and the Scandinavian countries, fertility fell markedly from about the third quarter of the nineteenth century. It remained high during the early stages of the Industrial Revolution, the textile boom. At that time child labor was still used in the factories (e.g. Tilly 1977). It was during the second state of the Industrial Revolution, beginning around 1850, when a change in the demand for skilled labor took children out of the factory system and put them into schools, that birth rates begin to decline substantially.

More recently, in Western Europe the annual population growth dropped from 0.56 percent in 1970 to 0.32 in 1975—a sharp reduction for a large area. (In four of these countries population growth has come to a halt.) In the United States the growth rate, which dropped from 0.90 percent in 1970 to 0.60 percent in 1975, continues to decline today.

2

Paths of Proletarianization: Organization of Production, Sexual Division of Labor, and Women's Collective Action

LOUISE A. TILLY

On 25 October 1880, the women cigar makers in the government monopoly tobacco factory in Lyon, France, sat down at their work with their arms folded.* The factory manager, along with the prefect of the department, met with a delegation of strikers and proposed a compromise. The workers refused and continued their strike. Their agitation increased until finally, the police forcefully evacuated the courtyard of the factory where the workers had gathered to demonstrate.

The manager and the prefect then requested that the government send an inspector-engineer from Paris with full authorization to bargain. This was done and the Paris delegate agreed that no new measures would be taken that directly or indirectly reduced worker's salaries. Nor would the striking women's delegates be punished for their role. The cigar makers then agreed to return to work.

Charles Mannheim (1902:420), a French scholar who wrote his thesis on the condition of workers in the state tobacco factories, remarked that the Lyon plant was in a state of "incessant agitation" from 1880 to 1883. In fact, a large section of his study is devoted to descriptions of strikes in the tobacco

*An earlier version of this Introduction appeared in *Signs*, vol. 7, no. 2, Winter 1981. © by The University of Chicago.

industry—twenty-seven of them—between 1870 and 1900. In all of the strikes, women workers played a dominant part. Michelle Perrot notes in her magisterial study of French strikes that "although they accounted for only .5 percent of the female labor force [in the period from 1870 to 1890] they [tobacco workers] supplied 16 percent of the female strikers" (Perrot 1974:329).

What a contrast to the often-assumed passivity of women workers! Although her chief concerns are elsewhere, Perrot is evenhanded in her evaluation of women as strikers. Nevertheless, she concludes that women were characterized by "timidity and lack of resolution" when it came to striking (K. Purcell 1979).[1] Why were the women tobacco workers such an exception to the common rule that women, relative to men, were unlikely to strike? What do the tobacco workers suggest about the conditions which *promote* female strikes?

This chapter focuses on women's collective action in response to the multifaceted process of proletarianization in France and the new organizations of production and household division of labor that accompanied it. It focuses exclusively on urban working-class women and primarily, but not exclusively, on workplace-based collective action. A systematic comparison of variations in the organization of production and in the household division of labor provide part of the answer to the central question, Under what conditions will women's participation in collective action be more or less likely? The chapter begins with the concept of "collective action" and its usefulness for understanding women's class-based action. The French economic-historical context for proletarianization and women's economic activity is the topic of the next section. Brief case studies of typical proletarian situations follow, each involving a different "mix" of organization of production and household division of labor. The cases proceed along a continuum from household organization of production, that setting least likely to promote women's collective action, to individual wage earning in industrial production, in which certain circumstances facilitated it. Typical forms of female collective action and different participation patterns are identified in each setting. The conclusion lays out some generalizations about the connections among organization of production, the household division of labor, women's propensity to act, and the form of that action.

COLLECTIVE ACTION

Many political historians ignore women—and men—who had no formal role in political structures. They focus on the power center of a polity, the capital, and confine their analyses to formal politics: legislation, day-to-day administration of government activity, officials, and policy and its enforcement. Those without a role are marginal from this perspective; if they appear at all, it is only incidentally, when they come into intermittent contact with formal politics. Historically, the political activity of women most often has been outside this central arena, for they have had no formal rights or duties as citizens. To observe women's politics, then, it is necessary to look beyond the formal arena and seek out a more comprehensive method of analysis. The concept of "collective action" as a struggle over control of resources among groups is the theoretical framework used here. (One of these groups may be government and members of the polity; others may be classes; still others part of a class, an interest group, a community, a region, or a religious sect.)

Collective Action is defined as a group's application of pooled resources to common ends. Acting in their own interests, groups apply their resources to other groups or to authorities at any level of government. Political power, then, is the return from the application of resources to governments. Violence occurs when governments or other groups resist the collective action of a mobilizing group, or when a mobilizing group deliberately chooses violent means (C. Tilly 1978).

ECONOMIC CHANGE, PROLETARIANIZATION, AND WOMEN'S PRODUCTIVE ROLE IN FRANCE

The eighteenth- and nineteenth-century Industrial Revolution initiated an enormous shift of labor and resources away from primary production—agriculture, fishing, forestry—toward manufacturing and commercial and service activities. The scale of production increased, and the factory eventually replaced the household as the most common unit of productive activity. In France, the pace of industrialization was very gradual; it affected groups and geographic areas at different rates and times.

For ordinary people witnessing the growth of industrial capitalism, proletarianization was the central social experience. *Proletarianization* is defined here as the process of increase in the number of "people whose survival depended on the sale of labor power" (C. Tilly 1979:29). Although proletarianization was a common experience, how it occurred in given populations varied markedly, as did the timing of the process. The paths or patterns of proletarianization were linked systematically to patterns of collective action. Although some degree of rural, agricultural proletarianzation was an integral part of the process, it is not discussed in the primarily urban case studies that follow.

Urbanization occurred in nineteenth-century France as the proportion of population in cities increased, but even at the end of the century, much manufacturing took place in the households of part-time peasants, craftsmen, and rural workers in domestic industry or in small-scale workshops. Because of the particular character of French industrialization, operating alongside continuing peasant agriculture, France's manufacturing population was scattered throughout the country in rural as well as urban areas; thus "the distinction between industrial and agricultural work is often artificial" (Fohlen

1973:26). Protoindustrialization—cottage industry, or the putting-out system, as it was called by the classic economic historians—had begun as a stratagem of merchant capitalists to tap underemployed labor power in needy rural households to produce cheap goods for distant markets. It lingered in France, in small towns and villages, even in the late nineteenth century, because it allowed high-quality craftsmanship and quick changeover of styles to match fashions, not to mention low wages. By the late nineteenth century, families working as cottage production units owned their tools, usually looms, and sometimes they hired an assistant or two. Despite these anomalies they were all proletarians, parents and children alike, selling their labor power with little control over their joint wage except putting additional family members to work or laboring longer hours.

Urban industrial growth had created new kinds of cities in France by the 1870s. The textile cities of the Nord, and mining and metalworking cities of the Nord and Pas-de-Calais (or of the Stephannois region of Central South), are examples. These cities, all products of industrial capitalist concentration, had very different labor-force characteristics. In the textile city, there was heavy labor-force participation by girls and women, including some married women. In the mining town, most jobs were men's jobs. Girls did some auxiliary work around the mines and shops or were servants; married women were seamstresses or store or cafe keepers, if they were wage earners. The division of labor by sex in the coal miners' or metalworkers' families was especially sharp. Men and boys worked in heavy labor removed from the household. Married women generally stayed in the home and were responsible for housework, childbearing, and child care.

In most towns and cities, public administration, commerce, and small businesses that produced directly for consumers were common. Women worked primarily in domestic service, the garment industry (young women in shops, married women in their homes), food processing, and paper and tobacco plants. Throughout the century there were also many urban women in informal, casual labor as carters, petty traders, street hawkers, and laundresses. Although consumer production and merchandising became large-scale in the nineteenth century, the specialization of sectors of these urban economies changed little. Unmarried women in cities usually earned wages for their work. The decline of the household organization of production in the urban sector meant that even if they worked at home—and the late nineteenth century was a heyday of sweated home industry—women were unlikely to be part of a family productive unit. Instead they labored as isolated individuals for employers who paid them a wage. Married women in the working class often worked intermittently doing laundry, cleaning, and the like, for they had heavy home responsibilities too. Women's work, then, had changed rather little: the majority of working women had low-skilled jobs in areas considered women's work for centuries.

The economic life of the manufacturing classes can be characterized by organization of production. First, household organization did not disappear in nineteenth-century France; craftshops continued household-organized production. Second, other household production units, particularly in handloom weaving and small metal production, were composed of proletarian wage earners. Third, individual wage earning was the predominant mode in urban industry. Hence, a distinctive characteristic of French economic production in the second half of the nineteenth century was that the household organization of production was preserved in some proletarianized production. That is the economic context for the first case in the typology of organization or production and women's class-based collective action.[2]

The cases to be examined next are those of household manufacture in the Cambrésis, the silk industry of Lyon and the Lyonnais, the large-scale textile industry of the Nord, the mining and metalworking industry, and the tobacco industry.

Household Manufacture in the Cambrésis

The linen handloom weavers of the Cambrésis in northern France seemed an anachronism even to their contemporaries. Here is an ethnographic account of these weavers' work and family life written at the turn of the century.

> The father of the family groups the community of workers, of whom he is the natural head, in the workshop, at the looms. He himself works too, giving each of his family the joint responsibility of working in the enterprise. All the family members collaborate to varying degrees, without exception, in the production of cloth.
>
> From an early age, the children of both sexes help their father do his job by producing the *trames*. This task consists of winding the linen thread on a bobbin, which is then placed in the hollow of the weaver's shuttle. Once they are thirteen, the children are rapidly taught how to weave by their own family and assigned to their own loom. . . .
>
> The mother is concerned above all with house work, aided in her many tasks by her daughters. The rest of the time, often rising before dawn, she also prepared the bobbins for the weavers' shuttles; if there is an idle loom, she hurries to replace a sick or absent worker.
>
> [In the family workshop] each person finds the task appropriate for his or her strength and intelligence. The children, far from being a burden for their parents, became very real resources for the family. Raised to be weavers, they become weavers [Blaise 1899:36–37].

Without the unpaid labor of his wife and the wages of his children, it would have been impossible for the male weaver to support a family. Wages were very low in the industry, reflecting its marginal relationship to the industrialized textile industry, located in the same area of France. Furthermore, there were sharp cycles in the trade, and in any ordinary year there were likely to be several periods of unemployment (ibid.: 53–55). In response, all family members were pressed to accept family goals, even if this meant sacrifice of individual hopes. Children were not schooled; they went to work very young. Their marriages could be delayed, or they could be sent out to find work elsewhere as their younger siblings took their places at the looms (Grafteaux 1975). The weavers' chief solutions to poverty, short of migration, were working long hours and having children who could work, too.

As their conditions degenerated, the weavers did act collectively in large strikes in 1889, 1895, and 1906. The strikes of the handloom weavers were largely male events; those who dealt with the bosses and paraded their demands through the small towns of the Cambrésis were the male heads of weaving households. They were accompanied by their sons but not by their wives and daughters. There was a strict division of labor in these households; the shop, even though located in the weaver's cottage cellar, was the male weaver's preserve. He was the boss, the person who carried on family contacts with the public world of the labor market. Although the children of these families earned individual wages, the wives did not. Children's wages were given to the mother to spend on household needs, as were the father's wages. The organization of production promoted familial orientations among the handloom weavers. Workers in the small, separate, household production units were slow to mobilize and strike. When they did, the women's role was minimal (see L. Tilly 1980).

Silk Industry of Lyon and the Lyonnais

There were some similar characteristics in the organization of production in the silk industry of Lyon. There the once proud and independent artisan silk handweavers were undergoing slow, painful proletarianization. For a time, the defense of their jobs met with some success, for the merchant capitalists benefited from the concentration of weavers in the city. Like the linen entrepreneurs of the Cambrésis, these merchants were hampered by the cyclical demand for their products, based on trends in fashion, which made them hesitate to invest in factories or big inventories (Sheridan 1979:120–23).

An economic journalist, writing in 1860, noted the continuing importance of the household as productive unit: "One fact is striking, right off; that is family life. The stable workers, owners of one or more looms, are almost all married. Since the assistance of a wife is indispensable for the multitude of tasks auxiliary to weaving, they marry young. By the nature of his work, the weaver stays in his home" (Audiganne 1860:44). Recent research shows that by this period, however, the household economy had been considerably modified. Between 1847 and 1866, there had been "a reduction in the proportion of residents in the household not related to the head of the household or to his spouse, and in the proportion of nonresident workers needed to weave the active looms ('familialization'), and a reduction in the proportion of males, both kinfolk of the head or spouse and nonkin, residing in the same household ('feminization')" (Sheridan 1979:111; see also Strumingher 1979:1–16). Women workers—kin of the master weavers or live-in wage earners who were part textile workers and part servants—performed the various tasks of preparing and winding the warp, and they did the weaving. George Sheridan concludes that "women played an especially important role in preserving the traditional household economy" (Sheridan 1979:113).

A second kind of productive unit, in addition to the household-organized silk workshop, was the convent weaving shop, located in the suburbs of Lyon. There nuns supervised women weavers and managed the business, which was financed by Lyon entrepreneurs (Strumingher 1979:8–9). A third productive unit was the silk *internat,* sometimes metaphorically called a convent factory. At these institutions, girls and young women boarded in dormitories attached to silk spinning and reeling mills, their work and personal lives strictly supervised, often by nuns (see Vanoli 1976:19–39; LeRoy-Beaulieu 1873:410–25; Perrot 1974:328). In both cases, women were greatly limited in their freedom of action because of supervision and threats of dismissal on the job and of lost wages and fines if they quit. At the same time, there were a growing number of large-scale mills, mostly in small towns but also in Lyon, where silk reeling, throwing, and the various spinning and twisting operations were done by local women and girls hired on a daily basis.

By the 1860s the repressive regime of the Second Empire and hard times in the silk industry had greatly reduced the level of Lyonnais *canut* (silk weaver) mobilization and action. It was only when new labor laws, which relaxed prohibitions on association, were passed in the last years of the Second Empire that a large strike of the *Fabrique* (the Lyonnias handweaving system) brought out urban *canuts,* rural domestic weavers, *and* women factory workers. The largest group of women who struck in the city were some 600 *ovalistes,* who performed a special twisting operation on the silk thread, usually in medium-sized shops. It was in the "revolutionary fervor" of 1869, in response to an organizing effort by the Lyonnais affiliates of the First International, that "for the first time, we witness large strikes of women workers, who held meetings, discussed issues, set up committees and organized unions" (Maritch 1930:253; see also Moissonier 1972). The petition of the *ovalistes,* which one historian calls an illustration of their "naiveté and inexperience," asked the prefect to arbitrate between them and their employers. The bosses pointed out that they were competing with lower-paid Italian workers and refused any concession. Some *ovalistes* who received room and board from their employer were evicted. The women gathered in menacing groups around his house, breaking windows and threatening to burn the building down. Several of the women were arrested, and the strike was broken by police action (Maritch 1930:221–22; Moissonier 1972:81–83). Given their circumscribed lives, such women ordinarily would not be expected to strike. The contemporaneous large waves of strikes made theirs more thinkable and offered them models of collective action.

Generally, neither the girls and women working in the proletarianized household production of silk nor those in the *internats* were often involved in collective action, even when male weavers were. The *internats* were set up such that they preserved women's social ties—frequent home visits were allowed—while isolating them from other workers (Hanagan 1976:276). Parents could be fined if their daughters left their jobs. The women were so closely supervised and overworked that it was hard for them to develop any solidarity. Lucie Baud, a silk union activist around 1900, was one who decried the effects of the *internats* on women workers' solidarity (Perrot 1978:139–46).

Later, in the 1870s and 1880s, however, there were women's committees among factory silk workers in Lyon and the surrounding region that affiliated with local union confederations *(chambres syndicales)*. Most of the southeastern strikes in that period were led by such groups. In the period from 1871 to 1890, one-third of the all-female strikes in France were in the textile and garment sector, and one-third were in the silk industry (Perrot 1974:326–27). When women workers organized with men, they struck with them as well. By the end of the nineteenth century, then, women engaged in industrial production. They earned independent wages, and though both their husbands and their parents often had a claim on these wages, the women mobilized and acted collectively in strikes.

Textile Industry of the North

Women constituted a large minority, sometimes even a majority, of mill-workers in the classic cotton and wool textile cites of the north. By the 1870s the industry was mechanized and located in large-scale shops. Michelle Perrot describes a favorite photographic study at the turn of the century—men and women flooding through the textile factory gates together at the end of the day *(sortée d'usine):* "[There were] crowds of workers of both sexes, young, gaunt, wrung out, underfed, but clowning crudely nevertheless, as if emboldened by their number, by the 'collective being' of which they were a part" (ibid.:352). Although both men and women were employed in these mills, the type of work done by each sex was usually quite different. Women and children did preparatory work; they were piecers and helpers. Proportionately fewer women did the central tasks of textile production—spinning and weaving. Those who did weave were more likely to work in a mixed setting. Women who worked in the mills were primarily young and unmarried, though toward the end of the period there was a clear tendency for more married women to work (L. Tilly 1979).

Women in the northern textile mills did strike with other workers. The published statistics prior to 1890 did not always report numbers of women in strikes that involved both women and men; nevertheless, newspaper and police accounts placed women in demonstrations and processions on the occasion of strikes. In the weavers' strike of 1867 in Roubaix, a strike directed against an employer speedup that required each worker to watch two looms instead of one, two of the ninety-eight persons arrested were women (Archives nationales 30 March 1867). Later the same year a woman, along with two men, was arrested for beating up a male weaver who had accepted the two-loom regime (Archives nationales 10 July 1867). In an 1880 city-wide strike in Roubaix, the commanding officer of the gendarmerie reported to Paris that all of the male and female workers, some 12,000–15,000 strong, were on strike in the spinning and weaving mills. He noted large groups of strikers clustering in the streets and parading about (Archives nationales 5 May 1880). Nevertheless, women did not strike in proportion to their numbers in the industry (Perrot 1974:318–19).

Women workers were in a difficult position in the northern mills. Male workers accused women of competing, at low wages, for men's jobs. Contemporaries, both workers and authorities, believed that women were less likely to strike. In 1886, for example, striking Roubaix weavers demanded that their employer fire one of the women workers who would not strike with them over a wage issue (Archives nationales 28 Jan. 1886). The boss refused to fire the woman. The police reports for a series of textile strikes during the fall and winter of 1899 in Roubaix and Tourcoing further illustrate male/female discord. The women did not strike often, but they were put out of work by the strikes. In only one of the strikes reported did women weavers join male workers—thirty-five women accompanied seventy men in the initial walkout on 20 November 1899. In Wattrelos on 4 December 1899, there were taunting serenades outside the homes of families whose daughters did not join the strike at the Motte wool-combing establishment in Roubaix. The parents were blamed for their daughters' lack of solidarity, an accusation that may have been justified in some cases; one of the fathers involved was himself a dissident from the strike (Archives departmentales 23 Nov. 1899, 4 Dec. 1899).

Women textile workers were also especially vulnerable because there were many young women seeking work. In a strike of women bobbin winders in December 1880, fourteen women protested the dismissal of one of their coworkers. Their employer promptly gave them their papers and replaced them with no difficulty. Moreover, most women workers, single or married, lived with families. Their families claimed their wages and loyalty and could influence, particularly among young women, their decisions about striking. That women were proletarian wage earners was not sufficient to promote their participation in collective action parallel to that of men. This was due less to personal characteristics, such as the female passivity so often invoked by contemporaries, than to situational factors. Young single women, in particular, were less likely to strike because of their economically vulnerable position, their relatively brief commitment to industrial employment, their lack of opportunity to develop solidarity on or off the job, and, finally, their reliance on the family for personal well being. The situation was different for married women. Although relatively few of them worked at any time, even in the textile industry, it is likely that over the years an individual women worked often enough to develop connections and a kind of solidarity with other workers, as well as lore about strikes, which could serve her when the occasion to strike arose. At this time, I have no evidence of differential participation rates in strikes by married women, but statistics indicate that there were more women strikers, proportionately, as the female textile work force came to include proportionately more married women after 1900.

Mining and Metalworking Industry

The metalworking and mining town, another prototypical industrial city, was characterized by quite a different industrial organization and household division of labor. Men and boys were the primary wage earners, and wives were concerned with the home, children, and food purchase and preparation. Young women could be coal sorters at the mine, or perhaps servants, but few other jobs existed for women.

The coal miner's wife was noted among workers' wives in her active role in work-related struggles. She had often been employed in the mine as a girl; she knew the work of the mine. As a married woman, she had to deal with the company as landlord, as owner of the store, as distributor of health services, and sometimes, even, as school board. Michelle Perrott writes that the mine strike was an "affair of the tribe: committed, the women demonstrated unequalled tenacity, seeking contributions for aid to strikers, organizing their slim resources, boosting the flagging morale of the men, involving themselves with the policing of the strike. At the time the workers' shifts changed, they stood across the roads, [and] blocked access of scabs to the pits" (Perrot 1974:405).

An incident illustrative of women's collective action occurred in April 1906, in Billy-Montigny, a mining town in the Pas-de-Calais. A month earlier, a disaster had shaken the pits of nearby Courrières. More than a thousand miners were trapped and died. A strike followed; the miners demanded that the companies attend to their workers' safety. The action was bitter and violent and included a dynamite attack on an employer's home.

On 10 April a group of five hundred women carrying red and tricolored flags trimmed with black crepe went to the train station in Billy-Montigny to meet a woman believed to be on the train from Bethune. Madame Ringard was returning from the *chef-leiur* (county seat), where she had given testimony to a judge against three accused bombers. She was not on the train, but the crowd searched the platforms, assembled to sing the "Internationale," and marched off down the street. The same day another group of women carrying black flags marched to petition the mine administration to hasten rescue efforts in the flooded pits, as some survivors had been found. The two groups joined. When police and soldiers tried to hasten the procession, "a great number of rocks were thrown at the soldiers (*Temps*, 11 April 1966).

The women who met the train at Billy-Montigny were seeking to discipline the woman who, they believed, had betrayed the striking workers. The second women's demonstration indicates the utter dependence of the wife on her husband's wages. The death of a husband was devastating to the miner's wife, who lived in a community where it was very difficult for a woman to support herself. The women were not wage earners; they could not strike, but they expressed their solidarity with striking workers through a demonstration.

Another homemakers' protest, a version of the food riot, was launched in 1911 in Ferrière-la-Grande, a metalworking city in the northern industrial belt near Maubeuge. Women from a nearby town dumped a merchant's goods when he refused to lower his prices. In Maubeuge itself, on 25 August, a crowd broke the windows of a butter merchant. On Saturday, 26 August, no butter or eggs were available in the market. A small group of women wearing red insignia marched into the marketplace. As they marched, they sang, to the tune of the "Internationale,"

> Rise, each mother of a family
> Arise and let us unite
> Let's march to fight the misery
> That the farmers have brought down on the country.
> And if one day we are victorious
> We'll show our dear husbands
> That all women have fought
> For the lives of their poor little ones.
>
> Forward comrades,
> Friends, rise with us,
> No fear, no riot
> We want butter at fifteen sous![3]

A wave of protest about food prices swept over the industrial departments, including a violent incident at Billy-Montigny on 30 August. There a crowd of women and men attacked a baker's wagon. The baker shot one of the demonstrators, and the crowd turned on him in fury. When he hid in a house, the crowd smashed the windows, looted the chicken coop, and set a wagon on fire before they were dispersed by gendarmes (*Temps* 31 August 1911).

Both the protest over food prices and the strike-related collective action originated among women in the households with a strict division of labor. The miners and metallurgists left housework and child rearing to their wives. The women, in turn, were expected to use male wages to purchase a comfortable living. The worker's home, like the bourgeois home, was a haven from work—a haven for which the wife was primarily responsible. With this household division of labor, the wife's role as wise consumer was salient.

This consumer interest recalls the role of women in the eighteenth-century grain and bread riot. Yet there are differences. The 1911 food protest began in industrial areas, not in agricultural marketing or administrative cities (Hanson 1976; Flonneau 1970:60–62; Perrot 1974:130–34) The object was less often the basic diet items of bread and grain and more often butter, milk, and eggs. The protestors were often connected with unions or parties—witness the red insignia and the "Internationale Butter." Indeed, the unions soon took over the movement and began formal, nationwide demonstrations. The early demonstrators tried to police prices, just as coal miners' wives policed the strike. Those who resisted their demands, who tried to elude the set price, were attacked. The reporters for *Le Figaro* who filed the report from Maubeuge on 27 August 1911 employed the strike metaphor when he wrote that the protest was "more than a strike but not quite a crusade" (*Figaro* 27 Aug. 1911).

Still other aspects of the 1911 collective action clearly distinguished it from the earlier grain and bread riot. The women's food demonstration, which had an elected committee and a designated chair, was organized in a more formal and almost bureaucratic fashion than was the food riot, a protest held together by the rioters' shared sense of justice and communal rights. It was the consumer interest of working-class wives which led them to protest in 1911, but the form of their action had more in common with other collective actions of the period than with the food riot of the Old Regime.

Tobacco Industry

We have seen women as purposeful actors in strikes and demonstrations in late nineteenth-century France. Whether, when, and how they acted was determined by their familiar position as well as by the organization of production. Their interests were often familial, whether they were supporting striking husbands, protesting high consumer prices, or striking (or choosing not to strike) on their own behalf. We return now to the tobacco workers, whose work situation pulled them away from family interest and placed them in a different relationship to their work.

The factories in the tobacco monopoly—which produced cigarettes, cigars, loose tobacco, and matches—employed thousands of people in one institution, the majority of them women. Women in the tobacco industry worked each day in shops far removed from their households. Although they were generally unmarried, as were most women workers, a disproportionate number were married women, as the jobs in the tobacco industry were relatively secure and skilled. Cigar makers in France apprenticed and trained for several years, and, unlike the comparable labor force in the United States, the majority of French cigar makers were women (Mannheim 1902:22). The privileges these skilled workers won were often passed on to their co-workers. A tobacco worker's daughter often sought a position in the same shop as her mother; working conditions and wages were superior to those of most female jobs (ibid.; 63; see also Perrot 1974: 329–30; Guilbert 1966: 93–99). Apprenticeship, parent-to-child continuity in the same occupation, and lifetime commitment to one job provided opportunities for the development of solidarity and association among women tobacco workers not unlike the opportunities of male craftsmen and skilled workers.

In fact, the tobacco workers founded mutual aid or friendly societies and then formed unions, just as did male skilled workers and artisans. In the Lyon strike described in the introduction of this chapter, a mutual club preceded the strike, and its leaders represented the women (Mannheim 1902: 421). The first union was set up two days after a successful strike in January 1887, in Marseille. The tobacco workers organized to improve conditions of work and to claim benefits such as paid maternity leave. The particularities of their work situation accounted for the assertiveness of these women in defining and acting in their interests. In addition, their average pay was closer to men's salaries than was the pay of other women workers. The tobacco workers' earning power continued to increase over most of their working lives because of their long-term work commitment. (To be sure, these factors could have been a result as well as a cause of their activism.)

The organization and scale of the tobacco industry also promoted association by grouping many women together and possibly even by segregating women in certain positions; teams of workers were paid as teams. It is not surprising, then, that tobacco workers organized in female or predominantly female groups. Theirs was one of the few unions in which women played a significant leadership role. Their activism was an ongoing affair, not tied to temporary mobilization and strikes. It led a male supervisor to complain, "Neither the privileges which the state worker enjoys nor the generosity and concessions which they have received have led them to moderate their demands" (quoted in Zylberberg-Hocquard 1978). These women knew what they wanted and were ready to fight for it.

CONCLUSION

The cases examined here, focusing on working-class women's collective action in different proletarianized situations—household manufacture in the Cambrèsis, the silk industry of Lyon and the Lyonnais, the large-scale textile industry of the Nord, the mining and metalworking industry, and the tobacco industry—illustrate the conditions under which such collective action was more or less common. They do not address the questions of women organizing and acting on women's issues but, rather, the ways in which industrial capitalism changed and shaped wage labor and households, men's and women's relations to each, and patterns of collective action.

Characteristics of the organization of production and the household division of labor were critical variables in women's participation in collective action. Women working in household production were isolated from other workers except family members. The chief of the household productive organization was also head of the family. Hence, in the strikes in domestic industry, the heads of household acted for the family as they did in other relationships with the state or with employers.

Some women in the large-scale silk industry of Lyon were isolated from their families when they were at work because they lived in dormitories at their place of employment. But these women were frequently working for their families or to save for marriage, which made them extremely vulnerable to possible employer retaliation if they complained or acted collectively. In the face of a massive class mobilization, however, such women did join a strike movement. As time went on, more women who worked in silk factories were older, "permanent" workers; that is, they worked for more of their lives, though not necessarily continuously. This gave them the opportunity to build networks of solidarity and association and, I speculate, a higher propensity to class-based workplace actions. Furthermore, the silk industry unions facilitated women's organization through women's committees.

In the Nord, women workers in the early years of the cotton and wool textile industry were more likely to be young and single. In the workplace their work differed from that of men, and they were less skilled. If employers tried to substitute female workers for male, the men blamed the women and perceived the only way out of the problem as eliminating or limiting women's work. Compared with men, women were shut out of workers' organizations. Their family connections also tended to isolate single women from other workers with similar class interests. Sometimes they were pressed to strike (or pressed not to strike) by family as well as class interest, or by personal inclination, but they lacked both independent associations and opportunities to build solidarity. Thus it is no surprise to find uncertainty and lower levels of strike participation among young women. The sexual division of labor in the household could act as a deterrent for married women workers, for they were obliged to do housework as well as wage work. There were also cases of husbands who intervened to prevent their wives' striking. Nevertheless, as the cotton and wool industry, like the silk industry, hired more married women, their lifetime commitment to wage work and the opportunity to build association gave women more chances to participate in collective action.

Paradoxically, perhaps a very strict division of labor in the household, such as that in the homes of metal and mining workers, seems to have encouraged wives to participate actively in workplace struggles because of their dependence on the wages of the male head of the household. The community of work in these industries included women, even if women were not themselves wage laborers. Women in this setting, and other wives whose major concern was managing household consumption also acted out of consumer interests.

Only in the case of the tobacco industry was there strong participation of women in class-based workplace collective action, which grew out of the special characteristics of their work, the organization of production, and their lifetime commitments.

This historical evidence, then, suggests that proletarian women will tend to act collectively more often when *as workers*

(1) they associate with others with similar interests;
(2) they can translate these interests into structured association;
(3) they have resources they can mobilize and deploy;
(4) their employers are dependent on their regular supply of labor;
(5) there is a favorable economic climate, which means that withdrawal of labor represents a real burden for the employer and, potentially, a real gain for the workers;
(6) their position is not extremely vulnerable;
(7) there is a general climate of economic claims; and
(8) their position in the household division of labor gives them the opportunity to act autonomously.

Furthermore, women will tend to act collectively more often *as members of households* when

(9) the household itself is mobilized in defense of interests that can be generalized as those of the household as well as of individual members.

These conclusions do not differ very markedly from those that predict higher participation rates by men. The chief difference is the case of defense of household consumer interest. Women were much more likely than men to participate in such collective action. Responsibility for household consumption was rarely a primary concern of men in an industrial economy. A general theory about comparative propensity to participate in working-class collective action, whether strikes or food protest, informs about women, too. No special psychological or gender-attribute explanation is needed to understand women's proportionately lower participation rates. Certain women, in positions and situations that promoted their readiness to act, did act. The paths of proletarianization shaped women's wage labor and their family responsibility and, consequently, determined both their propensity to act collectively and the form of action they chose.

Notes

1. See Purcell (1979) for comparable conclusions in present-day England but a model that explains low rates of female strike participation in terms of situational factors rather than personal characteristics.

2. The economic change described above is more fully discussed in Tilly and Scott (1978).

3. From *Le Figaro* (Paris), 27 Aug. 1911, quoted in Hanson (1976) and Flonneau (1970). The following citations from *Le Temps* and *Le Figaro* are also quoted in Hanson 1976.

3

Uneven Development: Class, Race, and Gender in the United States Before 1900

LEITH MULLINGS

It is by now well established that the modern world is characterized by uneven development—the development of Europe and the United States through the underdevelopment of Africa, Latin America, and Asia. Just as the popular explanations of this inequality have ignored the relationships of exploitation with the underdeveloped world, so too have these frameworks ignored the uneven development in the "developed" world, stemming from unequal exploitation and incorporation of labor. In the United States, stratification based on race and ethnicity as well as class and gender was both a prerequisite for and a creation of modern capitalist development.

During the nineteenth century, the United States entered a period of rapid economic development, becoming the most advanced capitalist country in the world. This set the stage for the imperialistic enterprises at the turn of the century that were to involve the invasion of the Philippines, the Spanish-American War, and, in the twentieth century, economic and military interventions in Africa, Asia, and Latin America. The wealth that enabled the build-up of military power was generated in part by the massive amount of free labor provided by enslaved Africans and Afro-Americans and indentured Euro-Americans, as well as the cheap labor provided by free immigrant Euro-Americans.

As the status of women all over the world was affected by the manner in which "development" took place, so too in the United States women's labor was an integral aspect of economic development. Since the structure of labor differed by race and class, as well as by gender, the experiences of women of different races and classes were fundamentally different.

The ways in which class and race have affected the lives of women have not been sufficiently recognized and studied by feminist scholars. "Radical feminists" in particular have tended to ignore these variables, suggesting that they are divisive. Patriarchy, stemming from the sex-ordered division of labor, is held to be the major form of oppression, equally shared by all women. In industrial societies, the private/public dichotomy is seen as a basic mechanism for maintaining patriarchy. Heidi Hartmann (1976) summarizes this view, which is fairly common among scholars of women's history in the United States: "In our society the sexual division of labor is hierarchical, with men on top and women on the bottom. . . . It is my contention that the roots of women's present status lie in this sex-ordered division of labor." Recently, scholars concerned with class and race have suggested that the "radical-feminist" perspective derives primarily from the experiences of upper- and middle-class Euro-American women and that the bases of gender oppression are a great deal more complicated. Bonnie Dill (1983), for example, suggests that "Minority women experience patriarchal society, but are denied protections that public patriarchy offers Euro-American women." Angela Davis's (1981) comprehensive work demonstrates the importance of race and class in any analysis of women in the United States.

This chapter follows the latter line of reasoning by examining the ways in which class and race conditioned the experiences of women in the private and public spheres during the period of industrialization in the United States. I will first discuss the period prior to industrialization—loosely called the colonial epoch—since it lays the basis for the developments we will find in the nineteenth century.[1] This is not meant to be a historical account, but rather one that will highlight certain ethnographic issues. Because Afro-American women have been omitted so often from women's histories, I give special attention to their lives before and after slavery.

COLONIAL PERIOD

Women came freely and in bondage to a world built on the land of the native Americans that was called "new." Patterns of labor exploitation that were to characterize the United States were established during the founding of the colony, giving women of different classes and ethnic groups, as well as their men, qualitatively different experiences.

The early colonial economy was characterized by small-scale agriculture and business. The economic conditions, along with the shortage of women, produced a marked flexibility in both public and household spheres for free Euro-American women, despite ideologies of gender differentiation. Women participated in economically productive work in the fields as well as in the house, and work was considered a duty for both married and single women. After the initial stages of settlement, work in the fields after the first crop was harvested became more infrequent for free Euro-American women, with custom decreeing that "only those wenches that are not fit to be so employed were put to the ground" (cited in Ryan 1983:27). As we shall note, unfit wenches included enslaved African women.

While it was true that ownership of land accrued predominantly to male heads of households, in some locations—particularly in states of the earlier settlements—land could be owned by women. For example, in Virginia in 1634, opposition to women's legal entitlement to land ownership was overcome (Spruill 1938:11). Villages in Massachusetts, Pennsylvania, and Maryland traditionally allocated land to women (Ryan 1983:23). Women could inherit lands from husbands and fathers, and widows often used such resources to carry on as independent traders and entrepreneurs. The elasticity in the way in which women's roles were defined allowed an important minority of women, particularly those in or near towns, to be employed outside the home in male-dominated commercial activities (Blau 1978:30; Foner 1980:8–9; Degler 1980:365).

Within the household, free Euro-American women were granted some protection by law, custom, and theology. The family was considered to be a cornerstone of society, and colonial courts intervened if men dealt brutally with wives, daughters, or female servants (Ryan 1983:37–38). Family handbooks of the seventeenth century advised husbands in their behavior toward wives "seldom to reprove: and never to smite her" (Spruill 1938:163). In New England some aspects of Puritan theology "worked to mitigate the domestic despotism of patriarchy," with wives admonished not to idolize their husbands (Ryan 1983:38).

As colonial land grants were exhausted and private enterprise developed, the distribution of wealth grew more uneven. This brought with it not only the widening chasm between male and female activities, but—as the planters' and merchants' elite was strengthened—the lives of women of different classes became more divergent. For free women of all classes, the developing separation of market and household spheres meant increasing centrality of the household. However, upper-class women could delegate most of the actual household work to servants and spend much of the day in leisure activities. Nancy Shippen Livingstone, the daughter of a prosperous Philadelphia merchant and the wife of a New York aristocrat, described her routine as follows:

This morning I gave orders to the servants as usual for the business of the day, then took a little work in my hands and set down before the fire to think how I should dispose of myself in the evening. The morning I generally devoted to working and reading, and I concluded to go to the concert. Then I considered what I would dress in, and having determined this important part, I felt light and easy [cited in Ryan 1983:93].

This lifestyle perhaps reached its extreme in the planter class, about which Chastellux commented that the "natural idolence" of Virginia women was augmented by the luxury of being served by a large number of slaves (Spruill 1938:76). The extent of available help is evident in the case of Elizabeth Pinckney, who, living alone after the marriage of her children, was said to keep a rather modest establishment. She described her domestic help as follows:

> I shall keep young Ebba to do the drudgery part, fetch wood and water, and scour, and learn as much as she is capable of Cooking and Washing. Mary-Ann cooks, makes my bed and makes my punch. Daphne works and makes the bread, old Ebba boils the cow's victuals, raises and fattens the poultry, Moses is employed from breakfast until 12 o'clock without doors, after that in the house. Pegg washes and milks [cited in Spruill 1938:77].

George Washington wrote of the necessity of hiring a servant to "relieve Mrs. Washington from the drudgery of ordering, and seeing the table properly covered, and things economically used" (Spruill 1938:77).

Indenture

The "drudgery" was generally performed by the unfree. In the early seventeenth century, the domestics on plantations were frequently indentured servants. One of every three passengers disembarking from the Atlantic passage in seventeenth-century Virginia was a woman, the majority of whom were indentured servants (Ryan 1983:22). Indentured servants were bound to work for a limited period. Death rates were high for indentured servants, though most of those who lived could look forward to freedom in the early period, and perhaps a subsidy of tools and land when their indenture was completed. The nature of the work of female indentured servants was usually determined by the status of the family for which they worked: the servant of a small planter might do some field work, while that of a wealthy planter would most often be a domestic servant.

Although female servants were undoubtedly vulnerable to sexual exploitation, the extent to which this occurred seems to have been limited by moral norms and legal protections (Carr and Walsh 1979:30): female servants could and did sue masters for support of children (Ryan 1983:42). Indentured servants, in general, possessed some rights to life and contract and could bring suit to enforce contract rights (Foner 1980:5). After the term of indenture ended, a female servant could, and often did, become a planter's wife. Particularly where there was a shortage of women, indentured servants experienced some liberty in making their choices (Kennedy 1979; Carr and Walsh 1979; Lerner 1979).

Slavery

Indentured servants did not meet the growing labor needs of the colony, and captured Africans were brought to the colonies against their will. In 1619, the first group of twenty Africans was brought to Jamestown, Virginia. They were indentured servants, but between 1660 and 1682, court decisions and special laws transformed African servants into slaves. By the end of the seventeenth century, domestics on plantations were predominantly enslaved Africans; and with the expansion of tobacco, rice, and indigo plantations after 1700, the number of slaves rapidly increased.

Among enslaved Africans, the concern for fullest exploitation and highest profits muted gender differentiation in the public sphere. As Angela Davis has put it, "the starting point for any exploration of Black women's lives under slavery would be an appraisal of their role as workers" (1981:5). The majority of slaves in the Deep South were agricultural workers, women frequently doing the same work as men. Owens notes: "A standard claim was that 'women can do plowing very well and full well with the hoes and equal to men at picking' " (1976:39). Julia Brown remembers: "I worked hard as always. You can't imagine what a hard time I had. I split rails like a man. I used a huge glut and a iron wedge drove into the wood with a maul, and this would split the wood" (cited in Yetman 1970:47).

The workday of the enslaved woman was very different from that of the Euro-American plantation mistress:

I never knowed what it was to rest. I just work all de time from mornin' till late at night. I had to do everythin' dey was to do on de outside. Work in de field, chop wood, hoe corn, till sometime I feels like my back surely break. . . . In de summer we had to work outdoors, in de winter in de house. I had to card and spin till ten o'clock. Never get much rest, had to get up at four de next mornin' and start again. Didn't get much to eat, neither, just a li'l corn bread and 'lasses. Lordy, you cain't know what a time I had. All cold and hungry. I ain't tellin' no lies. It de gospel truth. It sure is [Sarah Gudger in Yetman 1970:151].

Household relationships were, of course, constrained by the fact that slave families were at best uncertain: members could be sold, raped, or killed. Some indication of the prevalence of this disruption is evident in the post–Civil-War marriage records. Analysis of data on marriage registrations of 2,880 Afro-American couples by the Union Army in 1864–65 indicates that only 13.6 percent of the couples registered had been able to live together without disruption. Of those who had been separated from a previous spouse, over one-third of the marriages were broken by the slave owner, presumably through sale, and approximately one-half were disrupted by the death of a spouse. Similar results were indicated by a study of 450 slave marriages in

Louisiana, where 35.7 percent were broken by the slave owner and 51.5 percent were disrupted by the death of a spouse (Degler 1980:119).

For African and Afro-American women there were few protections in the reproductive sphere. In fact, as Davis (1981:7) points out, rape became a weapon of terrorism used against enslaved people to facilitate the exploitation of labor. These mothers bore children, but had no rights to them. A year after the importation of Africans was halted, a South Carolina court ruled that children could be sold away from their mothers because "the young of slaves . . . stand on the same footing as other animals" (cited in Davis 1980:7). Delia Garlic recalls:

Slavery days was hell. I growed up when de War come, and I was a mother before it closed. Babies was snatched from deir mother's breast and sold to speculators. Chillens was separated from sisters and brothers and never saw each other again. Course dey cry. You think they not cry when dey was sold like cattle? I could tell you about it all day, but even den you couldn't guess de awfulness of it [in Yetman 1970:133].

Yet people take conditions that have been thrust upon them and out of them create a history and a future. Recently historians have documented the processes by which Afro-Americans, using African forms where possible and creating new forms where necessary, put together families as best they could (see especially Gutman 1976). Some slave owners encouraged the formation of the completed family. No doubt this was sometimes for humanitarian reasons, but clearly many sought to maintain labor discipline by exploiting the affective bonds between family members with direct and indirect threats and incentives. After the escape of one of his slaves, a slaveholder observed, "he would not go anywhere remote from his wife, for whom he always indicated strong attachment" (cited in Owens 1976:85). Noah Davis, a slave whose master allowed him to travel and deliver sermons to raise money for his freedom, said, "How can I leave my wife and seven children, to go to Baltimore. . . . I thought my children would need my watchful care" (cited in Owens 1976:198). The family was, as always, a place of refuge, a source of strength, and an inspiration for rebellion—but also a means of control.

Notwithstanding affective bonds, men and women resisted slavery. Women with children were perhaps inhibited from fleeing slavery, but some did, sometimes pregnant and sometimes with children. The late Lathan A. Windley's publication of the advertisements for runaway slaves from the 1730s to 1790, in Virginia, North Carolina, Maryland, South Carolina, and Georgia, found a significantly higher number of male than female fugitives, but some of the cases of women were rather dramatic. For the five areas, 6,373 men, 1,258 women (including 26 who were described as pregnant), and 215 children under ten were advertised for as fugitives (Aptheker 1984:10). Flight of women alone was somewhat unusual, but it did occur. For example, in 1785 in South Carolina, Charles H. Simmons of Charlestown announced the flight of "THREE NEGRO WENCHES: JENNY, an elderly short wench; DIDO her daughter about 35 years of age, middle stature; and TISSEY, her grand-daughter with a young child at her breast." An announcement that six adult slaves had fled a plantation in Savannah, Georgia, pointed out that two of these were women and that Sue, who was about thirty-five years old, quite short, and "is now and has been for a long time lame with the rheumatism, even to her finger ends (but nevertheless) . . . carried her three children with her, viz. Juno, a girl of 10 years; Sarah, 7 years; and Dolly, 3½ years old" (ibid.:17).[2]

Although slavery often drove blood relatives apart, shared oppression brought non-blood relatives together in extended family groups. Generations later, the descendants of the slaves—faced with modern enclosure of land in the South and economic depression driving apart blood relatives—responded with fictive kin networks for collective survival. Life in the slave quarters, a welcome retreat from slave society, included adoption of relatives, socialization of children, and care of the elderly. Although there is some disagreement about the significance of gender-based division of labor, most recent findings support Davis's contention that with the household the "salient theme is one of sexual equality" (1981:17). The relative equality was reflected in the marriage vows recited on one plantation. The groom pledged to perform the "duties of an affectionate and faithful husband" and the bride similarly pledged to be "an affectionate and faithful wife" (cited in Ryan 1983:162) without assertions of obedience.

After work in the field and factory, both men and women had additional tasks to perform for their own households. Men often did extra hunting, fishing, or agricultural work to help provide the family with food. Women often had domestic tasks to perform. Yet even here, the division of labor does not seem rigid. Owens notes that many young women hunted with great success (1976:196).

Women had the extra burden of childbearing and frequently worked up until childbirth and soon afterward. Owens suggests that the general rule applying to enslaved women after childbirth was "make her do something, for as long as she hugs that sick house, she'll never get well" (cited in Owens 1976:40). Carrying their newborns on their backs, enslaved women returned to work in the fields and fed them as they could. Sometimes slaveholders permitted enslaved mothers to spend extra time caring for children, which would be made up by extra work by the father of the children (Owens 1976:200). The division of labor, to the extent that it existed, seemed geared toward facilitating the survival of the family. One of the ironies of slavery was that disenfranchisement of both men and women meant that the enslaved family possessed no means by which one gender could control the other.

Discussion

In this period, women of different classes emerge with clearly different experiences, options, and constraints. The lives of women of different classes are at least as different from one another in these respects as they are from the men of their own classes. For Euro-American women, class distinctions were becoming more salient and the public/private dichotomy was solidifying. In the early phases, women of the planter class had access to resources primarily through their husbands and fathers, but could command some independence through participation in manufacture, agriculture, and some commercial enterprises. The extent to which they were subject to the limitations of sex-role ideologies tended to be modified by demographic and technological conditions. The limited political rights of indentured servants, and later of poor Euro-American women, were shared with the men of their class. In the early period, the division of labor was probably less extreme, and availability of land allowed a certain flexibility in the mobility structure. In later periods, these women too were affected by the emerging segregation of roles by gender.

The lives of enslaved women were very different. These women shared with men of their class a complete lack of property rights or even rights over their own bodies. They often did what was considered to be men's work. They shared the reproductive burdens of both the planter's wife and the indentured servant, but they had no protection of their sexuality or their families, except that which they could muster themselves, within the confines of the slave system. Here we find a major distinction between the lives of the free and the unfree. The sex division of labor seems to have been greatest in the planter class. This was reflected in the household, and relationships seem to have been the most patriarchal in the emerging merchant, planter, and artisan classes (see Farber 1973).

Given the realities of the lives of enslaved women versus the ideologies of gender-based role differentiation, it is not surprising that stereotypes begin to emerge that we will find throughout U.S. history. Because Afro-American women performed tasks that were thought to distinguish men from women and possessed qualities that were considered taboo by womanhood of this epoch, symbols and later theoretical formulations defined the feats accomplished by Afro-American women as unfeminine and defined femininity in contrast to Afro-American women. Surely the images of the enslaved woman hewing wood and the shy, retiring plantation mistress, prone to fainting, have little in common.

INDUSTRIALIZATION

In the first half of the nineteenth century, slavery, wage labor, and small-farm and artisan labor competed for dominance. The victory of wage labor culminated in the Civil War, as industrial capitalism became the dominant mode of production. With industrialization and the rise of the so-called robber barons, who obtained government legislation authorizing them to seize natural resources and force out competitors, class differences were intensified.

Distinctions between women of different classes, certainly clear during the previous epoch, became further entrenched and functioned to signify and strengthen class differences. By mid-nineteenth century the majority of native-born women had husbands who were relatively comfortable farmers, shopkeepers, managers, clerks, and professionals, with only a small proportion being unskilled workers (Ryan 1983:148). During this period, employment opportunities for middle- and upper-income women decreased, as gender restrictions in businesses, trades, and professions became more stringent. Thus, for most women access to resources was largely a matter of the occupation of their husbands and fathers. However, in states such as Virginia, New York, and others where married women were granted property rights, women seem to have had some independent access to financial resources.[3] There were also some avenues to independent income; for example, urban middle-class wives often increased their income by taking boarders.

Domesticity: Elite and Middle Stratum Women

The cults of domesticity and true womanhood that proliferated during this period reflected ideologically the increased wealth that allowed some women not to work outside the home, the growing separation of home and workplace, and the nascent consumerism. Based on the assertion of the dichotomy between home and workplace, the contrast between male and female natures, and the idealization of motherhood (Harris 1978:33), the cult of domesticity affirmed, for all classes, the home as the only sphere of the "true" woman. Although elite and middle-class women were discouraged from pursuing careers in business and their professions, their access to financial resources—or to the fruits of them—gave them privileges that neither men nor women of other classes possessed. They clearly experienced a public/private dichotomy: their realm was the household. However, once again, much of the work was done by servants, leaving some leisure for pursuit of other interests.

Harriet Beecher Stowe, for example, who was by no means wealthy, plaintively reveals her boredom with the confines of domestic life, but also makes clear the extent of help from servants in her relatively modest household. In a letter to a Miss May, written 21 June 1838, she laments the change in her personality since becoming a wife and mother and describes her day:

> In the first place I waked about half after four and thought, "Bless me, how light it is! I must get out of bed and rap to wake up Mina, for breakfast must be had at six o'clock this morning." . . . "Dear me, broad daylight! I must go down and see if Mina is getting breakfast." . . . Then back I come to the nursery, where, remembering that it is washing day and that there is a great

deal of work to be done, I apply myself vigorously to sweeping, dusting, and the setting to rights so necessary where there are three little mischiefs always pulling down as fast as one can put up. Then there are Miss H— and Miss E—, concerning whom Mary will furnish you with all suitable particulars, who are chattering, hallooing, or singing at the tops of their voices, as may suit their various states of mind, while the nurse is getting their breakfast ready. This meal being cleared away, Mr. Stowe dispatched to market with various memoranda of provisions, etc., and the baby being washed and dressed, I begin to think what next must be done. I start to cut out some little dresses. . . . By and by the nurse comes up from her sweeping. I commit the children to her, and finish cutting out the frocks. . . . But let this suffice, for of such details as these are all my days made up. Indeed, my dear, I am but a mere drudge with few ideas beyond babies and housekeeping [cited in Stowe 1889:90–92].

While the work the women performed in the home contributed to the growth of an industrial society, it was the working class and enslaved men and women whose labor created the wealth that allowed the middle- and upper-class domestic lifestyles to exist. By the close of the eighteenth century, the first mechanized factories were taking entire families—including women—to work in conditions reminiscent of industrializing England.[4] Wages were determined by gender and age, with women and children making less than men (see Ryan 1983:84).

Euro-American Women Workers

By 1850, women worked in nearly 175 industries in manufacturing, through their low wages creating the surplus value that helped to build the economy. The extent to which women worked outside the home was conditioned by class, ethnicity, and marital status. For many Euro-American working-class women, leaving the paid labor force upon marriage was an ideal to strive for, although not always attained. It was, however, attained more frequently by those Euro-American working women whose husbands were able to make a so-called family wage. The cult of domesticity, disseminated through the church, the educational system, and popular literature, sought to define femininity for all classes of women, but also became the basis of the demand for the family wage that allowed women and children to stay at home.

For some, the ideal of the woman's sphere could become a reality. U.S. census figures of 1860 show only about 15 percent of adult women employed outside the home (Ryan 1983:117). A study conducted by the Bureau of Labor in 1887 found that 75 percent of the female industrial labor force was under twenty-five and that 96 percent of them were single. As of 1890 the average tenure of women's work outside the home was only eleven years (Ryan 1983:175–76).

These conditions, however, did not pertain equally to all strata of women. The Irish, for example, the largest group to immigrate during the earlier phase, faced some of the worst socioeconomic conditions among Euro-American groups. In the Irish-dominated Sixth Ward of New York in 1855, 44 percent of women between the ages of fifteen and forty-nine were gainfully employed, primarily in domestic and personal service. While most women working outside the home in this area were young and single, most married women took in boarders in order to supplement their income (Groneman 1977:85), a practice that was fairly widespread among urban working-class women (see Ryan 1983:147).

Studies increasingly suggest that married women, depending on their socioeconomic circumstances, participated in the labor force more frequently than was originally thought. In Lowell, Massachusetts, for example, by 1860 one-half of the households were female headed (Degler 1980:371). After the Civil War as many as half of all Irish women were without a spouse because of widowhood, desertion, or separation (Ryan 1983:156). It is reasonable to assume that such women moved in and out of the labor force as necessary. Working-class Italian women, on the other hand, tended not to work outside the home to the same extent as other groups (McLaughlin 1977). In 1890 in New York City, fewer than one in twenty Italian wives were employed outside the household; among Jewish wives, the figure was one in fifty (Ryan 1983:177).

These women, too, were responsible for the domestic sphere, but this probably meant doing most of the work without servants. The extent to which participation in the labor force gave working-class women greater autonomy in the household is not clear, but the hypothesis that working gained them some autonomy is not unreasonable. Young single women contributed a major portion of their wages to their family of origin (Ryan 1983:176), but their wages could also be used to gain power and privileges at home, to escape from social pressures, to leave home and decide how their wages were to be spent, and to have something comparable to a dowry in seeking a marriage partner (Kennedy 1979:16–17). Most married women were not in the wage-labor force, but often worked in the home, sewing or taking in boarders. In addition to the extra money made in this fashion, working-class wives usually had charge of the spending money for the household (Ryan 1983:180–81). This frequently meant the entire paycheck (Degler 1980:136), and women often had charge of most decisions. New research, unimpeded by the stereotype of the working-class male, is needed to clarify the extent to which working class men wielded power in the household.

Afro-American Women Workers, Slave and Free

While Euro-American working-class women toiled in the factories, and elite women adorned parlors, several hundred thousand Afro-American women,

men, and children were undergoing mass disruption. Individuals were sold away and families separated as export agriculture shifted from the upper to the lower South between 1815 and 1860. These enslaved laborers planted and picked the cotton for the mills in which the free Euro-American labor force worked. By the midnineteenth century, seven out of eight slaves—men and women—were field workers (Davis 1981:5). Enslaved labor was also used for industry. In textile, hemp, tobacco, sugar-refining, and rice-milling factories, in the lumber and transportation industries, and in foundries, saltworks, and mines, women did what was considered to be men's work (see Foner 1980:99). The following observation of a Carolinian was probably typical and accurate: "In ditching, particularly in canals . . . a woman can do nearly as much work as a man" (cited in Starobin 1970).

For free Afro-Americans,[5] who were not permitted to work as operatives in shops and factories, the industrial revolution did not change the types of work available to either men or women. In the South, free Afro-American women worked as cooks, laundresses, and housekeepers. In the North, the types of work available to Afro-Americans was not much different. According to the 1838 census of Philadelphia, among Afro-Americans, eight out of every ten working men were unskilled workers, with 38 percent working as laborers, 11.5 percent as porters, 11.5 percent as waiters, 5 percent as seamen, 4 percent as carters, and 10 percent in miscellaneous laboring capacities (Hershberg 1972:199). In 1847 less than .5 percent of the Afro-American male work force were employed in factories (Hershberg 1972:191). Of the women, more than eight out of ten were employed as domestic servants in day-work capacities. By 1880, one in every five Afro-Americans in this area lived and worked in a white household as a domestic servant, demonstrating the pervasive job discrimination that occurred at the same time that industrialization was providing widening job opportunities for Euro-American men and women (ibid.). Up to 1859 there were no Afro-American women employed in the cotton mills or other factories in the area (Foner 1980:105). This situation was typical of the industrial North, where Afro-Americans were excluded from the burgeoning industrial job market.

After emancipation, Afro-Americans in the South became sharecroppers and tenants. Like Euro-American working women who had struggled for the family wage, Afro-American women attempted to withdraw from the labor force and to demand for their men wages that would support a family. In 1865, an Alabama plantation owner complained to his daughter, "The women say they never mean to do any more outdoor work, that white men support their wives and that they mean that their husbands shall support them." A plantation mistress had a similar complaint about one of her exslaves: "Pete is still in the notion of remaining but chooses to feed his wife out of his wages rather than get her fed for her services" (Gutman 1976:167–68).

Inexpensive labor was important for getting out the cotton crop at the highest levels of profit. A Georgia planter predicted, "You will never see three million bales of cotton raised in the South again unless the labor system is improved. . . . One third of the hands are *women* who *now* do not work at all" (Gutman 1976:167). Boston capitalists worried about the effect of the withdrawal of women on their profits: "A very large proportion of the women have left the fields and stay at home in the cabins. This, in looking to the future, is a serious loss, one over which there is no control" (Gutman 1976:168). There was some control, and in some cases immediate and direct measures were taken to force women back into the fields. For example, a Louisiana planter instructed that rent be charged to the nonworking wives of exslaves who were working on his plantation (ibid.). Given the prevailing ideology that the woman's place was in the home, it is ironic that John deForest, a Freedmen's Bureau officer in Greenville, South Carolina, concluded that families needing bureau aid had gone "astern simply because the men alone were laboring to support their families" and that he worried about the "evil of female loaferism" (Gutman 1976:167).

Emancipation did not bring an end to job discrimination for Afro-Americans in the North, either. In most cities, Afro-Americans were confined by racism to lower-paying and more menial jobs, as a function of both wage differentials and job-category discrimination (see Mullings 1978). In the Boston of 1880, for example, considered to have had unusually favorable opportunities for Afro-Americans, 74 percent of all Afro-Americans worked as waiters, servants, barbers, laborers, porters, laundresses, and seamstresses; the largest group were servants. As compared with the Irish, the lowest-ranking Euro-Americans, almost three times as many Irish (19.8 percent) as Afro-Americans (7.2 percent) were skilled workers. A similar situation appears in other cities (see, for example, Gutman 1976:442–47).

In most U.S. cities, the constraints on the ability of the Afro-American man to earn a "family wage" forced Afro-American married women into the labor market in much greater proportions than Euro-American wives. By 1880 50 percent of Afro-American women were in the workforce as compared to 15 percent of Euro-American women (Degler 1980:389). While the majority of working women of both races were unmarried, significantly higher proportions of Afro-American wives worked. Data from the 1890 census show labor-force participation by white married women at a rate of 2.5 percent as compared to 22.5 percent among "nonwhite" married women. Separating out foreign-born women reveals a labor-participation rate of 3.0 percent among foreign wives[6] (Goldin 1977:88). By 1900 there was a 26 percent employment rate among Afro-American wives, as compared to 3.2 percent among white married women. Again, the comparison with immigrant wives sustains the contrast. In most American cities, the employment rate of Afro-American married women was four to fifteen times higher than that of immigrant wives (Pleck 1979:368).

Several factors may have had some bearing on the high labor-participation rate of married Afro-American women. Scholars have suggested that slavery conditioned Afro-American women to combine work and family (Goldin 1977), that Afro-American wives chose to work themselves and keep their children in school rather than have their children go out to work, as Italian-Americans did (Pleck 1979). It seems clear, however, that the major factor constraining the options of Afro-American women was the pervasive discrimination against both men and women, eliminating the possibility of a family wage. Within the limitations set by the society, Afro-American women made choices about how they fulfilled their responsibilities. For example, in most cities, Afro-American married women chose to work as laundresses rather than domestic servants in order to spend more time with their children (Gutman 1976:167–69). Despite some disagreement, most studies acknowledge that Afro-American women have had greater independence in the household, manifested in egalitarian decision making and the ability to terminate unsatisfactory relationships.

This period, characterized by rapid economic development, accelerated and sharpened class divisions and, as part and parcel of that, the distinctions between women of different classes. The development of the United States was based on concentration of wealth and differential exploitation of labor. Among those who lacked ownership of and access to wealth, differences of incorporation into the labor force, with minorities suffering greater exploitation, were rationalized by racism. It is only within this framework that the different experiences of women can be understood.

Perhaps the public/private dichotomy was most apparent among elite and middle-stratum women. This was the only group of women who could afford to stay out of the labor force throughout their life cycle. It is among these strata that the cult of true womanhood could be acted out and the strict separation of home and workplace maintained. Political disenfranchisement was more meaningful in these classes, where the men had power and wealth. True, most women had access to the fruit of these resources only as wives and daughters. Nevertheless, their class position gave them a life-style no other men or women could enjoy. Their responsibility for household, then, meant the supervision of workers.

Ironically, it was often sex-role symbolism that was projected to rationalize the maintenance of the unequal socioeconomic system. The glorification of "southern womanhood"—the celebration of upper-class Euro-American women and the alleged fear that they would be tainted—was a major element in the symbolism that rationalized a reign of terror against Afro-Americans after the Civil War (see Davis 1981 for an excellent discussion of sex-role ideology and lynchings). Elite women reaped the benefits of an unequal social order, and to the extent that they "bought into" the privileges the system generated, they accepted its structure.

For Euro-American working-class women, the public/private dichotomy was less clear. Unmarried women worked in the public sphere, and married women probably participated in wage labor more than is generally thought to be the case. For working-class women, the sexual division of labor meant sex-segregated (and lower-paying) jobs. Yet, particularly during the period of industrialization, the extent to which industries were dominated by men or women at a given point in time shifted with ecological and technological conditions and the decisions of employers. While it was certainly true that working-class men participated in encouraging sex segregation of the work-place, we need to look further into the role of employers in initiating conditions that encouraged these developments. Certainly recent studies have documented the active role of employers in segmenting labor markets.

Working-class women used the ideology of women's place to demand a family wage (see, for example, Baxandall et al 1976:17) that would allow them to withdraw from an exploited workforce at the same time that middle-class women's rights activists were condemning it. Working-class Euro-American women, too, were responsible for the household, but for them this meant doing the work of the household themselves. They, too, were politically disenfranchised relative to their men in later periods of history, when ownership of property ceased to be a condition for suffrage; however, in the absence of access to real political power, this had not the same salience.

Afro-American women, in a sense, were the least affected by the public/private dichotomy, as the prohibition against the employment of women never extended to them. During slavery they often did men's tasks, and after emancipation job segregation developed more slowly. In the initial postemancipation period, men and women were predominantly field hands in the South, domestic servants in the North. Sex segregation was certainly experienced as wage differentials. Because racism allows the rationalization of a superexploited labor force (Mullins 1978), Afro-Americans have never had access to a family wage and both men and women have had to work throughout their life cycle.

The double burden of women is most apparent in this population, where married women have historically worked in the public sphere and cared for their household without outside help. The fact that Afro-American women must do market work, but are forced to do so in sex-segregated jobs, has been expressed dramatically by Bonnie Dill (1983): "Minority women do not have the protection of private patriarchy, but are exploited through public patriarchy." Ironically, the conditions Afro-American women and men have encountered seem to have resulted in more independence in household relationships.

CONCLUSION

Some important issues arise when one examines class and race differences among women. In all classes there was a sexual division of labor. But what gives any division of labor significance is its link to a structure of differential and unequal rewards. In this sense, the sex-ordered division of labor may have been greatest in the property-owning class and least among Afro-Americans, among whom for much of this period the sex division of labor was relatively minimal. But when we examine the concrete results of the division of labor—access to resources and consequent ability to control one's life—the difference is perhaps greater among women (and among men) of different classes than between men and women of the same class.

It seems clear that production relations—that is, where women and their men stood in relationship to the process of production—determined the significance of reproductive relations. Women of the privileged classes, while confined to the household sphere, were guaranteed certain protections and possessed options within the household based on resources that no other class could command. At the other extreme, we find Afro-American women denied the refuge of the family and household, with respect to both protection of the family and the ability to choose not to enter the labor force. Yet within the household they may have possessed the greatest degree of equality in their relationships with their own men.

The class position of women, then, was basic to the way in which they experienced the events of this period. Race was intertwined with class: populations from various parts of the world were brought into the labor force at different levels and racial differences were utilized to rationalize special exploitation of men and women, producing a distinct experience for women of color. Although the ideology of the division of labor was universal, the way in which it was manifested in a given class was ultimately determined by the interests of the class in power.

This is not to suggest that sex-role behavior is determined simply from the top down. As is evident from the material discussed in this chapter, men and women actively participated in defining and redefining gender roles. But the ways in which women understood and participated in the struggle against gender oppression differed with class and race. As numerous scholars have pointed out, most middle-stratum women of this period focused on the struggle for political enfranchisement and the abolition of the private/public dichotomy within the limits of the socioeconomic system (see Lerner 1971; Davis 1981). To the extent that the source of injustice was seen to be the sexual division of labor, the perpetrators were judged to be men of all classes, and discussion of class and race were deemed unnecessary and divisive; these women were, to some extent, the forerunners of both the moderate and radical feminists.

Working-class Euro-American and Afro-American women confronted a system in which exploitation was not only determined on the basis of gender. For these women, who were linked to the men of their own class by the racist and class oppression that benefited men and women of the dominant class, struggles rarely took the form of attacks against patriarchy. For Euro-American women, the issue of equality was embedded in labor struggles; and for Afro-American women, it lay in the struggle for emancipation and for political and economic rights, campaigns they waged in unity with men of their class. The implications of these different orientations, arising out of divergent class experiences, are evident in contemporary proposals to gain women's equality in the United States, ranging from Heidi Hartmann's demand for a "bedroom to bedroom struggle" to Angela Davis's call for socialist transformation.

Notes

1. Periodization is used somewhat broadly in this chapter. Difficulties arise in comparing Afro-American women, for whom emancipation resulted in a major change of status, with Euro-American women, for whom it was industrialization that signaled significant transformations.

2. Herbert Aptheker analyzes the raw data collected by Lathan A. Windley in *Runaway Slave Advertisements: A Documentary History from the 1730's to 1790* (Westport, Conn.: Greenwood Press, 1983). Both Aptheker and Windley caution that these advertisements by no means reflected the totality of runaways. I would like to thank Dr. Aptheker for making his then unpublished paper available to me.

3. The extent to which women of this class had access to financial resources only through men is not at all clear. For example, Griffen and Griffen's (1977) study of Poughkeepsie, New York, between 1850 and 1880 indicates that wives had considerable control over financial resources and commercial ventures. Between 1869 and 1887, 33 states gave property rights to married women (Degler 1980:332).

4. In New England, the unmarried daughters of farmers became mill workers for a few years before retiring to marry or pursue other careers. The initial conditions under which they worked in such areas as Lowell, Massachusetts, lasted only for a few years, after which factory conditions deteriorated and the work force became primarily foreign-born. For an account of the Lowell mill workers, see Dublin (1979).

5. Between the 1790s and the Civil War, the number of free Afro-Americans grew to five hundred thousand.

6. There are some discrepancies, generally having to do with the definition of the labor force and the way in which populations are delineated (see Goldin 1977:88n), but the basic trend remains quite clear.

4

Runaway Shops and Female Employment: The Search for Cheap Labor

HELEN I. SAFA

Since the 1960s there has been a marked expansion in a new form of multinational enterprise, characterized primarily by the manufacture of exports in less developed countries destined for sale in overseas rather than domestic markets.* The availability of cheap labor is the prime determining factor for investment; hence this type of enterprise is generally found in countries where low wages, high unemployment, limited natural resources, low levels of unionization, and politically stable regimes prevail. Their governments encourage investment by lifting trade barriers and other impediments to the use of cheap labor (Trajtenberg and Sajhau 1976:16). Thus, most export-processing industries in developing countries enjoy tax holidays, subsidized credit, and export subsidies as well as freedom from import duties on raw materials, machinery, and other items necessary to production. In exchange, the developing countries expect to improve their foreign-exchange earnings and to generate employment in these largely labor-intensive industries.

Export processing represents a new path for certain less developed countries, one that has replaced import substitution as a means toward industrialization and economic growth. Import substitution fostered the formulation of nationalistic measures and protectionist legislation with the purpose of boosting national industries. The new trend seems to encourage foreign investment by minimizing the importance of national boundaries and

*An earlier version of this chapter appeared in *Signs*, vol. 7, no. 2, Winter 1981. © 1981 by The University of Chicago.

allowing market mechanisms to operate without constraints. Import substitution required the development of an internal market; it had to "be supported through the progressive provision or extension of purchasing power at home" (Frank 1978:1). In export processing, however, the market is external. It demands the maximum reduction of production costs, principally wages, to compete effectively on the international level. At the same time, labor-intensive industrialization counters the objections of those who criticized capital-intensive technology formerly sent to developing countries, a technology that generated relatively little employment (Helleiner 1973:23).

Despite considerable study by the International Labor Organization and others on the macroeconomic effects of export-processing industries, few have given attention to the type of labor force recruited, other than to characterize it as cheap and unskilled. Many studies do not even mention that the great majority of workers are women. The high rate of female employment represents a radical departure from the pattern of most multinationals, which generally employ men in highly mechanized, capital-intensive industry. The recruitment of women into these jobs is another stage in the search for cheap labor that characterizes industrial capitalism, particularly the more competitive labor-intensive industries. Export-processing industries, furthermore, have a variable impact on the status of women employed by them in Third-World countries.

THE GARMENT INDUSTRY

The history of labor-intensive industry in advanced capitalist societies helps us to understand the predominance of women in new export-processing industries in the Third World. Labor-intensive industries—garment manufacturing, textiles, food processing, electronics—have traditionally used female labor, from the earliest stages of the Industrial Revolution in England and France to the present day (Tilly and Scott 1978). Explanations for the predominance of female labor vary. Management usually reverts to sex stereotypes that depict women as having patience for tedious jobs, nimble fingers, and visual acuity. A far more adequate explanation, however, appears to lie in the higher profits that can be extracted from female labor due to low wages (Elson and Pearson 1981). Women have traditionally been paid less than men, reflecting both their subordinate position in society and the assumption that women are never the principal source of family income, but are dependent on men as providers. This pattern persists to the present day, even in areas of high male unemployment such as many developing countries, and even where, as in the Caribbean, a high percentage of women are heads of households and constitute the principal if not the sole source of support for their families. Thus, according to Ruth Pearson and Dorothy Elson, "women enter the capitalist labor market already determined as inferior bearers of labor" (ibid.: 29).

Cheap labor is essential to labor-intensive industries because they are highly competitive. While automation has occurred in food processing, textiles, and increasingly in electronics, they are still far more labor intensive than industries such as steel, petrochemicals, and automobile manufacture.[1] Garment manufacture has probably remained the most competitive of all labor-intensive industries, due to comparatively simple technology, low capital investment, and low-skill labor requirements, which make it relatively easy for new firms to enter (U.S. Department of Labor 1975a:3). The high turnover rate in garment firms is reinforced by the high risk involved in frequent changes in clothing styles and in fluctuating demands affecting certain sectors of the industry (such as women's dresses) more than others. Even in garment manufacture, however, there has been a noticeable increase in the concentration of production in larger firms, which are taking an increasing share of the industry's total business. The number of plants in the United States declined, in all major segments of the industry, from 27,521 in 1969 to 22,961 in 1973, with the top one hundred companies accounting for almost 30 percent of total sales (ibid.). If we separated shipping and distribution from production, we would probably find an even greater concentration. Much of the production process is still given out to jobbers and subcontractors. It is the unskilled phase of production that has increasingly been moved abroad, while shipping and distribution have been centralized in the United States, where the major market lies. For example, one garment manufacturer with production in both Puerto Rico and the Dominican Republic has shifted all shipping and distribution to the headquarters plant in the United States, with a corresponding shift of personnel out of production into these other areas.

If we trace the history of the garment industry in the United States, we can demarcate at least three stages in the process of labor recruitment. The runaway shop—as these new export-processing industries have been called—is merely the last stage in the industry's constant search for sources of cheap labor. The three stages include: (1) use of a native labor force, including recruitment from rural areas; (2) use of immigrant labor; and (3) the runaway shop. Each stage has used a different type of female labor force and has been characterized by a different pattern of capital accumulation.

Native Born Labor

Use of the native labor force in the early stages of industrialization depended heavily on recruitment from the rural areas. Thus, the earliest workers in the textile mills of New England at the beginning of the nineteenth century were generally daughters of farm families, single women who could be more easily withdrawn from agricultural labor and who usually stopped working as soon as they married. Women's lives were neatly divided into a paid productive phase and an unpaid reproductive phase. In the latter phase, their energies were largely directed toward the maintenance and reproduction of the labor force, which should have helped maintain a steady supply of native labor.

However, native white women also had to be provided with relatively good working and living conditions (women usually lived in resident boarding-houses), which grew too expensive for textile-mill owners as the industry burgeoned (Ware 1936:234). In addition, the supply of native white women was not sufficient to meet the demands of the growing industry, particularly since alternative sources of employment and domestic labor were available to workers. The garment and textile industry, therefore, had to seek another source of cheap labor.

Immigrant Labor

By the middle of the nineteenth century, immigration provided this new source. Immigrant labor was free from many of the restrictions governing native labor. The women had a greater need to work; and, thus, they accepted worse working conditions and lower wages. Many immigrant women worked after marriage, often sewing at home for exploitative piecework wages in an attempt to reconcile paid work with household and family responsibilities. It has also been argued that immigrant women had a different attitude toward work—that they did not regard it as incompatible with the female role in the way that many native white women of that period did (particularly women whose class background assured them of a choice in this matter). The proportion of gainfully employed immigrant women and daughters of immigrants increased steadily until 1910. Then reform movements, designed not only to improve factory conditions but to Americanize these women, began to take effect. Immigrant women, especially mothers, were encouraged to stay at home to take care of their children. They were encouraged to regard retirement from paid labor rather than job advancement as a sign of upward mobility (Kessler-Harris 1975:221, 229). Reformers voiced concern for the health of these women, which probably reflected a greater concern for the quality of future generations of laborers.

Reform movements also led to the initiation of protective legislation for women, which not only reduced the jobs available but made women more expensive to employ; it restricted the hours women could work, the types of work they could perform, and their working conditions. At the same time wages for men were increasing, making it easier for many married women to remain at home. The new ideal, which equated respectability with domesticity, mitigated class consciousness among women. They began to regard work as temporary and secondary to their family role and thus, permitted employers to regard their earnings as supplementary—that is, justifiably lower than male wages (ibid.: 223, 230; see also Safai: n.d.).

The period from 1890 to 1920 also witnessed a change in the pattern of factory ownership in the United States, brought on by the transition from competitive to monopoly capitalism. Factories passed out of the control of families rooted in local communities into the hands of distant financial centers and major retail outlets (Burawoy 1979:239). Many factories relocated to areas of cheap labor, as in the move of New England textile mills to the American South. Impersonal employer-employee relations replaced an old paternalism, and workers, including those in the garment industry, responded by organizing on a regional basis into industrial unions. However, the garment industry remained largely decentralized in small plants dependent on local labor, at least in the production phase. As Burawoy (1979:244) notes, "The rise of the large corporation in the monopoly sector by no means spelled the downfall of the small firm in the competitive sector." On the contrary, monopoly capitalism generated a corresponding competitive sector, through which it gained flexibility in adapting to changing demands. The competitive sector can produce more cheaply than the highly paid, strongly unionized monopoly sector. In this way, the garment industry provides cheap labor and flexibility and absorbs the risks of changing market demands for the garment retailers (Circel and Collins 1980:11).

Because of its status as a poorly paid, manual occupation, the garment industry in the United States has always provided a haven for newly arrived immigrants, who do not possess the language and educational skills needed in clerical and other types of service employment. Without the constant flow of new immigrants, the garment industry would probably find it difficult to survive. It is the lowest paying of any major industry group in the United States; at the same time, it is the largest industrial employer of women (NACLA 1978:7–8). In New York City, with the exception of some older women who have been working in the garment industry for many years, Jews and Italians have been succeeded by Hispanics. Puerton Rican women constituted one-fourth of all garment production workers in the 1970s (U.S. Department of Labor 1975b:81). The Puerto Rican women have been joined by an increasing number of Dominicans, Colombians, and other Latin Americans, often undocumented workers who are forced to work for low wages under poor working conditions because of their illegal status. Production in the garment industry has moved abroad, often to the native countries of these immigrant women. But it has also gone underground, into illegal sweatshops that employ nonunionized, often undocumented workers at less than the minimum wage (NACLA 1979).

Runaway Shops

The runaway shop represents a new strategy in the effort to recruit cheap labor. The shops are primarily located in peripheral developing countries, which have vast labor reserves brought on by high unemployment and population growth. The runaway shop exports jobs instead of importing labor, particularly to small countries: in Asia, to Singapore, Hong Kong, South Korea, and Taiwan; in the Caribbean, to Jamaica, Haiti, and the Dominican Republic; in Central America, to Costa Rica and El Salvador. In these countries, the possibilities for import substitution are limited because of the small size of the domestic market and, therefore, they are heavily dependent on exports (Helleiner 1973:25). However, even large Latin American countries such as Mexico have set up export-processing zones along the border (Kelly 1980).

The new international division of labor, which the runaway shop represents, was stimulated by a series of economic conditions in advanced capitalist countries, including (1) full employment, particularly during the economic boom of the 1960s; (2) a dwindling supply of immigrant labor, particularly after the passage of the Immigration Act of 1965, which greatly limited the admission of unskilled immigrants; (3) high wages, brought on by a scarcity of labor and the increasing strength of unions and of the working class in general—workers' demands for fringe benefits such as paid vacations, sick leave, and medical insurance drove labor costs even higher; (4) growth of the welfare state, which provided members of the reserve labor force, particularly women, with an alternative to poorly paid, manual labor (Santa Cruz Collective on Labor Migration 1978:106); (5) technological changes, which facilitated the development of a cheaper and faster international cargo transportation system; and (6) the deskilling of work (or the "massification of labor") through mechanization and scientific management, which fragmented production into relatively simple stages, each performed by a different operator. Fragmentation of labor has been going on in the garment industry for quite some time, resulting in the reduction of highly skilled trades to repetitive and monotonous operations—sewing one seam, adding hooks or buttons—some of which still require considerable skill. What is new is the way in which this fragmentation of production has been internationalized, with the more skilled jobs retained in the domestic sector, while the less skilled jobs are sent abroad. In the garment industry, for example, the cutting of garments, a job usually reserved for men, is most often done in the United States, while sewing is done abroad.

The new international division of labor in the garment industry has been greatly facilitated by items 806.30 and 807.00 of the United States Tariff Law. Under these items, tariffs on articles assembled abroad that are made up of components fabricated in the United States are limited to the value added to the product as a result of labor. Low wages abroad effectively minimize tariffs. In the garment industry, only the sewing process is taxed rather than the garment itself, which presumably is made of textiles manufactured and cut in the United States. The importance of these tariff laws in facilitating export processing of Third-World goods destined for the U.S. market should be evident. According to one report, item 807.00 is more significant than item 806.30; in 1969 it accounted for an import value twenty-three times greater than did the latter item (Helleiner 1973:38). These tariff provisions apply not only to U.S. manufacturing firms, but also to jobbers and to non–United States manufacturers, including many that subcontract to large retailing firms like Sears Roebuck and J. C. Penney. Despite increasing opposition from unions, those who argue for tariff provisions contend that they increase competitiveness in the American and international market of many U.S. firms—firms which could not otherwise compete with lower labor costs abroad.

Proponents argue further that, given the dwindling supply of low-cost labor in the United States, manufacturers should provide skilled jobs to Americans and recruit unskilled labor abroad (Wool 1976). The cost of female labor in postwar America rose considerably due to an almost insatiable demand for office workers—a demand that coincided with the bureaucratization of industry and the expansion of white-collar jobs in the service sector (Burawoy 1979:243). In the United States this has resulted in a shift from blue-collar to predominantly white-collar jobs, particularly among white, single women. Ethnic minorities—Afro-Americans, Puerto Ricans, and Mexican Americans—are still found largely in industrial and service occupations (Safa n.d.:130). It has also led to a dramatic increase in the percentage of married women in the paid labor force; they represented 58 percent of all U.S. working women in 1974 (U.S. Department of Labor 1975a:16). The demand for women as white-collar workers and the rising cost of living finally destroyed—or at least seriously weakened—the feminine mystique of women in the home (Kessler-Harris 1975:234).

Despite the increasing incorporation of women into the labor force, employment in the New York City garment industry has drastically declined. The industry has moved both underground and to cheaper labor areas in the United States, such as the American South and abroad. For example, in the 1960s workers in New York's apparel industry saw a 40 percent decline in jobs, a loss that continued at the rate of twelve thousand jobs per year through 1973 (U.S. Department of Labor 1975a:104–6). These figures appear to be related to the sharp decline in the labor-force participation rate of Puerto Rican women between 1950 and 1970, although precise correlations are not available (Safa n.d.:7). Meanwhile, imports totaled $8 billion in 1978 and were expected to amount to 22 percent of the U.S. market in 1979 (NACLA 1979:37).

The process of relocating industry is not confined either to the garment industry or to the United States. In West Germany, for example, a study of the new international division of labor for the textile and garment industry points to a 37 percent decline in employment during the period from 1960 to 1976, due largely to relocation (Frobel, Heinrichs & Kreye 1980:59). Another labor-intensive industry that has undergone massive relocation in recent years is electronics, which, unlike garment manufacture, has grown precipitously in the postwar period. Despite an overall increase in the electronics work force in the United States, the number and percentage of production workers has decreased, due to the relocation of production abroad (Snow 1980:14–15).

Both the garment and electronics industries generally employ women as production workers, and although there has been pressure by unions to curb imports, only when competition from abroad hit prime industries such as automobiles and steel was there a public outcry. The automobile and steel industries primarily employ men, and plant closings have devastated entire communities. Though not subject to the same tariff regulations as the garment and electronics industries, the decline suffered by these capital-intensive industries is also symptomatic of the new international division of labor, which has spurred competition among advanced industrial countries as well as between them and developing countries. This international division of labor also has implications for the sexual division of labor in Third-World countries, where a whole new category of women industrial workers has been created.

IMPACT OF RUNAWAY SHOPS ON THIRD-WORLD WOMEN

If the relocation of labor-intensive industries has had an adverse effect on women workers in the United States as well as other industrialized countries, what impact has it had on Third-World women in the areas to which these industries have moved? Are the new possibilities for employment improving their status in the society? What effect has export processing had on the traditional sexual division of labor and, in particular, on family structure in these Third-World countries? Is wage labor increasing the class consciousness of the women workers by removing them from the home and exposing them to an impersonal wage-labor market?

Most studies on the impact of runaway shops have focused on economic criteria—changes in the country's foreign-exchange earnings, employment levels, and access to training and technology. Few studies focus on women workers, partly from a lack of concern, partly from a lack of data (Frobel, Heinrichs & Kreye 1980:344). In the remainder of this chapter, I will attempt to fill in the gap by briefly summarizing some of the studies completed between 1978 and 1980 on women workers in runaway shops, chiefly in Southeast Asia, Mexico, and Jamaica (Lim 1978; Grossman 1979; Bolles 1979).

Critics of export processing as a strategy for development contend that it only intensifies the dependence of Third-World countries on advanced capitalist nations like the United States, because foreign companies, usually multinationals, have exclusive control of the markets. Furthermore, production is not linked to the domestic economy, except as it provides poorly paid jobs (Frobel, Heinrichs & Kreye 1980:367; Nayyar 1978). This does not balance the scales, Frobel, Heinrichs, and Kreye (1980:344) maintain, since the overwhelming majority of the workers—70 percent—are women between the ages of sixteen and twenty-five who are primarily employed in production as unskilled or semiskilled laborers. Export processing has not led to any appreciable reduction in the rate of male unemployment and has introduced a new category of workers—young women—into the industrial labor force (Grossman 1979:8).

Clearly, this is bound to have an effect on the sexual division of labor in Third-World countries, where women have not traditionally played a major role in the industrial labor force. It is more disruptive than the previous recruitment of cheap labor among rural or immigrant women in the United States, where in most cases rural and immigrant men were also employed and were not totally dependent on women's earnings.

Patriarchy

The limited data available suggest that the impact of runaway shops on the sexual division of labor in Third-World countries varies with the degree of male unemployment and the intensity of patriarchal tradition. Thus, in Mexico, disruption of traditional family patterns appears to be quite severe as a result of the unemployment of women in the Border Industrialization Program. Along the border, the Mexican rate of employment and underemployment combined reaches 30 percent. In Ciudad Juarez, along the Mexican border, the majority of men living in households of female assembly operators are either unemployed or underemployed, often working in some aspect of the informal economy. The lack of employment for men forces women into paid wage labor, though the Border Industrialization Program was actually instituted to provide an alternative source of employment for men dislodged by the elimination of the bracero program. The impact on family structure is unmistakable; in the Ciudad Juarez sample studied by María Patricia Fernández Kelly (1980:24, 27, 36), one out of three women employed by garment manufacturers was a head of household.

In Jamaica, however, where there is a tradition of female-headed households that dates back to slavery, the employment of women in export processing does not appear to have increased the formation of such households (Bolles 1979).[2] Although the majority of factory women live in visiting unions* or head their own households, factory employment appears to provide one of the few stable sources of income for women who would otherwise be forced to make a living through the informal economy, given the high rate of unemployment for both men and women. The absence of a strong patriarchal tradition in Jamaica and a long tradition of women working outside the home suggest that factory employment for women there has had a less disruptive effect on the sexual division of labor than in other areas.

Age and Marital Status

The impact of export processing on the sexual division of labor in Third-World nations also varies with the age and marital status of women workers. Female-headed households usually consist of older women with dependent children. It is possible that a job contributes to a woman's sense of economic autonomy

---

*"Visiting union," a term used in the English-speaking Caribbean, describes a relationship where a woman continues to reside in her own or her parents' home, but is visited regularly by a sexual partner.

and the ease with which she may dissolve a marital relationship; that is, working women may be more likely to end an unsatisfactory relationship, since they have the possibility of supporting their families on their own. However, most women recruited to work in runaway shops are young and single and contribute to their parents' income rather than sustaining families of their own. This pattern is less likely to have a disruptive effect on the sexual division of labor; as a daughter, a woman worker does not directly challenge the male role of economic provider (Salaff 1981:272–73). In many countries, such as Malaysia, the family remains in the rural area and women migrate to work alone, living in boardinghouses under very crowded conditions (Grossman 1979). By contributing a major portion of her earnings to her family, a young woman worker forms part of a multiple wage-earning strategy necessitated by the high cost of living and low rate of pay in Third-World countries, conditions that force most adult members of households into income-earning activities (Safa 1983; Wong, ch. 13).

Does their contribution to the family economy enhance their status in the family and in the larger community? Do these women enjoy greater independence as a result of their new wage-earning capacity? The studies reviewed here suggest that the impact of wage labor on the status of these women is very limited, due to the nature of employment in export-processing industries. The wages are very low, averaging $1 to $2 per day in 1975, much lower than those paid in industrialized countries (Frobel, Heinrichs & Kreye 1980:350). In some areas workers are forced to serve an apprenticeship, which can last as long as six months, during which they receive only half the normal wage (Grossman 1979: 10). Many women along the Mexican border are kept on temporary contracts and are periodically discharged, despite many years of employment in the same plant. In this way manufacturers circumvent the fringe benefits due a permanent worker, such as sick leave, vacation time, and severance pay (Kelly 1980:44).

High Rates of Turnover

The impact of industrial employment on the status of these women is also minimized by the high rate of turnover in export-processing industries, which is estimated at 5 to 10 percent monthly (Frobel, Heinrichs & Kreye 1980:10). Many workers cannot withstand the competition of piecework, or they are fired for being unable to meet their production quotas. In addition, these industries prefer young, single women with no previous work experience, rather than experienced workers who command higher wages (Grossman 1979:10; Wong, ch. 13). The reasons for this preference vary, but generally younger women are considered more docile and more productive, that is, more committed to a strong work ethic than older women. Older workers are also more likely to be married and burdened with family duties. There is generally no provision for women with such responsibilities; child-care centers are almost unheard of. In the electronics industry, workers suffer from impaired vision after several years of looking through a microscope. Many "burn out" before they are thirty. Electronics workers along the Mexican border are generally younger and better educated than garment workers, who represent a more marginal labor force (Kelly 1980). Alternative job opportunities for export-processing workers are practically non-existent, except in the poorly paid informal sector, so that even women with a college education are sometimes forced into factory work (Grossman 1979: 10). Advancement on the job is also limited because there are relatively few technical or supervisory personnel, and many of them are foreign (Lim 1978:21).

The instability of employment is increased by the fluctuating demand for the products of labor-intensive industries, such as garment manufacture and electronics, the most important product groups in export processing. For example, Linda Lim (1978:21; also Wong, ch. 13) reports that "during the 1974– 75 world recession, about 15,000 electronics workers were laid off in Singapore, nearly a third of the industry's labor force, and about two-thirds of all workers laid off in the whole Singapore economy." Physical plants involve minimal investments—they are often rented from the host government—and manufacturers search constantly for new sources of cheap labor. Both of these factors facilitate plant closings and relocation. In Southeast Asia, a labor hierarchy has already begun to develop, with more established sites such as Hong Kong and Singapore becoming regional headquarters for the electronics industry, providing high-skilled jobs and better wages. Meanwhile, Malaysia serves as an intermediary center for testing; and Indonesia, the Philippines, and Thailand represent the last frontier, with the lowest wages and worst working conditions (Grossman 1979:16).

A New Proletariat

Clearly, export processing is leading to the rapid formation of a large-scale female industrial proletariat in Third-World countries. Frobel, Heinrichs, and Kreye estimate a total number of 725,000 workers in free-production zones worldwide,[3] while female labor-force participation has risen to more than one-third in small countries like Singapore and Malaysia (Wong, ch. 13, table 13.1; Lim 1978: 16–18). Recognizing the potential impact of such a rapid increase in the female industrial labor force, some host governments have instituted harsh measures to restrain the growth of worker solidarity in new export-processing industries. The governments fear that labor unrest and higher wages will only induce companies to move elsewhere, as happened in Jamaica under the Manley government and in Puerto Rico with the extension of the federal minimum wage law to the island. In Southeast Asia, governments have actively and violently suppressed worker protest; they are backed by laws prohibiting strikes in vital industries, which normally include foreign-owned manufacturing plants (Grossman 1979:8). Labor unions may be prohibited by law or, as in Singapore and Malaysia, severely restricted or controlled by the government (Lim 1978:16–18). Aline Wong's analysis of the Singapore economy is particularly instructive, because it suggests ways in which the state, under the rubric of state economic planning, can supplant the older forms of family patriarchy by intervening "extensively in almost every sphere of social and economic life, influencing work and the family, as well as cultural values and psychological motivations" (Wong, ch. 13). A job may give a woman a degree of economic autonomy and loosen the bonds of a patriarchal family, but is also exposes her to a new form of capitalist exploitation and state control.

Planned Development

Singapore and Puerto Rico have served as models of planned development based on export processing, but both countries now face increasing competition from neighboring areas, which can offer still cheaper wages and attractive incentives to foreign capital. In order to retain a comparative advantage, Singapore has embarked on a second stage of industrialization, emphasizing capital-intensive, high-technology products, which can be produced by its more highly skilled and literate population. As Wong (ch. 13) explains, however, this type of industrialization does not lessen Singapore's dependence on export markets, and it is likely to reduce the demand for female labor, since many of these industries employ primarily men. Puerto Rico has also attempted to move away from a dependence on unstable, labor-intensive industries by inducing capital-intensive industries such as petrochemical plants and pharmaceutical companies to establish themselves on the island. However, Puerto Rico continues to be plagued by plant closings and rising unemployment—among men as well as women, since labor-intensive industries still employ primarily female labor. In the garment industry, even women in unionized plants sometimes work only a few days a week or are laid off for weeks at a time because of changes in the U.S. market and competition from production elsewhere. Even union women are paid only for the days they work. The Puerto Rican government, with ample assistance from the United States, attempts to subsidize marginal industries by supplementing low wages and periods of unemployment with food stamps, unemployment insurance, and social security. The government also supplies tax exemptions and even wage subsidies to hold industries on the island. Ostensibly subsidies to workers, these programs actually enable marginal industries to continue paying low wages, to cope with competition from abroad, and to weather declines in demand. Any reduction in these programs under the Reagan administration is bound to cause increasing labor unrest and migration to the mainland.

With the exception of a few strikes, which have often been met by police repression, worker resistance in export-processing industries has been largely limited to cases of "mass hysteria" in Southeast Asia and high rates of turnover and absenteeism in the Caribbean. In Asian countries with labor shortages, some plant managers try to cultivate the loyalty of their workers by emphasizing the "family" nature of the enterprise and by encouraging competition and consumerism among women workers through beauty contests, cosmetics classes, and bonuses for high productivity (Lim 1978:23–33; Grossman 1979:13). The westernization of these Asian women increases the social stigma attached to factory work and discourages such workers from developing solidarity with other workers.

CONCLUSION

Export processing may serve to integrate women into the development process by providing them with large numbers of new industrial jobs; it also enhances their possibilities for exploitation. In assessing the advantages and disadvantages of export processing as a development strategy in Third-World countries, it is important to assess its impact on women as well as its effect on conventional economic criteria such as foreign-trade earnings, employment levels, and access to technology. There are several important determinants of the impact of export processing on the status of women:

(1) the level of male unemployment, which, coupled with new jobs for women, could have a drastic effect on family structure, perhaps leading to an increase in female-headed households;

(2) the low wages, poor working conditions, instability, and limited job mobility offered by this new industrial employment, factors which could, if not carefully controlled, simply turn these industries into a new form of exploitation and subordination for Third-World women; and

(3) the state restriction of worker solidarity expressed in labor unions, strikes, or conditions by which women workers strive to improve their working conditions and wages.

It is important that these factors be taken into account if women are not to be continually exploited as a source of cheap labor, as they have been throughout the history of industrial capitalism. Runaway shops link the concerns of women workers in advanced industrial nations and developing countries, since an increase in jobs in the Third World generally implies a decrease elsewhere. Reaction to unemployment in the United States has generally taken the form of narrow protectionism, with unions and management exhorting the public to "Buy American" and urging the government to adopt a more restrictive policy on imports from the low-wage regions. The textile unions of the European Economic Community have taken a more creative approach by urging their governments to restrict concessions on import quotas to countries which comply with minimum ILO standards concerning wages, working conditions, and free-trade unions (*German Tribune* Aug. 17 1980). A similar approach has recently been advocated by a prominent U.S. labor leader who is seeking the support of the labor community to oppose extension of the Reagan administration's trade-incentive provisions of its Caribbean Basin Initiative to countries with proven antilabor records (Washington, D.C. Council on Hemispheric Affairs 1983). If adopted, such a policy would reduce the exploitation of workers in export-processing industries, restrict competition between low-wage countries, and gradually increase the wages and buying power in Third-World countries, making them less dependent on export markets.

The increasing number of countries dependent on export processing as a development strategy and the deteriorating economic conditions faced by both advanced and developing countries, however, make it highly unlikely that such a progressive policy will be adopted. Runaway shops are, after all, but one manifestation of an increasing international division of labor that pits countries and workers against one another on a global scale.

Notes

1. Michael Burawoy (1979:240) points out that "the process of deskilling proceeds unevenly, transforming sectors of the economy in different countries at different times and leaving some industries altogether untouched." Of course, "deskilling" can occur without automation, as in the fragmentation of different tasks in the garment industry.

2. The same appears to be true in Puerto Rico, where, in a study now being conducted among factory workers, we have failed to find any correlation between female employment and marital breakdown.

3. Frobel, Heinrichs, and Kreye (1980:302, 307) define free-production zones as "all those production sites in developing countries whose major function is the industrial utilization of labor in those countries for world market oriented production." Free-production zones are usually industrial enclaves screened off from their surrounding environment in order to control access of persons and products. Not all export-processing industries are located in free-production zones, which are also known as free-trade zones.

PART II
Reproduction and Production in Nonindustrial Societies

I is still common in cross-cultural studies of gender to treat societies whose internal economies are nonindustrial as if they remain uninfluenced by the relations of Western capitalism. At the same time, studies that focus on the impact of the West on different societies have too often given insufficient attention to particular culture histories, traditions, and interests and the part these play in a people's response to new difficulties and new options. The following section is intended to address both shortcomings by focussing on the ways in which women in different types of traditional economies are dealing with the changes in their economic and social roles.

Diane Bell's chapter on the Aborigines of north central Australia describes how women use their traditional ritual practices to fight against the loss of their rights vis-à-vis men that has been brought about by colonization. In the next chapter, on the Trobriands and Samoa, Annette Weiner shows how women resist the erosion of the kinship structure that has ensured them a sphere for independent action, by maintaining the important ritual exchanges of the valued goods they produce. Soheila Shashahani documents the loss of what independent base for action women had among a pastoral tribe of southern Iran that has been drawn into a market economy, and Simi Afonja analyzes the intersection of capitalist relations with historically changing gender relations among the Yoruba of Nigeria. A common thread running through the case studies is the trend toward, or increase of, male dominance in the nuclear family structure that is basic to the Western capitalist economy. Together the studies yield new insights into the ways women in different kinds of societies, or of different statuses in the same society, may accept or resist this trend.

5

Central Australian Aboriginal Women's Love Rituals

DIANE BELL

To appreciate the impact of the changes wrought by the colonization of Aboriginal land in Australia, one must first appreciate the quality of gender segregation in the Aboriginal society.[1] While devastating for Aboriginal men and women alike, segregation has affected the two sexes differently because of the sex-segregated nature of their society and the male-oriented nature of the colonial power.*

The twin assumptions that gender values are ordered in an unchanging, rigid, hierarchical structure and that men are the most important social actors have led some anthropologists to conclude that Aboriginal women are now and have always been a dominated sex. However, I suggest that while the division of labor by sex was fixed, gender values were (and still are to a limited extent) fluid. It is in the dynamic interweaving of sexual politics and social change that we find clues to the relationship between the sexual division of labor and women's marginal position today. In the ritual domain where women continue to engage in work that is distinctively theirs, the changing nature of women's work is starkly drawn. Thus, I look to the realm of religious ritual to probe the meaning of gender relations for the Kaititj women of Warrabri, a government settlement in the Central Australian region of the Northern Territory.

*An earlier version of this chapter appeared in *Signs,* vol. 7, no. 2, Winter 1981. © 1981 by The University of Chicago.

Underwritten by her critically important economic and ritual contribution to her society, Aboriginal women's independent manner, dignity, and autonomy of action once ensured that her voice would be heard and heeded. Although today women continue to assert their rights within their society and continue to celebrate these in their rituals, their position vis-à-vis men has been considerably weakened. For negotiations between the sexes are now conducted in an arena where white-male control is the norm, and the roles made available to women are restrictive and predicated on an image of women as sex object, wife, and mother. Where once there was interdependence, now there is dependence. The separation of the sexes that once provided a basis for woman's power now provides thé means for her exclusion.

THE CHANGING FACE OF ABORIGINAL SOCIETY

For tens of thousands of years prior to the establishment by the British of a penal colony at Botany Bay in 1788, the Australian Aborigines based their life and law on their complex relationship to land. They looked to the dreamtime, the creative era, when the mythical ancestors wandered across the land, named important sites and features, explained social institutions, and performed rituals. Today their living descendents must perform these rituals and celebrate the activities of the ancestral heroes in order to maintain and reaffirm the strength and relevance of the law as an ever-present and all-guiding force in people's lives. Under the law established in the dreamtime, men and women had distinctive roles to play, but each had recourse to certain checks and balances which ensured that neither sex could enjoy unrivaled supremacy over the other. Men and women alike were dedicated to observing the law that ordered their lives into complementary but distinct fields of action and thought: in separation lay the basis of a common association that underwrote domains of existence.

Today, plagued by ill health, chronic unemployment, a dependence on social security, and a general feeling of powerlessness, many of the two hundred thousand descendants of the original owners of Australia live as paupers, an enclave population within a rich and developing nation of fourteen million. The loss of land on which to hunt has been more than an economic loss, for it was from the land that Aboriginal people gained not only their livelihood but also their sense of being.

The spread of white settlement across the Australian continent has been uneven and often violent. In the Northern Territory some groups have lived in close contact with whites since the opening up of the north in the late nineteenth century; others have only recently come into sustained contact; still others have returned from centers of population density to their traditional homelands.

In Central Australia, where I have worked since 1976, the demands of the pastoral and mining industries have alienated the best lands and introduced ideas and goods not easily incorporated by the old law. Aborigines have found a precarious niche at the interface between the old law of the dreamtime and the new law of white frontier society. On the fringes of towns, in camps adjacent to homesteads, on cattle stations (ranches), herded together on missions and controlled settlements, many Aborigines have lived in refuge-like communities poised on the edge of what was once their traditional land. However, with the passage of the Aboriginal Land Rights (Northern Territory) Act in 1976 some land has returned to the Aboriginals, and they have the right to claim other parcels of land.[2] New and exciting life choices are now possible.

In the late 1970s Warrabri (then a government settlement, today Aboriginal land) was home to four different groups: the Warlpiri (Walbiri) from an abandoned mission 210 kilometers to the north, the Kaititj and Alyawarra from neighboring cattle stations to the east, and the Warramunga from the mission and the town of Tennant Creek. The enforced coresidence of peoples with such different backgrounds, yet all with traditional ties to land, engendered many tensions and conflicts. Alcoholism and violence constantly disrupted family life. In 1976 this mixed Aboriginal population of approximately 700 shared their lives with the 80–100 whites whose function it was to administer the affairs of the community and to deliver certain services, such as health, education, and law enforcement. Since the proportion of whites is so high, any analysis of the Warrabri Aborigines must take account of their presence.

The dominant feature of the new law is that it is male oriented, controlled, and delivered. The idea that men have certain roles and that women occupy a particular place are today as clear cut as they were in the past. Women's work is still women's work; men's work is still men's work. However, the context within which this work is undertaken and the way in which the work is evaluated have altered radically. Today a woman has no security as an independent producer but is dependent on social security payments that entail relationships over which she has no control. She is a member of a household, one with a nominal male head and notional breadwinner; she is a dependent. In the past women lived with men in small mobile bands where female solidarity was possible. Today women live in settlements, missions, cattle stations, and towns where male solidarity is given new support and additional opportunities to be realized. While women are recognized as the "feeders and breeders," men are groomed as politicians by their fellow white-male administrators and liaison officers. Further, because it is inappropriate for Aboriginal men and women to sit together in large mixed gatherings, most consultations with settlement communities take place between Aboriginal and white males (Bell and Ditton 1980). Aboriginal women have been cut out of much of the political life of larger settlements and left in their camps to produce babies and small artifacts. Such, in European reasoning, is the wont of women.

Today the sexual politics of Aboriginal society are no longer played out within the confines of that society. The ongoing dialogue between the sexes, the interplay, the exchange, the constant vying for power and status continues: male assertions of control and authority must still be balanced against female independence and solidarity. Women still actively participate in the construction of the cultural evaluations of their work, but they are constrained and defined by the male-dominated frontier society as the female sex, one necessarily dependent. In seeking to understand the changing role and status of Aboriginal women and the sexual division of labor, we need to explore not only the basis of female autonomy and solidarity within Aboriginal society but also to allow that claims to autonomy and expressions of solidarity now occur in a vastly changed and changing milieu (Bell 1983).

WOMEN'S WORK

In the Aboriginal communities of Central Australia today, as in the past, the usual pattern is that during the day men socialize with men and women with women, each in an area taboo to the other. In most hunting parties there is also a division whereby women hunt the smaller game and search for grubs, berries, roots, and wild honey, while men seek out the larger game. In the past in the desert regions it was the women who provided the reliable portion of the diet (up to 80 percent) and the men who occasionally brought home a larger animal (Meehan 1970). The sharing that women enjoyed with each other during the day, the solidarity they enjoyed with their sister co-wives, and their contribution to the food quest could not easily be shrugged off by men.

Today, as in the past, at evening time when men and women come together in family camps, women do so with confidence and dignity. Matters of common concern are discussed between husband and wife, and the produce of the day is shared. In the ebb and flow of daily life the independence and interdependence of the sexes is clearly illustrated. However, this pattern varies, as does the weight women may bring to bear on the final decisions taken in contemporary communities. When Aborigines live in small, relatively homogeneous family groups, as they do on some cattle stations and homeland centers, interaction between the sexes results in women's having a decisive role in family affairs—one which, due to group composition, makes them participators in community decisions. Women have no such role in the larger, more heterogeneous settlements where family and community do not coincide (Bell and Ditton 1980: 90).

Crucial to women's status is their relation to Aboriginal law. In seeking to make plain to whites the importance of their law, Aborigines draw upon an extended work metaphor. The law is termed "business" and is made up of "women's business" and "men's business." No pejorative overtones adhere to the qualification of business as women's. Ritual activity is glossed as "work" and participants as "workers" and "owners." The storehouse for ritual objects is known as the "office." Ritual is indeed work for Aborigines, for it is here that they locate the responsibility of maintaining their families and their land.

The separateness of the sexes, so evident in daily activities, reaches its zenith in ritual activity. Again men, this time anthropologists, have underestimated or underreported the religious life of women. Yet ritual is, I believe, an important barometer of male/female relations, providing, as it were, an arena in which the values of the society are writ large. There the sexual division of labor is manifested and explored by the participants, and men and women clearly state their own perceptions of their role, their relationship to the opposite sex, and their relationship to the dreamtime whence all legitimate authority and power once flowed. Both men and women have rituals that are closed to the other, both men and women allow the other limited attendance at certain of their rituals, and finally there are ceremonies in which both men and women exchange knowledge and together celebrate their membership in the one society and their duty to maintain the law of their ancestors.

THE RITUAL DOMAIN

The range of women's ritual activity in the desert is extensive. The most common is the *yawulyu* in which women celebrate the broad themes of attachment to country, maintain health and harmony within their community, and define their power to control and direct emotions. Rights to participate in these rituals are based on rights and responsibilities with respect to the land that a woman holds through the patrilines of both her mother and father. A woman has two "countries" but her rights and responsibilities in each are qualitatively different. She is *kirda* for the country of her father and is said to own that country. She is *kurdangurlu* for the country of her mother, and she is said to manage that country. Country is jointly owned with members of one's patriline and managed through the children of the senior women of the patriline. The *kirda* to *kurdungurlu* relationship entails a ritual reciprocity that binds together patriclans; it is the basic structuring principle of the land-maintenance ceremonies that both men and women must perform.

Yawulyu are staged quite independently of men, although the particiualr natural phenomenon or species of flora or fauna which is the focus of the ritual is shared with the men who are joint *kirda* and *kurdungurlu* for that dreaming country. Men and women thus share a knowledge of country encoded in the designs and songs which they jointly own and manage, but these are elaborated by each sex in their own closed and secret rituals so as to enhance their status as men or women. For women I found it was not the role of childbearer per se that was being celebrated. Rather, women were casting themselves as the nurturers of emotions, of country, and of people. As women "grow up" children, so they "grow up" country and relationships. Women see themselves as responsible for the maintenance of social harmony; hence their concern with health and with potentially explosive emotions. Any imbalance in these domains is a threat to their community. In the strife-ridden context of settlement life in Central Australia this is a truly awesome responsibility.

Within their own ritual domain women exercise complete autonomy and totally exclude men. The entire area of women's camps, including the nearby ritual ground, is taboo to men. In the case of the Kaititj of Warrabri this area is located as far as possible from the central facilities of the settlement and from other Aboriginal camps. The single women's camp, the *jilimi,* provides a home for widows, estranged wives, women visiting from other communities, unmarried girls, and in fact any women who have chosen to live beyond the control and purview of men. Between 1976 and 1978 approximately 25 percent of adult women at Warrabri were living in the various *jilimi* of the settlement. The *jilimi* is thus the home of a high proportion of important and influential women. Within those camps women are ritually independent and were once, and are still to a degree, economically independent of men (Bell 1983). Thus, the role of the *jilimi* as a power base and refuge for women is obvious. Yet, paradoxically, since most ritual activity is initiated from these camps, it is little wonder that men are vague about women's ritual activity. Moreover, Aboriginal men will not and cannot discuss women's business: male anthropologists may not be made aware of the activity, let alone be invited to attend. As a result the image of women as lacking any important ritual responsibilities has been perpetuated by the male orientation of research.

An understanding of male/female power relations and the sexual division of labor in Aboriginal society has often been sought by anthropologists within the context of arranged marriages, wherein old men are depicted as cheerfully allocating scarce resources and arrogating to themselves the right to bestow women's services in marriage (Meggitt 1962: 264–70). It is thus possible to postulate an enduring and constant relationship between women's work and the cultural evaluations of her role, a relationship which makes both secondary. The institutions of polygyny and gerontocracy, sanctioned by the male control of the ritual domain, then become the means by which men control women. However, Aboriginal women do not endorse this analysis, and my own observations offer support for their self-assessments.

For instance, women play a decisive role in maintaining the promise system of marriage through their politicking and ceremonial activity during male initiation (Bell 1983). Elsewhere I have argued that, seen from a woman's point of view, marriage is an evolving serial monogamy wherein women progressively contract marriages that are more and more to their perceived benefit (Bell 1980). In so doing they actively establish alliances and cement relationships that they deem desirable. Marriages resulting from such female-initiated action are correct within the kinship system. They are "arranged" marriages contracted between families of the couple, not "promised" marriages formally agreed upon at the time of male initiation. Women also organize male/female relations deemed legitimate by society through a particular form of women's ritual known as *yilpinji.*

During my period of field work, 80 percent of extant marriages were correct within the kinship system and 20 percent incorrect, but promised marriages accounted for only 5–10 percent. Formal business contracts entered into at initiation time did not organize the totality of marriage arrangements. In their own way, both men and women sought to regulate and thereby, so they hoped, to contain male/female relations and to gain control over the activities of the opposite sex. Women stated that they used love rituals, *yilpinji* business, to establish and to maintain marriages of their own preference. In these rituals women clearly perceived themselves as independent operators in a domain where they exercised power and autonomy based on their dreaming affiliations with certain tracts of land. These rights are recognized and respected by the whole society. Women are not, and never were, the pawns in male games, and they have always been actively engaged in establishing and maintaining male/female relationships of their own choosing, that is, they have engaged in women's work.

The focus on promised marriage has obscured and distorted the role women play in establishing and maintaining relationships deemed legitimate by the whole of Aboriginal society. In part this has been because women's love rituals have been seen as "love magic," as a deviant and illegitimate activity pursued on the periphery of the real decision-making domain of men. According to Phyllis Kaberry (1939: 265–67), love magic was a safety valve and at times a form of vengeance. To Geza Roheim (1933: 208–9) it was the sort of activity in which women indulged. It was magic; it could not be religion because women did not have access to the dreamtime power. Although Kaberry (1939: 220–21, 276–78) and Catherine Berndt (1965: 238–82) have challenged this aspect of Roheim's characterization of women's lives, the designation *magic* with all its perjorative overtones, has persisted. Love magic continues to be viewed as a haphazard activity, lacking any structure or purpose. It provides background noise, a low level of interference for descriptions of the activities of men. Women's ritual activity, their work, has been seen as of concern to women only, while that of the men is seen as of concern to the whole society. Men celebrate themes of a broad cohesive nature; women have narrow, personal, and particularistic themes and interests (Munn 1973: 213). Such an interpretation of ritual misreads the way in which women state their role and the way in which that role is evaluated by Aboriginal men and women.

It might be analytically convenient to set up an opposition whereby men controlled the formal arrangements (i.e., marriage) and women controlled the informal (i.e., love rituals), but the formal and informal are not so easily separated. Women take part in marriage arrangements and men perform love rituals, but each does so with a particular purpose in mind (Strehlow 1971). It is this which distinguishes men's work from women's work in the business of marriage.

Through an analysis of the themes, imagery, symbolism, and structure of women's love rituals, I demonstrate that *yilpinji* concerns the whole of Aboriginal society, that it is underwritten by the dreamtime law, and that it concerns

emotional management, not love magic. Women's business, like men's business, has to do with the maintenance of Aboriginal society as a whole; both
work to uphold the law.

YILPINJI AND COUNTRY

Women who worked magic were called witches by missionaries who banned
such activities; unhappily, it is a label still in vogue at Warrabri today. Many
Warrabri residents who lived at the Baptist mission at Phillip Creek during the
1940s before the establishment of Warrabri tell of the lengths to which women
would go to perform *yilpinji* and of the trouble this caused because the
missionaries and some Aboriginal converts were deeply opposed to it. One
reason for the opposition to *yilpinji* lay in the sexual nature of its subject
matter; yet of the three hundred Kaititj love songs that I have collected in the
field and translated, only a few have to do with actual consummation of sexual
relations. Major themes are longing for country and family, sorrow, anticipa-
tion, agitation, concern, shyness, and display. Country is both a basis of
identity and an analogy for emotional states. Love is, in fact, a very poor
translation of *yilpinji* but one that has found acceptance in the anthropological
literature and has been fed back into the indigenous conceptualization, reinforcing the male notion of what women ought rightly to be about. For white
itinerant road gangers and station hands with whom some Aboriginal women
have had sexual liaisons, love magic has been a smutty joke. It was something
for which one could pay to enjoy. It clearly marked women as sex objects.
Meanwhile, debasement of *yilpinji* as love magic allowed Aboriginal men an
avenue by which it could be defused. Thus, white men encouraged *yilpinji*,
and Aboriginal men could, with this newfound male support, construe *yilpinji*
as magic. Aboriginal men were thereby able to score telling points in their
ongoing tug of war with women.[3] In the process Aboriginal women's religion
was stripped of its actual complexities.

Kaititj women are not explicit in their sexual references but employ euphe-
misms like "going hunting together." They also use gesture: a graphic hand
sign or one to indicate that a woman is being led away by the wrist. They may
dance holding a rhythm stick or bunched-up skirt before them as a mock
penis, but consummation is always offstage or obliquely indicated. Had I
asked for love songs and love myths, I am sure I would have collected fewer
songs, but they would have been more explicitly sexual. The songs and myths
glossed by the Kaititj as *yilpinji* have more to do with the common core of
values underpinning and shaping male/female bahavior than with the playing
out of strictly sexual relationships.

Love and sex are aspects of *yilpinji*, which itself encompasses the sweep of
tensions and emotions engendered by male/female relationships. Such relationships, however, must be seen in their cultural context, where country is a
major symbol of attachment. Devil's Marbles and the surrounding area, known

as *karlukarlu,* for instance, is a focus for rain dreaming. It is spectacular country, where enormous round rocks stand in the desert. During rains numerous small streamlets run from the rocks and ridges, wild figs grow from the devices, and water collects in the rock holes and depressions high on the Marbles. The desert lives. The colors and contrasts are sudden and dramatic; red rocks and green water heavy with slime weed, tall ant hills and spinifex plains. The country is extremely rich in dreaming sites and ancestral activity, but when the road was built from Alice Springs to Darwin it was located through the very center of the Marbles so that important sites are no longer accessible to the Kaititj. Sorrowfully the women claim that they can still hear the old people crying from the caves. This loss has meant that certain important rituals can no longer be performed, but, since the area is within a day's travel of Warrabri, women may still hunt, camp, and dream there. Nonetheless, by losing access to important sites where they could express their attachment and whence they can draw power, women have been weakened. One ritual object associated with this area was so powerful that it was believed a man would meet a violent death if he came within close range of it. This terminal sanction is no longer available to women. Men have, however, retained their own violent sanctions and apply them during initiation time.

The ritual objects that act as title deeds for country are, for the men, mostly kept at the site to which they belong. Today many are kept in the ritual storehouse on settlements, for "the country" is often many inaccessible miles away from where people now live. Women, on the other hand, have always kept their ritual objects in their immediate care. On settlements fire risk is high, as is the danger of discovery, and so women are restricted in the range of objects they can safely maintain. Guided by male-oriented research, government officials have conceded that men need storehouses or "offices"; thus on all settlements there are brick, fireproof storehouses for men, but not for women. Only in 1977 was the first women's ritual storehouse opened at Yuendumu. This recognition of the value of men's ritual gear and disregard for women's ritual needs have placed restrictions on women while encouraging men in their ritual politics.

Settlement life also restricts women's access to country more than it limits men, since the latter may seek licenses and thus have access to vehicles, while women will not generally seek licenses from white police. Some do have licenses, however, and have managed to acquire vehicles. Once owned, a vehicle is kept as exclusively women's property, and this right is respected. On settlements such as Warrabri, where the village council is all male,[4] women have difficulty in obtaining permission to use community vehicles. Many visits to country are aborted because women can neither gain access to a vehicle nor provide a woman driver to take them on women's business.

In short, women have unequal access to the resources provided by the new law; moreover, they are denied a role as co-workers in the emerging social order of Northern Australia and are depicted as second-class citizens within their own society. Aboriginal men have successfully co-opted the white-male representatives of the new law, who in their ignorance have provided new weapons for the male half of Aboriginal society. The negotiating position of Aboriginal women has been undermined, and their loss of land amounts to more than a loss of foraging grounds. To add insult to injury, their tie to land is deemed by many white observers never to have existed.

YILPINJI STRUCTURE AND RANGE

In discussing and analyzing any aspect of women's ritual domain, I am confronted with the problem of using material that is restricted as either secret/sacred or as exclusive to women. When this difficulty arises I have provided generalizations without giving details of song texts or describing the content of the rites. Besides, most women's rituals have a publicly known structure, which can be briefly outlined. Owners and managers, *kirda* and *kurdungurlu*, for a particular dreaming or country gather in the women's secluded ritual areas to prepare the ritual paraphernalia, paint their bodies, sing the country, do their secret business, and discuss the procedure and myth. They then proceed to a more public arena for the display of the painted boards and bodies that encode the myths, a singing of the country which sketches the travels and exploits of the ancestors, and an indication in sign and gesture of the broad categories into which the songs fall. Finally the boards are rubbed clean, the power absorbed, and the ritual objects returned to the women's ritual storehouse. The performance of such rituals consumes valuable resources: ochre, fat, psyhic energy. It is, in short, hard work.

Yilpinji may be performed for a number of reasons other than that of attracting a lover. *Yilpinji* may force a wayward husband to return, remind a wife of her duty to family and country, or even repulse the unwanted advances of a spouse or lover. In Central Australia the focus of *yilpinji* is the community, not the individual for whom the ritual is performed. Both men and women respect its power. Great care is taken by women after a performance to nullify the power of *yilpinji* by throwing dirt and cleaning away all traces of the activity. It must bring about immediate consequences only for the subject of the ritual, not for the whole community. The latter will benefit rather from the restoration of harmony and maintenance of correct marriage alliances. Consultation before a performance is undertaken to determine the rectitude of *yilpinji* in the particular case. I have never heard women admit that they sing for a "wrong-way" partner, although such a union can result if the power is not properly controlled. Warlpiri women were forever accusing the Kaititj of making trouble with their *yilpinji* by the indiscriminate singing of songs. Although the Kaititj appear to exercise enormous care in *yilpinji,* these accusations have forced them to desist from using several powerful songs. Residence on the settlement in this way also has limited their range of expression and played a part in narrowing the recognition of women's religious activities.

Yilpinji is achieved through a creative integration of myth, song, gesture, and design, against a backdrop of country. The circle, the quintessential female symbol, finds expression in the body designs, gestures using rolling hands, and patterns traced out by the dancing feet. Certain *yilpinji* and health/curing designs are the same, because, as Kaititj women recognize, love, health and sexual satisfaction are intertwined at the personal and community level. Exclusively *yilpinji* designs concern agitation, excitement, and longing. Such feelings are said to be located in the stomach that quivers and shakes like the dancing thighs of women or the shaking leaves of men's poles at initiation or the shimmering of a mirage or the iridescence of a rainbow.

YILPINJI AND MYTHS

The following discussion of myth develops the argument that women are claiming a right to express feelings that may superficially seem ambivalent. Ownership of myth and the rights to perform rituals provide the power base for women's claims, while the content of the myths explores women's autonomy and the nature of male/female encounters. Women in the myth encapsulate two warring principles that underpin women's identity. On one hand, there is autonomy; on the other, there is the desire for social intercourse involving men. No invariable sequence is apparent in the mythic representation of encounters, although women's loss and pain are consistently present. Myth provides an explanation for male violence but not its justification. It serves rather as a warning of the treatment women may expect from men and of the danger they face when leaving their own country.

In extracting a story line from the ritual performances and presenting it in the form of a myth, which has a beginning and end, I am doing violence to the ritual's cultural conception. My justification is that, short of a lifetime spent as a woman in women's camps, it is impossible to comprehend the kaleidoscopic range of nuances, ramifications, and elaborations of behavior by which the dreamtime ancestors act out *yilpinji* myths. By organizing the fragments I gleaned into such a form I was able, by way of clarification, to ask further questions of the women. On several occasions I have read back to the women my rendition of the myths; they have nodded assent but declared my version to be written text, which constitutes a form peculiar to Europeans. Their telling of the myth in ritual emphasizes the richness of country, rather than the development of plot or character: two cultural views are thus encapsulated in "myth as action" compared with "myth as text." Country and the sites are part of a metaphysical knowledge system that is totally unlike the European system. The latter elaborates meanings and ideas about society and the significance of life through focusing on persons and their seemingly highly individual actions; Kaititj women's ritual myths look to country dreaming and other spiritually empowered events to discuss themselves and their relations to men.

I should also point out that by presenting the myths in this form I am providing an overview that no individiual woman could recite. The different dreamings are the responsibility of different women, and although each is aware of the content of the dreamtime activity and characters of others, one may only rightly speak of one's own dreamings. Because I was able to record dreamings from all the women of the Kaititj group, my synthesis is not the product of one person's knowledge and would not occur in this form. Women would correct me if I misplaced the dreamings of others but would not comment on the content of the dreamings of others.

There are no occasions on which a woman would sit down and tell *yilpinji* myths, although there is a corpus of songs which are glossed *yilpinji*. There are ritual practices, designs, gestures, and ritual paraphernalia which are used only in conjunction with *yilpinji,* and certain conditions which are said to eventuate exclusively from *yilpinji.* I have put the myths together from actual performances I attended, subsequent discussions and translations of songs and symbols, women's explanations of ritual action and song furnished during performances or while listening to a tape. Once the women had decided I was a suitable candidate for investment into ritual knowledge, they were prepared to elaborate more than usual during actual performances. They were dedicated to my learning the business straight and to informing me of the background knowledge that a woman of my age and status should have.

As the mother of a son nearing the age of initiation and a daughter nearing the age of marriage, I was in a position to begin a course of important ritual instruction. I discovered quite late in my fieldwork that I was deemed a suitable candidate because, as a divorced woman in receipt of a government pension, I approximated the Aboriginal model of women ritual leaders. Like women resident in the *jilimi,* my economic independence was marked with receipt of a pension. It is important that men are kept in ignorance of many of the women's activities, and this can be assured only if a woman lives basically with other women. Aboriginal women assume that white women tell their husbands of their daily activities and therefore that they cannot be entrusted with women's secrets. I was warned that I must not discuss certain ritual practices with men. During most of the first year of my stay I was on trial. Little wonder, then, that male fieldworkers gain only a superficial understanding of women's rituals, that young single fieldworkers are given information appropriate to their perceived age and status, and that married women are given the advantage of ritual participation without necessarily the accompanying ritual explanation.

The two interrelated myths that provide the scenario for most *yilpinji* songs, designs, and performances belong to the *Kurinpi* (old women) dreaming and the *Ngapa* (rain) dreaming. These dreamings belong to and are managed by the women of the Nampijinpa and Nangala subsections, all of whom trace descent from the founding drama of the Stirling Swamp and Devil's Marbles area. The behavior glossed as *yilpinji* (in myth) occurs only in the Devil's Marbles area, because, say the Kaititj women, Kaititj dreaming for that area also has rainbow, whereas Warlpiri rain dreaming (farther west) only has rain. The privilege prompts jealousy and suspicion on the part of Warlpiri and pride for Kaititj. On settlements it provides a further wedge for men to drive into women's solidarity.

The Kurinpi Myth

Although I would like to provide a detailed analysis of the *Kurinpi* myth as it exemplifies the dilemma or warring principles facing women, in that they want the advantages of children and the company of a spouse but fear the unpredictability of men and men's challenge to their independence and autonomy, I shall discuss here only that portion of the *Kurinpi* myth which concerns *yilpinji*, women's claims to feelings as their right, and an exploration of the complexities of male/female interaction:

> *In the* Kurinpi *myth two elderly, knowledgeable, and respected women, known as the* Kurinpi, *wander about in the Stirling Swamp naming the country and performing such rituals as are their responsibility. Their life is one of ritual observance and celebration of the bounty of their country. Their power is manifest in their ability to turn red as they rub themselves with fat while traveling from their swamp home in search of company. On their journey they observe the ritual relationship of owner to worker, experience sorrow at death, and come into conflict with members of the younger generation and the opposite sex.*
>
> *Once out of their swamp homeland they cease to name the country and travel more warily. They poke the ground with spearlike sticks. As they pass through another swamp area closer to Devil's Marbles, they enter a patch of tall spear trees. Fearing that perhaps someone might see them, they clutch their ritual packages to themselves and continue. Several young boys appear and dance flanking them, just as did the* kudungurlu *for the* kirda *in their previous encounter with this ritual relationship. The boys are carrying spears similar to the women's. The women teach the boys to throw spears in an overarm action. The women wonder why the boys, who are also carrying ritual packages, continue to travel with them. The young boys have ritual packages such as are the right of older people. At the meeting and while traveling with the boys the women feel a mixture of shame and curiosity. Finally each reveals to the other the contents of their packages. The* Kurinpi *attempt to leave, but the boys beg them to stay so they can show them everything. "No," say the women, "you are too young and we are leaving." Suddenly the boys disappear and reappear as initiated men. The women look on in amazement, since these men are wearing their ritual headbands and armbands. Again the women hasten to leave and again the men beg them to stay. The women fear that these men might spear them, for they now have long strong spears such as men*

carry. The men follow the departing women, who soon leave them far behind. "Never mind," say the men, "we shall sharpen our spears, harden them in the fire and spear the women when we catch them."

The women say to each other, "Come. Let them go their way. We have everything we need." As the men travel they say, "Let them go. We have all we need and can easily catch them later when we learn how to throw these spears." As the Kurinpi *dance on they see and join another group of women who are performing* yawulyu *rituals. The men with the spears are unsuccessful in catching the women because they are not prepared to violate the restrictions of the women's ritual area.*

The meeting with the boys has many connotations, but here I shall comment only on the significance of the myth for women's perception of themselves in their social function and in relation to men. Before encountering the boys the women had never felt shame. They had confidently and authoritatively known their country and their relationship to it. The status of the boys, already ambiguous, becomes doubly so after their transformation, without ritual, into men. Each is prepared to respect the ritual packages of the other, but the men rather fancy the women and decide to pursue them. The women continue to display their power by their rubbing of fat into their bodies and by their color changes. The men decide to use force and a new technology to win the women but are thwarted when they discover that the women have sought sanctuary in the company of other women.

In another encounter of the *Kurinpi* with men, they do not escape but are overpowered. These two encounters are not considered to exist in any temporal sequence but, like the women's ability to turn red and take on the colors of the desert, the stories are in constant flux, an ever-shifting and dynamically constituted power on which women may draw. The two accounts are not considered conflicting versions of the same myth but rather are taken to be an illustration of the vagaries and complexities of male/female relationships:

The women were returning to the camp from a day of hunting when some men began throwing stones at them. "What is this?" asked the women. "We want to get food, not to run away." Unaware of the presence of the men, the women continued home and on the way dug for grubs. One man ran after one of the women and stood on her digging stick and asked the woman for food. The woman felt shamed because she had never met a man like that before. He told the woman to get up, promising that they would dig together. "Don't be shy," he said, "We shall go together." He gently took the woman by the arm and they all continued together. But as they traveled and the woman left her country behind, she held back and tried to go the other way. The man crippled the woman with a spear. As she lay naked and complaining of this cruelty, he began to beautify himself so that she would love him. He brought her animal skins to warm her body and sat with her. She tried to straighten herself, but it hurt too much. She looked back to her country but knew she must leave with her husband.

It is worth noting that hitherto in the myth the women were depicted as old. Here they appear to be younger, but this is of little consequence since in both myth and reality older women and men court each other but also younger partners. Women regard themselves as desirable regardless of age.

In women's perception, men are so insecure that violence is their sole means of expressing emotion. Roheim (1933:237) would interpret this myth as a description of the wild being tamed, but if seen within the context of land and of male/female interaction as a power relationship, the myth argues the importance of women's power base and also shows that, through marriage, men can disrupt women's lies to land. The once kind suitor who took the woman by the arm now spears her. Her tie to her country is also damaged. In being crippled by the spear wound the woman is also deprived of her land. In the loss of land she loses her autonomy and power base, but he gains a wife to whom he can now afford to show affection and from whom he now seeks love by beautifying himself. In her crippled state, she feels pain, loss of autonomous movement, and loss of land. As they continue together she sees his country, like a mirage, before her, and he begins instructing her in the wonders of his country. Through men, women may thus gain knowledge of another country, but the price is high. It is worth noting that after marriage men in reality often do not succeed in carrying off young wives to another country. Frequently they take up resident in their wife's country.

The Ngapa Myth

In the section of the *Ngapa* (rain) myth which concerns *yilpinji*, a complex series of relationships is played out. The wise rain father, known as Jungkaji, attempts to restrain his overly pretentious sons, the rainbow men, who come into conflict with their older brother, Lightning, while pursuing young girls to whom they are incestuously related. Rain's wife, as mother of the boys, finally lures them from the dangers of their exploits by feigning illness. Their duty to their mother overwhelms them, and they return, only to die at the insistence of their stern father. There are important themes involving the flouting of a father's authority over his sons and identification of devotion to the mother with the sons' destruction, but I shall concentrate on the aspects of male/female relationship that are explored in the myth. During the pursuit, both men and girls, in contemplating the possible outcome of their behavior, express fear, ambivalence, tenderness, aggression and insecurities.

The rainbow men, as older and younger brother, travel around in circles in the Devil's Marbles area from Dixon Creek to Greenwood Station. Their father warns them not to venture too far, but they ignore his warning. "Rainbows should stay close to rain," he says, "Let Rain rain himself," says the sons. "We shall travel further." They travel up so high that they can see the sea. They sit on top of the clouds and display their brilliant colors. They swoop into the green water below. They hide from rain in hollow logs and from the girls in creek beds and behind ridges.

In most of the encounters the girls, who are classificatory sisters but not identified as younger and older, are unaware of the presence of the men, who creep closer and closer to them. The younger brother warns the older not to go too close lest he frighten the girls. "Hold back," he warns. The older brother counters, "Don't be silly." To their delight the women are picking sweet fruits. "You'll frighten them if you go any closer," warns the younger brother. "Wait for rain before showing yourself." The men have rubbed themselves with red ant hill to dull their brightness and thus not frighten the girls. As they add marks to their bodies, they reflect on their own beauty and wonder if the girls, will like them. "Why don't they love us? Have we shown ourselves for nothing?" they wonder. The younger brother questions the correctness of the pursuits of the girls. "They may be of the wrong subsection," he suggests. "We can take wrong skins," says the older brother, but the younger still holds back.

Finally the girls separate. One goes to dig yams, the other to swim. The older brother descends upon the girl who is digging, and such is his brightness that she closes her eyes. He woos her and finally convinces her that she should accompany him. As she leaves she looks back in sorrow for her country but also, like the Kurinpi, *she knows she must leave with her husband. The younger brother goes to the water where the other girl is swimming, but she is too frightened to go with him and attempts to escape. He spears her in the leg, and while she lies naked before him, he beautifies himself with body scars, all the while gently wooing her with tender words.*

In the exploits of the rainbow men their brightness and its malleability are the subject of constant reference. They can overpower women with it. They can thus tear women from their land. The *Kurinpi* women, on the other hand, change color in a way that demonstrates their power over their bodies and over men. One of the stated reasons for this extreme power of Kaititj *yilpinji* is this access to color in the rainbow myth.

In yet another encounter, the young girls are camped with their mother, who remains in camp while they go in search of spring water for her. They return very tired and do not realize that men have been working yilpinji *for them. Like most dreamtime women (and women today) they have carried their ritual packages with them but because they are so tired, they have decided to leave them behind in the camp, high in a tree. The next day they return from hunting with two men they have met during the day, only to find their packages missing. The girls are reluctant to go with the men, who then spear them; finally they travel, along with their mother, into the men's country.*

In this myth women's power, in the form of their ritual packages—that is, their tie to the land—is stolen, thus rendering them comparatively helpless.

Women in Myth

In many of the exploits of the rainbow men, the girls are actually working the *yilpinji* for the men, who follow them through the scrub or who are far away. In a dream a man may see his beloved wearing her *yilpinji* design and hasten to join her. As he returns to her she makes a bed for him so that they may comfort each other when reunited. "Make my heart still," she pleads. "Lie with me." Or as he travels he may hear the sound of her voice like music from afar. He may fish by throwing grass into the water to attract the fish and see his loved one instead. Or she may have prepared a ball of the green slime weed that she threw out to him from a distance, and this has now reached him.

When they are finally reunited, he kneels before her, woos her, and gently encourages her to appreciate his charms; he may make a pillow of his *woomera* (spear thrower) or swish away the flies with it. Sometimes the girl is afraid, but he reassures her. In one song she lies in a tight ball, but he soothes her and covers her until she relaxes. He asks, "Do you love me? If not I shall go away forever. Please tell me." Such behavior is a far cry from the single-mindedness of the songs and myths discussed by Ronald Berndt and C. H. Berndt (1951) and Roheim (1933), in which the end point is always copulation. In the women's songs a man may even feign illness in order to gain his loved one's attention, hoping that she will eventually come to love him.

Yilpinji: Themes and Symbols

A major symbol of *yilpinji* is color and its power to attract. The whiteness of the headband and feather twirled by the opening woman dancer is contrasted to the bursting color of the rainbow men, which must be dulled with green slime weed so as not to dazzle women in the myth. Thus, paradoxically, in ritual practice women throw balls of green slime to attract a lover; in fact both men and women use green slime to attract. Like the men's colors, the women's colors are not static. They shift and change hue. The *Kurinpi* turn red, the color of the country. The rainbow men burst dangerously with all colors, but use red of the ant hill and green from the water to dull their brilliance. Women see their own and men's colors as dynamic, not fixed in a color spectrum but fluid, unpredictable, dramatic as the country itself and ever changing.

The shining of watchbands and buckles, the sparkling of lightning, the lure of blond hair, the blackening of eyebrows, and the reddened legs of women dancers all induce a lover to notice and appreciate the charms of a possible partner. A major theme of ritual is display. Decoration and display have found expression in terms of both traditional and introduced items. The traditional male hair-string headband has been replaced in reality and in some songs by the scarf or band from a stockman's hat. The arm bracelets adorned with feathers formerly celebrated in song may now apprear as the shining watch that winks across the desert. The pubic cover which is pushed aside by the impatient lover becomes the shining buckle, which is seductively left open but catches the sun and shines. A woman's digging stick may now be a shining crowbar; her wooden carrier, a metal billy can. Such items glisten as women travel and attract the attention of a lover. In the same way bald heads are said to shine in the sun and to attract lovers.

The intrusion of such themes and items, which are often associated with a particular person, has been construed by C. H. Berndt (1950:43) as evidence of the nonreligious nature of love magic. I think it has more to do with the manner in which women dream and with the ever-present nature of the dreamtime. In ritual the dreamtime moves concurrently with the present so that the appearance of introduced goods and their evolving meanings is not a contradiction so much as proof of the relevancy of the dreamtime law. Many of the songs belong to, or depict, actual living people; in time these songs will become part of the repertoire and their characters will be given kin terms, as are the characters of the songs already accepted by male anthropologists as bona fide dreaming songs. The mixture of songs suggests to me that these present-day themes are in the process of achieving the nonspecificity and vagueness that characterize the dreaming. The innovative themes have a relevancy for today's world. One Kaititj/Alyawarra woman commented to me as I watched in amazement while money, an alien concept, was added to a ritual exchange, "It does not matter what it is. It is what it stands for that is important!" However, the accommodation of such modern items within ritual lulls women into believing that they have retained control over the power to attract, a power demonstrated by successful liaisons with white men. For women this belief strengthens their self-image and demonstrates the power of *yilpinji;* for men it strengthens the destructive image of woman as a sex object.

EXEGESIS

In these myths various admired female stereotypes are presented. The *Kurinpi* are the ritually important women, while the young girls exude sweetness, youth, and the ability to hunt proficiently. In ritual the desirability of these qualities is celebrated by women for a number of reasons. In both the *Kurinpi* myth and the rainbow myth men are portrayed as cruel, unsure, vain. They continually ask each other, "Will she like me? Will we frighten them?" Insecure about their ability to woo and win, they win, then woo, beautifying themselves after wounding the women. Once they make contact there is no standard response. The stable, symbolically ordered positions on the axis become freed and negotiable. Like the shifts in color, like the unpredictability of the country from which women draw their power, men are inconsistent. One brother uses soft words and beauty. He has been the confident one all along. The other uses physical force but soft words.

In an Aranda men's song cycle recorded by Theodor Strehlow (1971:4), the sequence of attraction, violence, consummation, and travel to a new country is followed, but the male perception and articulation casts woman as the passionate partner, so passionate in fact that she leaves her own country to travel with him. When sorrow fills her as she leaves, he empathizes and beautifies himself to console her. Thus, men also recognize that in marriage women may lose land but in the song explain it as women's passion and credit themselves with tenderness. In Nancy Munn's (1973:47) account of Warlpiri male *yangaridji* (closely related to *yilpinji*), the crippling motif is said to be used to ensure fidelity. Uniting both the male and female versions of *yilpinji* myths is the depiction of love as crippling and the use of land—also an actual living resource—as a central symbol. By evoking their control of land, women may attract men.

The display of color so powerful in the myths about the rainbow men and the *Kurinpi* women is given form in the body decorations and secret rituals of the women. In *Kurinpi* performances women redden themselves, and, like the *Kurinpi*, have the power to attract and face possible violence or escape to the closed world of women. Women's ritual practices, unlike the action of men in myth, are deemed invariably successful. Such differentiation and separation of the qualities of powerful, cruel/gentle men in myth is dynamically opposed to powerful, irresistible women who give the myth form in the rites. Like the *Kurinpi*, women may remain apart or seek a spouse; like the girls in the rainbow myth, they may lead a man to destruction or entrance him with their sweetness. It is their choice.

The conflicts and tensions that arise when men and women must enter into the direct negotiation of rights, privileges, and obligations with each other burst forth in violence such as that seen in the jealous fights common in many communities, but they also find expression in the ritual statements of women in *yilpinji*. In everyday life men fear that if they really hurt a woman she may take ritual action. If a women turns away from a man she usually has good reason. Her response will certainly have been the subject of much public discussion. If she acts rashly, she will incur the censure of other women and will have no security in their camps. Women are not considered to be fickle in the eyes of men or women, and if a woman uses *yilpinji* against a man he knows he has deserved it. Fights begin with accusations of infidelity (a vastly expanded possibility in settlements), not fickleness. The heightened suspicion of women's infidelity, like the debasement of *yilpinji* to love magic, has been imposed on women; stereotyping of the women's highly predictable responses to maltreatment has been achieved without consideration of their perceived feelings or their attitudes toward the diminution of their enforceable rights.

In *yilpinji* women not only articulate their models of social reality but also attempt to shape their worlds. This latter aspect is, I believe, apparent in the way in which women comment on ritual as it proceeds. At one level they discuss the myth as I have delineated it, and at another they comment on the power and efficiency of the rituals. These two levels are interwoven in the seamless web of life that encompasses the now of today and the now of the dreaming. Particular songs or combinations of songs and actions are remembered as having been sung at a particular place for a particular person and with a particular result. Two older women married to much younger men did not see the action of a man taking an older wife as duty but saw it as a man desperately in love with an irresistible woman. Such is the women's perception of the affair. They do not see themselves as being shuffled around but as capable of deciding whether or not they will go to a younger man. Since women exercise wide choice in second and subsequent marriages it is hard to believe that they go to younger men merely to uphold the gerontocracy. They go if they wish. To ensure the success of the match they work *yilpinji*. The two older women mentioned above are celebrated cases of *yilpinji*, but all the women with whom I worked would admit to having used *yilpinji* to achieve results they desired and all attested to the success they had.

As songs are being sung, women comment on the possible outcome of the ritual and the action in the ritual. They assert their rights to feelings. "That is my feeling," I have heard women say in explanation on many occasions. "If you want to stay you may." If a woman wants to get out of a marriage which she finds distasteful because the man is playing around, taking a second wife, or acting violently, a wife may ask for her ritual group to perform *yilpinji* to make him turn away from her. These are powerful actions, and they are allowed only after the women have weighed the case. However, if a woman says, "That is my feeling," her words are respected.

In the myths, the lovers are often improperly related. Roheim (1933:209-10) cast *yilpinji* as a holiday from the rules, but in my experience, love rituals are very carefully used and then only after extensive consultation and consideration of the merits of the request. *Yilpinji* only induces certain states; it does not have the power to condone "wrong-way" unions, which, in any case, are rare, notorious, and generally short-lived. *Yilpinji* is used to establish correct unions. It is therefore feared by men, because *yilpinji* impinges upon the set of relationships that men claim to control through marriage alliances. They know that they cannot negate women's *yilpinji* and often do not even know they are being performed. At any time a woman may thus overturn the plans of men. Men do not attempt to prevent women from staging *yilpinji* but rather turn to their own sphere of control of male/female relations and intensify demands in the domain of promised marriages. Women respect the marriage codes but not necessarily the plans of men. In using *yilpinji* for correct unions they are upholding the moral order but not endorsing men's rights to determine actual marriages. The charge made by the women and accepted at face value by some anthropologists that women use *yilpinji* for "wrong-way" unions obscures women's endorsement of central values.

CONCLUSION

In exploring women's mythology I have argued that women represent their world as one which is self-contained, known, and secure. The authority to control this world and the power to exclude men from this domain are underwritten by the dreamtime—the all-encompassing law of the past and now. In acting out the responsibilities conferred upon them as women by this law, women engage in work which is distinctively theirs. In the past this ensured that they would be recognized as full members of their society. Today, although they continue to work in their domain, one which remains separate and distinct from that of the men, they no longer enjoy their former status. For Kaititj women the sexual division of labor is, on the one hand, dynamic and changing, much affected by colonization and white patriarchial practices. On the other hand, these women remain firmly oriented toward the age-long values of renewal and bound to people, law, and the land. To the extent that women's rituals endure and encode crucial aspects of gender relations and therefore of Aboriginal culture, women and their rituals contribute most significantly to the continuity of Aboriginal structures in a colonial frontier society.

Notes

1. The research for this paper was undertaken when I was a postgraduate scholar in the Department of Prehistory and Anthropology, School of General Studies, Australian National University. I gratefully acknowledge the Department's assistance and that of the Australian Institute of Aboriginal Studies in funding my fieldwork. For criticisms on the various drafts I am particularly indebted to Caroline Ifeka and my fellow participants in the Wenner-Gren Conference, August 1980. Finally I thank the women who sat with me in the field, taught me, and cared for me.

2. Under this act, Aborigines in the Northern Territory may claim unalienated crown land and land in which all interests other than those held by the crown are held by or on behalf of Aborigines.

3. By locating *yilpinji* within the context of land and interpreting the myths in terms of power symbolisms, I have not dwelt upon the explicit themes of sex, as have some previous analyses of male/female relationships (see Berndt and Berndt 1951).

4. Aboriginal councils established in the 1950s are now assuming greater powers in the running of settlements and are demanding legal recognition and status through incorporation (see Bell and Ditton 1980:1–15).

6

Forgotten Wealth: Cloth and Women's Production in the Pacific

ANNETTE B. WEINER

WOMEN AS PRODUCERS OF WEALTH IN THE TROBRIANDS

In 1971, during the first days of my field research in Kiriwina Island in the Trobriands, Papua New Guinea, I found that Kiriwina women produce and control the distribution of a form of wealth—objects made from banana leaf fibers. In 1980, I undertook fieldwork in Western Samoa to explore the possibility that women's wealth in Kiriwina was not an isolated phenomenon. My comparative hunch proved correct. A particular kind of wealth, made by women from the leaves of pandanus and trimmed with feathers, still has economic and political value today. These discoveries force a reconsideration of traditionally accepted views on the relations between women's production and the division of labor.

After all the reevaluations and reanalyses of Bronislaw Malinowski's classic Trobriand studies, who would have thought that Kiriwina women owned anything of economic value? Exchange theory assumes that reciprocity—involving important wealth objects—occurs between men. If male informants do not tell us about banana leaves as wealth, the ethnographer remains very comfortable with his or her guidelines of exchange between men. The anthropological history of Trobriand ethnography illustrates the ease with which a primary form of wealth can be ignored. That this wealth is produced by women certainly was a major reason for its absence in the ethnographic literature. Of equal importance, however, is the fact that fibrous wealth as a physical object may not appear culturally significant to an outsider's eyes, even to those of a trained anthropologist. The exchange of *kula* shells among men no doubt seemed far more impressive to Malinowski and others than the flimsy-looking bundles of banana leaves that women distribute after someone dies. It is not very difficult to conjecture why Malinowski or Harry Powell (who did Trobriand field research in 1950) did not write about women's wealth, when they both saw women involved in these distributions (Weiner 1976).

Now that the role of Kiriwina women and their production of bundles of banana leaves have entered the ethnographic corpus, we do not need to belabor the issue of forgotten wealth. However, another problem remains. Given that women produce a primary object of wealth, how is the power of women to be defined in relation to men's power and to political power?

From the earlier ethnographic literature on the Trobriands, we have a view of a society where men are the producers of yams, which are the major source of food and also the major object of exchange between affines and between chiefs and their followers. Some men, especially chiefs, also participate in *kula*, the network of overseas partners who exchange armshells for shell necklaces. Women or women's production was not thought to figure centrally in any of these activities. We now know that Kiriwina women produce and control their own wealth, which is connected directly to men's yam production and which affects the accumulation of men's wealth (Weiner 1976; 1980a). Even with their own wealth, however, women do not participate in the political domain in the same way that men do. Women are not chiefs, although this may not always have been the case,[1] and women do not enter into formal public disputes over land control and ownership. Kiriwina women do not go on overseas expeditions associated with *kula* transactions. Yet women's wealth is connected in important ways to these events and statuses (Weiner 1983a).

Many feminists would write off the case of Kiriwina women's wealth as merely one more example of women's universal secondary status. Other anthropologists have argued that although Trobriand women use skirts as wealth, it is still men who exchange the *real* wealth and who have the *real* power (e.g., Powell 1980: 700–702). In *Women of Value, Men of Renown* (Weiner 1976), I emphasized that Kiriwina men control events in what I called "historical time and space," the social domain, while women control "ahistorical time and space," the cosmological domain where the regeneration of lineage identity occurs. I also pointed out that because women's wealth has economic value, women enter profoundly into the male historical domain. In using these categories I was attempting to escape from the connotations of dichotomies such as "private/public" and "nature/culture" in which notions of male dominance and the political still are grounded in nineteenth-century assumptions that separate women and the symbolic from the *real* world of politics. My goal was to extend the notion of the political and to determine how power is constructed within a cultural system, and how much power is regenerated through time. Given a situation where rank is firmly established,

what objects serve as the validation of rank and the social relations that
support rank?

In thinking further about these processes, I always returned to the unusual
phenomena of bundles of banana leaves in their use as a limited currency, as a
statement of social relationships connected to yam production, which involves
the labor of men, and as a validation of the regeneration of matrilineal *(dala)*
identity. Following every death, the blood relatives of the dead person must
distribute thousands of bundles of banana leaves to all individuals who were
not members of the deceased's lineage, but who were connected to the dead
person through a final or patrilateral relations, fictive kinship, or friendship.
The accumulations of bundles worth hundreds of dollars depends upon the
production of individual women. Men, however, must take their wealth objects—such as yams, pigs, manufactured goods, and trade store items—and
exchange them for bundles of banana leaves. These bundles they then give to
their wives to increase the size of their wives' distributions.[2] The higher
ranked and the more politically powerful a man is, the more important it is for
him to secure large amounts of bundles for his wife (see Weiner 1983a). The
production and distribution of women's wealth act as a leveling device,
periodically depleting the wealth of men, including chiefs. That the production
of women's wealth is still intact and even inflated after over a hundred years of
Western contact must be carefully considered. Why should an object such as
banana-leaf bundles, with no apparent use value, necessitate the vast expenditures of men's wealth, including large amounts of Western cash? Clearly,
bundles of banana leaves must have a cultural value that exceeds the value we,
as anthropologists, place on the political. If women are the producers and the
recipients of this wealth, what is their role and the power of their role in the
total social system?

Recent data from other societies in the larger Kiriwina region, known as
the Massim, illustrate the uniqueness of bundles of banana leaves. In islands
such as Sudest and Vakuta, women's fibrous skirts are used as objects of
exchange (Campbell: 1981; Lepowsky: 1981). Only in Kiriwina, however, are
both skirts and bundles of banana leaves considered wealth. On Woodlark and
Tubetube islands women directly participate in *kula* and in other kinds of
public exchanges involving stone and shell valuables that in Kiriwina involve
only men (Damon 1983; Martha MacIntyre, per. com. 1981). In general,
throughout the Massim, women have a higher status than elsewhere in New
Guinea, as Malinowski (1922, 1926) and Seligman (1910) originally pointed out.
In Kiriwina, however, the system of ranking and inherited positions of chiefs
reaches a level of integration unlike that found anywhere else in the Massim
and unusual throughout the rest of Papua New Guinea. Only in Kiriwina do
women produce bundles of banana leaves which circulate as a limited currency. What then is the relation between this form of wealth and political
stratification? Does women's production of *cloth wealth* play a fundamental
role in the development of stratification?[3]

USES OF FIBROUS WEALTH

Although the relationship between women's production and stratification seemed to make sense in the Kiriwina case (Weiner 1983a), comparative data supporting this view was needed. Elsewhere in the Melanesian literature, there are scattered references to woven mats as wealth. Codrington (1891) noted the use of "mat money" in the New Hebrides (see also Layard 1924; Rivers 1914; Speiser 1923). A most intriguing early description from Coote (1883) concerns Aurora, where "women are the mat-makers and mats represent wealth." In the production process, special kinds of mats, used only in initiation societies, are allowed to rot through a method of slow, carefully controlled burning in which black incrustation adheres to the mat and "hangs down in stalactic forms called by the natives 'breasts'" (Coote as quoted in Quiggin 1949: 132). The recent work of Margaret Rodman (1981) on the importance of mats in East Aoba, New Hebrides, demonstrates the contemporary high value of mats for both women and men in exchanges marking important events such as birth, initiation, and death. Mat-work and plait-work currencies have also been reported in the Marshalls and in the Solomon Islands (Quiggin 1949: 133–34), and the loom traditionally was used in Kusaie, in Santa Cruz, and on the Banks islands, where woven girdles and mats functioned as currency.[4]

Unfortunately, these important data from island Melanesia are too brief for comparative analysis. In 1978, however, I had the opportunity to view a slide presentation depicting the exchange activities surrounding the inauguration of a Western Samoan chief.[5] Particularly rivetting was the central role that women seemed to be playing in the exchange proceedings. Particular slides showing women presenting huge fine mats were not only strikingly impressive in their magnitude, but visually jarring in their uncanny similarity with Kiriwina women carrying skirts as wealth payments during mortuary distributions. While watching the slides, I experienced a sensation of déjà vu, taking me back to that first day when Kiriwina women had told me that skirts and bundles are "just like your money." Depite the enormous differences that exist between Samoan fine mats and Kiriwina bundles of banana leaves, the similarities in their use are fascinating.

A dramatic picture emerges as one turns to the literature on Polynesia. Scattered throughout early historical sources and ethnographic reports are descriptions of fibrous wealth produced by women. Yet even though fine mats, barkcloth, and woven cloaks occasionally are referred to as "prestige goods," they are only briefly mentioned and are then ignored[6] (but see Gailey 1980 for an analysis of traditional women's wealth that includes barkcloth in Tonga). The reasons for discounting the consequences of fibrous wealth are multiple. In some cases, European contact immediately disrupted local cloth production with trade in European cloth and blankets. Still today, however, in islands such as Samoa, Tonga, and Fiji, the production of barkcloth and mats remains important. These fibrous cloth objects continue to be used in exchanges central to kinship relations and political alliances. Among the contemporary Maori, traditional woven cloaks still circulate in mortuary distributions for individuals of high rank (Metge 1967). In Eastern Polynesia, in lieu of bark-cloth, cotton appliqué quilts designed and produced by women are exchanged at important political events and at births, marriages, and deaths (Hammond 1981).

As in the Trobriand example, plaited and woven objects and barkcloth are producucts of women's labor, rather than men's. No doubt this reason played a large part in the dismissal of such production as unimportant. The forgotten wealth of Polynesia also reflects a contemporary and naive Western view of cloth as a mass-produced commodity and therefore as an object lacking any power to effect individual kinship and political consequences.

Early sources on Samoa contain references to the importance of fine-mat exchanges at birth, marriage, death, and at the taking of a chiefly title. In fact, Margaret Mead reported that fine mats are "Samoan Currency" (1930: 73). She noted that the age of a fine mat, the lineage status of the woman who weaves it, and the history of the exchanges in which each mat has been involved all "ceremonially" enhance its economic value. "Setting aside their secondary value derived from association, the Samoan fine mat is an excellent illustration of a currency originally founded upon labor value" (ibid.).

Yet this account by Mead was ignored, partly because exchange theory as developed by Malinowski (1922, 1926) defined objects as either "ceremonial" or "utilitarian." An object that had no use value, that was thought of as an "heirloom," that was physically perishable in contrast to stone or shell, and that was produced by women, drew little interest. Anthropologists were interested in *real* wealth and *real* power, and forms of cloth seemed inap-propriate to these concerns. However, once we recognize that bits of banana leaves, pandanus threads, and barkcloth pounding are significant cultural features, we must reevaluate traditional views.

BANANA-LEAF BUNDLES AND SOCIAL RELATIONS

Taking women's production of wealth seriously and returning to the Trobriand example, we find an important set of comparisons in relation to Samoan cloth wealth. Banana-leaf bundles are produced through a labor-intensive process (Weiner 1976:239–41) from the leaves of one variety of the banana plant. Unlike male valuables, such as *kula* shells and stone ax blades, which must be obtained through long-distance trade and exchange partners, bundles are produced locally. The rate of their production is connected to death, for only after a death are huge amounts of bundles necessary for formal distribution.[7] All women connected to the dead person through kinship ties must make bundles. At the same time, the men who are married to these women are buying bundles from other women, who are unrelated to the deceased. These women make bundles expressly to pay for the items women's husbands are using to procure additional women's wealth. In this way, each death triggers the production of bundles by women and the expenditure of wealth by men.

Bundles, however, are tied to death in a more profound way than economics. What makes bundles and skirts objects of a different order than the shells and stones of men's wealth is their ultimate reference to the cultural processes that validate rebirth in the face of death.

In a society where rank as a principle of birth is well integrated, yet where individual positions of power and status are always being negotiated, the strength of one's lineage support must be demonstrated publicly. At no other time is such strength felt to be under attack than when someone dies. All deaths, except for those of very old people, are thought to result from personal attacks of sorcery. Only at a death do members of a particular matrilineage appear publicly as a distinct group. Only at a death does the size of a matrilineage and the wealth of individual members become visibly prominent in all the exchanges that continue for four to eight months after burial.[8]

In Kiriwina, the *reproduction* of matrilineal identity, property, and social relations with "others" not of one's own matrilineage depends fundamentally upon women's wealth. As a general concept, my use of the word *reproduction* refers to the way societies come to terms with the processes whereby individuals give social identities and things of value to others and the ways in which these identities and values come to be replaced by other individuals and regenerated through generations. I take as my basic premise a view of society as a system cyclically integrated through culturally defined processes of birth, growth, decay, and death. Rebirth, which I formally call *regeneration,* constitutes the replacement of these values at death so that some measure continues, i.e., is regenerated for the living. As a matter of course, women play as central a part in these processes as do men.

Reproduction is never perceived as automatic or as solely biological, but is a process that demands continuous work. Such work involves production associated with the processes whereby identities and objects are given to individuals and, in the course of generations, are reconstituted and recirculated. From an ego-centered perspective, each individual is made more than her or his natal identity by the accumulation of additional resources, such as physical growth and identities perceived to occur through others, material objects, networks of social relations, ritual associations with ancestors, and significant kinds of knowledge and talents.[9] In this way, the basic relationships central to the processes of reproduction involve each ego in relation to all "others" who during the course of the ego's life will contribute to the physical, material, social, and cosmological growth of the ego. Through this process, one's own identity is expanded through "others," who have access to different resources and skills. Through a life cycle, each ego not only accumulates these resources, but also divests them by giving them to others. At death, resources associated with the deceased may be replaced by the living so that they continue to circulate beyond one person's lifetime.

In the Kiriwina case, land controlled through generations by members of the same matrilineage as well as the detachable paraphernalia of matrilineal identity—such as personal names, decorations, and magic spells—are given to others to use who are not members of the giver's lineage. For example, men and their sisters give a man's children the use of land, personal names, and decorations. In this way, lineage properties and rights are detached from the original lineage and circulate among others who are not members of that matrilineage. Death is the moment when the reclaiming of these things occurs. In the mortuary distributions that take place after each death, bundles and skirts publicly mark all the relations that the dead person had during her or his life with others and all of these relations in terms of the circulation of matrilineal properties. In this public way, bundles and skirts validate the strength and wealth of a matrilineage, marking the ability of individuals identified with the matrilineage to give to others in repayment and replacement for what was given to the deceased throughout her or his life (see Weiner 1980b).

The example of bundles and skirts illustrates that certain resources objectify the general societal processes of reproduction. These resources document and legitimize the fundamental condition whereby ego and others are tied together. To mark these relations and transfers of property through succeeding generations, the resource must be a material object with some physical property of durability. The primary value such an object acquires—its "fetishism," in Marx's terms—grows out of its direct association with the processes of reproduction and regeneration. By isolating these objects and analyzing their circulation through time, the dimensions of the relation between ego and others can be ascertained. From a comparative perspective, the degree of hierarchy achieved in a particular society and the limitations for expanding hierarchical potentialities in the relations between an ego and others can be examined (see Weiner 1983b for an example of this view taken from an egalitarian society).

What makes banana-leaf bundles in Kiriwina a resource of primary value is their fundamental attachment to death and regeneration, their ability to document the wealth and social relations of a matrilineage. Value constructed at the primary level of death and rebirth underwrites the ongoing exchange value and currency value of the very same objects. Regardless of their periodic control over men's wealth, Kiriwina men, including chiefs, are never free from the exigencies of death, where women's wealth is redistributed and where women's needs for wealth accumulations drain men's wealth in order to fulfill these needs. In Kiriwina, women's wealth forms the basis for the integration of a system of chiefs by validating the rights, powers, and prosperity of matrilineal identity at the time when a lineage is in its weakest position. The drain on men's wealth, in an attempt to defy such weakness,

limits the degree of hierarchy that can be achieved within the Kiriwina system
of chiefs. Resources of movable wealth, unattached to lineage controls, such
as *kula* valuables, cannot be accumulated to any large degree (Weiner 1983a).
Therefore Kiriwina chiefs must rely fundamentally on the power of their
matrilineage identity, a power tied directly to women and women's wealth.
Kiriwina men dominate women when the political arena is examined in and of
itself. When the political is seen as inextricably tied to death, however, the
roles of domination are reversed, for women limit men.

The degree of limitation for both women and men is reflected in the extent
to which women's wealth can reproduce the specificity of historical circumstances. Women's wealth lacks any value associated with individualization.
Bundles and skirts do not carry any formal coding relating each object itself to
historical events or to the names of specific social relationships, or even to the
identity of a particular matrilineage. Bundles and skirts document the processes of replacement. The amounts of wealth distributed publicly record the
present state of particular social relations. The categories of bundles that are
distributed consist only in the separation of bundles into "clean," "dirty,"
"new," or "old." When these different categories of bundles are distributed,
they refer to certain kinship distinctions between the matrilineage and others
and to certain kinds of exchanges that involve men's wealth (for details see
Weiner 1976). New bundles have a higher value than the other kinds, so that
with each death, the most important bundles are those that have just been
produced. Over the course of several years, one woman's new bundles will
eventually become another woman's "clean" bundles, and finally "clean"
ones become "old" or "dirty." Even with these changes, the life trajectory of
bundles remains relatively short.

The objects themselves never represent the histories of statuses of relationships through generations. The material objectification of matrilineal identity and the processes of reproduction are only partially achieved. The relative
"thinness" of the historical and social content that women's wealth addresses
mirrors the anonymity that exists in traditional notions of conception (Weiner
1976:121–36). An unnamed ancestral spirit is thought to cause conception
when it enters a woman's body. This spirit *(baloma)* is identified only as
matrilineal "blood" rather than as a particular ancestor. In this way, matrilineal identity is regenerated through unmarked, ahistorical time.

Ultimately, in the domain of death as the political, women fare no better
than men, for history and social relations have no long-term, generational
form. Where the specificity of history and the social relations between matrilineage identity and others occurs is in the male domain of land ownership
and control. The results that men achieve in obtaining labor and resources
from others, however, are periodically undercut by death and the constant
need for women's wealth by all women and men.

CLOTH AS WEALTH AND POWER IN SAMOA

A comparison between Kiriwina bundles and Samoan fine mats isolates a
striking set of differences. Fine mats in Samoa act as currency for all goods,
including land and services. Kiriwina bundles can only be used as limited
currency, for bundles cannot obtain land, services, or certain kinds of men's
wealth. Fine mats are presented at all major activities throughout a life cycle,
in addition to death. Fine mats last for several hundred years; therefore, the
qualities of permanence and the recording of histories and titles are an
essential part of the value of fine mats.

A few examples will illustrate the economic importance of Samoan fine
mats. Mead (1930) presented a list of common equivalences she found in 1920;
one fine mat was given for one large pig, ten bed mats, a kava bowl with twelve
legs, and twenty large baskets of food. In 1980 (during my field research) fine
mats were sold for cash at the market at Apia. Large ones sold for from $150 to
$200. These fine mats, however, were not thought to be of exceptional value,
for only old fine mats, of the highest technical quality, are prized.

Despite the use of cash in all important transactions today, fine mats still
retain their significance. In 1978, at a marriage involving the families of two
high-ranked descent groups ('āiga),* three thousand fine mats were presented
by the bride's relatives. In the same year, seven hundred fine mats were
distributed at the death of a man who held a high title. Important specialist
services, such as a house or canoe building, must be paid for in fine mats.
According to Stair (1897), the final ceremony of the tattooing of a chief's son
often cost as much as six hundred to one thousand fine mats. Krämer (1902)
reported that the cash equivalence of fine mats for payment in Samoan house
building was as high as 5,000 to 10,000 German marks. Today, fine mats still
accompany such services, even though cash may be included. In 1979, at the
building of a new church, the head carpenter was paid five hundred fine mats
and $12,000.

In its circulation as currency, fine mats remain tied to social relations. For
large accumulations of fine mats, the head (ali'i) of an 'āiga[10] controls the
distributions. Every individual household owns a stock of fine mats. Unlike
the Trobriands, however, where women retain full control over the distribution
of bundles, in Samoa, final control is vested in the highest title holder (the
chief) of an 'āiga. When fine mats need to be presented for services, payment,
or for a birth, marriage, or a death, all members of the 'āiga bring fine mats to
the house of the ali'i. The number and quality of the fine mats brought from
each individual household are determined by the woman of the 'āiga. Al-

---

*An 'āiga is a descent group related through a male and female line.

though the head of the *'āiga* presents these fine mats, he or she becomes indebted to each person who brought fine mats. In this way, the autonomy of a chief remains dependent upon, and obligated to, those who are beneath him in rank and title. An enormous degree of strategy and manipulation occurs in the distributions of fine mats, as each mat is graded in terms of its quality, history, and title. Given that five hundred or more fine mats may be distributed during one occasion, strategy itself remains a complex task.

Nowhere is strategy more predominant than at the taking of a title *(saofa'i)*. Krämer (1902) presented an excellent illustration of the problems of securing political legitimization. In Krämer's example, the question posed by Samoans involved in a difficult decision over the taking of a title was, Let us see where his families are. The question meant, How many families will support the title holder? The answer would be declared publicly in the number of fine mats the members of the *'āiga* present. In each presentation, the quality of each fine mat—its name and position among the other fine mats given—demonstrates how the givers feel without any verbal discussion. The strength of a person's support is expressed in fine mats.

A special category of fine mats operates totally within the political domain. Fine mats called *'ie o le mālō* (the fine mats of government) are exchanged at the taking of high titles and at the death of those holding the highest-ranked titles. These fine mats have special names, which stand for a series of events that happened to the members of the *'āiga* at some unknown time in the past. These stories are secret knowledge, but the presentation of such a fine mat when its name is called out is indeed a powerful moment.

Fine mats must be understood as repositories of myth and history. They are documents stored away for fifty, one hundred, or even two hundred years. The older a fine mat becomes—that is, the browner the white pandanus turns, the deeper its patina, the more patched in places where aging has rotted the original material—the more valued the mat is. In addition to the historical weight that gives value to fine mats, these objects also possess a sacred power. "One fine mat saves a thousand lives," is a statement often made to me. When a murder occurs, the highest titleholder of the murderer's *'āiga* covers himself with a valued fine mat and approaches the house of the highest titleholder of the dead person's *'āiga* to ask forgiveness for the crime.[11] An informant once questioned me, "Why do you think Samoans attribute so much significance to strips of pandanus and feathers of birds? They have no use at all." Then, answering his own question, he continued, "Fine mats are more desired than your gold. A fine mat is protection for life."

WOMEN, CLOTH PRODUCTION, AND HIERARCHY

In Samoa, the transformation that occurs in the production of cloth wealth, when compared with Kiriwina cloth wealth, gives rise to an object that can become a historical document. The production of one fine mat takes from six months to a year of women's work.[12] Women work together as a group; traditionally, this group *(aualuma)* was an integral and politically significant part of village organization. In Kiriwina, women usually work informally and often alone. A skirt can be woven in three or four days and one bundle takes a half hour to produce after the drying process is finished. In the Samoan case, greater physical durability is achieved through more intensive labor applied to more complex technologies. The durability of Samoan fine mats is further enhanced through the recognition that age, in addition to fine work, increases value. The sacredness and the political power of Samoan fine mats are linked to past genealogies and myths. In this way, fine mats validate the regeneration of the past, while, at the same time, they document present events. This primary value, vested in the process through which death and regeneration are culturally achieved, gives value to this object in its circulation as a full currency and in a wide range of competitive and potentially challengeable sociopolitical situations.

In Kiriwina, by means of a form of cloth, which lacks the specificity of historical identity but contains the basic values of matrilineal identity, women produce the conditions for hierarchy. Bundles and skirts remain the wealth of women only, but this form of cloth wealth subsumes men's wealth. In Kiriwina, women do not move into the male domain and become chiefs; neither do the men who are chiefs exercise the kind and degree of domination over men and women that occurs in Samoa. Bundles and skirts remain intrinsically tied to death. They support, yet limit, a degree of hierarchy that is unique in the Massim and rare throughout the rest of Melanesia. Throughout Polynesia, however, hierarchy and political stratification are much further developed.

In the Trobriands, to be born into a particular matrilineage secures one the right (dependent upon age) to become a chief. In Samoa, the right to a title is far more complex, with many lines of possible access and many competitors. The circulation of fine mats signifies support, ability, and ultimately, in the circulation of the "fine mats of government," the highest power. Samoan fine mats not only reproduce the conditions for hierarchy, as in the Trobriand case, but also reproduce the history that records hierarchy. In Samoa, some women occupy the same positions of power that some men occupy as titleholders; and traditionally, women as sisters hold important sacred positions of power.

Fine mats are the wealth of *both* women and men, but final control over the circulation of fine mats is appropriated by a titleholder. Women hold titles as well as men, but men are the more frequent titleholders. In 1500 A.D., however, a woman, Salamasina, accomplished what no man has ever done. Salamasina held the four highest titles of the Samoan Islands (Krämer 1923) and politically controlled all of Samoa. The history of women's roles in Samoan society has been difficult to piece together because missionary reforms, begun in the midnineteenth century, dramatically weakened the status and prestige of women, as Penelope Schoeffel (1977, 1981) has illustrated. The traditional village organization of women *(aualuma)*, where the production of fine mats was controlled by senior women, was undermined by the church, because of women's power as "sacred sisters" in relation to their brothers and the highest titleholder of their natal (or adopted) *'āiga*.

Political power in Samoa is vested in the possession of titles and, traditionally, in the sacred power of women as sisters. Each title is hierarchically ranked with its own genealogical, historical, and cosmological foundations. The degree of power associated with a title may rise or fall depending upon the relationship between one titleholder and another as well as those who support each title. A woman who is the sacred sister of the titleholder has the right to veto her brother's decisions and to cause or assist in preventing sickness and death among her brother's family members. The "curse" of the sacred sister is feared because it is thought that such a curse could destroy the male side *(tamatane)* of an *'āiga*. The sacredness of women as sisters protects (and may destroy) titles and lives just as the sacredness of fine mats, produced traditionally by sisters, can provide "protection for life."

In general, as rank emerges into precise levels of integration, the complementarity between men and women becomes objectified in objects of exchange that take their primary value from the forms in which death and regeneration are culturally perceived. The power generated by these objects enables cloth to become currency and to be used in sociopolitical contexts that may have nothing overtly to do with death. Regardless of particular situations, however, the demand for production is tied to essential developmental stages in a life cycle. The tension between production and reproduction should not be thought of totally as individual coercion and domination. In the Trobriand case, death rather than any one individual, still remains the major source of domination. In a funeral in 1980, a Kiriwina woman told me with great mournfulness in her voice, "It just is not fair that we have to spend so much money for only one dead person—just one death and we have to work so hard."

The objects that take on these values and properties are not random. Rather, they must be particular kinds of resources signifying abstractions of the "self." In his essay, "The Notion of Body Techniques," Marcel Mauss wrote, "The body is man's [*sic*] first and most natural instrument. Or more accurately, not to speak of instruments, man's first and most natural technical object, and at the same time technical means is his body" (1979:104). From a similar perspective, cloth, in all its varied abstracted forms found in the Pacific, such as banana-leaf bundles, fine mats, feather cloaks, and bark cloth, becomes both the object and the means by which identification of the social self can be used to validate and record past and present social actions.

The object, however, is not only a recorder of circumstances, but circulates among others. In this way, its very path of circulation creates meaning and history. In their movements through time and space, forms of cloth address the processes whereby legitimization of rank is fixed, whereby ancestral identities are incorporated into present situations, and whereby the social histories of relationships are documented.

The absorbing of action in this way gives weight to cloth, enabling it to become an economic value in its own right. As cloth takes on greater properties of durability (both in physical and cultural forms), each object becomes a repository of greater historical content, thus enabling the object to act directly, not only on the processes of death and regeneration, but on regeneration as a political priority of chiefly (or kingly) inauguration. In the Pacific, the production of such cloth for the most part was and still is the work of women. The interrelationshps between female and male domains of power in view of cloth-wealth production vary, as I have briefly sketched, in accord with the role of cloth as a historical document. Extended labor gives to cloth the possibility for durability. The value of age gives cloth the ability to outlast a human life. When this occurs, cloth wealth documents the past and the present for future potentialities.

In each case presented here, the circulation of cloth wealth elevates some women into powerful positions that are complementary to, or are the same as, male positions of power. What this means is that the question of male dominance over women in small-scale societies is far more complex than has been realized. Kiriwina women and Samoan women—at least, in the latter case, before the advent of missions and colonization—have (or had) decision-making powers and control over an object of wealth that is more fundamental than the wealth of men.[13] Cloth wealth is a resource firmly attached to the core social identities which culturally are the foundation for each of these societies. The limitations for women in terms of domination must be accounted for with equal emphasis on the limitations for men. As cloth production allows for the circulation of large amounts of wealth, its economic and political advantages are apparent. Yet the primary value of cloth vis-à-vis death and rebirth means that the political remains tied to death and to women.

CONCLUSION

I have contended that Pacific forms of cloth are not the plant-fiber stuff of other than the real world of the political, but rather are the very stuff supporting rank and hierarchy. The labor-intensive process of plaiting, weaving, pounding, and dyeing is not mere symbol of the names, genealogies, cosmologies, and myths, but creates the very warp and woof of reproduction and regeneration. Certainly Homer understood these dynamics as he wrote of Penelope weaving by day and unweaving the same fabric by night in order to halt time, to neither bury her husband, marry a suitor, nor change the relationship between gods and humans.

In 1971, I sat in a village in northern Kiriwina, wondering anxiously how I would ever understand what I was supposed to understand each time a woman pushed some banana-leaf bundles into my hands and shoved me into the center of a mortuary distribution. When a Kiriwina woman said to me, "*Nununiga* (banana-leaf bundles) are just like your money," what did she mean? I asked myself that question a thousand times in the course of my field research. Now I ask similar questions about bark blankets in the Pacific Northwest, animal skins in East Africa, textiles in West Africa, carpets in Turkey, fabrics in India, and cloth in Ancient Greece. I wonder what role they once played in establishing religious and political hierarchies, and what nexus of female and male relationships resulted from the varying kinds of female and male controls over production and distribution? How have we as anthropologists been misled by the effects of colonization and industrialization with its trade "gifts" of European fabrics and the establishment of textile factories and mass-produced cloth? The Trobriand question once made me anxious. Today the same question elicits a strong feeling of excitement. There is much important work to be done.

Notes

(The research in this chapter was funded by the John Simon Guggenheim Foundation. An earlier version was written while I was a Member of the Institute for Advanced Study, Princeton. An expanded version, "Plus précieux que l'or: Relations et échanges entre hommes et femmes dans les sociétés d'Océanie," can be found in *Annales* 37 (1982): 222–45. I thank both of these institutions for their support, and also the national governments of Western Samoa and Papua New Guinea for making this research possible. I am deeply indebted to those Trobrianders and Samoans who generously gave of their time and interest. I also thank the Wenner-Gren Foundation for Anthropological Research for their support of the conference for which this material was originally written and for the stimulating interaction that took place at the conference.)

1. In the oral history of chiefly lineages, there is a reference to a woman who was once a high-ranked chief (Austen 1940). Informants I questioned could not explain the circumstances of this woman's chiefly reign and I could not find any evidence of other women who were chiefs. A large part of the problem is that genealogies are often shallow, and written histories and reports began only at the turn of the century.

2. *Valova* is the Trobriand word for the exchange of wealth, food, or other goods for payments in banana-leaf bundles. Today, men take Western cash and buy trade-store items which they in turn sell to villagers for bundles. As one young man once told me, "If women would stop needing so many bundles, then men would have enough cash to do other things." (Weiner 1976: 78–80; see also Weiner 1980a for a discussion of the impact of colonialism on *valova* and women's wealth.)

3. The importance of cloth and its relationship to political evolution can be found in John Murra's (1962) insightful essay on the Inca state and cloth production. See also Mona Etienne's (1980) study of cloth production among the Baule, Ivory Coast, prior to and after colonization, illustrating the dramatic changes that occurred in the role and status of women when European cloth replaced locally produced cloth and textile factories hired men rather than women. Eleanor Leacock (1979) raised a central issue concerning the production of cloth and its relation to the development of class society, noting the ease by which cloth can be "transformed into a commodity."

4. There are indications that in Micronesia women's production of cloth played a role of importance. On Palau, mats were used as currency (Einzig 1949: 39–42). Glen Petersen (1982) recently called attention to the traditional economic value of mats on Ponape.

5. Slides were presented by Sharon and Walter Tiffany at the Association of Social Anthropology in Oceania, Eighth Annual Meetings, Clearwater, Florida, 1979.

6. Not only has the role of women in cloth production been ignored in Polynesian ethnography, but the role of exchange has been totally neglected. Irving Goldman stated: "The economic primitivism of Polynesia appears in strongest relief against the picture of economic specialization in the much smaller societies of Micronesia, Melanesia, and New Guinea . . . Aboriginal Polynesia had no entrepreneurship in goods, no system of finance, no concepts of interest, no currency, no credit-debtor relationships, no systematized trade, and none but the most elementary systems of temporary accumulation" (1970: 477). In Sherry Ortner's (1981) recent article on Polynesian hierarchy and the role of women, she, too completely ignored women's economic role in production and exchange.

7. On Vakuta Island, located directly south of Kiriwina Island, but part of the Trobriand group, women distribute skirts as wealth in mortuary payments, but they do not use bundles of banana leaves (see Campbell n.d.). As Campbell notes, the size of networks of relationships that must be attended to following a death is much smaller than in Kiriwina. Here we see a case where a change in technology allowed women's wealth to reach larger and larger numbers of individuals.

8. Other distributions without women's wealth continue for five, ten, or even twenty years after each death. These distributions are commemorative for all the recently deceased within a clan. The events are organized by men, but both women and men are the recipients (Wiener 1976: 80–84).

9. In Kiriwina, men give their children things from their own lineage, such as decorations, magic spells, knowledge, and rights to land use. A man's sister also contributes to this growth process through performing beauty magic on her brother's children.

10. The subject of the definition of the Samoan descent system has a long argumentative history in the anthropological literature. See, e.g., Sahlins (1958), Ember (1959), D. Freeman (1964), Weston (1972), Schoeffel (1981), and Shore (1983). Also see Davenport (1959) on nonunilinear descent groups. In briefly presenting a definition of 'āiga, I refer to a descent group tracing identity back to an original brother-sister sibling set, each of whom initiated a "foundation title" establishing the tamafafine (uterine side) and tamatane (agnatic side) of the descent group. In addition to birth, individuals may also be considered a member of an 'āiga through adoption, marriage, or service. The chief of each 'āiga or branch of the 'āiga is called a matai, and a chief with one of the highest-ranked titles associated with noble families is called ali'i.

11. See Shore (1983) for a description and analysis of a murder and the use of fine mats in the way I noted.

12. For descriptions of the technology of Samoan fine-mat production, see Buck (1930). Traditionally, the red feathers necessary for decoration on the fine mats were also imported from Tonga via Fiji, where they were obtained from paroquets (Coriphilus frinqillaceus) (see Hjarno 1979–80; Kaeppler 1978 on this trade network). Today red feathers are obtained by dyeing chicken feathers. See Weiner 1976: app. 2 and 3, for descriptions of the way Kiriwina bundles and skirts are made.

13. Eleanor Leacock emphasized this problem in relation to food production carried out by women. "[T]he participation of women in a major share of socially necessary labor did not reduce them to virtual slavery, as is the case in class society, but accorded them decision-making powers commensurate with their contribution" (1972b: 34).

7

Mamasani Women: Changes in the Division of Labor Among a Sedentarized Pastoral People of Iran

SOHEILA SHASHAHANI

The person who worked, found her/his essence.
—Mamasani proverb

Among peoples where the women have to work far harder than we think suitable, there is often much more real respect for women than among our Europeans. The lady of civilization, surrounded by false homage and estranged from all real work, has an infinitely lower social position than the hard working-woman of barbarism, who was regarded among her people as a real lady and who was also a lady in character.
—Friedrich Engels

Changes in the status of women among the Mamasani, a formerly pastoral nomadic people of southwestern Iran, parallel those that have been found generally to accompany colonialism. As Leacock (1979:189) put it, "[O]ne of the most consistent and widely documented changes brought about during the colonial period was a decline in the status of women relative to men." In part, the causes were indirect, as "the introduction of wage labor for men, and the trade of basic commodities, speeded up processes whereby tribal collectives were breaking up into individual family units, in which women and children

111

were becoming economically dependent on single men." In part the changes were directly caused, "aided by the formal allocation to men of whatever public authority and legal right of ownership was allowed in colonial situations."

Such a realization on the part of anthropologists and social scientists working on the Middle East has been hindered by perspectives that fundamentally rationalize and justify the policies of the United States in the area (Schaar 1979).[1] "Tradition" is seen to be the major problem faced by women. Beck and Keddie (1978:18) write that "what most Middle Eastern women lack when compared either with their wealthier and better educated compatriots or with Western women of many social classes, is freedom of choice regarding basic life decisions." However, they do not see the solution in political or economic terms, but in terms of a break with tradition: "To break with tradition so that the majority of women, children and also men become freer than they are today, programs must be sought in which those now tied to tradition can actively and willingly participate. This not only could modify current value systems, but in many areas is a prerequisite to material improvement and rising incomes" (ibid.: 14).

Elsewhere (Shashahani 1981) I have criticized such a position. In this chapter I document how changes in the "traditional" division of labor among a tribal people of Iran, the Mamasani, has increased women's dependence on men and has reduced their arena for independent decision making.

THE MAMASANI

Mamasani Township is located near the southern end of the Zagros Mountains. It covers 8,032 square kilometers and in 1972 had a population of some ninety thousand. This population was approximately 5.5 percent urban, 11 percent transhumant, and the rest rural.

I conducted my research in 1977–78 in the village of Oyun in the subdistrict of Bakeŝ. In 1972 there were 684 villages in Mamasani Township. Its only city, Nurâbâd, was established in Bakeŝ in 1962 from twenty-five villages. Oyun, in the plain of Nurâbâd, had 120 hectares of agricultural land and four orchards. Herbs were gathered daily from the fields. There were two herds of seventy goats and a few sheep. About half of the population owned cows, almost strictly for domestic use. Three years before my fieldwork an agricultural cooperative was established in the area, and the agricultural lands of Oyun became part of the cooperative. There were about forty households in the village, and a total population of about 246.

The following discussion of the economic activities and division of labor by sex among lower-class Mamasani is a reconstruction of the time when the villagers were part of a peasant and pastoral nomadic society. Hunting was an elite activity; gathering was practiced daily; raiding was a source of income;

and herding and agriculture were the two basic forms of production. The society was not self-sufficient, so I consider exchange as well as reproduction, and the processing of foods and other goods.

In my discussion, I shall emphasize sex-line crossing. My assumption is that, when both sexes participate in the same task, one sex stands less chance of being alienated from the activity and thus exploited for his or her ignorance and lack of access to its resources. The specific work is not mystified, as it is in relationships where either the producer is enslaved, or the producer exclusively appropriates the product of work.

WORK AND ITS MEANING

A lazy person, man or woman, lower or upper class, is not well regarded among the Mamasani. However, just working is not valued highly unless it is accompanied with *zerangi,* that is, a clever, quick, dexterous, smart, and cunning quality. A person who also possesses *mardom dari* can become really successful. *Mardom dari* is behavior that attracts people's support, trust, and goodwill, although for a lower-class person a term translating as "hospitable" would be more commonly used.

Some of the women I worked with closely were *bibis,* that is, descendants of a *khân,* and therefore of the upper class in tribal society. Their work consisted of organizing and administering their households, although their image was that of rich people who did not work in the sense of engaging in daily chores. A *bibi* who performs chores is considered stingy, because it is inferred that she does not want to pay a servant. The *zerangi* of different upper-class women becomes clear when one compares two with similar backgrounds who gained different economic status. One *bibi* was neither *zerang* nor *mardom dar,* so her household was practially a ruin. Another who had started at the same level worked very hard and was *zerang;* however, since she was not also *mardom dar,* she was only moderately successful.

A lower-class *zerang* woman works hard, quickly, and cunningly. She participates in a wide range of productive activities and does not become a slave; instead she becomes needed. Her position is very different from that described by Bossen for "modernizing" societies, where women

> can be "idle," poor and powerless such that their productive functions are devalued or not counted. . . . Typically this means specialization in domestic service, including child-bearing and rearing, and other kinds of services. It is by virtue of this specialization that women become an easily exploited surplus labor force. If female labor is in oversupply relative to the needs of society, then the status of all women will be lowered [1975:591].

ECONOMIC ACTIVITIES

Agriculture

Men and women of the lower classes participated in farming, with landless families doing most of the work. The *khân* went to the fields for supervision; the *bibi* went occasionally. Similarly, the village chief often went to the fields, and his wife less often.

Men were responsible for the heavier work in agriculture, ploughing, spading, and irrigating the fields. Women did the lighter work, such as sowing, weeding, harvesting, and picking fruit. From spring through fall men and women went to the field almost every day. The crops they grew were wheat, barley, rice, cotton, a variety of pulse, sesame seed, and some opium, as well as vegetables. Fruits grown were mainly citrus.

Herding and Dairy Activities

Wealthy farmers possessed flocks of goats and sheep. Landless households owned none, but their members might work as shepherds for the more prosperous classes. Cows, from two to seven a household, were owned by everyone except the shepherds and wage-earning farmers.

Herds were taken daily to the pastures around the settlement. Men and women of all ages, except for young women with children, might do this task, although it was most often the men who engaged in it. When the dwellers of Oyun moved their herds, the four richest families went to Daŝt Arjan, a two-day trip. Other families went only ten kilometers away, beyond the western hills of the village.

During the spring and summer, women were occupied daily in dairy activity. Every day, from 4 to 6 a.m., noon to 1 p.m., and 6 to 7 p.m., they milked the cows, goats, and sheep, and boiled the milk to make yogurt. From this yogurt they made butter, cheese, clarified butter, and other products. Men did not participate in dairy activities.

Spinning, Weaving and Tanning

The women spun goat hair, sheep's wool, and cotton; from the yarn they wove tents, floursacks, cloths on which to prepare bread, bedding, and floor coverings. Women also made almost all the clothing. In addition, they tanned goatskin and sheepskin to make containers for carrying and storing water, and for churning butter. There was some specialization in these tasks. Not all women knew how to do all the processes involved.

Hunting and Gathering

Hunting the wild goats and partridges common in the area was a male occupation. However, it was only performed during the fall and only by those men who were not busy and who had guns, i.e., the *khâns* and the rich men of the village. Women did not participate.

Gathering brought in wood for burning, weeds for cattle, and vegetables for daily food. Men brought in heavy logs and women brought branches and light logs from nearby groves. Women and girls gathered herbs used for daily cooking. Any available member of the family gathered cow weeds—boys and girls, men and women, although men did the least. Acorns were used before wheat became the sole grain for bread, and they were still gathered in famine years. Anyone might gather them, but the job was usually done by adolescent boys.

Fetching water in the morning was a female task. Men never participated in it, since women often stayed for a while to wash and to talk at the spring.

War and Raiding

"To ensure one's daughter's future subsistence, one would not give her to a man who did not have a good background," an upper-class elder informed me. "Just as today people have recommendations and diplomas, formerly people would be asked in which raid they had participated." Many rules for raiding were observed, from the area or people one could raid to the percentage of the take given to the *khân*. Special behavior was observed on the warpath and special attire worn on the occasion.

Warfare was largely an upper-class undertaking. According to Bonte (1977:42–43), "Les sociétés d'éleveurs nomades sont souvent des sociétés au sein de laquelle les activités guerriéres jouent un role important. . . . L'utilisation et souvent la possession des animaux de guerre sont parfois reservées à une aristocratie et constitue un aspect important de son pouvoir." There was a distinction between raiding and stealing. A raid was a group undertaking, and it required the entire group's decision and cooperation. The objects taken—guns and accessories, woven objects, utensils, metals, and herds—were divided among the participants for their use or later sale, with a percentage going to the *khân*. Stealing, by contrast, involved only one or several individuals who might take a goat and slaughter and eat it without delay. "I vowed to Hazrat Abolfazl that I would never go stealing," a poor man of Oyun told me.

In connection with raiding, women might inform men about the objects others had and where they were located, in return for a percentage of the take. Should this percentage not be given in the promised amount, a woman could discreetly inform the original possessor and receive a gift from him.

The rules of warfare included respect for women. "If there is a woman in a caravan that one is going to plunder, one must cease the undertaking in respect for her," contended a *khân*. "If one has plundered a tribe or a village and a woman comes asking for her belongings, everything that she claims must be returned to her." Women were never violated after a victorious battle, nor taken as tribute. The only time in recent Mamasani history that women felt threatened by their opponents was in 1836, when they were attacked by government forces (Fasâ'i 1972:244).

Generally women did not participate in offensive warfare. Yet the last important intertribal war, which caused eleven deaths, was said to be caused by a woman. A young *khân* reported, "I remember that women were sent on limited war expeditions, especially against government forces. This was a jest to encourage tribal men to attack the enemy." Furthermore, women's participation in warfare was reported for a neighboring tribe, the Kohgiluye (Safi-Nejâd 1355). Women did participate actively in defensive warfare, and horseback riding and shooting were not unfamiliar to them. They also prepared food for the men and through their *kel zedan* (high-pitched cries used at times of excitement), they incited and encouraged men to action.

Since women were not shot at or beaten, they went to the battlefields to search for their wounded or dead and brought them back for nursing or burial. It is evident that though warfare was a male task, it was not totally alien to women, who also knew its reality.

Exchange

Women were not only importantly involved in economic production among the Mamasani; they also participated in the exchange and distribution of their products, or gave them to their menfolk to sell in town for products the family needed. In the summer men took extra wool or cotton, tents, bedding, or carpets to sell in a nearby town, and used the cash to buy material for clothing, shoes, utensils, tea, and sugar. Women directly purchased these goods, as well as inexpensive jewelry and medicinal herbs, from peddlers *(pilevar)*. Women seldom went to town and welcomed peddlers, although these sold their goods at higher prices than did the shopkeepers in town.

Women also engaged in economic interactions within the village in relation to goods in daily use, such as wheat, woven objects, goats, cows, milk, and vegetables. I observed two women bargaining over the price of a carpet. Exchanges of milk, vegetables, utensils, and so on between neighbors and close relatives were objects of exact calculation, even if carried out in the form of gift giving. No large-scale exchange occurred without the knowledge of both spouses.

Exchange between lower-class women and the *bibi* (or between their men and the *khân*) was conducted in the form of gift exchange. *Galleh begir* (a tax for the use of the *khân*'s pasture) was given to the *khân* at New Year in the form of a gift of lamb, kid, or clarified butter. In times of difficulty, certain "gifts" were given by the *khân* to people in need in the form either of goods for use or of waiving the pasture tax. At such times, women would perhaps pray at home that the *khân* would be generous, while men dealt directly with the *khân*'s envoy in the fields. In cases of extreme difficulty, however, women directly supplicated the *khân* or his envoy. Either women or men would also go to the *bibi* for economic aid.

Curing

Women were the healers among the Mamasani. At an early stage of my research, when I was making a lexicon and asked about the names of plants, I was advised to consult women. Herbal knowledge was their specialty. The boundary between food and medicine was not sharp, for many herbs used in daily food had medicinal properties. *Malva sylvestris* (known locally as *tula*) is an example. In season, this medicinal herb was used daily to season rice.

Two women in the village were the most knowledgeable healers, skilled in midwifery and the setting of joints, as well as in herbal medication. However, the average woman knew about forty plants that she administered to her children and other ailing individuals. Medication included dressing of wounds, tonics for newborn babies, petrurients, and the use of particular plants for bodily disorders such as sore eyes, stomach aches, and colds. Herbs were either gathered or procured from a peddler or spice seller in a nearby town.

Reproduction

According to a local proverb, "The child of one person will not be anyone else's child." In other words, do not expect anybody else's child to do for you what you would expect your own child to do. Another proverb states of children, "A hundred is not too many and one is not too little." In traditional Mamasani culture, children were prized highly. The more their number, the more *main d'oeuvre* one had, and the more family relations one could expect to have in the future. It is not surprising that the upper classes had the largest number, especially the *khâns* with more than one wife.

It is not the case, however, that reproduction took most of a woman's time, as Raphael has implied (1975:1). It was not "reproduction" as such, but the production of use values, that consumed a woman's time.

Production for Use

Preparation of objects for use by the members of a household, washing, cleaning, cooking, mending, were activities that occupied women for many hours. Bread, which was baked several times a week, took at least two hours each time. The simple food cooked once a day took about an hour of preparation. Washing dishes and clothing, which were done once or twice daily, took at least a half hour each time. Sweeping house and yard took another half hour, and finally there was putting utensils, clothing, and other household items in order. The less the possessions, the less the time spent on their care. However, the higher the social class and the more the possessions, the greater the likelihood of having servants.

In addition to these daily activities, there were seasonal or occasional activities. The preparation of goatskins for fetching and storing water was a month-long process on which several women worked together. This task and butter making were late-winter activities. All household utensils and bedding were washed before the New Year. In early spring rose petals were collected and dried, to be put together with feathers in pillows. In late summer pomegranate seeds for cooking were dried on the roof. In autumn lemon and sour orange juice were made and stored. New clothing for members of the household was mostly made before the New Year. There was also the sewing of different bedding items. Finally there was the preparation of large quantities of food for the vows that were usually taken during the month of Moharram.

The extent to which men participated in these activities is a crucial question. As "nonproductive" activities, such tasks are usually evaluated as less valuable than "productive" activities. Though time-consuming and essential, they are not appreciated highly. Furthermore, they are repetitive activities in which, after a certain degree of excellence in their performance has been reached, a higher level is not aspired to.

Although Mamasani men were capable of cooking and washing, they did not ordinarily engage in them. Only when their service was needed for a social occasion or an emergency in their household did they perform these tasks. Sex-line crossing occurred, but not as a common phenomenon; daily household tasks were all feminine. As for the *bibi,* she knew well how to do all such tasks, but her function was supervising the others who did them. The *khân* was even further away from such activities.

The significant point to be made here is that modernization among the Mamasani led to an increase in women's household activities and production of use value and a decrease in their productive activities for wages or exchange.

DEVELOPMENT AMONG THE MAMASANI

The effects of modernization upon the Mamasani pastoral nomads have pervaded all domains of life. Changes have followed primarily from (1) political measures that undermined the chiefdom system and established government administrative bureaus, a gendarmerie, and an office of justice; (2) economic measures that undermined the traditional farming and herding system without a national program that would effectively replace it; (3) the effects of these on class and kinship relations and the relative loss of meaning of participation in social events; and (4) the ideological effect of schooling, the radio, and urban contacts in devaluing tribal and peasant ways of life and glorifying urban life and "civilized" ideologies.

A few words on the economic reforms are necessary. The principal purposes of the land reform and nationalization of pastures introduced in Iran in 1962 were to get rid of local chiefs who were threats to the *shah;* to introduce agricultural cooperatives, and later agribusiness, which would put the government and external investors in control of agriculture and would create the need for food imports; to destroy the possibility of a rural popular uprising against the regime; to open up the rural areas as markets for consumer goods; and to drive the rural population to urban centers and create an urban proletariat.

With respect to the last purpose, it is striking that no one from the seven big landowner households of the village has left, while almost all of the men between ages twenty and forty in the thirty-three households with very little or no land have left the village for work. It is noteworthy that they started working elsewhere in 1975, one year after the establishment of the agricultural cooperative.

The effect of the economic changes upon women is illustrated by considering three age groups. First, there are eleven young women of thirteen to eighteen years of age in the village who work as farm labor. They work eight hours a day for approximately fifty days a year on beet and cotton farms, or picking fruit such as pomegranates and oranges. They are paid on a daily basis. None of these girls are educated. Educated girls, if not still in school, would consider such work beneath their dignity. Second, there are nine women over forty years of age who work on their own land from eight to eighty days a year. They complain about not getting properly paid by the head of the agricultural unit to which they, as small owners, belong.

These two groups, the oldest and the youngest, participate the most actively in economic production, and both are doomed to disappear. The young women will get married and leave the village (four did before I left the village), or will become housewives primarily engaged in the production of use values. Younger girls are becoming more educated and therefore will not engage in farming as they grow older. The older women, the second category, will soon be too old to work, and they will not be replaced.

The third and predominant category of women is those with young children. About half of these women have one or two cows. They do family-dairy work and they or a child take the cows to pasture every day. They milk and make yogurt daily; occasionally they make clarified butter. Children ten to fifteen years old often help them cut weeds for feeding the cows, and daughters gather wild herbs, in season, for use in daily cooking. In fall these women pick fruits from the jointly owned gardens or for a large landowner.

The observed data indicate a marked decrease in women's involvement in production. In part, this is because of the decrease in herds (there are only two herds in the village and only one transhumant herder), and in part because so many men no longer work in the village. Women would help their husbands in the fields, but do not go when the lands are no longer considered theirs. The older women who still farm do so with the older men who are still in the village.

The cash-earning activities of women, conducted at home, have become trifling. Only two women, one close to forty and one older, earn cash from dairy activities, principally from selling clarified butter. Two women still sew leather buckets. Sewing has become a specialized activity, demanding the possession of a sewing machine; one seamstress earns approximately one-sixth of the yearly income of her lower-class household. A major preoccupation of women in the production of use values has become sewing sumptuous clothing, especially for important social events. The *bibi* in particular spends many hours and much money sewing regional clothing, and lower-class women do their best to imitate the latest fashion. Skirts take between twelve and twenty yards of cloth and on special occasions no less than four skirts are worn.

CONCLUSIONS

The Mamasani, then, are no exception to Boserup's statement that "economic and social development unavoidably entails the disintegration of the division of labor among the two sexes traditionally established in the village" (1970:5). The modernization of agriculture and migration to the towns means that "a new sex pattern of productive work must emerge, for better or worse. The obvious danger is, however, that in the course of this transition women will be deprived of their productive functions, and the whole process of growth will thereby be retarded." Mamasani women have lost considerably as producers in their household economy. Previously, their production of goods, especially dairy products and woven objects, brought in a considerable amount of cash. Now their formal economic productivity is minimal, and their daily tasks have become those of the production of use value and consumption. The first group of men who left for work returned with cash and consumer products such as material for clothing, curtains, blankets, tape recorders, and much-prized cheap cigarettes and whiskey. Therefore, their wives favored their migration, and one man who would have preferred to stay and work on the land left because of his wife's insistence.

As for women's reproductive function, children have become an economic liability. Raising children has become much more expensive than in the past, and since children now go to school, they do not help in production. A national motto of the 1970s declared, "The less the children, the better your life." However, lower-class women do not have the facilities upper-class families do for effective birth control, and they are not successful in their use. They have more children than the upper classes, which weakens their families economically. From the female perspective, therefore, the woman's unique capacity for reproduction has become a problem and she herself looks at her capacity as a nuisance. Women told me repeatedly, "If you have too many kids, you cannot keep them all clean, and send them to school, and expect them to have a good life in the future."

Finally, with the coming of modern medicine, women have lost their role as healers. Women no longer use traditional medicines, nor do children born since 1975 take the mixture of herbs infants used to be given. Instead, women consider their own knowledge as backward and uncivilized. Yet the doctor at the health center attached to the agricultural cooperative confided to me, "We lack almost everything; we do not have aspirin, sterilized water, medicine for sore eyes." Furthermore, I observed the doctor and his assistants prescribing medicine without examining the patients and treating women in a very degrading manner. Most degrading were the doctor's constant remarks that the women were dirty and did not keep their children clean, although the "dirt" was often no more than dust.

To summarize, development among the Mamasani of Iran—as has been shown for other regions of the developing world—has had an adverse effect on women. As Tinker has stated, "Development, by widening the gap between the income of men and women, has not helped improve women's lives, but rather has had an adverse effect upon them" (1976:22). Through changes in the division of labor among the Mamasani, women's economic contribution has been reduced and their dependence on men's wage labor has increased. Further studies are needed of the political, social, and ideological domains in order to have a fuller picture of the ways in which development has affected women's status among these and other sedentarized pastoral peoples.

8

Changing Modes of Production and the Sexual Division of Labor Among the Yoruba

SIMI AFONJA

Analysts of the sexual division of labor have recently begun to acknowledge that modernization theory in studies of women and development provides only a limited explanation of sexual inequality, in part because of its assumptions about the basis of the sexual division of labor.[1] Underlying modernization theory are two basic notions: (1) that capitalist accumulation and expansion determine the sexual division of labor in all societies and (2) that historical process and the direction of change are the same throughout human history.* The first assumption has given rise to the tradition of explaining women's status chiefly in terms of the degree to which females participate in production roles outside the home. However, recent comparisons of development patterns in advanced industrial nations and in Third-World countries have revised this explanation of female subordination. In examining divergent patterns of development, these studies have made conceptual and methodological refinements that distinguish between the sexual division of labor as the cause of female subordination and the sexual division of labor as the effect of female subordination. These revisions have generated a new set of assumptions: that analysts must identify more than one causative factor of change;

*An earlier version of this chapter appeared in *Signs*, vol. 7, no. 2, Winter 1981. © 1981 by The University of Chicago.

that a universal theory of change must be based on an understanding of autonomous historical processes; and that gender relations in both production and reproduction must be examined, because change in one sphere signals change in the other.

In their reappraisal of Ester Boserup's work (see chap. 9), Lourdes Beneriá and Gita Sen argue that Boserup ignores the significance of women's role in biological and social reproduction by concentrating on the sphere of production outside the home. International development policies based on this approach that encourage women to enter the work force to earn some income for their basic needs are also considered ineffective because they are only concerned with how women can be useful for development. This perspective has persistently dominated studies of women and development because little attention has been given to specify the relationship between production and reproduction (Deere & de Leal, 1981). The resulting gap in theoretical development has made it difficult for most researchers to reconcile women's low status in the domestic domain with their high participation rates in the public domain. Gloria Marshall and Peggy Sanday identified this contradiction between the two domains in the case of the Yoruba of Southwest Nigeria, but could not reconcile the findings with their theoretical perspective. Boserup, too, acknowledged low status in the domestic sphere in Africa without explaining how this affected the restructuring of positions in the colonial period. In order to explain the relationship between the cause and the effect of female subordination, therefore, one must analyze the continuity between historical and contemporary patterns of the sexual division of labor in production and reproduction. This is imperative in African studies, because the labels "traditional" and "modern," "colonial" and "precolonial," draw arbitrary lines through the historical process of change and, as Audrey Smock and Alice Schlegel suggest, encourage the analyst to transpose the phenomena of the present onto the past.

These theoretical limitations distort current assessments of the role of Yoruba women in distribution in a preindustrial subsistence economy. The concentration of women in marketing, an economic activity outside the home, gave rise to the popular notion that Yoruba women enjoyed considerable autonomy before the colonial era. But this general interest in women's marketing activities is one of the by-products of the discovery of exchange economies in preindustrial societies and of liberal economists' tendency to attribute phenomena such as interests and capital, individual choice and contractual relations, to noncapitalist societies. Conspicuously absent in such works is analysis of the social aspects of production that are of critical importance to distribution—an economic process with social and political connotations. What is missing in studies of Yoruba women's economic activities, therefore, is an explanation of how trade is integrated with other areas of production and reproduction in an economy characterized by a low level of specialization. Also missing is an analysis of the social relations generated by this integrated economic structure and of the ways in which these relations have been altered by the transformation to commercial and industrial capitalism.

The introduction of factors such as interests, capital, individual choice, and competition into studies of subsistence economies raises the issue of the relevance of Western values to the economic activities and economic relations in a preindustrial society. Adopting this classical economic model in such an analysis discounts cultural values which are meaningful in traditional kinship and sociopolitical relations between men and women. For example, Annette Weiner (see chap. 6) studies the cultural value of women's products among the Triobriands and points out that observers tend both to underestimate the functions of these products in reproducing and regenerating social relations and to assess the products against the ethics of rationality and individualism in contemporary capitalist societies. In order to account for cultural values without overlooking the possibility of some degree of individualism and rationality, Weiner adopts a model of reproduction in which an ego-centered perspective remains integrated with a societal perspective, and in which individual interaction, transactions, strategies, and motives are played out. Reproduction is thus seen as part of a complementary role structure in which men and women share tasks for survival rather than compete for goods and services. This model of reproduction encourages the analyst to extract the pattern of the sexual division of labor from the realities of the particular society. But a historical analysis of the sexual division of labor must include an explanation of how the process of capitalist accumulation and expansion changes a society's pattern of complementary roles and rewards into a competitive and individualistic structure.

As suggested earlier, the model required for this type of analysis must articulate traditional patterns of the sexual division of labor with new forms and thereby show how the sexual division of labor in reproduction forms the basis for contemporary patterns. The model I have chosen for such a study among the Yoruba is the model of the political economy that is currently gaining wide acceptance in African social studies. According to Steve Langdon (1974), it emphasizes the "intermeshing of so-called political, economic and social factors of change in one on-going historical process." This multidimensional approach is considered an improvement over modernization theory because it erases the arbitrary line between traditional and modern Africa and thus explains the realities of the colonial and postcolonial eras in light of all the major processes of the two periods.

In using this model to characterize the sexual division of labor within different Yoruba socioeconomic formations, I examine the social relations of production and women's role in reproduction during early trade with the Arab world, in the period of the Atlantic slave trade, in the period of legitimate trade, and in the present. My categorization of this entire historical process into two modes of production—the African and the capitalist—is meant to highlight the critical stages of African involvement in the capitalist system of production. By treating each mode of production as an articulation of different socioeconomic formations, I am able to demonstrate the continuity between traditional and modern Africa.

THE AFRICAN MODE OF PRODUCTION

Claude Meillassoux's and Catherine Coquery-Vidrovitch's descriptions of the African mode of production represent two different conceptualizations of economic formations in a precapitalist society. Meillassoux's work was structured by his interest in deemphasizing distribution and in projecting the socioeconomic formations associated with production (1975). He therefore argues that subsistence agricultural societies value land as an instrument of labor for human reproduction and vest land control in the older members of the family or lineage—the unit for reproduction. According to Meillassoux (1964:100), the social conditions of agricultural production within subsistence economies and the use of land as an instrument of labor ensure the "priority of the relations between people over the relations to things, lifetime duration of personalised social bonds, concern for reproduction, notions of seniority and anteriority, cult of ancestors, fecundity, etc."

Coquery-Vidrovitch criticizes Meillassoux for underestimating the volume of economic exchange in Guro society. "The specificity of the African mode of exchange," she writes, "is located in the combination of a patriarchal community economy with the exclusive control of long distance trade by one group" (1975:57). Mobility through migrations and through long-distance trade, she claims, are unique aspects of African societies that were suppressed by colonialism and colonial institutions. Coquery-Vidrovitch convincingly argues that these different types of long-distance trade had profound influences on socioeconomic institutions of both coastal and interior societies, which were linked in a relay system. Thus, like liberal economists, she defines a heterogeneous mode of production, unlike the homogeneous subsistence agricultural mode defined by Meillassoux.

These two representations of the African mode of production are perhaps not as irreconcilable as they appear to be. The two accounts can in fact be seen as two different stages in Africa's development, with subsistence agricultural production preceding the heterogeneous mode. There is no doubt that Africa experienced revolutionary economic changes after the fifteenth century, due in part to the influence of long-distance trade. But there were regional variations due to differences in various kingdoms' exposure to such trade and to differences in the scale of the trade over time. Thus by introducing the temporal dimension into the analysis of African production before the fifteenth century, and by acknowledging differences in the scale of social organization, one may reconcile Meillassoux with Coquery-Vidrovitch and suggest that subsistence agricultural production was the dominant mode before the fifteenth century, with craft production and market exchange as subsidiary economic activities.

As Meillassoux himself explains further in a later paper, "Economic formations can be, and usually are a combination of several modes of production,
one being dominant, i.e., governing the basic relations of the society at large"
(1975:98).

In spite of the basic differences between Meillassoux and Coquery-Vidrovitch, they both agree that subsistence agricultural production and internal
trade, the most basic elements of the African mode of production, did not
produce sufficient surplus to cause any significant transformations in the
social structure. The technology for agricultural and craft production was so
poorly developed that there were no major projects comparable with those in
the Middle East and Asia. The need did not arise for people to exploit the
resources of the land beyond the basic requirements for subsistence and for
the maintenance of social and political ties with neighboring lineages and
kingdoms. Long-distance trade, which was essentially trade in luxuries, also
could not alter the economic structure as dramatically as the trading relations
that developed after the fifteenth century. The luxury goods traded were not
used in the production of other goods; they were consumed by the aristocratic
classes and the entire trade was highly intermittent (Straffa, 1972; Wallerstein
1976). The question at this point is, What was the pattern of the sexual division
of labor in the lineage-based subsistence mode of production?

Terray's and Hopkins's images of economic relations in subsistence economies support Meillassoux's analysis and underscore the importance of reproduction within such economies. According to Hopkins (1973), the
predominance of subsistence agricultural production in Africa before the
fifteenth century precluded a system of capital accumulation. Terray (1972)
describes self-subsistence as an economic situation where circulation—the
link between the production unit and the consumption unit—is not mercantile,
where the production and consumption units are homologous and coter-
minous. The absence of mercantile relations within the self-subsisting unit
makes society's major goal the production and reproduction of the material
conditions of existence, of the community's members, and of the structural
organization. The relations of production and community organization are
based on the control of the means of production and reproduction (subsistence and women), as Meillassoux (1975) suggests. There is a complementary
structure in the division of labor: men and women share the tasks involved in
physical production, but women bear the burden of reproducing the members
who join the goals of production and reproduction. The amount of cooperation
within such a system depends on the type of crops, the agricultural processes,
and the time allocated to farming relative to other duties.

This cooperation does not preclude inequalities in the distribution of
responsibilities, although these inequalities are hardly perceived from within
because they are culturally legitimized. Both Terray and Coquery-Vidrovitch
point out that the load of responsibility usually falls more on women than on
men and more on the younger members of the community than on the elderly

members. These inequalities are also reflected in the reward structure, particularly in patrilineal societies, where women are excluded from property inheritance and from the control of land, the main instrument of production. Inequalities in the reward structure are also evident in the disbursement of the products, because they are controlled by men to their own advantage. Thus, how much to consume and how much to declare as surplus for exchange are determined by the head of a household.

Although this basic pattern of the sexual division of labor derives from Meillassoux's case study of the Guro economy in the precolonial period, one can use Yoruba economic formations and relations of production from the twelfth century to verify some of his ideas. Before colonial rule, the Yoruba of Southwest Nigeria were organized into semiautonomous kingdoms in which centralized bureaucratization was circumscribed by the segmentary lineage kinship structure (Lloyd 1955). This kinship structure prevented the emergence of a feudal structure, which usually implies the exploitation of subjects by despotic rulers as in the Asiatic mode.[2] Land, the instrument of production, was vested in the lineage and was distributed to individual members through the extended family heads. Agriculture was the predominant economic form, although the scale of social organization encouraged subsidiary economic forms such as craft production and trading. In fact, the products of the lineage-based craft guilds were as important in Yoruba internal trade as the agricultural goods produced by families. Economic production was certainly not based on blood relationships alone, but subsistence and social reproduction still took precedence over economic profit.

The Yoruba traded with their northern neighbors in the savanna and with sisterly kingdoms such as the Edo, but historians have yet to provide sufficient information on the diversity of such trade and on the extent to which this exchange altered the social organization before the fifteenth century.[3] External trade was restricted in volume and was limited to a few luxuries consumed by the rich and powerful. The brass castings that the Yoruba exchanged with their Edo neighbors were used on ceremonial occasions by the Edo monarchs, just as the purple velvet purchased from the Edo was an item on the list of Yoruba royal regalia.[4]

The character of external trade among the Yoruba supports the earlier suggestion that most subsistence economies are usually concerned with the tasks of production and reproduction of family and community members. This is reflected in the household division of labor in which all members shared the tasks of agricultural production. Men were responsible for the heavy work of clearing the bush, women and children participated in planting and weeding. Women harvested, processed, and marketed the products and, contrary to popular opinion, female help on the farm was strongly institutionalized in the Yoruba social structure. Thus women contributed to production and reproduction through farm work as well as through bride wealth and through the property rules that prevented women from owning land, even in societies with bilateral kinship relations. Land, a fixed instrument of production, passed through the men, who also controlled the usufructs of the land.[5]

Before the fifteenth century, then, the tasks of production and reproduction dictated the pattern of division of labor in the Yoruba subsistence economy. The responsibilities of family members complemented each other, which encouraged cooperation for family and lineage survival rather than competition between the sexes. This pattern in the sexual division of labor explains the egalitarianism of such a precapitalist society. Women contributed to the survival of the system, and such contributions were recognized in different ways. The salient point to be considered in understanding the subsequent transformation to an inegalitarian structure is that men, particularly in patrilineal households, exploited their position as guardians of family and lineage values, status, and resources. The sexual division of labor within the household was inadvertently the basis for the new structure.

From the fifteenth century onward, the African subsistence mode of production began to take a different shape, mostly under the influence of changing long-distance trade patterns; however, neither development produced any major changes in the sexual division of labor until the late eighteenth century. Trans-Saharan trade, which had started in about 100 B.C., had much less influence than European trade on the indigenous economic structure because of the limited variety in trade items, the low purchasing power in West Africa, the costs of desert travel in terms of human lives and money, and the impossibility of transporting perishable goods over long-distance routes (Hopkins 1973). The aristocracy's monopoly of trans-Saharan trade until the nineteenth century also limited the influence of this economic activity on Yoruba production modes. If anything, the Islamic religion, which trailed the paths of the trade, only reinforced the ideology of production relations in the household.[6]

European trade later gained the upper hand in volume, organization, and regional spread, but did not transform the economy until the beginning of legal trade during the nineteenth century. The Atlantic trade had started in the late fifteenth century with slaves as the major export. Slaves were exchanged for luxuries, consumer items, and weapons, but this trade relayed through only a small number of wholesalers whose links in the hinterland were the aristocrats who had monopolized trade with the Arab world. This monopoly was challenged in the Yoruba country during the eighteenth century by a new class of military chiefs who raided neighboring smaller kingdoms for slaves. Their appearance marked the entry of commoners into the Atlantic trade, a process that led to radical changes in the nineteenth century.

The participation of commoners in slave trade and the internal wars in Yorubaland forced more citizens into new economic activities. Isola Olomola, commenting on the effects of the trade on Eastern Yorubaland, says: "The raids endangered traditional economic activities as men and women no longer freely cultivated the fields or visited the distant markets for fear of capture.

Able-bodied men abandoned their usual economic activities for the seemingly more lucrative slave raids" (1977). The women who benefited most from the slave trade were daughters and wives of aristocrats and warlords. They enjoyed the wealth from the trade but were also relieved from domestic chores and farming by the available slave labor. In his account of social change in Abeokuta during the nineteenth century, I. I. Delano (1963) discusses the privileged style of living in one warlord's household and the deprivations the family suffered during the depression that followed the abolition of slave trade.

The nineteenth century is usually described as the era when primitive capitalism gained a foothold in Africa, a time when traditional economic formations underwent significant changes in response to new economic processes. The abolition laws and the initiation of legitimate trade helped expand trade beyond traditional lines. Africans exported agricultural products in place of slaves, and new consumer goods were imported into Africa. The demand in Europe for African agricultural products and the existence of alternative sources of subsistence reduced the value of food products relative to cash crops and thus created a new class of farmers. Supplies from Europe fostered the development of a new generation of small-scale traders who operated in the towns and cities. These changes in the scale and unit of trade and in the structure of agricultural production had remarkable influences on the sexual division of labor, particularly on women's participation in trade relative to other economic activities in the domestic and public spheres.

THE CAPITALIST MODE OF PRODUCTION

To understand the development of the capitalist mode of production, one must synthesize the adapted indigenous modes that emerged in the eighteenth and nineteenth centuries and the capitalist mode that emerged in the colonial era. The development of trading factories and of a brokerage system, the institution of the middleman, and the increase in the amount of imported goods advanced on credit stimulated the development of "separate economies" in the forest zones and along river basins (Newbury 1969). Although these economic institutions were limited, they formed the foundations of the contemporary African capitalist structure. The continuation of these eighteenth- and nineteenth-century forms within present-day institutions in fact explains why Lionel Cliffe (1976) analyzes capitalist development in Africa in terms of an "articulated mode of production." Various economic formations—those of the labor reserves, of petty export commodity areas, of former feudal societies, and of frontier communities—are synthesized with industrial capitalism.

The sexual division of labor within the new capitalist mode is therefore conceived as an articulated form, which varies from region to region according to the nature of the interaction between the precapitalist and the capitalist modes. These regional variations create remarkable differences between the coastal regions, which were centers of commerce, and the hinterland, which had relatively less exposure to early trade. There are similar differences between the cash-crop and the food-crop regions and between urban centers of commerce and political organization and rural areas. The following sections will describe the sexual division of labor in four major areas of the economy: subsistence farming, cash-crop production, trade, and wage labor.

Subsistence Farming

The traditional pattern of economic cooperation in subsistence production was altered as the Yoruba moved into the nineteenth century. But the changes did not destroy the relations of dependence among members of the household. Women still participated in agricultural work, although this activity had decreased relative to trading. The increase in female trading has hitherto been explained in terms of a single factor: the insecurity of women on the farms during the civil wars. This explanation, which derives from J.F. Pedler (1955), has been overemphasized relative to other equally important determinants of the sexual division of labor. B. W. Hodder (1962) and Gloria Marshall (1964) use the same argument to justify the predominance of women in trade and the clear-cut division of labor in which women were traders and men were farmers. Marshall argues further that the civil wars only intensified an existing pattern of division of labor. The flaw in this and other similar analyses is that they underestimate the amount of female labor in agricultural production before the nineteenth century and the effects of the economic transformations of the century on the sexual division of labor. Additional varieties of foodstuffs, the decline in the number of food-crop producers, and the growth of towns and cities are important but often neglected considerations. The presence of domestic slaves on farms and in homes also reduced the amount of time women spent on housework and in agricultural production.

The withdrawal of women from agricultural production proceeded faster in the towns and cities than in the rural areas. Rural women continue to combine agricultural production with rural marketing. A. Oshuntogun's (1976) studies in three Yoruba villages show that women still spend 20 to 40 percent of their time on their husbands' farms. But a commercial relationship is defined to the extent that women are remunerated for this service. Sarah Berry (1975) too, found that 84 percent of the women in Orotedo, a Yoruba village in a cocoa-growing belt, said they helped their husbands with farm work, compared with 43 percent and 25 percent, respectively, in the nearby villages of Abanata and Araromi-Aperin. Relatively few women in the latter village were engaged in farm work because several had inherited their fathers' cocoa farms and relied on paid labor. Some of these women were also in the commercial production of palm oil and kernels.

Cash-Crop Production

Cash-crop production can be considered one of the earliest forms of African capitalism because West Africans controlled and organized new commercial agricultural ventures based on their existing economic formations. The middlemen in Atlantic trade diverted their resources toward production of cash crops at the beginning of legitimate trade. Freed slaves went into the enterprise, and peasant farmers used old and new methods in cash-crop production. This widespread production of cash crops changed the values associated with the means of production, land, labor, and capital. Land was no longer an instrument of production for subsistence, but a means of production for capital accumulation. Thus lineage control over land and over family labor loosened. Women's and children's labor was now valuable not only in subsistence agricultural production but also in cash-crop production and in other areas where indigenous capitalism emerged. Paid labor replaced family labor in most areas of cash-crop production, but farmers relied on family labor when there was a labor shortage or at harvest time when the labor requirement was high.

Unlike subsistence production, cash-production farming usually carries some remuneration for women's labor, initially in kind (e.g., a cloth gift) and later in cash. Such cash rewards were invested in trade, thus giving wives of cash-crop farmers an edge over the wives of peasant farmers.

The commercialization of land and the increasing emphasis on individual property ownership gave women access to cash-crop production. Women in societies with a bilateral kinship structure inherited cocoa farms and were able to use virgin land for commercial agricultural production. Berry gives the example of one of the wives of the *bale* (chief) of the Araromi village who inherited ten acres of cocoa and also some uncultivated land on which she planted nine more acres of cocoa. In addition, she purchased a three-acre farm of mixed tree crops. Respondents at Ile-Ife also confirm the trend toward the relaxation of inheritance laws. According to Chief Omisore, it was unheard of for commoner women to own landed property and houses in the past.[7] Today, women own farmland and land and buildings in the town.

This is not to suggest that women are as involved in cash-crop production as men. Male control of technology and capital ensures the predominance of men over women in this area. But the question is, What gave men and not women access to technology and capital? The answer to this lies in the control that men had over women's labor and reproduction in the subsistence economy, not solely in the opportunity given by the colonial administration, as Boserup suggests. Traditional values persist first because women's role in reproduction continues to be emphasized, and second because men were able to take advantage of their control of capital, land, and family labor in the subsistence economy when foreign technology was introduced.

Boserup bases her interpretation of women's position on the assumption that the colonial administration organized cash-crop production. Economic historians have shown in more recent writings that the entire enterprise was initiated by Africans themselves with adequate knowledge of how to adapt local institutions and factors to the new products. Their success in fact contrasts with the failure of foreign plantation managers in West Africa. Women's limited participation in this sphere should therefore be explained in terms of institutional factors related to women's position in the subsistence economy, factors which provided the basis for the division of labor that ensued during the colonial period.

Trade

General interest in the power women gain through market exchange has encouraged many writers to conceptualize West African trade as a homogeneous structure. However, the history of the division of products, the availability of capital, and the amount of income generated by trade exposes a trade structure with clear divisions by sex.

Women in the subsistence economy controlled items of subsistence: food, cloth, pots, etc. Men controlled the most valuable products of the farm— particularly those that helped to generate capital—and had exclusive control of long-distance trade items until the nineteenth century. Such differences in the types of items men and women traded were common in most African societies, as epitomized in an Akan popular saying: "It is the business of a woman to sell garden eggs and not gun powder" (Daaku 1971). Samuel Johnson (1921) shows that the Yoruba made similar distinctions. Men and women participated in trade, but each sex had its own line, and this division partly explains the inequality between the sexes.

The unequal structure of trade suggests that the physical presence of women at the market is not a sufficient indicator of their status in the community. The source of the wares, the amount of capital input, and the value of the items for capital accumulation are neglected factors in evaluations of the impact of trade on African women's status. The data collected so far in this study suggest that trade in the subsistence economy was an integral part of women's reproductive services. It did not engender widespread individualism, the profit motive, and competition until the expansion of trade in the nineteenth century. The amount of power derived from internal trade was until then limited by the low volume of trade, which could not alter family economic relations.

Women's economic power was also limited because their articles were exchanged for use value rather than for manufacturing profit. Men were therefore at an advantage when they entered the Atlantic trade. Their dominant position continued into the twentieth century, with the control of wholesale trade. Since such large-scale trade gave men the opportunity to accumulate capital and managerial experience, they were able to take over from the European commercial houses after independence. However, women continued to dominate retail trade, particularly as the sector expanded into the lowest tier in the hierarchy.

The capitalist economy now features three distributive channels: the open market, small retail shops, and large-scale department stores. The first is the domain of women, whether the products are farm or imported consumables. An increasing number of women now operate small retail shops as well, but men own the more capital-intensive shops. Department stores are under the exclusive ownership of corporate bodies.

Wage Labor

Yoruba women first entered paid employment in the late nineteenth century as porters of exported and imported products from the hinterland to the coastal regions.[8] Evidence also shows that they were part of the forced labor used for construction during the colonial period.[9] Poor work conditions and access to alternative economic activities discouraged women from large-scale participation in this sector, a trend that continued throughout the colonial period when low levels of education and cultural and personal factors became the most important deterrents to female employment (Afonja 1976). Records show that in 1950 less than 2 percent of all paid employees were women. The 1966 estimates show that they constituted about 7.2 percent of the total labor force. This low participation rate is also shown in the proportional distribution of established staff in the Federal Civil Service in 1974: only 11.5 percent of the 122,914 positions were occupied by women.[10]

Women's placement within the occupational hierarchy is as important as their unequal representation in the labor force. Men are generally more skilled than women, and they occupy the positions of greater power and authority as well as the more highly paid jobs. The majority of women are employed in the service sector as typists, secretaries, teachers, and nurses. Only 2.9 percent of all the professionals in Nigeria in 1966 were women. In 1968 only nine women held managerial positions in the private sector in comparison with 181 men.

A corollary of the small proportion of women in the formal sector is their predominance in the informal sector, which is equally stratified. Although jobs in the informal sector are often said to be more adaptable to women's domestic responsibilities, women hold the poorest of these positions and have greater difficulty in maintaining a steady income because they must intermittently leave these highly competitive jobs to bear children.

The entry of women into commercial agriculture, new forms of trade, and informal- and formal-sector occupations are nineteenth- and twentieth-century developments that have not relieved women from their traditional responsibilities. Thus women's tasks of reproducing and nurturing the family, which were established in the subsistence economy, have primarily determined their subordinate position in new production roles. The competitive social relations within the new economic structure also thrive on the inequalities built in through the use of women's labor in production and reproduction. Internal and international class relations strengthen these inequalities and increase the competitive economic relations among family members. The persistence of a value structure that defines women's primary task in society as biological and social reproduction and that allocates higher rewards to production roles in the public domain continues to give men an edge over women. The double burden of assuming these traditional roles as well as the new continues to ensure women's subordination.

CONCLUSION

This analysis of the sexual division of labor in an African society shows the continuity between the past and the present in explaining the impact of development on African women. By taking into consideration external and internal factors of change since the fifteenth century, one can explain the cumulative effect of culture and socioeconomic formations in establishing contemporary patterns of gender relations in production and reproduction.

The transformation from a lineage mode to a capitalist mode was not effected by capitalist expansion alone, but also by the internal economic and political changes accompanying state formation and expansion. The strife brought on by these changes altered preexisting formations and introduced the element of class into the eighteenth and nineteenth centuries. By examining cultural, economic, and political factors, we can see that the norms and values associated with production and reproduction in the lineage mode persisted into the twentieth century.

Notes

1. The study reported in this chapter is financed by the Ford Foundation, Lagos, Nigeria.

2. Coquery-Vidrovitch (1975) points out that the most salient features of the Asiatic mode—village communities based on collective production, a regime capable of forcing the population to work collectively, and generalized slavery under a despotic ruler—have not been found anywhere in Africa. See also Buttner (1970) for a discussion of the stagnation in the development of feudalism in Africa.

3. See Fage (1962) on early trade between the delta and the Yoruba waterside.

4. A. Oguntuyi (1952) claims that the red velvet was introduced into the kingdom of Ado-Ekiti during the reign of the Ewi Owamuaran between 1490 and 1511.

5. Goody and Buckley (1973) claim that this is the practice in most patrilineal societies where women did not inherit land.

6. See I.A. Ogunbiyi (1969) for a comparative assessment of the freedom of movement of Hausa women before and after the Jihad.

7. This respondent is over seventy years old. His explanation for female property ownership is in terms of the patterns of residence, lineage structure, and the structure of Yoruba towns. The extended family compound, he suggests, did not allow a woman to construct her own residence or own a whole apartment.

8. Ile-Ife women traders recount their experience on the trade routes to the coastal town of Ejinrin.

9. J. A. Atanda's (1973) findings have been confirmed by respondents on Oyo. The women claim that women labored under difficult conditions, often without food, sometimes losing the babies that they carried on their backs.

10. The latest estimates are reported by the Federal Ministry of Manpower Development.

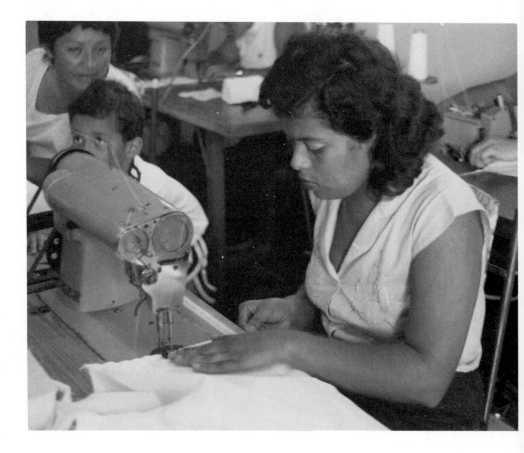

PART III
Women and Development in Third-World and Socialist Societies

I t is commonly assumed that the increasing incorporation of women into the paid labor force is a sure sign of the improvement in women's status and naturally accompanies the process of economic development. The authors in this section, however, question this assumption. They point to the under-estimation of women's involvement in productive activities in preindustrial societies, often as unpaid family workers on peasant farms or in the informal economy. Women often lose this productive role with the shift toward commercial agriculture and capital-intensive industrialization, which favor skilled male labor. Even the large numbers of women employed in the growing service sector or in the newer export processing industries in Asia, Latin America, and the Caribbean are usually poorly paid and have little opportunity for upward mobility.

Another critical issue in determining the impact of paid employment on women's status is the relationship between production and reproduction, or the dual responsibilities of women as workers and as housewives and mothers. Participation in paid labor often intensifies women's work, resulting in "the double day", since they are not relieved of their household responsibilities. Even in socialist countries, where Croll notes major efforts have been made to incorporate women into the labor force, governments have not fully addressed the issue of women's reproductive role. As a result, the gains anticipated from increased female employment have not been fully realized, and women in socialist countries still find themselves subordinate to men.

This is not to argue that women should withdraw from the paid labor force because there have been no gains from employment. For most women, in both Third-World and advanced capitalist societies, there is no choice: they are forced to seek paid work to support themselves and their families. In fact, one explanation for the increasing number of women in the labor force is women's need to work to supplement the declining real wages of men or to replace male breadwinners who are unemployed. Thus, male unemployment plus the rising cost of living pushes most poor women into the labor force out of necessity rather than choice. However, traditional assumptions about the sexual division of labor (i.e., that men were the principal breadwinners and women the housewives) still prevail and, as Benería and Sen note, condition women's secondary status in the labor market.

The evidence presented here indicates that the increasing incorporation of women into the paid labor force is a necessary but not sufficient condition for sexual equality. Paid employment brings women some measure of financial autonomy, but often intensifies their work load and the degree of exploitation. The barriers to fuller sexual equality are both ideological and economic. So long as women see themselves and are seen as supplementary wage earners, they will continue to be discriminated against in the labor market and utilized as a source of cheap labor. The traditional sexual division of labor needs to be broken down not only by incorporating women in the labor force, but by reducing their responsibility for domestic work.

9

Accumulation, Reproduction, and Women's Role in Economic Development: Boserup Revisited

LOURDES BENERÍA AND GITA SEN

More than a decade has passed since Ester Boserup's book, *Woman's Role in Economic Development* (1970), was published.* Probably no single work on the subject of women and development has been quoted as often. Given the importance of the subject and the appearance of a considerable amount of new material since 1970, it is now possible to evaluate the book from a fresh perspective; indeed such an evaluation is necessary. In this chapter, we propose to summarize Boserup's main contributions, but also to present a critical analysis of her approach, particularly in view of recent scholarship on the subject.

When Boserup's work was published in 1970, it represented a comprehensive and pioneering effort to provide an overview of women's role in the development process. First, Boserup emphasized gender as a basic factor in the division of labor, prevalent across countries and regions: "Even at the most primitive stages of family autarky there is some division of labor within the family, the main criteria for the division being that of age and sex. . . . Both in primitive and in more developed communities, the traditional division

*An earlier version of this chapter appeared in *Signs,* vol. 7, no. 2, Winter 1981. © 1981 by The University of Chicago.

of labor within the family is usually considered 'natural' in the sense of being obviously and originally imposed by the sex difference itself" (Boserup 1970:15). Despite the existence of stereotyped sex roles and the universality of women's concentration in domestic work, Boserup pointed out significant differences in women's work across countries and regions. She criticized the "dubious generalization" that attributes the provision of food to men in most communities; women too have been food providers in many areas of the world. Her comparative analysis was particularly illuminating for Africa and Asia, where she emphasized the fundamental role women played in African agriculture in contrast to their lesser role in Asian countries and in Latin America as well.

Second, Boserup analyzed a variety of factors behind these differences. One of the most frequently quoted parts of her analysis is her comparison between the "female" and "male" systems of farming, which correspond to the African system of shifting agriculture and the Asian system of plow cultivation. In Africa, low population density, easy access to land, and less class differentiation than is found in Asian societies resulted in a division of labor where men cleared the land for cultivation and women actually culti- vated the subsistence crops. In Asia—a region characterized by high popula- tion density—a ready supply to landless laborers available for hire and the "technical nature of farming operations under plough cultivation" dis- couraged women's involvement in agricultural tasks and encouraged segrega- tion of the sexes, including the seclusion of women in some areas (ibid.: 26).

Boserup's analysis pointed to the correlations between women's work and factors such as population density and land holding. Although she was not always explicit about precise connections, she did suggest the existence of a relationship between these factors and different forms of women's subordina- tion. For example, in her discussion of the economics of polygamy in tradi- tional Africa, Boserup argued that polygamy made it possible for a man to control more land and labor, because each wife was assigned a plot of land to cultivate. Thus, her analysis pointed to an economic basis for polygamy and the bride price. Boserup's analysis did not explain polygamous arrangements in which wives seem to represent a cost rather than an economic resource for the husband, but it created a challenge for others to do so.

Third, Boserup's book began to delineate the negative effects that colo- nialism and the penetration of capitalism into subsistence economies have often had on women. She pointed out that European colonial rule, rather than being a "liberalizing" factor for African women, contributed to their loss of status: "Europeans showed little sympathy for the female farming systems which they found in many of their colonies." Women often lost their right to land as a result of "land reforms introduced by European administrators" (Boserup 1970:54,60). These reforms, Boserup explained, were based on the European belief that cultivation was properly men's work. She argued that the introduction of modern technology and cash crops benefited men rather than women by creating a productivity gap between them; women were relegated to the subsistence sector of food production using traditional methods of cultivation.

Fourth, Boserup, among others, emphasized that "subsistence activities usually omitted in the statistics of production and income are largely women's work" (1970:163). Although there is a tendency for official statistics to under-report all subsistence activities, whether carried out by men or women, some of these activities tend to be specific to women, particularly domestic work and participation in agriculture as "unpaid family labor."[1] Despite some efforts to include subsistence work in statistics of production and labor-force participation, women's work continues to be underreported and underesti-mated, particularly in the area of domestic production. In addition, the con-ventional theoretical concepts that underlie statistical categories are ideologically biased toward an undervaluation of women's work (Benería:n.d.) Boserup, therefore, raised an issue that is essential to a proper understanding of women's participation in economic life.

Finally, Boserup's comparative analysis projected the different sexual divisions of labor encountered in farming systems onto patterns of women's participation in nonagricultural activities. For example, she called attention to the influence of farming systems on migration patterns and on the participa-tion of men and women in urban labor markets. African women's involvement in food cultivation generated a pattern of predominantly male migration, leaving women and children in the village. In contrast, Boserup argues, the Latin American pattern in which women participated less in farming involved a high degree of female migration, due also to the employment opportunities for young women in urban centers. Boserup's generalization, at times over-stated, encouraged far more detailed analysis. Her scholarship inspired a great deal of the empirical and theoretical work that followed.

Despite Boserup's obvious contributions, critical analysis reveals three major weaknesses in her work. First, the book is essentially empirical and descriptive, and lacks a clearly defined theoretical framework that empirical data can help elaborate. Although Boserup fails to identify an explicit frame-work, her underlying analytical concepts are often neoclassical. This seriously limits her analysis. Second, Boserup takes as given a unique model of develop-ment—the model that characterizes capitalist economies. Finally, despite her concern with the position of women in the development process, Boserup does not present a clear-cut feminist analysis of women's subordination. By concentrating on the sphere of production outside the household and ignoring the role of women in reproduction, her work fails to locate the basis of this subordination. In what follows we will elaborate each of these points in more detail.

THEORETICAL FRAMEWORK

A common criticism of Boserup's book is that it is repetitive. This problem becomes acute because the book fails to go beyond the data that it presents;

Boserup rarely attempts to derive any overall theoretical or conceptual structure from her empirical data. These data are rich in insights about the patterns and variations in women's work across Africa and Asia, but ad hoc introductions of values and ideology often take the place of explanations. In discussing the growing dominance of men over women in agriculture during Africa's colonial period, for example, Boserup contends that gender-based prejudice on the part of the colonialists caused them to teach advanced agricultural methods only to men.

When Boserup does use theoretical concepts, they tend to fall within the framework of neoclassical economics. In her discussion of the labor market and wage differentials between women and men, she suggests that the individual preferences of employers and workers determine the nature of women's work, and hence their earnings. Boserup (1970:113) analyzes demand in the labor market, stating that employers often prefer male labor over female labor; she analyzes supply by stating that women prefer to work in home industries rather than in large enterprises.

This emphasis on preferences constitutes a limited view of the forces that influence the labor market and the process of wage formation. There are many cases in which employers prefer women over men: examples include tea plantations, textile-manufacturing firms, and labor-intensive industries operating in many areas of the Third World (ILO 1970; Heyzer: n.d.; Safa, ch. 4; Arizpe & Aranda, ch. 11, Wong, ch. 13). Many of these are in fact large enterprises. Therefore the factors influencing preferences must be explained. They range from the temporary character of employment among young, unmarried women—an important factor in hiring policies of multinational firms—to the tendency of women workers toward submissiveness, avoidance of tensions, and acceptance of low wages. In addition, women's own preferences need to be seen in dynamic perspective, and cannot be taken as given. They are the result of changing factors such as access to land, household work, family structure, family income, the availability of employment, and women's perception of the economic and social roles.

Boserup does go beyond a narrow focus on individual preference in her examination of hiring practices and wage formation in the export sector:

> It seems that the clue is to be found in considerations of costs in the plantation sector. . . . In Africa, the methods of food production are such that women can do nearly all the operations unaided by men. It is therefore possible to economize on labor costs in plantations (as well as in mines and industries) by employing only male workers, leaving the dependents . . . to be supported in the home village by the able-bodied women. The Asian pattern is in sharp contrast: there the predominant agricultural system requires the presence of men in the village. . . . Hence the plantation owner must face the fact that the whole family must get its livelihood from the plantation and this, of course, can be arranged most cheaply by

having every able-bodied member of the family working on the plantation. Thus, in the Asian as well as the African case, the plantation (or the European farm) can avoid paying the male wages sufficient to support a whole family (1970: 77–78).

The theoretical implication of such an argument is that the wage is not just a payment for productivity—the result of market forces of labor supply and demand. It is determined as well by the costs of maintaining and reproducing the labor force. This supports a Marxist theory of the wage rather than the neoclassical explanation, and is a concept that is compatible with a patriarchal vision of the male wage as the main source of family income. Women's wages, then, are viewed as complementary rather than primary, which explains women's willingness to work for a lower wage, and helps to explain why women's wages often remain barely above 50 percent of male wages in cases where women's productivity is as high as, if not higher than, men's (ILO 1970).

Boserup (1970: 107, 147–51) also hints at the existence of both wage differentials due to job segregation by sex, and labor-market hierarchies related to race and nationality as well as gender. Her empirical insights appear to support a theoretical model of fragmented labor markets rather than a model of a competitive labor market, which would suggest a neoclassical framework. Yet Boserup makes no attempt at reconciling her various and apparently contradictory descriptions of wage differentials and hiring practices. Her underlying neoclassical categories do not allow her to integrate her rich empirical observations within a coherent analytical framework. Similar limitations in her analysis result from her assumption of a unique development model.

MODEL OF DEVELOPMENT: MODERNIZATION VS. ACCUMULATION

Boserup's general argument is that women workers are marginalized in the process of economic development because their economic gains as wage workers, farmers, and traders are slight compared to those of male workers. Hence, policy efforts should be directed to redress this problem, so that women share more fully in the fruits of modernization. Underlying this is the view that modernization is both beneficial and inevitable in the specific form it has taken in most Third-World countries—a notion that has been extensively criticized by radical social scientists over the last two decades (Baran 1959; Frank 1967; Amin 1977).[2] The modernization approach has two negative effects on Boserup's analysis. First, she tends to ignore processes of capital accumulation set in motion during the colonial period, and the effects of such processes on technical change and women's work. Second, she does not systematically analyze the different effects of capital accumulation on women of different classes.

Of the many variants of modernization theory, Boserup's work is one based on a technological determinism that uses cultural values as filler for conceptual holes in the analysis. The technological determinism in her argument is clearest in her discussion of indigenous farming systems. Though Boserup argues that there is a negative correlation between the use of the plow and the extent of field work done by women, the basis of this correlation is never clarified. Nor does she discuss the possibility that there may be deeper causal reasons for the empirically observed correlation. Instead, one is left to presume that technical variation exercises some powerful, if mysterious, impact on the division of labor by sex. This sort of unexplained correlation is rife in modernization theory. The processes of modernization—in this case, the effects of plow cultivation on women's work—are rarely explained. Rather, the more modern is usually held up as the model against which the more backward is judged. To Boserup's credit, she does not make this last step. Instead she sees modernization operating concurrently with women's loss of economic independence.

However, this insight is not located in any coherent theory, but only in a sharp empirical intuition. Boserup holds cultural prejudices to blame for women's marginalization; overall the process of modernization is viewed as beneficial. Indeed, Boserup regards modernizing technical changes, such as the shift from hoe to plow cultivation, as the inevitable products of population growth.[3] But nowhere does she confront the causes of growing population density, particularly the Malthusian belief that population growth is somehow inherent in human nature.

Viewing the Third World from this perspective involves ignoring effects on population growth and density of the alienation of land and its private appropriation during the colonial period. The direct effects were felt most sharply in regions such as Southern Africa, where most of the land (and, inevitably, the best land) was taken over by settlers, squeezing the indigenous population into shrinking reserves and leaving high person-to-land ratios (Palmer & Parsons 1977). The indirect effects have been felt in most regions where the privatization of land, labor, and subsistence have generated incentives for higher fertility among peasants (Mamdani 1972).

Such changes in the social organization of production and in the appropriation of the means of production also have powerful effects on the division of labor by sex and age. What appears to Boserup to be a technically determined correlation between plow cultivation and women's lower participation in field work has its roots in the social relations of production and reproduction. To be sure, Boserup does note that "the plough is used in regions with private ownership of land and with a comparatively numerous class of landless families in the rural population" (1970:26). This, she says, creates the possibility of substituting hired workers, male and female, for the farm wife in field labor. But she does not explain why and through what processes this possibility is realized.

In fact, in her entire discussion of women's agricultural work, Boserup makes a rather artificial separation between women from landed-peasant households and women from agricultural-labor households. It is not clear why she focuses on the former when defining male and female farming systems, and discusses the latter in another section. Surely the landless women should also be part of the criterion by which a farming system is defined as male or female. This is especially true where women constitute a significant proportion of the agricultural wage-labor force in regions of plow cultivation.[4] In fact, the further along one reads in Boserup's book, the more it appears that the crucial distinguishing feature between African and Asian farming is not, as she suggests, the tools used—hoe versus plow—but the forms of appropriation of land, of surplus, and of women's reproductive capacity. The sexual division of labor is related to these factors.

Similarly, although Boserup discusses the economic roots of polygamy, she fails to examine the process of change in this system as the possibilities of capital accumulation multiply. In some precolonial African communities, a large number of wives gave a man status and possibly a greater voice in the village councils. But women had at least partial control over the product of their labor. With the coming of long-distance trade and private appropriation of land, women's labor could be used to produce a surplus, which formed a basis for accumulation of land and wealth (Ciancanelli 1980). In turn, class differentiation began to intensify, women came to have less and less control over the product of their labor, and additional wives became, in fact, simply additional field workers who facilitated the accumulation of use-rights to more land. These changes probably indicated a major alteration in gender relations to the detriment of women. By failing to examine such matters, Boserup's argument remains divorced from any coherent analysis of the interconnections between the social process of accumulation, class formulation, and changes in gender relations.

Another example of her work's weak conceptual basis is Boserup's discussion of women's declining status under colonial rule. The biases of modernization theory are evident in her presumption that the introduction of commercial agriculture was generally beneficial, except for the consequent decline in women's status. This presumption ignores entirely the long history of resistance to forced cultivation of crops such as cotton and coffee in Africa and other Third-World regions (Nzula, Potekhin, & Zusmanovich 1979). Cultivation involving the increased use of land and labor in the production of commercial crops was a major mechanism for the transformation of land relations and class differentiation, and it opened possibilities for exploitation by commercial capital. The active intervention of the colonial state in such cultivation and in attempts to disseminate technological improvements is hardly surprising. The subsistence crops of the local people were not a source of surplus value. Subsistence farming drew the government's attention only under two circumstances: first, whenever the labor and land used for subsistence crops acted as a barrier to the expansion of commercial crops; and second, whenever subsistence production deteriorated to the point where there was excessive migration to the urban areas, or eruptions of political resistance (Bernstein 1979; Van Allen 1972).

Teaching the women better techniques in subsistence cropping, as Boserup suggests, would have been like treating cancer with a Band-Aid. That such teaching did not take place could hardly be the cause of women's worsening situation under conditions of rapid land alienation and class differentiation. Nor is Boserup correct in implying that all men benefited from commercial production. The possibilities of accumulation inherent in commercial farming undoubtedly enabled some men to raise themselves up in the indigenous class hierarchy, but most men did not experience such mobility. The narrow truth of Boserup's thesis is that while some men could be integrated into the ruling class, almost no women could be, at least on their own. The concentration of women in subsistence farming undeniably caused this unevenness. That commercial cropping came to dominate over subsistence cropping was a product not of European patriarchal culture, but of the process of capital accumulation. Thus, women's loss of status results from the interweaving of class relations and gender relations.

Recent scholarship emphasizes the close connections between processes of accumulation and changes in women's work and in the forms of their subordination. The single most powerful tendency of capitalist accumulation is to separate direct producers from the means of production and to make their conditions of survival more insecure and contingent. This tendency manifests itself in new forms of class stratification in rural areas—between rich peasants and capitalist farmers, on one hand, and poor peasants and landless laborers on the other. Capitalist accumulation can have a variety of effects on women's work depending on the specific form accumulation takes in a particular region.

In some areas, the sexual division of labor may change and women's workload may be intensified. For example, Jette Bukh (1979) shows how the concentration of men in commercial crops and male migration to urban areas in search of work have forced women in Ghana to take up additional tasks in subsistence agricultural production, lengthening and intensifying their work day. The pressure on women in these largely female-headed households is aggravated by increased school attendance among their children, which has induced changes in the crops cultivated. For example, women have begun to substitute cassava production for labor-intensive yam production, though cassavas are less nutritious. They have also decreased vegetable production. Furthermore, as land becomes privately appropriated, common sources of water, fuel, and food are lost to poorer peasants and landless laborers, forcing women to spend more time and labor in finding, fetching, and foraging (Sen: n.d.).

In other areas, women may lose effective control over productive resources and over the labor process and its product. Kate Young (n.d.) describes the changes in the sexual division of labor that resulted from the penetration of merchant capital and its interaction with local capital in the Mexican region of Oaxaca in the 1920s. Merchant capital was already taking away women weavers' control of their terms of purchase and sale. The shift from traditional crops to market-oriented coffee production introduced new changes; women's work shifted from weaving to seasonal participation in coffee production. As a result, they lost control over economic resources and over the labor process, and became secondary and marginal workers in agricultural production.

A third possible effect of capital accumulation involves a new division of labor in which young women become migrant wage earners. The increasing internationalization of capital offers vivid examples of woman's place in the capitalist labor process. Noeleen Heyzer (n.d.) describes the participation of young migrant Malaysian women in the labor-intensive industries of Singapore. Migrant workers make up 51 percent of the total manufacturing work force in Singapore, and about 45 percent of the workers in this sector are women working at the bottom levels of the wage structure. Heyzer's analysis illustrates the conditions under which women are becoming important participants in the industrialization process taking place in Third-World countries. As Dorothy Elson and Ruth Pearson have pointed out (1981), women's employment is a logical outcome of the increasing fragmentation of capitalist production, in which technology enables industrialists to shift the labor-intensive processes of production to the Third World. Female labor meets the needs of capitalists searching for a disciplined and low-cost labor supply. Helen Safa (ch. 4) illustrates this point in her discussion of runaway shops in Latin America and Asia, where about 80 percent of the employees are women. A common feature of this type of employment is that it is temporary, either because contracts are of limited duration or because there is a high turnover of workers. In addition, working conditions are oppressive. Heyzer describes the prevalent "atmosphere of compulsion" and the alienation of the workers. Safa describes the lack of public transportation, inadequate health care and other social services, and management resistance to unionization.

In some areas capital accumulation may weaken traditional forms of patriarchal control over women and introduce new forms. Carmen Diana Deere, (1977; also Deere & de Leal 1980) shows how changes from servile to capitalist relations of production in midtwentieth-century Cajamarca, Peru, loosened patriarchal controls over women's work. Increasing male migration to the coastal plantations gave women greater autonomy, but access to land shrank, and a new structure emerged by which women became dependent on male wage earners. Similarly, in Southeast Asia patriarchy within the family has been replaced by a capitalist control that takes very patriarchal forms; young women's lives and sexuality are circumscribed by the firm's labor-control policies.

Finally, class differentiation accompanying the capitalist transformation of a region provides a new basis for differentiation between women. This is well illustrated by Ann Stoler in her study of Javanese women. In analyzing the impact of agricultural change on labor-force participation, Stoler states that "for the poorer majority of village society, both men and women suffer as more and more land is concentrated in the hands of the wealthier households. However, the decline in female employment opportunities is more easily observable" (1977). While Boserup points to the ability of some women from landed households to withdraw from field work when landless laborers are available, she does not point out the implications of this situation for women who are landless laborers. Poor and landless women, for example, are often forced to seek agricultural work despite declining employment opportunities due to mechanization of agriculture (Sen: n.d.).

In brief, these studies show the specific ways in which women are affected by the hierarchical and exploitative structure of production associated with capitalism's penetration in the Third World. Modernization is not a neutral process, but one that obeys the dictates of capitalist accumulation and profit making. Contrary to Boserup's implications, the problem for women is not only the lack of participation in this process as equal partners with men; it is a system that generates and intensifies inequalities, making use of existing gender hierarchies to place women in subordinate positions at each different level of interaction between class and gender. This is not to deny the possibility that capitalist development might break down certain social rigidities oppressive to women. But these liberating tendencies are accompanied by new forms of subordination.

ANALYSIS OF SUBORDINATION: REPRODUCTION

One of the most pervasive themes of the present feminist movement is the emphasis placed on the role of reproduction as a determinant of women's work, the sexual division of labor, and the subordinate/dominant relationships between women and men.[5] It is precisely this emphasis that is lacking in Boserup's book. As a result, her analysis does not contain a feminist perspective that speaks directly to the problem of women's subordination. To be sure, the book is about different forms subordination can take, but it fails to elucidate the crucial role of the household as the focal point of reproduction. Nor does it explain the social relations among household members in the making of "the woman problem" and in determining women's role in economic development.

Boserup's analysis of polygamy in Africa offers an illustration in this regard. Her analysis, as mentioned earlier, is grounded in economic factors, namely, the greater access to land and labor resources provided by each wife. Boserup's interesting insight, however, is not accompanied by an analysis of the significance of this type of household arrangement for the dynamics of male domination. Nor does it explain why polygamy can also be found in Middle Eastern countries where women are secluded and do not represent an addition to land and labor resources. In these cases, polygamy becomes a luxury that not all households can afford. A similar situation can even be found in parts of Africa where women are secluded, such as the Hausa region in northern Nigeria, where polygamy has been on the increase during this century (Longhurst: n.d.). In the Middle East and in the Hausa region, polygamy might be related to social reproduction, that is, to the access each wife provides to family networks and resources. Seclusion may be an effort to control female sexuality for the purpose of identifying paternity and transmitting resources from one generation to the next.

Thus, Boserup's analysis falls within a traditional approach to women's issues (and echoes traditional politics). This approach focuses on nondomestic production as a determinant of women's position in society. Consequently, the solution to women's oppression is seen in the sphere of economic and social relations outside the household. Recent feminist analysis points out the shortcomings of this approach, stressing that it is one-sided and does not address itself to the root of patriarchal relations. In the three areas discussed next— domestic work, spheres of production and reproduction, and population and birth control issues—the emphasis on reproduction has contributed to an understanding of women's economic role, of the material base of their oppression, and of its implications for policy and action.

The Domestic Sphere

During the past decade, feminist attempts to understand the roots of women's oppression have resulted in a growing body of literature on domestic labor and household production, as well as on the patriarchal structure that controls them. Most of this literature is based on conditions prevalent in industrialized, urban societies, where the nuclear family has been, until recently, the most basic form of household organization, and wage labor has been the most important source of family subsistence. Under these conditions, the great bulk of domestic work consists of the production of use values through the combination of commodities bought in the market and domestic labor time. The goods and services produced contribute to the reproduction of the labor force and to its daily maintenance. Thus, domestic work performs a crucial role for the functioning of the economic system. It is linked with the market both by way of what it purchases and by what it provides—the commodity labor power that is exchanged for a wage.[6] In the average household, this work is done by women and is unpaid. Women's unique responsibility for this work, and their resulting weakness in the labor market and dependency on the male wage, both underlie and are products of asymmetric gender relations.

The form, extent, and significance of domestic work, however, vary according to a society's stage of economic transformation. In a subsistence economy, the materials used for domestic production are not bought in the market; they are transformed in such a way that household and nonhousehold production are closely linked—to the extent that it is hard to draw a line between them. Domestic work extends itself into activities such as gathering wood for the domestic fire, picking vegetables for daily meals, and baking bread in village public ovens for family consumption. Domestic work also becomes part of the agricultural labor process when, for example, the meals for agricultural workers are cooked in the home and transported to the fields. Similarly, the agricultural-labor process may extend itself into household production, as when cereals are dried and agricultural goods are processed for family consumption.

In agricultural societies, then, the degree of production for the household's own consumption is higher than in societies where a good proportion of home production has become commoditized. In farming areas domestic and agricultural work contribute most to subsistence needs. The African female farming system places the burden of subsistence largely on women. In most cases, despite a clearly defined sexual division of labor, men's and women's work is integrated in time and space. The separation between productive and reproductive activities is often artificial, symbolized, perhaps, by a women carrying a baby on her back while working in the fields. By contrast, under the wage-labor systems of industrialized, urban societies, the burden of subsistence falls upon the wage; domestic work transforms the wage into use values consumed in the household. A clear separation between domestic and commodity production exists, and unpaid housework becomes more and more isolated and differentiated from nonhousehold production.

Despite these differences, the extent to which domestic work is performed by women across countries is overwhelming. Women perform the great bulk of reproductive tasks. To the exent that they are also engaged in productive activities outside of the household, they are often burdened with the problems of a double day. As mentioned earlier, Boserup includes an interesting discussion about the tendency of conventional statistics to underestimate subsistence activities, including domestic labor, which represent a high proportion of women's work. Yet nowhere does she indicate how central women's primary involvement in household activities is to an understanding of their subordination and of their role in the economy.

Reproduction and Production

The emphasis on reproduction and on analysis of the household sphere indicates that the traditional focus placed upon commodity production is insufficient to understand women's work and its roots in patriarchal relations. In order to understand fully the nature of sex discrimination, women's wages, women's participation in the development process, and implications for political action, analysts must examine the two areas of production and reproduction as well as the interaction between them. An example from the field of economics—the internal labor-market model of sex differentials in the work force—illustrates this approach.

This model represents a step forward from neoclassical explanations of women's secondary status in the labor market. It focuses on the internal organization of the capitalist firm to explain sex segregation and wage differentials, rather than on factors of supply and demand developed by other models (Blau & Jusenius 1976). The dynamics of this internal organization tend to foster the formation of job ladders and clusters that create hierarchies among workers. Sex is one factor by which workers can be separated. In this model, occupational segregation, wage differentials, and other types of discrimination by sex are viewed as resulting from the hierarchical and self-regulatory structure of production.

Two policy implications can be drawn from this model. Radical policy would involve elimination of the hierarchical structure of production, perhaps by some form of workers' control and equalization of wages. To the extent that this would eliminate or reduce differences among workers, it would tend to eliminate or reduce differences by sex. A less radical policy would involve equal opportunity/affirmative action plans that take the structure of production and the labor hierarchy as given, but would make each job equally accessible to men and women. Both of these policies have a major flaw; they focus only on the structure of production and do not take into consideration women's role in the area of reproduction. If women face a double day and if child-care facilities are not available to them, neither of the two policies is likely to solve fully the problem of women's secondary status in the labor market, given that their participation in paid production is conditioned by their work in and around the household. All of this points out how necessary it is to eliminate discrimination within the reproductive sphere. Domestic work must be shared between women and men, child-care services must become available, and both patriarchal relations and gender sterotyping in the socialization process must be eliminated.

Within the Marxist tradition, it is interesting to note that the Engels (1972) thesis does contain an analysis of the interaction between reproduction and production. Engels's view of the origins of women's subordination links the productive sphere—the introduction of private property in the means of production and the need to pass it on from one generation to the next—with reproduction, that is, with the need to identify paternity of heirs through the institutions of the family and the control of women's sexuality and reproductive activities. The Engels thesis can be projected to situations, such as those prevalent in industrialized societies, where large segments of the population do not own the means of production, but where there are still a hierarchy and class differences within the propertyless classes. It can be argued that to the extent reproduction implies the private transmission of access to resources—education, for example—the need to identify the individual beneficiaries of this transmission remains.[7]

Engels himself did not extend the analysis in that direction. For him, as for Marx, the production of means of subsistence and the reproduction of human beings are the two fundamental levels of human activity. However, both assumed that the elimination of private property and women's participation in commodity production, made possible by industrialization, would set the preconditions for their emancipation. Thus the initial connection between production and reproduction found in Engels became blurred with the assumption that transformation of productive structures would automatically erase women's oppression. Traditional Marxist thinking and traditional leftist and liberal politics have followed a similar pattern. The new emphasis on reproduction is the result of the questions posed by feminists; it can be viewed as an elaboration of the simplifications inherent in Engels's initial formulation.

A variety of recent studies on women in Third-World countries have focused on the interaction between production and reproduction to analyze women's work. Maria Mies's (n.d.) study of Indian women lace makers in Narsapur, Andhra Pradesh, for example, shows how the seclusion of women has conditioned their participation in nonhousehold production. Although lace making is a producing industry geared toward the international market, it is highly compatible with seclusion and with domestic work. Women are engaged in lace making as much as six to eight hours a day, in addition to their household chores. Their average daily earnings amount to less than a third of the official minimum wage for female agricultural laborers. This situation persists even though the industry has grown considerably since 1970 and now represents a very high proportion of the foreign-exchange earnings from handicrafts in the region. Many of the women are the actual breadwinners in their families. Mies argues that this highly exploitative system has in fact led to greater class differentiation within local communities as well as greater polarization between the sexes. The system is made possible by the ideology of seclusion that rigidly confines women to the home, eliminates their opportunities for outside work, and makes them willing to accept extremely low wages. A strict focus on the productive aspects of lace making—this is Boserup's approach—to the exclusion of reproductive aspects, such as seclusion, presents only a partial picture of the nature of women's exploitation.

Population Control and Birth Control

The 1970s were particularly fruitful in highlighting the issues of reproductive freedom in the advanced capitalist countries; movements for abortion rights, safe contraception, and adequate day care, and struggles against sterilization abuse abounded. For women in the Third World, however, the question of reproductive freedom has been complicated by the issue of overpopulation and by opposition to imperialist-dominated programs of population control. This is, of course, also true for poor women from ethnic and racial minority groups who face the threat of sterilization abuse within the advanced capitalist countries. Much of the literature on Third-World countries has focused on the question of population control without directly addressing the problem of reproductive freedom for women or the possible contradictions between class and gender (Gimenez 1977; Mandani 1977). A feminist perspective can modify the analysis of population growth and control in the Third World.

The concept of reproductive freedom includes the right to bear or not to bear children and, by implication, the right to space childbearing. To the extent that children are potential laborers, or inheritors for the propertied classes, decisions about childbearing affect not only the woman but her entire household. For example, in very poor peasant households that possess little land and that are squeezed by usury and rent payments, the labor of children both on and off the peasant farm may be crucial to the ongoing ability of the household to subsist and maintain land. Pronatalist tendencies in rural areas may have a clear economic basis. Even neoclassical economists are becoming increasingly aware of the effect of class-related factors—level of schooling, size of landholdings, and access to technology—on fertility rates (Rosenzweig 1977). Marxist writers have shown the conflict between the economic rationality of the individual household and social programs of family planning and population control (Mamdani 1977). This conflict may be expressed in subtle ways, such as ignoring available contraception, or in more overt resistance to programs of forced sterilization. While leftists have correctly opposed forced sterilization and have pointed to the social causes of unemployment— the real population problem—there has been a tendency to ignore a critical aspect of childbearing: it is performed by women.

It is true that decisions about childbearing may affect the survival of the entire household over time; still, the most immediate burden of multiple pregnancies falls on the mother. In conditions of severe poverty and malnutrition where women are also overworked, this can and does take a heavy toll on the mother's health and well-being. The poor peasant household may survive off the continuous pregnancy and ill-health of the mother, which are exacerbated by high infant mortality. The mother's class interests and her responsibilities as a woman come into severe conflict (Folbre 1979, 1980).

The result of this conflict is that a poor woman's attitude toward birth control, contraception, and even sterilization are likely to be different from those of her husband or mother-in-law. Research on these problems in the Third World should address questions such as: (1) Who makes decisions about childbearing and birth control within rural households, families, and communities, and on what basis are the decisions made? (2) What indigenous forms of family limitation are available to poor women, and how are they used? (3) Are there differences of opinion and interest between the childbearers and other family members? (4) How does childbearing affect women's participation in other activities?

Answers to these questions require careful empirical research of a sort that is barely beginning in the Third World. The insights gained from empirical research must affect one's assessment of birth-control programs, especially the more enlightened programs that focus on the health and education of the mother. Reduction in the infant-mortality rate, improvements in health and sanitation, and better midwife and paramedic facilities can give poor, rural women more options than having to resolve class contradictions through their own bodies. Such programs, however, clearly cannot be a panacea for the basic problems of extreme poverty and inequality in landholding; the contradictions of class and capital accumulation in the countryside can be resolved only through systemic social change.

CONCLUSION

In our analysis we have assessed the positive contributions of Boserup's work to a decade of feminist research on women in the Third World. We have also tried to show the limitations of her analysis, which arise from a flawed and inadequate conceptual basis.[8] There has been a great deal of fruitful research in the past decade that is thoroughly grounded in theory, particularly in class-based and feminist perspectives, which provides a richly textured understanding of the position of women in the Third World.

It is very important to delineate the policy implications that emerge from this analysis. Boserup's own conclusions on policy emphasized women's education as the major mechanism by which modernization would begin to work to women's advantage. Through education, women can compete more successfully in urban labor markets and can gain access to improved agricultural techniques in the rural areas. This conclusion ignores two crucial features that an analysis based on the concepts of accumulation and women's role in reproduction would highlight. On one hand, it ignores the high incidence of unemployment among educated people in the Third World. Unless the systemic causes of unemployment are removed, women's education by itself is purely an individualist solution; it attempts to alter the characteristics of individual women rather than those of the system of capital accumulation. On the other hand, even if there were dramatic systemic changes, education by itself would not alter women's position, in that education cannot address issues of child care and domestic work. The high incidence of the double day in countries like the Soviet Union and China supplies ample evidence of this policy's limited success.

Short-term programs involving the basic-needs strategy have definite motivational limits, but they cannot be ignored entirely.[9] Since the principal outcome of tensions between gender and class are that women are overworked and in ill health, systems of water provision, electrification, and sanitation and health are immediately beneficial. One must remain aware, however, of how such programs are implemented and whom they benefit. Strategies that involve the self-organization of poor women for control over such programs are crucial.

The long-term goal, however, remains, and that is the elimination of class and sex hierarchies through a radical transformation of society, a struggle that requires not only an analysis of class and of accumulation, but a recognition of the importance of reproduction at all levels. We can no longer ignore the questions of what goes on within households, nor the interweaving of gender relations and class relations. The feminist analysis of the Third World in the past decade has lent support and clarity to this vision.

Notes

1. Where extended families prevail, adult men may also engage in unpaid family labor.

2. The modernization approach to economic development is based on a perception of social change as a linear movement from backwardness to modernity. Specifically, it calls for the adaptation of technology, institutions, and attitudes to those existing in the advanced capitalist countries of the West. The theory does not emphasize changes in class relations or the contradictory effects of the capitalist development process, nor does it acknowledge the possibility of alternative development models. In contrast, the capital-accumulation approach analyzes the growth of interconnected processes of production—both quantitative and qualitative—motivated by profits, extension of the market, growing social division of labor and modes of production, and the proletarianization of the labor force. Private ownership of resources, and hence of the surplus generated in production (profits, rent, and interest), leads to class differentiation between owners and nonowners of the means of production. Private ownership also signals the private appropriation of productive wealth, and growing inequalities in the distribution of income and power.

3. See Ester Boserup's earlier work, *The Conditions of Agricultural Growth* (1965). In this book, exogenously given population growth provides the major impetus for technical change in agriculture. Boserup's argument is intended to be anti-Malthusian: rising population density in a region is followed, not by the Malthusian checks of war or famine, but by technological adaptation (shorter fallow, higher cultivation intensity, the shift from hoe to plow) designed to facilitate greater food production.

4. In India, for example, plow cultivation coexists with wage-labor in agriculture that is one-third female. See India, Committee on the Status of Women in India (1974).

5. Reproduction here refers not only to biological reproduction and daily maintenance of the labor force, but also to social reproduction—the perpetuation of social systems. Related is the view that in order to control social reproduction (through inheritance systems, for example) most societies have developed different forms of control over female sexuality and reproductive activities. This control is the root of women's subordination.

6. For an elaboration of these points, see Beechey (1977), Fee (1976), Himmelweit and Mohun (1977), and Mackintosh (1979).

7. See Benería (1979) for an elaboration of the point. This notion can explain, for example, why sexual mores are less strict among the poor than among middle and upper-class people in many urban as well as rural areas.

8. For an earlier critique of Boserup's discussion of farming systems, see Huntington (1975) and Croll (ch. 14).

9. For a clarification of the basic-needs strategy, see ILO, *Employment, Growth and Basic Needs: A One-World Problem* (1976).

10

Capitalist Development, Family Division of Labor, and Migration in the Middle East

MONA HAMMAM

The extent to which Arab women are drawn into the wage-labor market cannot be considered a function of cultural variables attributed, as is often done, to the seemingly inviolable laws and traditions of Islam. Rather, it reflects the interplay of social and economic forces, at the base of which lies the sexual division of labor within the household. The plethora of ways that this division of labor is affected by—and in turn affects—the creation, expansion, and growth of the wage-labor market as well as women's absorption in it, is conditioned by the uneven development of capitalism in the Middle East, and the different rates at which the Arab countries have been integrated into the world market.

While the protracted process of capitalist development gradually destroys the hegemony of precapitalist forms of subsistence and houshold economies, and eventually supersedes them, the dominant relations of production, on a world scale, impede latecomers to the market from effecting a complete transition from one mode of production to another. One of the many consequences of this impediment on the social division of labor in the Arab countries is the distorted development of "modern" social classes. It deforms them as it fosters capitalist growth of a dependent type.

DEPENDENT CAPITALISM

What is referred to as "development" is actually the supersession of precapitalist forms by capitalism of a dependent type. In the transition, however, precapitalist forms, where women actively share in the production process both for subsistence and simple commodity exchange, are not entirely superseded by the capitalist mode of production. Rather, precapitalist forms coexist and articulate with capitalist forms in a complex network of interrelationships that, necessarily, modifies and transforms them.

Such a framework recognizes at the outset the structural and functional linkages that exist between women's unpaid labor in the household, their economic participation in the informal sector, and the rate and extent of their absorption in the formal wage-labor market. At the level of the household, women actively engage in the production of use values (simple commodities outside the sphere of market circulation) for the family's direct consumption and, occasionally, for exchange (mainly in the informal sector or local market). In the urban informal sector, women preponderate in personal, individualized services (as launderers, domestic servants, seamstresses, midwives, soothsayers, etc.) and as petty producers and traders. In both sectors, women constitute a "reserve army of labor" and appear on the economic scene in a range and diversity of roles that elude adequate enumeration. As casual laborers, the marginally self-employed, seasonal workers, unpaid family workers, the unemployed, and so on, they, like their male counterparts in this labor reserve, serve the function of depressing wages in the formal sector, thus yielding to the capitalist a higher rate of surplus value extraction.

Not only does women's availability as a potential and flexible supply of labor reduce the cost of reproducing labor power to the capitalist, but their economic activities, as petty producers and traders, effectively do the same: women produce those articles of consumption necessary for the basic survival of the laborer and household (i.e., necessary for the reproduction of labor power). These are sold in the informal market and/or provided, at the level of the household, at a lower price than would obtain in the formal market. These economic activities of petty commodity production and trade, whether in the household or informal market, help maintain a low cost of living for the poor. Therefore, wages can be kept low and, in effect, women's economic activities act as a cost-of-living subsidy to the capitalist market. Low wages, in turn, serve to accelerate the proliferation of the informal sector as an alternative or secondary source of cash income to supplement meager earnings, or as the sole source of cash income for the household.

Such a situation of dire economic need *compels* those women, who are otherwise constrained from entering into the formal wage sector, to seek access to income in the informal sector (where it is sporadic, irregular, and unregulated) in order to supplement their husbands' earnings or, in cases where the woman is the sole earner, as the only source of cash flow into the household.

Thus, in Egypt, for instance, it is a common pattern in working-class families to find that the husband, in addition to steady wage employment, takes on a secondary occupation in the informal sector, while his wife raises chickens (on rooftops or in stairwells) both for the family's direct consumption and for exchange. She might also take on casual labor as a washerwoman or work as an unpaid producer or trader in her husband's secondary occupation. An estimated one-fifth of the urban population of Egypt, or roughly nine hundred thousand households, live below the poverty level. For most of these, informal sector occupations provide the only source of income.

On the other hand, low wages also perpetuate household economic activities (where women assume the major responsibility) as a dire necessity. This situation *constrains* women from seeking wage employment in either formal or informal sectors, simply because the private work they perform within the household is essential to the family's survival; and outside employment would threaten household viability. Thus, it is estimated that in North Yemen, in an average-size family of six to eight persons, the labor of two women is required to carry out the minimum household chores necessary for subsistence: fetching water (a scarce resource, often obtained at great distance and, particularly in the mountainous areas, an extremely arduous task), caring for livestock, collecting animal fodder, and gathering fuel. The labor of a third woman is required for crafts production (making pots, baskets, and utensils), light farming, and so on. Hence, the sexual division of labor within the household effectively bars women from access to regular wage employment, for only if there are three or four women can the household afford to release one woman for outside labor (Carapico & Hart 1977).

In addition, an age-specific sexual division of labor within the household can impose restrictions on women's availability for outside employment. Thus, in rural Egypt, women drop out of *field work* at age twenty, particularly those who until then had been working for wages, and assume other chores such as care of livestock or poultry or food processing. The vast majority of rural working women, however, are unpaid family workers: they account for 82 percent of the female workers (Harik 1979).

Structural constraints are further buttressed by institutional ones: *access to credit* for the overwhelming majority of the economically active in the informal sector is severely limited due to eligibility requirements and to the time it takes to process loan applications. Hence, informal credit markets, which are generally at a higher rate of interest than commercial sources but are faster to obtain, inflate the cost of production in small-scale and family enterprises (rural and urban), while outputs of goods and services are cheaper than in the capitalist formal sector. Thus, a survey of squatter settlements and informal financing for housing construction in Cairo indicates that the rate of interest, in the informal credit market, ranged from 10 to 20 percent at a time in

1977 when commercial interest rates were set at 6 percent (Joint Housing Team 1977; Hammam 1979).

When one considers that roughly one-half of Egypt's rural population, approximately 1.5 million families, is landless (Richards 1980—figures are for 1972). and approximately one-quarter of these live below the poverty level (Harik 1979; Radwan 1978), ineligibility for loans is obvious. In the Jordan Valley, 60 percent of the farmers are tenants and one-third of the agricultural labor force are women (the majority of these are Palestinian and they are often heads of households). And yet, among those who applied for loans (most do not), they received less than 10 percent of all loans made by the Jordan Valley Farmers' Association in 1978. A survey undertaken that year indicates that 75 percent of farmers applying for housing loans from the JVFA were either tenant farmers or sharecroppers—i.e., not landholders (Hammam 1979)— hence ineligible to qualify.

Access, or lack of access, to credit is more a function of class than of sexually discriminatory practices in the Arab World. Under Islamic law, women are granted full autonomy in owning and disposing of property. These rights, however, are severely circumscribed by the tradition of preserving property *intact* within the *agnatic* kin group. Hence, a property owner would have access to credit but she would not be able to exercise full control over her share of the family's property in land. Among the vast majority, who do not own property or who own very little, access to small sums of ready cash is often accomplished through the formation of informal rotating-credit cooperatives *(gam'eyyas)*. These *gam'eyyas* consist of groups of women who pool their resources to extend credit to one of their members. They put in the same amount of money every month, thus extending credit to another member, then a third, and so on, until the loans to all members have been paid off. These loans are interest free, and defaulting is unlikely because of the women's interdependencies. However, the amount of funds that can be mustered is limited, so *gam'eyyas* tend to be a last-resort strategy for coping with poverty, or a convenient and occasional means for acquiring goods and services whose costs outstrip the family's monthly budget.

Another institutional mechanism constraining those employed in the informal sector is lack of access to national, regional, and export markets. *Access to markets* is not only circumscribed by the restrictions on credit accessibility just noted; but also such associated factors as transportation costs, steady supplies of raw materials and capital goods, and exploitation by suppliers, employers, and middlemen. In Egypt, for instance, a survey of rural households undertaken in 1961 indicated that one-third of all rural households derived their *primary* earnings from off-farm employment in such small-scale industries as food processing and textiles (where women preponderate as producers), as well as woodwork and metalwork (where men predominate) Yet the majority of these enterprises are not linked to national or regional markets. Furthermore, a general lack of basic skills (literacy and arithmetical)—more acute in rural areas, and higher for women than for men—as well as a lack of skills in marketing, accounting, and management, constitute further problems for these small-scale family enterprises.

In the Arab countries as a whole, it is estimated that less than 30 percent of the economically active population, excluding women, is in the work force (Birks & Sinclair 1979). In Egypt, the proportion employed is 33.5 percent; for Syria, Yemen, Jordan, and Morocco, the figures are 25 percent, 28.3 percent, 20.4 percent, and 24 percent, respectively (ibid). Women's work-force participation rates in the Arab world as a whole was roughly 10 percent in 1975. The figures for Egypt, Syria, North Yemen, Jordan, and Morocco, were respectively 6.9 percent, 11.1 percent, 4.4 percent, 6.4 percent, and 13.1 percent (ICRW 1980).

As has been demonstrated earlier in this chapter, structural and institutional constraints on absorption into the capitalist sector inflate the ranks of those engaged in informal-sector occupations (casual and seasonal work, petty-commodity production and trade); these constraints also perpetuate household-based productive activities. The latter is a double-edged sword: it not only impedes women from joining the wage-labor market when the demand arises, but also restricts their access to education, and thereby ensures that when they do enter the capitalist sector, they enter at the lowest levels of skills and pay.

Widespread unemployment and underemployment, the inability of the capitalist sector to absorb informal-sector occupations, population pressure (particularly acute in Egypt and Morocco), and a host of other social and economic factors in Arab countries rich in labor and poor in capital have contributed to a growing worldwide phenomenon: the internationalization of labor. This phenomenon is particularly marked in the Arab countries since 1973, as a result of the increase in oil prices and the concomitant growth in the demand for labor resources to meet the production, construction, and service needs of the oil-rich Gulf States. Egypt, Jordan, and North Yemen are the largest labor exporters, and out-migration is predominantly male.

We shall examine the impact of this out-migration on the sexual division of labor in selected Arab countries. Before we proceed, however, we shall briefly turn to a historically informed discussion of the factors *inducing* women's absorption into the wage sector. Since Egypt was the first of the Arab countries to undergo the protracted process of capitalist transformation, initiated in 1816 through a complex system of state monopolies, we shall deal with the impact of this transformation on the sexual division of labor. A further justification for including this brief overview is that it succinctly demonstrates that even the most ideologically entrenched and culturally prescribed tradition of sex division in society gives way to the force of economic determinants.

CAPITALIST TRANSFORMATION AND THE GENDER DIVISION OF LABOR IN NINETEENTH-CENTURY EGYPT

1816–1848

Under Mohamed Ali, statist industrialization was put into effect during the period 1816–48, in an attempt to forge the economic basis for Egypt's independence from Ottoman rule. Industrialization was accomplished in a period of great labor scarcity (the entire population of Egypt at the time was roughly two million), through a system of monopolies, which resorted to corvée drafts and which brought all the productive sectors, including agriculture, crafts manufacture, and trade, under the direct control of an increasingly powerful and bureaucratic state.

During this period textile, sugar, tobacco, saltpeter, and gunpowder factories were established, as well as iron foundries, creameries, metalwork, and the Alexandria arsenal. The expansion of areas under cultivation, particularly for the cultivation of long-staple cotton, required the construction of huge irrigation systems, canals, and dams.

Since women were already the main producers of textile crafts, they were immediately absorbed into the network of state monopolies, both in a putting-out system (where they worked at home for the mill) and through forcible recruitment to the newly established textile factories, where they worked alongside men. Corvée drafts also brought women into the tobacco and sugar industries. The types of work in which they were engaged were not so competitive with men as to depress wages. They were engaged in areas of work generally regarded as uniquely adapted to women, such as spinning, carding, bleaching, and weaving yarn and cloth in the textile industries; stripping cane in the sugar industry; and sorting tobacco leaves and packaging cigarettes in the tobacco industries. Paid piece rates by the sheikh el-Balad, they received roughly two-thirds the wages of men, but because their work (except in the tobacco industry) was seasonal, their annual wages were roughly one-third those of men. Conditions at the factory were so deplorable that Mohamed Ali regarded factory work as one form of penal servitude. In protest, workers often set factories ablaze (Tomiche 1968).

Women who worked in the putting-out system generally owned and continued to use their own instruments of production. They were forced to purchase their raw materials from the government and to sell their finished products, at a fixed price, back to the State. They, too, were paid piece-rate by the sheikh el-Balad. In 1823, women workers in the province of Sharqeya organized themselves to protest the embezzlement of their wages by the sheikh el-Balad and to press their claims for prompt payment of their embezzled wages (Tomiche 1968).

State-set demands on production, coupled with military and corvée drafts, meant that the burden of production, both for the family's own subsistence and to meet state demands, fell on peasant women and their children. The scarcity of labor at the household level combined with production quotas for the state had deleterious effects on the ability of the household to provide for its own subsistence, and family subsistence suffered. In addition, crafts manufacture, which had generally served as an independent economic base for women, was also being undermined. When production fell short of state demands and/or when peasants could not pay for raw materials, taxes and other government levies (such as poultry and livestock) were extorted from the peasantry as payment. When draft animals had to be given up, women took their place. In the grain industries, women were used to turn the mills (St. John 1841).

Not only did women do the work of draft animals, but the scarcity of labor at the national level drew women into public-works construction through corvée drafts: irrigation networks, canals, and dams. Alongside men, women were assigned to clear away the earth, carrying and transporting heavy loads of mud and sand on their heads (Hamont 1843).

Second Phase of Industrialization

The first phase of Egyptian industrialization came to an end when the combined pressures of the major European powers and the Ottoman Porte forced Mohamed Ali to accept a capitulatory regime. This ensured unfettered penetration of foreign capital into Egypt, eventually transforming the country into a raw-materials appendage to the British colonial metropolis. This also thwarted the fruition of capitalist relations within Egypt, whose seeds had barely been sown. Toward the latter half of the nineteenth century, the Civil War in the United States and the subsequent cutoff of U.S. cotton supplies ushered in the second phase of Egypt's industrialization. The area under cotton cultivation was greatly expanded. This, in turn, required the construction of more irrigation networks, the reopening of processing plants, and the building and extension of transportation networks. Though this phase was short-lived, women did not stand outside the historical process. They made sugar, cotton, and cigarettes. Their largest concentration was in the textile industry, where they, as well as children, were employed in sorting, pressing, and straining cotton. They worked seasonally, from September to February, for as long as *15 hours per day*. In the cigarette factories, they were employed as sorters of tobacco leaves and as folders of cigarette packets. They worked for 8½ hours in the winter and 10 hours in the summer. And, just as in the Muhammed Ali era, women were also drawn into construction work where, as described by Vallet, "[T]hey were responsible for transporting building materials (cement, bricks, sand). . . . In single file they climbed up the scaffoldings carrying their load in a round basket which they balanced on top of their heads. In this particular enterprise which employed 150 workers, masons or carpenters, 27 were women" (1911:84–122).

The experience of Egyptian women in the nineteenth century, under conditions of primitive capital accumulation, is not exceptional. Some of the same factors that impacted on the sex division of labor at that time, particularly those that undermined cultural proscriptions, continue to operate in the Arab countries today.

UNEVEN RATES OF DEVELOPMENT: WOMEN AND MIGRATION

Differences in the rate and stages of capitalist transformation is reflected in the range of GNP per capita. According to the World Bank, this stood at a high of $16,000, in Kuwait, to a low of $250, in North Yemen. Figures for Saudi Arabia, Bahrain, and Iraq were, respectively, $4,400, $2,140, and $1,390, while those for Tunisia, Syria, Jordan, and Egypt were $840, $780, $610, and $280, respectively (Birks & Sinclair 1979).

As indicated earlier, labor force participation rates for the region as a whole stood, in 1975, at 30 percent for males and roughly 10 percent for females. The percentage of the economically active population that is female in the Arab countries is indicated in Table 10.1, by employment status and occupation. Figures from 1975 for the total activity rates for women range from a high of 19 percent in Tunisia, followed by Morocco (13 percent) and Syria (11 percent), to a low of 3.2 percent in Algeria. In the category of "employee," which represents the best indicator of regular access to cash income, the figures are highest for Morocco at only 14 percent, followed by Tunisia and Syria, at 13 percent. Women are heavily represented in the category "unpaid family worker," with Syria exhibiting the highest rate at 62 percent, followed by Libya and Tunisia (60 percent and 55 percent, respectively). Figures are similarly skewed upwards in professional and technical occupations (followed by the services sector), with women's highest representation exhibited in Kuwait at 34 percent, followed by Jordan and Egypt at 30 percent and 24 percent, respectively. The figure cited for Kuwait may be rather misleading since expatriate labor accounts for almost 70 percent of the economically active population in the country (Birks & Sinclair 1978). The figure cited for Jordan may also be inflated because of the numbers of Egyptian women working in Jordan at the professional and technical levels as well as the numbers of Palestinians.

Intraregional variations are reflected in the degree of urbanization, which ranges from a high of 45–50 percent and more in such countries as Jordan, Egypt, Tunisia, and Kuwait to a low of 2 percent in North Yemen. Illiteracy rates for populations aged fifteen and above range from a high of 89 percent in North Yemen and Saudi Arabia to a low of 32 percent in Jordan. Female illiteracy rates stand at 85 percent in the region as a whole, ranging from a high of 98 percent in North Yemen and Saudi Arabia to a low of 40 percent in

TABLE 10.1
Percentage of Economically Active Population That Is Female, by Country; Employment Status, and Occupation

Country/Year		Total Economically Active	Employment Status			Economically Active (excl. family workers)	Occupation (excl. family workers)					
			Employee	Self-Employed	Unpaid Family Worker		Agriculture	Nonagricul. Production	Sales	Services	Admin/Manag./Clerical	Professional/Technical
Algeria	66	3.2[a]	5	2	9	4	1	4	1	13	11	21
Bahrain	75	5.4[b]										
Egypt	66	6.9[a]	8	3	11	7	3	3	6	14	9	24
Iraq	75	4.2[a]										
Jordan	61	6.4[a]	6	13.3[c]	16	5[d]	5	4[d]	1[d]	11[d]	5[d]	30[d]
Kuwait	75	8.5[a]	13		1	12	0	0	1	20	10	34
Libya	73	6.7[a]	6	1	60	4		1[d]	1[d]	10[d]	4[d]	19[d]
Morocco	71	13.1[a]	14[e]	6[e]	21[e]	15[d]	11[d]	15[d]	4[d]	38[d]	23[d]	15[d]
Saudi Arabia	75	4.9[a]										
Syria	75	11.1[a]	13	4	62	8		5[d]	1[d]	10[d]	9[d]	23[d]
S. Yemen	75	5.3[a]										
N. Yemen	75	4.4[a]										
Tunisia	75	18.9[a]	13	20	55	16		24[d]	3[d]	28[d]	19[d]	22[d]

SOURCE: Dixon 1979a,b.
[a] From ICRW 1980.
[b] From ECWA 1978, p. 2.
[c] From Labour Force Survey 1975.
[d] Includes unpaid family workers.
[e] Data from 1960.

Jordan. Variations are also reflected in the degree to wich women's mobility is proscribed by legal or cultural constraints. Thus, while Tunisia and South Yemen have formally abolished the veil, and the majority of women in Egypt, Morocco, Kuwait, Bahrain, and Syria do not wear the veil, most women in Saudi Arabia and North Yemen continue to do so. Differences are also reflected in the degree to which governments are committed to formulating and, more importantly, implementing policies designed to involve women in all aspects and phases of national life.

Bearing these intraregional variations in mind, all the countries under our purview are experiencing a similar phenomenon that is global in scope: the internationalization of labor. This phenomenon is particularly accentuated in the Arab countries, as is evidenced in the volume of migration, most notably since 1973:

> In 1975, there were over 2.5 million Arab workers and their dependents living in the Arab States—half of whom were employed. Since then, their number has risen by about 9% a year. An estimated 1,570,000 Arab workers were living abroad in early 1979. Another 975,000 non-Arab migrant workers were employed within the Arab World in Janaury 1979—a total of over 2,500,000 migrants in the Near East [Birks & Sinclair 1979:65].

Expatriate workers account for 40 percent of the economically active populations in Saudi Arabia, 60 percent in Kuwait, 81 percent in Qatar, and 85 percent in the United Arab Emirates. Arabs account for 75 percent of all migrants and most workers in Saudi Arabia (57 percent), followed by Kuwait and Libya (37 percent). Egypt, Jordan, and North Yemen account for 73.5 percent of the total Arab migrant work force; their share of emigrant labor represents 3.7 percent, 27.1 percent, and 28 percent of their respective work forces at all skill levels (Birks & Sinclair 1978).

Except among professionals and technical cadres, migration tends to be sex-selective and predominantly male among unskilled, semiskilled, and skilled workers. Families generally accompany professional and technical workers, however; and qualified Arab women in this category also migrate for employment in the oil-producing states. In 1975, female expatriate workers in Saudi Arabia and the United Arab emirates represented less than 2 percent of the expatriate work force; while in Kuwait, they were roughly 13 percent (Ecevit 1979). But the sex ratio of Egyptian teachers working in Qatar, Kuwait, and Saudi Arabia was slightly more than 100 percent in favor of women, and the sex ratio of all Egyptians employed in Jordan was 100 percent (they were filling critical shortages that resulted from out-migration of Jordanians, mainly among the skilled and professional (Birks & Sinclair 1978, 1979).

The sex selectivity of the latter group was later reinforced by legislation in Saudi Arabia to forestall permanent settlement of migrants who, potentially, might constitute a politically disequilibrating force. Hence, there was increasing recruitment of Asian, and especially Korean, workers, to Saudi Arabia. These workers are physically separated in "work camps." There is also an increasing trend to stipulate that Arab migrant laborers be single and to set limits on the maximum duration of their stay.

Thus far, the pattern of Yemeni migration—which, as noted earlier, constitutes roughly one-third of the economically active population—has consisted of a two-to-four year stay, mainly in Saudi Arabia. Migrants have been almost exclusively male. Roughly one-half to two-thirds of them are married. They leave their families behind and generally return during the harvest season (McClelland 1978). Usually they are between eighteen and thirty-five years old; most have had little or no formal schooling and are unskilled or semi-skilled (Ecevit 1979).

By contrast, the pattern of Algerian migration to France consisted (before the recent moves to repatriate these workers) of a ten-year stay. In 1970 the vast majority were unmarried. Of those who were married, almost one-third had French spouses whom they had met and married during their stay (Birks & Sinclair 1979).

The consequences of this predominantly male out-migration on the individual economies of the countries in the Near East are beyond the scope of this chapter. However, the impact of the internationalization of labor on changing and redefining women's economic roles—and, to a lesser extent, their social roles—has only just begun to surface.

IMPACT OF MALE OUT-MIGRATION ON GENDER DIVISION OF LABOR AND CLASS STRUCTURE

One of the major consequences of out-migration, and the subsequent increase in the share that remittances play in capital formation (through savings and investment), is the introduction of new class differentiations, which are reflected in the redivision of labor and in the reorganization of property relations. These, in turn, are often bound to, or modified by, their confluence with the dominant patterns of foreign investments and trade in the region.

Thus, while agricultural productivity has declined in some areas of rural Yemen and Upper Egypt due to labor shortages resulting from male out-migration, this decline has been reinforced by the availability of *imported* basic goods, including principal staples such as sorghum (in Yemen) and wheat (in Egypt), priced lower than locally produced equivalents. Competitive foreign goods, particularly of food stuffs, undermine the self-sufficiency of the rural household, at the same time that they increase its dependence on an assured and regular inflow of cash income, since families will consume a greater proportion of market goods for meeting their basic needs than they will produce themselves. Remittances are one source of cash inflow into the household to meet the heightened dependence of the household on market goods. According to the OECD Staff study cited earlier (Birks & Sinclair 1979), some areas of rural Algeria are totally dependent on remittances for their livelihood. In Tunisia, the governorates of Medinine and Babes (impoverished rural districts) derive 21 percent and 16 percent of their respective incomes from migrants (ibid.:109).

Existing below this group, whose main or sole source of cash income is derived from remittances, are the mass of households who could not, and still cannot, even afford to finance the departure of family members or their release to migration. Predictably, these households constitute the class most adversely affected by the general commercialization of the economy: inflated prices in land as well as in consumer and capital goods (much of which are imported, including basic foodstuffs); in short, by the general rise in the cost of living, and, one might add, in the standard of living, neither of which they can meet or approach.

Existing above both these groups are the families of migrants who spend a portion of personal income transferred to buy consumer goods and/or to pay off debts setting aside a portion as savings. Usually it is the migrant who saves and then sends back a sum of remittances specifically earmarked for the purchase of a particular item; or he purchases it himself locally or in the country where he has been working. Typical investments of savings are in land; in housing construction, where the quotient of imported construction materials is very high; in transportation equipment (trucks and tractors for personal use and for rentals, to serve as taxis); in irrigation pumps and other farm equipment; and in consumer durables, especially television sets. Another pattern is to either open a shop or set up a stall to sell imported consumer goods; watches, clothes, soaps, cigarettes, etc.

New class differentiations also occur within the urban areas as a result of savings accumulated by expatriate workers. These range from itinerant workers and small-scale enterprises selling imported goods to large investors, primarily in the construction of residential buildings, in land, and in farm machinery for the absentee landlords among them. Characteristic among the nouveaux riches is the pattern of conspicuous consumption. Most notably in Egypt, very little of the capital accumulated by these nouveaux riches is invested in production (Richards 1980).

In the rural areas, these modifications in property relations induce changes in the division of labor within the household. Depending on the amount of remittances a family or household receives, on its regularity and its investment, the out-migration of males has relieved some women of the necessity to work either as family producers and/or for a wage, at the same time that it compels others to assume increased work loads. Thus, acquisition of land or expansion of landholdings may accentuate dependence on family labor, or it may increase the options of the household: to rent out the land and/or to hire day laborers. Land use is a determining factor: land may be used for the cultivation of either subsistence crops, where women assume the major responsibilities, or cash crops, which are generally less labor intensive, depend more on male than on female labor, and are increasingly becoming mechanized.

In North Yemen, for instance, the volume of male out-migration is lower in the wealthier rural districts, where cash crops predominate, and highest in the poor southern districts, where subsistence agriculture, particularly of sorghum, prevails. In the wealthier areas, those who derive a lucrative income from cash crops—whether as owners or wage laborers—can "afford the prestige of secluding their women and hiring daily labour" (Myntti 1979:59). In the Hujariyya area, where male out-migration is high, resultant labor shortages as well as mechanization have accentuated the division of labor in subsistence farming *and* have significantly modified this division in off-farm rural employment. Thus, in the absence of farm machinery, it is the older men who do the plowing and threshing (although women are increasingly assuming these chores), while the women continue to do the bulk of agricultural chores necessary for sorghum cultivation: planting, thinning, weeding, harvesting, winnowing, pulling out roots, and collecting, transporting and applying manure. When farm machinery is introduced, it is the men's tasks that are mechanized (plowing and threshing), while the chores women perform are not relieved in either time or energy. Off-farm employment, on the other hand, particularly in the construction of irrigation networks, has drawn Yemeni women into wage labor because of shortages in the supply of male labor in the Hujariyya area. Women work alongside men at construction sites, carrying water and mud. They earn cash, but only half that of men (Myntti 1979). In a few areas, Yemeni women are also being drawn into wage labor (payment in money or in kind) or work as family producers in the cultivation of cash crops (cotton, in the Tihama; qat, near Taiz; and vegetables on family plots in the Amran area). Their absorption is due to labor shortages caused by male out-migration (ibid).

In some areas of Upper Egypt, for instance, where male out-migration, mainly to Kuwait, is high (ranging between 50 and 75 percent of the economically active populations of Beit Alam and Haraga), labor scarcity and the concomitant rise in the price of hired labor has accentuated dependence on the unpaid family labor of women and children. Agricultural real wages in Egypt have risen by 350 percent in the period between 1968 and 1978 (Richards 1980). However, as noted earlier, permanent agricultural wage laborers constitute a very small percentage of all rural wage earners, and women are even less represented; the latter preponderate as unpaid family producers and, to a much lesser extent, as casual and seasonal wage laborers. The range and extent of women's participation in agriculture and agriculture-related chores is indicated in Table 10.2, comparing Upper and Lower Egypt.

When women do not alleviate temporary labor shortages, machines may do so. However, mechanization also leads to labor displacements of both men and women, thus fueling the ranks of the unemployed and increasing rural-to-

TABLE 10.2
Work Participation of Rural Women in Upper and Lower Egypt

Activity	Lower Egypt		Upper Egypt	
	Number	Percent	Number	Percent
Plowing	8,300	49.7	1,000	10.9
Harrowing	8,300	49.7	3,800	41.3
Drilling	9,100	54.5	3,800	41.3
Cultivating	10,500	62.9	3,100	33.7
Irrigating	10,400	62.3	3,200	34.8
Fertilizing	9,500	56.9	3,500	38.0
Resowing	10,700	64.1	3,200	34.8
Thinning	11,100	65.8	3,200	34.8
Hoeing	9,300	55.7	3,400	37.0
Insecticide spraying	9,300	55.7	3,500	38.0
Reaping	11,300	67.7	3,500	38.0
Transporting crops	11,700	70.1	2,500	27.2
Packing crops	10,900	65.3	3,800	41.3
Milking	10,100	73.2	3,700	55.2
Poultry raising	13,200	79.0	7,500	81.5
Home agricultural manufacturing	10,700	64.1	4,200	45.6

SOURCE: Abou el Seoud, K., and F. Estira, "A Study of the Role of Women and Youth in Rural Development with an Emphasis on Production and Consumption of Nutritive Elements." FAO/Middle East Office, 1977–1978.

urban migration. Because of the lack of expansion of the productive sector noted earlier, this migration accentuates the proliferation of informal-sector occupations.

Another major consequence of male out-migration is its contribution to the increasing incidence of households which are, de facto, headed by women. It is estimated that in the Middle East and North Africa such households represent 16 percent of all households in the region (Buvinic & Youssef 1978: Youssef et al. 1979). While we have noted earlier the new class differentiations that occur among the families of migrant workers and the subsequent redivision of labor, a substantial number of these families depend not only on remittances but on the wage labor of women—be it in informal-sector occupations, including seasonal and casual work or in regular employment.

Women who are forced to assume sole or major financial responsibility for the household are clearly evident in North Yemen. The largest single employer of women, apart from the government, is the Chinese textile factory in San'a, a factory that hires only women. After a massive radio campaign launched by the Chinese to advertise job openings at the factory, six hundred women presented themselves at the factory gates and were employed. The overwhelming majority of these women were heads of household due to divorce, out-migration of males, or widowhood.

In the absence of regular wage-employment opportunities, women heads of household hire themselves out as itinerant workers. They work as seam-stresses, bride decorators, street cleaners, and donkey-cart drivers carrying water to residential neighborhoods; or as producers and traders: baking bread, making pottery, and selling fresh produce (Myntti 1979).

In Algeria, it is reported that between 1968 and 1973 self-managed farms relied heavily on female labor, doubling women's rates of work in agriculture during the period, as a result of heavy male out-migration to France (UN 1978:22).

CONCLUSION

Social consequences of male out-migration on the sex division of labor in the Arab countries have received even less attention than economic consequences in empirical research. Data on Tunisia, for instance, attribute the decline of fertility rates (from 2.8 to 2.2 per thousand) to male out-migration (Birks & Sinclair 1979). Data on North Yemen reveal that along with other inflated prices fueled by remittances, the *mahr* (bride price) has also risen (Socknat & Sinclair 1978). We noted earlier the proportion of Algerians who marry French women during their sojourn in France as expatriate workers. The most recent population census in Kuwait (1977) reveals that increasing numbers of Kuwaiti women are marrying non-Kuwaitis (as noted earlier, expatriate labor accounts for 60 percent of the work force). Saudi women are increasingly entering into the educational stream (sex-segregated) to offset the country's reliance on in-migration of women professionals. Fields of study at King Faisal and King Abdul-Aziz universities' colleges for women are limited to education (includ-ing administration), medicine, nursing, liberal arts and sciences, and theology. Patterns of consumption have changed, leaning increasingly toward conspic-uous consumption, particularly of imported goods. Canned soda pop, for instance, selling for 45 piasters when first introduced into the Egyptian mar-ket, became a status symbol for families across the social spectrum, replacing bottled soda pop, then selling for 3.5 piasters. Patterns of consumption have since outlived this phase, becoming increasingly sophisticated, or at least more luxurious. One would speculate also that many of the women whose husbands migrate for employment abroad feel more autonomous themselves, even if they are not so in actuality, while the husband is away. And it is reasonable to expect a rise in the age at marriage for both men and women, reinforced by increased expectations for the *mahr*, increased demands that migrants be single, the increased propensity for women to seek wage employ-ment, and other factors. This in turn would negatively affect fertility rates.

As a way of summing up, one should ask, as Gertrude Stein purportedly did on her deathbed, "What was the question?" For the Middle East, just as for the rest of the Third World, "development" begs the real question, which is, Can inequities be overcome within the existing dependent capitalist social formations? And one might answer, with Peer Gynt: "Backwards and forward, the road's as long; / In or Out, the road's as narrow."

11

Women Workers in the Strawberry Agribusiness in Mexico

LOURDES ARIZPE & JOSEFINA ARANDA

In recent years, the women's movement the world over has stressed the need to provide women with increased access to salaried employment in order to improve their living conditions.* In some industrialized countries, however, the recession and long-term economic trends are making it more difficult for women to get adequate employment, because, among other reasons, many of the jobs traditionally held by women in industries—particularly in textiles, garment manufacturing, and electronics—are being relocated in developing countries (UNIDO 1980). In some cases, many of the labor-intensive agricultural activities in which women worked as wage laborers have also been shifting to developing regions. In the latter, as the economic structure maintains high levels of male and female unemployment, most governments welcome capital investments that will create employment and bring in foreign currency through exports.

Behind this movement lie both the market pressures that forced companies into a constant search for lower production costs, and the rationale of "comparative advantages," according to which different economies are advised to specialize in those products that they can sell profitably in the international market. But it so happens that in the case of women, such "advantages" are closely linked to the cheap labor costs that come from the discrimination against them in the labor market. Thus, it could be said that women in developing countries are gaining the jobs that have been redeployed from

*An earlier version of this chapter appeared in *Signs*, vol. 7, no. 2, Winter 1981. © 1981 by The University of Chicago.

industrial countries. In fact, companies are using women's liberation slogans in deprived areas to justify giving jobs to eager young women rather than to older women or men who also desperately need jobs (Lim 1978).

The main issue raised by these events—whether the fluidity of the international labor market has become more of a zero-sum game for women than for men—cannot be fully discussed in this chapter, but some light can be shed on it by examining the extent to which such a "gain" for women in a developing country actually improves their status and living conditions. A survey through interviews of young Mexican peasant women who have recently entered salaried employment in the strawberry-export packing plants of Zamora in the state of Michoacán helps us to understand the changes created by salaried work in their consciousness, their living conditions, and their situation within family and community.

AGROINDUSTRY AND RURAL EMPLOYMENT IN DEVELOPING COUNTRIES

Worldwide, the optimism generated in the 1950s by the projects for rural community development and, after that, by the increase in agricultural production due to the Green Revolution, came to an end in the 1970s. Meanwhile, in the last three decades rural unemployment, movement of peasants toward the cities, demographic growth, and the marginalization of rural women from the technological and economic benefits of development have increased rapidly in many countries of Latin America, Africa, and Asia.

Import-substitution policies as a strategy for development in such countries led to rising foreign debts due to the high costs of technology and of capital goods imported from the industrialized countries (Todaro 1977). The governments of developing countries, in order to acquire foreign exchange to improve their balance of payments, have encouraged export-oriented agriculture, which has led to food scarcity in many rural areas of Africa, Latin America, and Asia (Lappe et al. 1977). Attempts to compensate for this scarcity by purchasing food from abroad have only perpetuated the vicious circle of dependency and poverty (George 1977).

Technological improvements from the Green Revolution increased yields and efficiency in rural production, but also led to higher concentration of agricultural resources in the hands of capitalist entrepreneurs (Palmer 1977; Hewitt de Alcantara 1978). In many countries this concentration has displaced small family producers who have become agricultural laborers or migrants surviving precariously in the outskirts of overpopulated cities (Arizpe 1978). The expansion of this surplus population in rural and urban areas is being attacked through massive family-planning campaigns, even though it is clear that population growth is closely linked to the conditions of extreme poverty and insecurity that prevail on the land. Another solution now being proposed to stop the rural exodus lies in the creation of rural employment through agroindustries, a policy sponsored both by national governments and by multinationals who have found a fertile field for investment.

Following this trend, in Latin America the per capita production of subsistence crops decreased by 10 percent between 1964 and 1974, while that of agricultural products for export increased by 27 percent (Burbach & Flynn 1978:5). During the same period U.S. capital investments in agriculture for export in this region increased considerably, since investments in the food industry provide a 16.7 percent profit abroad, compared to an 11.5 percent return within the United States (Feder 1977). Since World War II, food-processing companies have invested more in Mexico than in any other country of the Third World. An example of this type of investment is the strawberry industry in Zamora, which since 1970 has provided employment for approximately ten thousand young peasant women in its packing plants. As in the textile and electronics industries, which are also redeploying their production units abroad, the employment of women rather than men is clearly preferred in these agroindustries (Lim 1978; George 1977). Why are young women preferred? Is it sufficient to say, as do the managers of such plants, that it is because they are "more dexterous" and "less restless"?

PEASANT WOMEN AND RURAL DEVELOPMENT IN LATIN AMERICA

According to recent census statistics in Latin America, women's agricultural work shows a relative decrease in all countries and an absolute decrease in many (IL0 1980). Partly, this may be due to inadequate census registration of rural women's activities, but it also reflects increased female migration from rural areas, as well as the shift to other self-employment (especially petty trade) and intermittent domestic service—occupations that fall between the borders of organized economic activities and unpaid female domestic and community work (UNDP 1980; Massiah 1980). Another important shift in rural women's activities has been reported among small family producers, where the agricultural labor of household women is intensified in order to increase or maintain productivity in deteriorating market conditions (Deere & León de Leal (1981). Finally, a fourth trend is also becoming widespread—wage labor in agricultural and livestock production or in agroindustrial activities entered by poor, rural women (Ronner & Muñoz 1978: 327–34; Silva de Rojas & Corredor de Prieto 1980: Medrano 1980: Roldan 1980).

These four trends appear separately or in combination in different countries and regions. But all of them stem from the same process: the economic crisis of small peasant family production in rural areas throughout Latin America. Discussion of the causes of this crisis is beyond the scope of this chapter, but the major trends in the status and employment of poor rural women in Latin America must be understood in the context of strategies these households use to survive in an increasingly difficult environment. There are also, of course, large numbers of women who have broken completely with their parents' or their husbands' households and who live and make decisions on their own. We find them, for example, along the Mexican–U.S. border or in the shantytowns of all the major Latin American and Caribbean cities (Kelly 1983). Their choice of economic activity and life-style constitutes an individual decision-making process that should be analyzed as such within the narrow limits set by widespread unemployment and underemployment, cramped housing, and strict social pressures.

But in agrarian societies, there is little room for individualistic response. Especially in the case of young peasant women, the decision to work or to migrate is either made by the family patriarch or through permission granted by him. In any case, even more than sons, daughters are bound to their parents' households by religious and social norms that prescribe absolute obedience, docility, and service toward others. In fact, we argue in this chapter that it is precisely these qualities that make young women so attractive a work force. The data that follow should make this abundantly clear.

STRAWBERRY PACKING AND FREEZING PLANTS IN ZAMORA

The strawberry agribusiness in Zamora began to expand in the mid-1960s, first through U.S. capital and later through Mexican capital. Its competitiveness in the international market comes from the fact that Mexican strawberries are cultivated in the winter and that their transport and especially their labor costs are very low (Feder 1977). Production is completely dependent on U.S. companies: the seedlings are imported from California; the export trade is handled entirely by six U.S. commercial brokers who have stopped attempts by Mexican plants to sell directly to the European market; and the strawberry prices are dictated by conditions in the U.S. market, especially by the success of the California strawberry harvest.

Eighteen packing and freezing plants for strawberries functioned during the 1970–80 cycle in Zamora and in Jacona, a neighboring village. Among them the hiring characteristics and working conditions for women, as well as male personnel, vary little: for example, some pay $14.70 (U.S. $.66) per hour of work on the conveyor belts and others $14.00 (U.S. $.63) but the lower wage is counterbalanced by payment of bus tickets and by better treatment for the workers. As Marta Rodriguez put it: "X is the packing plant where women workers are treated the worst, and that is why they have many problems in hiring people. Even though they pay more there, the girls prefer better treatment, such as they get at Bonfil, where no overtime or commissions are paid. At X the bosses are almost Nazis." It is interesting to note that firm X is the one that consistently shows the highest productivity and efficiency; it is the only one, for example, that has devices under the roofing to prevent swallows from nesting there. In most of the plants there is a minimum investment in installations: they are prefabricated metal structures that can easily dismantled. Everything reflects short-term investment.

Fifty percent of production for export in the 1978–79 cycle, which produced 88 million pounds of frozen strawberries (though the official figure given for exports was lower, 72.7 million pounds), was handled by the six companies we studied. Of these, three hire as many as 900 women workers at the height of the season, one hires 650, and two hire up to 350. One of the worst conditions of work women face in these plants is the acute annual fluctuation in labor demand according to changing conditions in cropping and in the price of sugar (sugar is added to the frozen strawberries). Figure 11.1 shows the typical annual fluctuation in Frutas Refrigeradas, one of the companies surveyed. Except in special conditions, all plants are closed from four to six months each year and have a peak season for hiring from March to May. Later on we shall see how the hiring is organized and how the women workers adjust their working lives to such conditions.

THE SITUATION OF WOMEN WORKERS IN THE STRAWBERRY PLANTS

Approximately 10 percent of the personnel in the plants do administrative work; of these usually all managers and accountants are men, and the secretaries are young, single women from the town of Zamora. In production work, except for the young men who unload the strawberry crates from the trucks and those in charge of the refrigerators, the great majority of workers are

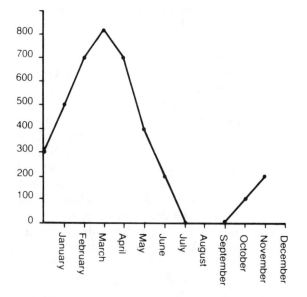

FIGURE 11.1 Annual fluctuation in number of female workers employed in the Frutas Refrigeradas plant.

young peasant women who live in outlying villages of the Zamora valley and the region.

The three-hundred women workers interviewed were selected at random from each of the six plants. On the average, between 5 and 10 percent of the total female workers in each plant were interviewed, with the exception of El Duero, where 18.3 percent of the women were surveyed. Interviewed in proportional numbers, they perform the different tasks described next:

1. *Stem removers.*—Women who remove the stems of the strawberries do piecework, that is, they are paid $5 (U.S. $.23) per crate of strawberries, each weighing seven kilograms. A worker with magic hands is able to remove the stems of up to thirty-five crates of strawberries per day; one with slow hands can barely manage five crates per day. But the number of crates available to work on varies from week to week. For example, on 4 February 1980, the four-hundred workers at Frutas Refrigeradas were assigned only one crate of strawberries each, because it had rained the previous week and very few strawberries had been harvested. On days like this the expenses of the workers for transportation and food are the same, but they earn only according to the number of crates they finish. On average, 80 percent of the women workers in the plants do this type of work; in the sample taken for the survey, they represent 75 percent of those interviewed.

2. *Supervisor.*—These women are chosen by the head of personnel, or by the union leader, to check whether the strawberries tossed into the canals have had the stem properly removed. They represent 4 percent of those interviewed, which is equivalent to the proportion of women working as supervisors in most plants.

3. *Selectors.*—Once the stem is removed, strawberries float along canals filled with water and disinfectant until they reach the conveyor belts, where the selectors pick out defective or rotten strawberries. As in the case of the supervisors, the selectors are chosen by the head of personnel or by the union leader, both of whom frequently show favoritism toward their friends or toward women from their own villages. This type of work is done by about 15 percent of the women workers in the plants and by 18 percent of those surveyed.

4. *Tray workers.*—From the conveyor belts the strawberries are put in tins or small boxes to be frozen, the best being placed on trays and frozen individually. This work is done by women who are selected in the manner described for those performing the two previous tasks. The women who performed the last three tasks mentioned were paid hourly, at the rate of $14 (U.S. $.66) per hour during the 1979–80 cycle. Though a stem remover who works with amazing dexterity might earn a higher wage than women engaged in the other tasks, normally supervisors, selectors, and tray workers earn more. Those who work on an hourly wage enjoy greater prestige because they earn more and are closer to the higher-level employees. Many of the stem removers would prefer to work on the conveyor belts, especially those who,

because of their age, are no longer able to work at high speed. But seniority normally is not taken into account for either promotion in tasks or other fringe benefits. The younger workers sometimes resent the favoritism, not so much for personal reasons, but rather because of loyalty to their villages: "See here—why aren't there more from Tinguincharo on the conveyor belts?" But others say that it is a tiring job. For instance, Berta Olivares prefers working as a stem remover, because, "We can at least go and walk around a little when we go get a crate for strawberries to de-stem . . . . but those on the conveyor belts are damned uncomfortable, they don't even let them move, they can hardly even sigh. We can even sing."

Now that the scene of the work has been described, the first questions to be answered are, Who are these women? Did they work before? If so, what jobs did they hold?

Occupational Background of the Workers

Of the women surveyed, 61 percent stated that they have never worked before. It must be noted that these included those who, because they are very young, had not yet entered the work force. Those who had worked before going into packing and freezing plants (41.3 percent) performed the types of jobs indicated in Tables 11.1 and 11.2. More than half worked in agriculture previously, and a third passed through paid domestic service. Their agricultural wage labor in the region has been replaced by immigrant labor, but this is not the case in paid domestic work, since housewives in Zamora repeatedly complained that "you just can't find servants around here anymore."

Table 11.2 shows that of the formerly wage-earning women who the strawberry agroindustry has attracted, most have been servants and agricultural laborers. We can now ask, Why have they taken jobs in the strawberry plants? Most of the female employees prefer to work in these plants rather than as servants because, Irma Cortes said, "We are not subject to the will of *la patrona* [the employer] and we can live in our own homes in the village where we have friends." Some of them like working in agriculture, but they find the work harsh. One of them said she preferred work in the fields "because we are out in the air, and not under the discipline of the factory, even though it is much more tiring work; for example, pulling out the weeds growing in the fields is awful hard work, and one ends up with one's back real tired."

Did they change jobs because of wage differentials? The income of 76.6 percent of those interviewed increased with their employment in the plants, while that of 7.6 percent remained the same. The high percentage of those who earned lower incomes (16.6 percent) can be partly explained by the fact that many of these had only recently joined the plants and had not yet acquired the necessary skills, while others attended work irregularly. Of those who previously held jobs, 66.1 percent worked in their own community, 28.2 percent in the region, and only 0.7 percent in another state, in Mexico City, or

TABLE 11.1
Workers' Previous Employment by Sector

Sector	Cases	
	(N)	%
Agriculture	69	55.7
Services	38	30.7
Industry	7	5.8
Trade	7	5.8
Agroindustry	2	1.7
Handicrafts	1	0.3
Total	124	100.0

TABLE 11.2
Workers' Previous Occupations

Position	Cases	
	(N)	%
Agricultural laborer	52	41.9
Servant	25	20.2
Unpaid family worker in agriculture	17	13.7
Office or shop employee	13	10.5
Factory worker	11	8.9
Trader	2	1.6
Others	4	3.2
Total	124	100.0

in the United States. Clearly, the strawberry companies have not brought back women working outside the region, nor have they attracted migrants from outlying regions, for the recruitment system precludes doing so. In fact, only 6.7 percent of the female workers were born in another state, and more than half (60 percent) were born in Zamora and Jacona, or in Ecuandureo, a neighboring municipality. The rest come from other municipalities in the same region.

None of the women workers live by themselves or with friends. With one exception—a woman who was adopted by the family with whom she lives—they all live with family or kin. The fact that they still live with their families is due to a very deeply rooted social rule that forbids a young woman's leaving her father's home except through marriage. But their choice of residence is also directly enforced by the acute housing scarcity in Zamora and Jacona and by the fact that the wages they earn are insufficient to permit living in a boardinghouse, the only socially acceptable form of habitation for single women living away from home.

Age, Marriage and Schooling

Most of the workers, 68.7 percent of the sample, are between fifteen and twenty-four years of age (Table 11.3). Managers of the plants stated that they prefer to hire young women because of their higher productivity, and because they are "very quick with their hands" and "concentrate better than the men." In fact, the younger women's manual dexterity is crucial in the task of removing the stems, but it is of only secondary importance in selecting and packing the strawberries; older women could do the latter tasks just as well. In only two of the plants, however, were older women predominantly chosen for these. Additional factors that influence the preference for hiring young women are analyzed in the next sections.

Girls usually begin to work in the plants when they are twelve to fifteen years old, and they work until they marry, normally between the ages of seventeen and twenty-one. As one of them put it, "The women marry before they are twenty because at that age the men say we have already missed the last boat." Those who do not marry continue working, and a few young married women return to work in the plants.

Of the female workers interviewed, 85.3 percent are single, 9.0 percent are married, 3.0 percent are divorced or abandoned, and 2.7 percent are widows. Almost all workers over the age of thirty are widowed, divorced, or separated from their husbands. Most of them support their children, and perhaps their parents or siblings as well. The few married women workers state that their husbands do not send back enough money from the United States, where they are working.

One older woman told us that in the early times of the packing plants women stood in long lines outside of the plants hoping to be hired:"There

TABLE 11.3
Ages of Female Workers

Age	Cases (N)	%
12–14	30	10.0
15–19	141	47.1
20–24	65	21.6
25–29	16	5.3
30–50	39	13.0
51–80	9	3.0
Total	300	100.0

were little girls, young girls and adults, even old women." But at present, the increase in the number of plants has led to a relative scarcity of women workers, particularly during the peak time of the season. At this busy time, plants hire women of all ages, including twelve-year-olds and older women. Then, as strawberries begin to come in at a slower rate, the management begins to eliminate workers: "First the little girls, then the lazy ones, then others begin to drop out by themselves when they see that there is very little working time left," one worker told us.

Sixteen percent, mostly the older workers, have not been to school at all, while 31 percent attended primary school up to the third grade. This low average in schooling can be explained by conditions in their communities, but it is significant to note that 3.7 percent have reached the high-school or preparatory-school level, since in theory their education should have given them access to jobs with higher incomes and prestige. But the fact is that very few such jobs are available in Zamora, and, besides, these women explained that they earn more money working at a fast pace in the plants than they would working in a shop or an office.

Although they seem to recognize this, the great majority of the women are convinced that their low degree of schooling prevents them from getting other jobs, and they complain bitterly that their parents, especially their fathers, did not allow them to go on studying:"Women are not allowed to finish [school] because our parents say it does not pay for itself because we then go and get married, and it has only been a waste." "If I were to study," said another, "I could be a secretary, and I would stop doing this very tiring job." The mythical nature of this hope becomes clear if we realize that, as has happened in other developing countries, an increase in levels of education would lead to an increase in job-entrance requirements, and consequently, the same proportion of less qualified women—even if their educational level were higher in absolute terms—would continue filling the lower-level jobs.

This hypothesis is further strengthened if we compare the plant workers surveyed in Zamora with a group of female agricultural laborers, surveyed in the state of Aquascalientes north of Michoacán, who pick grapes seasonally. The profile of marital status among the grape pickers resembles that of workers in the strawberry plants: 80 percent are single, 8 percent are married, 3 percent are divorced or separated, and 9 percent are widowed (Ronner & Muñoz 1978:331). In ages and schooling, the percentage distribution is also similar, but there are significant differences.

The similarities in both age structure and schooling indicate that roughly the same social group of women enter either of those jobs (Tables 11.4 and 11.5). But more women with higher schooling between the ages of twelve and nineteen enter strawberry-factory work in Zamora. The foregoing suggests (1) that many young, single girls enter agroindustry who otherwise would not work for wages and (2) that strawberry-plant work attracts women whose higher educational levels make it unlikely that they would accept work in

TABLE 11.4

Ages of Women Workers in Aguascalientes and Zamora

Age	In Zamora %	In Aguascalientes %
12–19	57.0	52
20–29	27.0	21
30–39	7.7	10
40 or over	8.3	17
Total	100.0	100

SOURCES: For the Aguascalientes: Lucia Diaz Ronner and Maria Elena Munoz, "La Mujer asalariada en el sector agricola," *America indigena* 38 (April–June 1978): 327–34. Other statistics from authors' research.

TABLE 11.5

Schooling of Women Workers in Aguascalientes and Zamora

Schooling	In Zamora %	In Aguascalientes %
None	16.0	32
1st–3d grade, primary	31.0	28
4th–6th grade, primary	49.3	40
Secondary or preparatory	3.7	——
Total	100.0	100

SOURCES: See table 11.4.

agriculture. However, additional data not included in the surveys on the educational levels in the communities would be necessary to confirm the latter hypothesis.

Social Attitudes toward Women's Work in the Factories

When the strawberry industry first began, it was very difficult for the plant managers to recruit enough women workers. The could get those who were already working in other jobs but were unable to attract young women whose families were not in dire need of additional income. The women's reluctance to enter paid employment was due to the very real fear, confirmed by women's experiences, that unaccompanied young women in public places would be "stolen." Carmen Garcia summarizes it neatly: "Previously, it was really rotten for the girls, because they were frequently stolen when they were going to fetch water, or to wash clothes or to bring the *nixtamal* [maize dough]. . . . They were even stolen with the help of a gun or a machete. They were taken into the woods and then the men would come to ask their parents for the girl [in marriage]. Most of the girls did marry them, even if they did not want to, and here divorce is out of the question. If they don't get on together, the woman just puts up with it. Here it is customary for the husbands to beat the women when they are drunk, they say that blows make women love them more." Yet, as it happens, the fact that the young girls are no longer "stolen" as often in the peasant villages of the region as they were in the past is attributed mainly to their working in the strawberry plants, although no one ever explains exactly why this is so.

Af first, the fathers flatly refused their daughters permission to work in the factories. One woman told us: "The parents are not used to one's working and in the village people gossip alot, they say that the women who go out to work go with many men." Not long ago it was still forbidden for men and women in the villages to address one another on the street. What the parents most feared, did occasionally happen. An experienced worker, Ines Gomez, explained: "When it [work in the plants] began, it turned out that many of the girls got pregnant because they did not know how to look out for themselves, and we move in an environment of 'machismo' and paternalism, it happened frequently. . . . but now the girls know how to handle themselves, now they even want to study and improve themselves." The young women workers see their situation in a different way and complain bitterly: "All they do is spread rumors about us. Many boys say they won't marry those who work in the plants, and all the girls from the village work there, but of course later they themselves are after us. They spread many untrue stories about us. Some of our nieces even went around saying that we were pregnant, and that we had left the children at the social security."

The young women workers' situation is further complicated by the migration of most of the marriageable men: "The girls don't go north [to the United States] because people talk badly about them. Even if we just go to Zamora they talk badly, we can never go anywhere. . . . The boys are allowed to go north and they come back real proud, some of them shack up with the American girls over there. They say they are very loose, that they even go after the boys. Others do return here to get married."

Initially the local priests were opposed to the women's factory work, too. One incident illustrates the situation very clearly. The strawberry plants in Jacona were unable to get female workers because every Sunday the local priest thundered that women would go to hell if they sinned by going out to work in the factories. It is said that the problem was solved when the owners of the plant spoke with the priest and offered to pay for the cost of a new altar for the parish church. Since that day, the local priest has exalted the dignity of work.

Wages and Expenditures

As has been noted, the workers' wages are subject to the rate at which the plants buy strawberries during the year and to their own level of skill. The monthly average wage among workers surveyed is $1,126 (U.S. $51.18). Eleven percent earn an average of $1,750 (U.S. $79.51) per month, 26 percent earn an average of $750 (U.S. $34.09), and 8 percent earn an average of $350 (U.S. $15.90). These wage levels are very far below the legal minimum wage, which amounted to $4,260 (U.S. $193.63) for the region in 1980. Since a single person, let alone a family with children, cannot survive on this income, such low wages can only be considered as complementary to the main income of a family.

Worse still is the fact that the wages these women get vary enormously on a day-by-day and week-by-week basis. The season begins in November or December and lasts until July or August. However, during that period there are "bad months," as the women call them—November, December, January, February, August, September—in which they earn an average of less than $500 (U.S. $22.72) per month. During the good months they may earn as much as $2,200 (U.S. $90.90) per month. Most of the women are not hired at the plants for the whole year; 56 percent work from seven to nine months; 5 percent work from ten to twelve months; 16 percent from four to six months; 11.6 percent from one to three; and 11.3 percent do not get to work even one month per year. Many of those in the last group work only on Saturdays during the peak season, or they are younger sisters of the workers, and tag along a few days per week.

During the months when there is no work in the plants, 75.3 percent remain at home helping with the domestic work; some do embroidering or knit pieces for sale. The surprisingly large number of women who follow this pattern indicates that these families do not urgently require a constant income from the women workers. In some cases—as, for example, one where the daughter supports herself and her mother—the income earned in the plant in the months of seasonal work is sufficient to keep them during the three months without work. Among the 24.3 percent of the workers who do work during these months, 7 percent work as servants, 11 percent go harvesting in the fields as day laborers, 1.0 percent work in offices, and 0.3 percent migrate to the United States. The remainder work in the informal sector in a variety of ways.

To what extent do these predominantly peasant families depend on the women workers' income? The majority (61.6 percent) answered that their work only partially supports their families, 20.7 percent replied that they give no financial help to their families, and 17.7 percent stated they offer major support. It is usual for one of the younger girls to hand over the entire weekly wage to her father or mother, who then little by little lets her have whatever

TABLE 11.6
Proportion of Workers' Wages Given to Parents

Monthly Wages (Pesos)	All	Almost All	One-Half	A Little	Nothing
200–1,000	36.9*	15.7	23.8	10.5	13.1
1,001–2,000	30.1	25.3	27.4	12.4	4.8
2,001–3,000	38.2	27.4	25.4	7.2	1.8
Over 3,000	11.2	44.4	11.1	22.2	11.1
All wage categories†	31.0	24.0	25.7	11.0	5.7

*Numbers given in percentages.
†2.6% of workers surveyed did not answer this question.

money she requires for her expenses. Table 11.6 shows that the correlation between the amount a worker gives her parents and the amount she earns is not significant.

How are their wages spent? What the workers keep for themselves, they spend on fashionable clothes, costume jewelry, romantic comics and stories, and beauty products. But the larger part of their wage, handled by their parents, goes into buying household consumer goods. This has helped the shops selling furniture and electric appliances. Some of the consumer goods purchased in the poorer households are basic items such as gas stoves, beds, wardrobes, and sewing machines; in other households the goods may be televisions, radios, blenders, and record players. Only a few households buy luxury items such as enormous consoles, fancy furniture, porcelain figurines, wine glasses, and so on. The survey indicates, however, that the parents buy these items not only for prestige but also because they can sell or pawn them when times get hard. It must be noted that the commercial boom in Zamora is due only in part to the women workers' income; it is mainly a result of the income in dollars sent back by the male migrants working in the United States. Even so, the pattern of consumption is the same in both cases.

Recruitment of Workers for the Plants

Women workers are recruited each season through social networks in the communities. In the plants that have unions, the union secretary chooses women delegates in each village or hamlet; in plants that don't have a union, the head of personnel chooses these delegates. Once the word is sent to them that they should begin recruiting, these delegates go around the village letting everyone know that they are hiring. They list the names of those women who want to go to work, purportedly giving preference to experienced workers. But Antonieta Castro complained that previous experience matters little:

"Some of the new ones are given preference by the bosses, because they give them *gollete* [some present]. We don't get angry about this, we only feel hurt." The "loyalty" that a worker has shown toward the general secretary of the union or the company is also taken into account during compilation of the lists, as are personal preferences and group rivalries within the community. In hiring, the company follows the list made by the delegate, moving through it progressively as the season advances. The recruiter in the village, usually an older woman, is socially responsible for the young girls she recruits as workers. Parents sometimes allow their daughters to go only if they trust the recruiter. This responsibility also gives the latter the power to decide who will work in the plant.

Conditions of Work

Hiring conditions and benefits in most plants are clearly below legal requirements stated in Mexican law. In the first place there are no contracts or permanent jobs for the workers. (According to the law the companies should pay the minimum wage, establish fixed working schedules, and hire the workers permanently during the entire year.) In the second place, fringe benefits are nonexistent: plant workers have no Social Security, nor do they have adequate medical services. More mothers could work if the plants had nurseries, and by law factories must provide one whenever there are more than thirty permanent women workers. When the women ask for a nursery, however, they are turned down. One manager said: "We saw that the nursery was not really necessary because only two or three children come along with their mothers, and that is why we did not put one in."

Women's Perception of Their Work in the Plants

Although these conditions persist, and in spite of the fact that many of the women employed in the plant consider the work to be tiring and oppressive, they prefer it because their only alternative is to remain shut in their homes doing domestic work or to work in jobs that are even more underpaid. Of the workers surveyed, 65 percent said that they prefer to work outside their home. As Amalia Vega put it: "We like so much to go out and work in the packing plant that when we return to our village in the evening we skip along the road dancing and singing. We don't mind about being tired [after a working day of eight to eleven hours]; because we have earned our few pennies and have left the little ranch for a while, we are very happy. In the village you get bored by seeing the same faces all day long and listening to the same gossip. By working we entertain ourselves." This is, in fact, a very fair assessment of the situation. When asked what type of work they like best, 59 percent answered that they prefer to work in a strawberry plant; only 4.5 percent prefer to work on the land, and 36.5 percent would prefer to be employed in an office.

Although four out of every five workers interviewed said they wanted improvements in their working conditions, particularly in wages and in the treatment they receive from their bosses, there are no real channels for protest. Only half of them belonged to a union, but this was due to the fact that only four of the six plants had a union. However, less than half of the workers (46.7 percent) thought that unionization could help them get better working conditions. This distrust reflects the fact that the existing unions closely collaborate with management. The pragmatic attitude of the union leaders, some of them women, is evident in the statement of one woman leader. Asked how she and other leaders got along with management, she said: "Fortunately there has always been a good relationship. People get to understand each other by talking. Also, we are interested in the company not having a loss, otherwise, we don't get *utilidades* [a profit-sharing government scheme]." In actual fact, workers rarely receive *utilidades,* which are sometimes used to pay for the annual fiesta and mass in the plant. As a result, workers hardly participate in union activities: "We get bored going to the meetings," one worker told us. "We don't understand anything and we get nothing out of it. We just waste our time."

Almost all the younger workers consider their job in the agroindustry as a stage in their life that allows them to get out of the daily routine of the village. More than half (58 percent) answered that they do not plan to go on working once they get married. As one of them told us, "Why, that's what I'm getting married for, to stop working!" Of those who say they may continue to work, many said they might marry a "bum" and end up having to support their household.

CONCLUSION

Why does the strawberry agroindustry predominantly employ women? It is true that the jobs of removing stems and selecting strawberries require manual dexterity but so do surgery, dentistry, playing musical instruments, and other predominantly male occupations. There are, then, other reasons why this industry employs women. In the region of Zamora, agroindustry cannot compete with the wages paid in the United States in order to attract and retain migrant male labor. At the same time there is a large population of young women who have very few alternatives for work. The strawberry plants do not have to compete with urban wages for women workers, since the emigration of women from the region is not frequent; male emigration largely covers the deficit in the budget of most peasant families. Moreover, the great majority of young women in peasant families have access only to paid domestic work or to wage labor on the land, both of them unrewarding jobs.

Therefore, a major reason for employing women is that they can be paid much lower wages than those stipulated by law, and can be asked to accept conditions in which there is a constant fluctuation in schedules and days of work. Here it seems to us that the companies take advantage of the traditional idea that any income earned by a daughter, wife, or mother is an "extra" over and above the main income of the father, husband, or son. If such wages were paid to male workers, the low income and the instability of the job would be untenable in the long run; workers would either move to other jobs or organize and strike for higher wages.

Other results of the analysis support this view. The fact that the percentage of women household-heads in the packing and refrigerating plants is very low—5.7 percent as compared to 12 percent in the region as a whole—suggests that the wages paid by the plants cannot constitute the central income of a household. Of course, it also reflects the factories' preference for young, unmarried workers.

Thus, the plants attract many young women—approximately one-half of the women workers—who normally would not enter wage-labor if the plants did not exist. Or so it seems, at least, from a comparison made with a group of agricultural laborers from Aguascalientes and from the fact that 42.4 percent of the workers surveyed gave only half or less than half of their wages to their households. Further support for this hypothesis is found in the large majority of women workers who do not seek alternative work during the months they are not employed in the plants.

Another advantage for the plants is the constant turnover among women workers. This impermanence allows a company considerable savings in wage increases due to seniority as well as in payments for maternity, illness, or disablement and in old-age pensions. Importantly it also prevents the workers from accumulating information and experience that would lead them to organize and to demand improvements in hiring and working conditions. Meanwhile, the traditional culture itself reinforces this turnover by making marriage the only aspiration for women.

Clearly, the strawberry agroindustry in Zamora is very profitable because cheap female labor is readily available. This conclusion coincides with that reached by Ernst Feder (1977), who points to the low cost of labor as one of the most important factors in making the Mexican strawberry industry competitive internationally. Thus, the "comparative advantages" of this industry in the international market are closely associated with the "comparative disadvantages" of young inexperienced, rural women who face social, legal, and economic discrimination. From a sociological point of view, what the agribusiness capitals have done is to make use of certain social and cultural characteristics of the region, that is, the high demographic growth, the traditional cultural values that assign a subordinate role to women, the family structure of the communities, and the local patterns of consumption. The key question to be asked is whether this way of using resources will improve the living conditions of the women and of their communities.

Have conditions of life for these women changed with their entry into salaried industrial work? This study shows that they have changed very little.

The great majority of workers continue to live in their parents' homes; very few have gone to live with other relatives in Zamora, and always under the same conditions of subordination and restriction they experienced in their own homes. About half of them hand over the greater part of their wages to their parents or use their earnings to support their own families. Thus they have only slightly increased their personal consumption. Their families, of course, have an improved standard of living, at least temporarily.

Although the women have more freedom when working outside of their homes, they are harassed by the men in the streets and are not free to move around the town or the villages on their own. Even when traveling to and from the plants the young women are closely supervised by recruiters and union leaders. There have been some changes: the young girls are not "stolen" as frequently as before, and apparently they have a more decisive voice as to whom they will marry. Also, some have become eager to study and to get ahead.

However, for the majority of women, work in this agroindustry is no way to get ahead. There are no promotions; the workers get no encouragement or help in acquiring skills or education; and the instability and low wages of the jobs do not offer any prospects for improvement in the future. Predictably, under these conditions no significant cultural change is taking place. On the contrary, the lack of prospects for promotion in the agroindusty, the low wages and the high level unemployment only push the workers back into the traditional hope of marriage as the only road toward a better future. Only a few of the young women, mostly those who have not married, have acquired new aspirations about employment possibilities and life styles. For them, however, it will be very difficult to find employment once the strawberry industry declines. The fact that the strawberry companies take advantage of the traditional values and conditions that subordinate women means they have an interest in reinforcing this traditional order. In fact, it is in their interest to oppose any initiatives to change the passive, submissive role of women in Zamora. In this sense, no "modernization" of women's roles is evident in the region.

What has been the impact of the strawberry agroindustry on the communities of the region? In the short run the industry has provided a better standard of living for rural families. The majority use the women's incomes to improve their housing and, particularly, to purchase household goods—furniture and electric appliances—which also serve as a form of saving. The worker's wages, then, flow rapidly through the merchants of Zamora toward the urban industries that manufacture these consumer goods.

But while the market for consumer goods has expanded, the poorer groups in the region have not been brought into the market. Because of the hiring practices in the plants, work is not given to women heads of household, nor to the poorer male and female laborers—those who most require an income. Rather, since the survey shows that the majority of the workers do not support themselves, it suggests that jobs are given mostly to young women from the mid-level peasant families, whose wages serve to improve their families' standard of living. Although such a gain is not to be underestimated, it benefits only minimally those households whose economic survival depends entirely or partially on women's wages. As a result, older female heads of household are pushed back into the strenuous, harsh, and even more poorly paid job of strawberry picking in the fields.

The strawberry agroindustry is not creating conditions for the future development of the region. It is not training workers, nor is it promoting or improving social services. It has not stopped the emigration of men to the United States. Finally, it has tended toward the concentration of land and capital while displacing and undermining production in small landholdings.

Thus, it seems to us that the strawberry agroindustry has provided some short-term improvements, but in the long run—aside from the profits that flow mainly to U.S. agribusiness concerns and to affluent local entrepreneurs—it will leave behind nothing but ashes when it collapses. According to two plant managers, the collapse is expected in three to five years. It is difficult to refrain from apocalyptic forecasts when we can see that the decline of this agroindustry will plunge the region back into underdevelopment; peasant household incomes will fall, massive unemployment will force countless women and families to migrate, and the hopes for a better life that have been raised among women will, once gain, be destroyed. Basically, nothing will have changed for women. Since the strawberry industry requires female workers whose income is not essential for the household, it bypasses the needy and predominantly employs women from middle-income groups. Since it requires submissive and docile workers, it reinforces patriarchal and authoritarian structures. Since it benefits from a constant turnover of workers, it does not oppose the machismo that confines women to home and marriage.

Two dilemmas emerge from a feminist analysis. The first is that much of the data—for instance, Amalia Vega's touching description of the joy she and other women feel at being allowed to leave the narrow horizons of their villages—show that the plants improve the lives of women and therefore, from a feminist point of view, should be defended. At the same time, salaries and working conditions at these plants are dismally exploitative, comparing unfavorably both to the norms set down by Mexican law and to actual situations elsewhere in Mexican industry; for this reason they should be denounced and opposed.

An even more painful dilemma faced by women's movements in situations such as this is that women whose consciousness has been raised by temporary employment will be left stranded when economic and social survival again becomes difficult if not impossible, when such industries move to regions populated by another group of docile and disadvantaged women. Thus, by the time the strawberry agribusiness—or the U.S. assembly plants along the Mexican border, for that matter—move to other countries that offer still lower production costs, the jobs Mexican women had temporarily gained from the loss experienced by their U.S. counterparts will also be lost to them. The jobs will then become a temporary gain for, perhaps, Haitian or Honduran women.

In this way, women's "comparative disadvantages" in the labor market in any given country can, at some time, be translated into "comparative advantages" for companies, capitals, and governments in the international markets. but when disadvantaged women organize to get even minimal improvements in wages and working conditions, the "comparative advantages" are lost, and investments go elsewhere. Clearly, all women lose along this chain. This being the case, one can only conclude that discrimination against women in employment, reflecting as it does the disadvantages women suffer from attitudes about gender, from social customs, and from their lack of political power, cannot be fought effectively in one place or country unless an appropriate international perspective is developed.

Notes

The research underlying this chapter was financed by the Rural Employment Policies Branch of the International Labor Office in February 1981.

12

The Articulation of Gender and Class in the Philippines

ELIZABETH U. EVIOTA

This chapter is about what it means to be female and poor in the Philippines. In more analytical language, this chapter is about the articulation of gender and class.[1] My intention is to point out the socioeconomic processes which have aggravated the impoverishment of large numbers of people and to show how women, both together with and apart from men, are affected by and respond to these processes. Because women have a subordinate position in familial and societal structures, they comprise the poorest of the poor.

THE ROLE OF WOMEN

Two key relations structure women's position in the Philippines: one is situated in their role within the family; the other, in their access to productive resources. Both these relations combine to place Filipino women in a subordinate position vis-à-vis Filipino men.

By role expectations culturally emphasized in the society, the Filipino wife/or mother is responsible for the care of children and the maintenance of the household, while the Filipino husband or father is primarily responsible, as head of household, for providing its material needs. In such an arrangement, the man's relationship to economic assets and resources (and by extension to the public sphere of politics and power) is direct, while the woman's is indirect, and mediated through her husband. Such, however, is the "ideal"; in fact, in the majority of households, economic necessity requires that the woman also engage in economic activity. In these households, then, the woman comes to have a direct relationship to economic assets and resources.

However, the conditions and terms of this relationship are both qualitatively and quantitatively different from those of the man's. First, economic responsibility is added on to a woman's household and child-care obligations, thus putting constraints on her time and energy. Second, since the household is a woman's primary responsibility, her economic involvement is taken as a secondary responsibility; and her relation to the labor market is as earner of a secondary income. Consequently, a woman is usually paid less for her efforts, is channeled into low-paying women's jobs or discriminated against, and is either easily dispensed with or readily recruited as suits labor-market demands. Third, women may have a direct relationship to economic assets and resources but not to the fruits of those assets: for example, numerous women in agriculture and services work as unpaid family labor.

Thus women's subordinate position, rooted within the family, is reproduced in the larger society. While this reproduction is maintained by means of such social mechanisms as values, norms, and socialization patterns (the ideology of "Women's place is in the home"), the material basis for women's subordination today lies largely in the requirements and consequences of the capitalist process.[2]

Capitalism profits from the subordinate position of women in three ways: it profits from their unpaid housework, from their unpaid family labor in non-household work, and from their work as low-paid wage-earners outside the home. First, at no cost to capital, women perform menial housework and look after the personal needs of their husbands, who have to sell their labor power outside the home. At a minimum cost to capital, women take care of children and raise a new generation of workers. Second, many women work on farms and in family enterprises as unpaid family labor, thereby performing productive work at practically no cost to capital. Third, because work outside the home is seen as secondary to women's primary duty to husband and children, women provide capitalists with a large, elastic, and usually compliant pool of marginal and low-paid wage labor outside the home. As a reserve army of labor, women are easily recruited or just as easily laid off, depending on capitalist demands.[3]

One must note, however, that the experience of the Philippines with capitalism, like that of most Third-World countries, is with a dependent type of capitalism, one that produces markedly uneven development. In turn, this uneven development further exacerbates the subordination of women.

PHILIPPINE ECONOMIC DEVELOPMENT

Economic development in the Philippines, especially since the end of World War II, has been decidedly uneven in structure. In some part this is a legacy of Spanish and American colonialism, but in greater part it is a consequence of Philippine integration into the international political economy of the postwar period. In the colonial period, the weak industrial sector and the rural sector were linked to each other and to the outside world through trade. In the postwar period especially, the natural resources in the rural sector (land, minerals, and forests) were used to produce the food and raw materials required to purchase imported capital goods for a growing industrial urban sector. While the industrial urban sector kept up with the modern world through relatively active involvement at international levels, the rural sector remained backward and underdeveloped. In fact, the small urban sector may be said to have advanced at the expense of the rural sector and its oppressed and uprooted peasantry.

In the urban sector, development was encouraged with the adoption of import-substitution policies from 1950 to the 1960s. During this period, the country was experiencing record increases in population. Measured by conventional aggregate criteria, the growth of the Philippine economy as a whole was healthy. In human terms, however, economic development has failed. Two kinds of problems have arisen. One is that growth rates have been accompanied by more and more inequitable outcomes in terms of employment and income distribution. Second, the overall unevenness of growth has led to the stagnation of the rural sector.

Import-substituting industrialization was biased in favor of capital-intensive, large-scale industries, especially those that were located in urban centers and that produced commodities mainly for the domestic market. The use of scarce capital in these industries was excessive. This led to the inadequate participation of medium- and small-scale industries, which tended to be labor intensive and less productive, and therefore less able to compete. Thus industrial growth could not absorb the expanding labor force. The rural sector, also increasingly penetrated by capital, was unable to overcome the effects of growing population pressures on available land. The end result of these development policies and practices was a growth in the numbers of unemployed and underemployed and a stagnation in real wages.

In the rural sector, "creeping capitalist invasion" in agriculture was phrased as a policy of agrarian reform. There was a drive to increase productivity through the promotion of modern farm technology, a rise in foreign investments, and a general growth in the market economy. However, this increased activity and productivity only served to sharpen income inequality (Ofreneo 1980a). Between 1956 and 1971, the decrease in the share of the national income of the poorest 20 percent of households was particularly pronounced among rural families.[4]

Development in the Philippines has resulted in the concentration of economic assets and resources controlled by a relatively cohesive class of industrialists, merchants, and agriculturalists; and in deterioration of living standards for those at the other end of the spectrum. The brunt of this uneven development has been borne largely by the major subclasses of the Filipino poor: the landless and near-landless agricultural workers and the marginal wage earners and self-employed in the urban-services sector. These groups make up roughly half of the country's total working population.[5]

GENDER AND CLASS IN THE COUNTRYSIDE

Of the close to 50 million people in the Philippines, some 65 to 70 percent live in rural areas. The major source of employment for most of the rural working force is derived from the land. However, only a minority of rural workers own the land they till. The majority either are tenants on marginal land or are landless agricultural workers.[6]

The landless class traces its roots to an iniquitous land-ownership structure during the colonial period, but in recent years a combination of factors has led to a massive increase in its numbers. These factors are: the accelerated expansion of agribusiness in the countryside and large-scale expropriation of lands by local and multinational firms; the gradual displacement from the land of farm families resulting from market competition (Ofreneo 1980b); increased population pressure on limited land; and the indebtedness of small farmers, resulting first in the fragmentation of land and ultimately in its abandonment.

By 1975 there were approximately 3.5 million landless agricultural workers (Espiritu 1978), representing 47 percent of all agricultural workers and 25 percent of the total labor force. Roughly one of every three landless workers (with higher proportions in rice and corn areas) is a woman.[7]

According to average annual incomes for 1974, the highest incidence of poverty was among landless agricultural workers.[8] The overriding goal of landless worker households is to produce enough to eat or to earn enough to pay for it. Since marginal farmers produce hardly enough to eat and landless workers do not earn enough to pay for food, family members have to help out. A wife takes on any available economic activity, including becoming a farm worker herself, and children discontinue schooling in order to work. Some families move from farm to farm in search of work. The combined efforts of family labor, however, are often insufficient, and three meals a day are not always possible. Malnutrition and poor health are especially prevalent among sugar-cane-plantation wage workers, whose child-mortality rates are high.

In general, rice farming provides higher remuneration, especially if wages are paid as a share of the crop. Coconut growing offers slightly lower wages, and sugar planting tends to pay the least.

The extent to which women participate in agricultural production depends largely on property and ownership and such factors as their age and the types of crops grown. Paddy production offers ample opportunities for paid labor for women, coconut growing the least. Wage rates for women laborers are consistently lower than for men (Carner 1980). For full-time workers the average weekly cash earning for women in 1975 was 27 pesos ($1.35), for men 40 pesos ($2.00).

Rice Production

Share tenants in Central Luzon use nonfamily rather than family labor.[9] The use of nonfamily labor is rational from the tenants' viewpoint because the tenant is both farmer and laborer. As farmer, he hires more laborers than might seem necessary because as laborer, he expects to be called to work on other farms. Household members also hire out their labor to other farms. Because of high rates of indebtedness to landlords, a tenant cannot make sufficient income from the land he cultivates. The wages are paid to fellow villagers not as a cost of farm management but as disguised compensation for their efforts on the farm. Thus, in share tenancy, women rarely work on family farms but instead join labor gangs on a wage basis.

This form of tenancy, however, is changing. With an increase in productivity, resulting from new rice technology, and the reduction of the landlord's share, resulting from a shift to fixed rent, the cultivator's share has increased, and there is a corresponding tendency to use family labor. At transplanting and harvesting times, the farmer orders his family members, mainly wife and children, to work as extensively as possible so that he can reduce his total payment for wages. This development tends to have adverse effects on the employment of landless agricultural workers. It is particularly hard on female heads of household or primary-income earners who are landless workers in rice (and corn) agriculture. In the absence of secondary adult-income earners, female-headed households are poorer than average landless worker households. On the average, women household heads work longer hours than male workers. Women are also reported to scavenge among threshed stalks of rice, gleaning any kernels that might remain (Bautista 1977).

Sugar Plantations

Sugar-plantation workers are the lowest paid of the landless agricultural workers.[10] In the sugar haciendas of Negros, 80 percent of the workers are paid on a contract basis: the contractor sets a flat rate for a given quantity of work. On the average, a plantation worker earns P4.69 per day, or approximately 67 percent of the minimum wage. Thus the contract system is a way of undercutting the minimum-wage law.

While there are no available statistics on women's and children's labor in haciendas, one study shows that women usually work eight or ten hours a day for 2.00 or 3.00 pesos, while eight- or nine-year-old children work for the same number of hours for 0.75 to 1.00 pesos a day. Often father, mother, and small children work together in the fields, taking home a total of 7.00 pesos per day. Thus in some cases, where sugar-plantation owners reported that they pay a minimum wage, they failed to add that they pay it to one person for the work of three or four people.[11]

Banana-Export Industry

The banana-export industry is organized on a different basis from rice and sugar agriculture. Numerous growers in the southern Philippines have direct links to multinational agribusiness; the deteriorating working and living conditions of their labor force are a consequence of these links. A study of grower/multinational ventures reports that 40–44 percent of the small growers are totally or primarily dependent on bananas.[12] For these small growers, indebtedness to a multinational corporation has been an unavoidable result of the shift from production of staple crops to production of bananas for export. The multinational advances the money needed for the costly conversion of rice or corn lands to banana production, as well as for fertilizers, pesticides, and other needs. The growers, however, are unable to meet the resulting debts at harvest time because price increases for agribusiness expenses outrun price increases for bananas. The grower then tries to save on costs and to increase production. What emerges as the most common and convenient way is the use of family labor: wife, children, and other relatives are recruited to work on the farm. However, the cash share which the grower receives from the company, after expenses are deducted, is barely enough to constitute a subsistence wage. This is doubly exploitative considering that the labor expended is not only the grower's but also that of his family.

The nature of banana production also severely limits efforts at income-augmenting activities, particularly for women. Chemicals used in agribusiness are hazardous for workers and often fatal to livestock. Therefore, it is risky to grow vegetables in the backyard. For fear of contamination, most grower households purchase all the food they eat.

In multinational factory operations within the industry, women—particularly the young, single, and better educated—are contracted (often subcontracted) as casual or piece-rate workers. These workers are assigned to the "delicate" operations (dehanding, cleaning, weighing, and packing of bananas). They sometimes work 24-hour days. When bananas have to be shipped, in an average eight-hour day some of these women may receive minimum wages, but only because they work at high speed.[13]

Thus the recent push for capitalist expansion in staple-crop and export agriculture has continued to result in disadvantageous conditions unique to women because of their position in familial and societal structures: women are the supplementary workers in family farms, the only adult workers in households which they maintain, secondary wage laborers in plantations, and casual workers in agribusiness factory operations.

GENDER AND CLASS IN THE CITY

As possibilities for survival in the village dwindle, rural poor households are faced with the necessity of leaving. Movement may be in stages: a son or daughter is sent elsewhere or the husband begins a seasonal migration to other areas. Remittances sometimes help in augmenting the earnings of those who stay. But often even these earnings are not sufficient, and entire households of income earners decide to move.

It is not known how many of the rural poor actually make their way to the city. Most move from farm to farm, village to village, or province to province in search of economic opportunities, and it is usually the younger and more educated who migrate to the cities. Those landless workers who do find their way to the city add to the large number of workers who cluster in low-paying services and unorganized-sector occupations.

Females dominate in the movement from countryside to city, primarily because males have more reason to stay behind.[14] Faced with further fragmentation of agricultural land and dwindling economic resources, household strategy has been increasingly to concentrate marginal landholdings in the hands of sons. If resources are available, daughters may be given an education.[15] This strategy is supported by the limited options open to unmarried women in agricultural work.[16]

Literally pushed out of the rural sector, poor women who lack resources, proper education, and relevant skills often find themselves in marginal, low-paying occupations in the city. The extent to which the urban sector draws on the supply of labor provided by poor rural migrants is seen in the structure of the urban labor market.

The service sector is the most important provider of jobs after agriculture.[17] During the past decade or so the service sector has increasingly absorbed labor, the decline in the share of agricultural employment being roughly matched by the expansion of service employment.[18] But this growth has not brought about any significant changes in the organization of the large, low-wage, unorganized sector, which contrasts with a relatively small, high-wage, organized sector. Average income differentials between the two groups remain large.

The Unorganized Sector

Women dominate the unorganized subsector: while their proportion in the total national work force was about 33 percent in 1974, their proportion in the services sector was about 60 percent. A consistently high percentage of women are urban maids, self-employed, or unpaid family workers in petty commerce (mainly small retail *sari-sari* stores, hawking, peddling, and street vending). Men, by contrast, are concentrated in government, community, business, and recreational services. The extent to which males are increasingly being absorbed by the organized sector is reflected in the percent change from self-employed to wage and salary workers—from 30 percent in 1956 to 64 in 1974. For females the change was only from 40 to 42 percent.[19]

Women also earn less than men. The wage differentials in each of the service categories were biased toward the male, with the biggest differential in domestic service, the least in government and allied services.[20] Women's wages also experienced a lower percentage increase in domestic and personal services: 25 percent from 1956 to 1974, compared to men's wages, which rose 36 percent in the same period.

The gap in labor productivity and in wages between organized and unorganized commerce reveals the peripheral nature of the petty-commerce activities of the service sector, in which women predominate. Output per person in organized commerce is about six times as high as in unorganized commerce. The wage difference between a general grocery store and a *sari-sari* store is about four to one; between these and petty selling even greater. In petty commerce the ratio of self-employment to wage employment for males fell between 1959 and 1967, then rose again from 1967 to 1971, while for females it rose steadily over the entire period.[21] In addition, the ratio of female family employment to wage employment rose through the whole period. Thus the unorganized-services sector, with its low earnings, low capital intensity, and long working day, affords a convenient venue for capitalist accumulation and expansion and depends heavily on female labor.

A glimpse of the economic and social life of poor urban women is provided by studies of hawkers and vendors and of life in squatter and slum colonies—the urban space which provides a "haven" for the poverty ridden urban masses. Thousands of hawkers and street vendors ply their trade in Manila, the country's principal city. A 1973 study estimates that approximately two out of three of these hawkers are female (Guerrero 1975). They are relatively older than the males and tend to specialize in commodities such as food, which, on the average, generate less earnings. Hawkers barely make enough to constitute a minimum daily wage; two out of three earn less than one Philippine pound a day (the legal minimum wage at the time of the survey was about 15 pesos). They usually work from nine to twelve hours. Almost a third have been hawkers for ten or more years. For practically all, peddling is the sole occupation. Hawkers have very little education and usually peddle because they know of no other way to make a living. Four out of five either had no previous employment or were formerly working in low-skilled occupations such as domestic service. Since the type of work a hawker performs does not fit the city's model of order and efficiency, the hawker is constantly subjected to apprehension or harassment by law-enforcement agents. Hawkers invariably live in squatter or slum neighborhoods.

The urban space occupied by hawkers and other urban poor provides the most visible evidence of uneven development within city limits. In 1970 roughly 32 percent of Manila's population lived in slum and squatter colonies. This was approximately 184,000 families or 1.1 million persons (Laquian: n.d.). The average yearly family income of this population ranged from 1,200 to 1,800 pesos in 1971 (Guerrero 1975), while the average income of city residents was 5,200.

Survival Strategies of Squatters

A study of a squatter area by Lopez and Hollnsteiner (1976) gives some insight into the survival strategies of these families. Only 44 percent of both spouses in the area were regularly employed (and even this was often on a day-to-day

basis in jobs like scavenging or vending); 16 percent were sporadically employed; the rest were unemployed. A third of the women worked at home
either part of the time or exclusively, mostly taking in laundry. Eight out of ten
mothers had preschool children, which may explain why they restricted their
work to areas around the neighborhood. The household's daily per capita
income of 1.93 pesos was below the minimum of 2.33 pesos set by the Food
and Nutrition Research Center as the cost of a basic minimum diet. Income
was augmented by the maximum use of labor in the family; children had to
discontinue their schooling to help out. Still, families tried to economize on
purchases and curtail wants to eke out some savings. In emergencies families
relied on kin for help or resorted to informal sources of credit at exorbitant
interest rates, usually 20 percent a week. Dwellings were in a deplorable state,
toilets were nonexistent, open drainage was common, and electricity and
piped water were largely unavailable. The physical costs to these urban
dwellers were malnutrition and poor health. Their condition provides a stark
contrast to the amenities afforded by affluent residences and high-rise apart-
ments, a contrast similar to that between subsistence agriculture and industrial agribusiness and corporate farms in rural areas.

CONCLUSION

When an estimated 45 percent [22] of a country's households experience poverty, general indices of economic growth become almost irrelevant. How can a
country's pattern of economic growth be deemed satisfactory, when it has
been accompanied by the widespread experience of the poverty here briefly
presented? The examples given, however, serve merely as illustrations, and do
not deal with numerous other varieties of poor, such as subsistence fishermen,
upland farmers, and cultural minorities.

Within poor households, the experience of poverty is different for women
and for men. However, while emphasizing differences among households with
different access to economic assets and resources generates little argument in
the Philippines, pointing out differences between women and men usually
does. It has been argued that with all the inequalities existing in the Philippines, inequalities between women and men are the "lesser" of the country's
problems (Castillo 1979). It is a mistake to think in these terms. True, it is not
useful to dwell exclusively on the inequalities between women and men; but it
is necessary to deal with gender inequalities if one is to understand the
structure of inequalities generally.

As the foregoing illustrations demonstrate, Filipino women experience
poverty differently from men because their relations within the family affect
their relations to the large society. Because the housewife role is historically
and culturally central to the identity of women, they constitute the unpaid and
necessary core of a surplus labor pool available for manipulation by capital.
As wives and mothers, poor women are invariably household workers as well

as unpaid family labor or wage earners. In marginal farm households, where family labor is maximized to increase production, women generally work as unpaid family labor. In landless agricultural and share-tenancy households, women join labor gangs or do plantation wage work. In nonagricultural work in urban areas, women constitute a pool of low-paid labor as marginally self-employed or as wage earners in the unorganized-service sector. In every case, women earn less than men.

The situation becomes doubly oppressive when women are the only adult income earners. Female-headed households, estimated to be between 10 and 15 percent of all households,[23] tend not to have an unpaid family worker or secondary income earner. Thus, it is not surprising to find that the most impoverished households are generally headed by females.

A time-use survey I conducted (Eviota 1979) demonstrated that when women take on outside economic responsibilities, their supposedly primary responsibility in the household is not diminished. Employed Filipino women spent an average of twenty more hours per week than their husbands in combined household and nonhousehold work. Their double day created extreme time pressures, not to mention physical strain, for these women. The amount of time devoted to relatively fixed economic and social responsibilities was more than doubled when the demands of housework and family were added to the time spent at paid work. Yet husbands were not inclined to do their share; husbands of employed women reported little more involvement in housework than husbands of employed women. And when husbands did perform some chores, they were the more peripheral activities; the wife remained responsible for the core of household obligations.

The plight of women, with their bond to the household and their consequent double shift, cannot be more clearly demonstrated than in the use of their time. Women's work in the home makes possible at no cost to capital the material and social-psychological reproduction of the labor force. And when social production is added to domestic production, exploitation is doubly acute.

The pace of economic development is accelerating in the Philippines, and women in particular are readily exploited through their position in the familial and societal structure. In many cases, the availability of abundant and low-paid female labor has been an important attraction to multinational corporations. Multinational electronics firms, for example, employ thousands of young women workers at barely minimum wages under sometimes difficult conditions of work (Eviota 1980). Most of these firms have already exploited young women workers of other Southeast Asian countries. As wages in a country rise, firms move to other countries. It will not be long before wages in the Philippines will seem high, prompting multinational firms to look elsewhere for lower-paying labor. However, the skills which women have learned are characteristically fragmented, limited to a particular operation, and not applicable to other types of work.

In sum, the existence of a large pool of low-paid labor, of landless agricultural workers, and of low-income self-employed and unpaid family workers is a consequence of the type of capitalist development path the international political economy opens up and which local class interests in the Philippines choose to follow. This development has favored urban centers and commercial and industrial sectors, while it imposes great hardships on the rural population. It is a development from which international capital and a local dominant class profit at the cost of the absolute impoverishment of large masses of people. It is also a development which has not simply overlooked the situation of poor women; instead it has pushed them into an increasingly disadvantaged position.

Notes

1. The principal criterion in the definition of class is the relation to the means of production. Lenin (1952) states:

Classes are large groups of people differing from each other by the place they occupy in a historically determined system of social production, by their relation (in most cases fixed and formulated in law) to the means of production, by their role in the social organization of labor, and consequently, by the dimensions of the share of social wealth of which they dispose and the mode of acquiring it. Classes are groups of people one of which can appropriate the labor of another owing to the different places they occupy in a definite system of social economy.

2. The capitalist mode of production has ideological and political characteristics, but it is the manner in which capital appropriates labor that is emphasized in this chapter.

3. Szymanski (1976) also mentions other ways capitalism profits from sexist ideology: sexist degradation and dehumanization serve, as does racism, as safety valves for venting the frustrations of men; and sexism is seen as motivating male workers to perform, with relatively little resistance, with women presented as rewards for achievement.

4. The following table shows this decrease compared to the change for the top 20 percent:

Percentage of Income Accrued	1956			1965			1971		
	Total	Rural	Urban	Total	Rural	Urban	Total	Rural	Urban
Lowest 20 percent	4.5	7.0	4.5	3.5	5.0	3.8	3.8	4.4	4.6
Highest 20 percent	55.1	46.1	55.3	55.4	47.2	57.5	53.9	51.0	50.7

SOURCE: Calculations from ILO (1974), based on Family Income and Expenditure Survey data, National Census and Statistics Office.

5. This estimate is calculated from table 3 of Bautista (1977) on farm laborers and from table 30 of ILO 1974 on employment in organized- and unorganized-services sector.

6. Near-landless families—those with small holdings or insecure tenant rights, represented 52 percent of the rural families in 1971 (Esman 1978). Although these families have their own land to till, with factors such as the structures of land reform, population pressures, and a state of indebtedness, they are likely to join the ranks of the landless in the near future (Bautista 1977). In this chapter, the term "landless agricultural workers," unless otherwise indicated, includes the near-landless.

7. The following table shows the 1975 proportions of female farm laborers by crop area.

Crop area	Total	%	Female	%
Rice/corn	2,364,546	69.0	928,396	39.3
Sugar/cane	381,344	11.0	77,285	29.3
Fruit, vegetables, root crops	297,347	8.5	141,663	47.7
Coconuts	294,183	8.5	64,734	22.1
Tobacco	88,827	2.5	37,261	42.0
Abaca	19,269	.5	2,791	14.5
Total	3,445,516	100.0	1,252,130	36.3

SOURCE: National Census and Statistics Office, cited in Bautista (1977).

8. The two main criteria used for deriving a poverty line are the consumption of the "representative poor" and the "least-cost" consumption basket necessary to meet specified minimum needs. In each case the major component of the consumption basket is food. The poverty line for a household is the cost for a typical six-member family. The poverty incidence rate is the proportion of households below this line (World Bank 1980).

9. The source of my discussion on share tenants is Takahashi (1977).

10. Data on sugar-plantation workers are from Tejada (1977) and Ledesma (1980).

11. As Tejada (1977) points out, however, because the contract system is recognized by the government, it is legal to pay below the minimum wage.

12. Information on the banana export industry (mainly Stanfilco, a subsidiary of Dole) is from David et al. (1980) and ICL (1979).

13. A study by Utrecht (1977) on plantation export agriculture (pineapples) found that in factory operations, the multinational agribusiness firms of Dole and Del Monte seek still other ways of saving on already low labor costs. These companies put pineapple workers in the position of "beginners" or "nonregulars" for as long as possible in order to skip the minimum-wage-law provision. In cannery work, women workers suffered from discrimination and were reported to be receiving lower wages than men.

14. The extent of the dominance of females in migration and the implications of this dominance are explored in Eviota and Smith (1980). The estimated net emigration in thousands in 1979 was 42.6 for men and 58.6 for women. The biggest differential occurred between the ages of twenty and thirty-four years.

15. See, for example, Smith & Cheung (1981).

16. A high share of the nonagricultural activities in rural areas is concentrated in manufacturing and a particularly high share of rural employment in manufacturing—67 percent—is female (ILO 1974).

17. Parts of this section on organized and unorganized sectors are from ILO (1974).

18. However, the average number of hours worked in agriculture for both sexes went up from 40.7 in 1964 to 42.4 hours per week in 1972. The increase for males was 43.8 to 44.8 hours and for females from 30.4 to 33.9 hours weekly. Thus, there was an average total increase of 1.0 hour for males and of 3.5 hours for females (ILO 1974).

19. Statistics on the services subsectors are from Jurado and Tidalgo (1978).

20. Domestic service presents a situation where women of a particular class have an immediate participation in subordinating women of other classes. Women and men of wealthy and even intermediate classes exploit women of the working, peasant, and poor classes in the use they make of servants to help minimize conflicts they face in their professional and family role enactments and to further their own class interests.

21. The following table shows the proportion of the ratio of self-employed workers and of family workers to wage and salary earners in commerce.

| | 1961 | | 1967 | | 1971 | |
	SE/WE	*FL/WE*	*SE/WE*	*FL/WE*	*SE/WE*	*FL/WE*
Total	235	55	230	67	240	59
Males	157	21	117	24	143	16
Females	140	100	419	138	433	142

SOURCE: ILO (1974).

SE = self-employed; WE = wage earner, FL = unpaid family labor.

22. Of this, 47.5 percent are in rural areas and 40 percent are in urban areas (World Bank 1980).

23. A multinational study on the subject, supported by the U.S. Agency for International Development, calculated this estimate from 1970 census categories.

13

Planned Development, Social Stratification, and the Sexual Division of Labor in Singapore

ALINE K. WONG

Singapore, a city republic of 2.3 million, has recently captured the interest of social scientists because of its rapid economic development since 1965.* Under British colonial rule, Singapore had thrived as a major commercial center and entrepôt port in Southeast Asia. Shortly after independence and separation from the Federation of Malaysia in 1965, the government of Singapore embarked on extensive programs of industrialization. As a result, the economy has grown rapidly, and Singapore is now ranked among the middle-income countries by the World Bank.[1]

As Singapore industrialized, the population experienced a rapid decline in fertility that brought the natural rate of increase from 2.3 percent in 1966 down to 1.2 percent in 1979. Changes in fertility, together with rapid economic development and a rising level of education, have significantly altered the lives of men and women in the republic. While some of the social and economic changes have benefited women, the effects of others are questionable. A number of important issues arise in the following discussion of the role of women in Singapore's development and the impact of development on the sexual division of labor and on women's status. Here, as in other countries, women's roles and women's status are intrinsically linked to their productive and reproductive activities, their class and ethnic affiliations. A brief descrip-

*An earlier version of this chapter appeared in *Signs*, vol. 7, no. 2, Winter 1981. © 1981 by The University of Chicago.

tion of development planning in Singapore must preface discussion of women's roles.

PLANNED DEVELOPMENT IN SINGAPORE

Like most other developing economies, Singapore began with import substitution as a mode of industrial development. The government, however, soon realized the shortcomings of this development strategy, particularly in light of Singapore's lack of natural resources and its small domestic market. Thus, beginning in the early 1970s, it adopted an export-oriented industrialization strategy, with a heavy reliance on the inflow of foreign capital and technology (J. Wong 1979:71–75). By offering tax incentives and appropriate factory sites, providing efficient infrastructural and public services, and strictly controlling labor unrest, the government was able to attract the foreign capital that has since laid the foundation for Singapore's industrial growth (Lee 1973; Keng-Swee 1972; Yoshihara 1976). In 1978, although foreign-owned or joint-venture firms constituted only 33 percent of manufacturing establishments, they accounted for 82.7 percent of the total output value, and 78.4 percent of the value added. Furthermore, they accounted for nearly 68.7 percent of total industrial employment and 91.8 percent of direct export value of manufactured goods (Dept. of Statistics 1978).

The inflow of foreign capital and technology has taken place in Singapore within a broad framework of state economic planning. Initially socialist in orientation, the People's Action Party (PAP) has remained the single dominant political party since 1959. The PAP government has carefully orchestrated the pattern and pace of economic development—investing heavily in the public sector, creating special economic institutions, and directly participating in economic activities. Social planning is also seen as an integral part of national economic planning. The government has centralized education and relocated the majority of lower socioeconomic groups into massive public housing projects. It has instituted a highly successful national family-planning program and has legislated social policies, planning for social development in accordance with population and labor-force projections and with a perception of the necessary cultural basis for a rugged Asian society. In other words, the government has intervened extensively in almost every sphere of social and economic life, influencing work and the family as well as cultural values and psychological motivations. Political dissent, labor movements, and mass organizations have been effectively controlled to provide a stable political climate conducive to the steady inflow of foreign capital. In the process, a majority of the citizens have come to accept the firm, guiding hand of a strong government; they have become increasingly depoliticized (Heng-Chee 1975:51–68; 1976).

Even though Singapore owes much of its industrial success to a unique combination of historical, economic, and social factors, as well as to effective political leadership, its experience with development offers a number of instructive lessons to other developing countries. The neighboring countries in Southeast Asia, in fact, look to Singapore as a model of development. Similarly, Singapore's dependence on the industrial West—be it economic, social, or cultural—is a common experience shared by many Third-World countries, just as the city-republic shared with them a recent colonial past. And Singapore demonstrates the validity of a widely held belief: that in general, women are adversely affected by strategies for economic development (Tinker & Bramsen 1976).

ECONOMIC DEVELOPMENT AND WOMEN'S WORK

There is a consensus developing among social scientists that indicators of women's roles and status should be included in overall measures of socioeconomic development—indicators such as the rate of female labor-force participation, marriage age and life expectancy, and rates of fertility and divorce. Any construction of composite socioeconomic indicators has inherent problems and weaknesses. What is questionable here is an underlying assumption that there is a direct ratio between the level of economic development on one hand, and the economic participation of women and women's status on the other. Although a woman's economic activity may bring her a certain measure of economic independence as an individual, the overall pattern of women's participation in the labor force may actually indicate that women's work is not sufficient for autonomous economic development, as in the case of dependent economies, or that it at best reinforces existing class and ethnic cleavages, as in both the developed and developing countries.

The rate of economic activity among women aged fifteen years and above has increased impressively since Singapore began to industrialize in the late 1960s. In 1957, only 21.6 percent of the women were economically active. But by 1970 the rate had risen to 29.5 percent, and by 1979 to 41.9 percent (table 13.1). Increasingly, women are employed in industry and commerce. Gains in

TABLE 13.1
Female Labor-Force Participation Rates in Singapore

Economically Active Women	1957 (%)	1970 (%)	1975 (%)	1979 (%)
As proportion of total female population aged 15 and over	21.6	29.5	34.9	41.9
As proportion of total number of women and men employed	17.5	23.5	29.6	33.6

SOURCES: P. Arumainathan, *Report on the Census of Population* 1970 (Singapore: Department of Statistics, 1970), vol. 1. Ministry of Labour, *Report on the Labour Force Survey of Singapore* (Singapore, 1975, 1979).

TABLE 13.2

Distribution of Female Labor Force by Industry

Industry	1957 N	1957 %	1970 N	1970 %	1975 N	1975 %	1979 N	1979 %
Agriculture, forestry, fishing	9,819	11.7	4,796	3.1	5,033	2.0	4,305	1.3
Mining, quarrying	165	0.2	205	0.1	271	0.1	291	0.1
Manufacturing	16,301	19.4	48,121	31.3	86,210	34.9	131,464	38.4
Electricity, gas, water utilities	77	—	533	0.4	758	0.3	1,061	0.3
Construction	1,761	2.1	2,817	1.8	3,085	1.2	4,659	1.4
Commerce	13,246	15.7	28,986	18.9	55,958	22.7	83,129	24.2
Transport, communication	1,112	1.3	3,943	2.6	11,311	4.6	17,158	5.0
Finance, insurance, business services	2,013	2.4	5,305	3.5	17,480	7.1	29,325	8.6
Community, social, personal services	39,551	47.0	58,843	38.3	66,511	26.9	71,129	20.8
Others	165	0.2	63	—	379	0.2	62	—
All industries	84,210	100.0	153,612	100.0	246,996	100.0	342,583	100.0

SOURCES: See Table 13.1.

TABLE 13.3

Distribution of Female Labor Force by Major Occupational Groups

Occupational Group	1957 N	1957 %	1970 N	1970 %	1975 N	1975 %	1979 N	1979 %
Professional, technical workers	8,328	9.9	21,818	14.2	26,572	10.8	32,777	9.6
Administrative, managerial workers	259	0.3	645	0.4	1,569	0.6	1,789	0.5
Clerical workers	5,616	6.7	26,029	16.9	61,586	24.9	90,097	26.3
Sales workers	8,630	10.2	16,433	10.7	30,306	12.3	44,237	12.9
Service workers	30,112	35.7	35,884	23.4	40,318	16.3	47,877	14.0
Agricultural, animal husbandry, fishing industry workers	10,057	11.9	4,950	3.2	6,169	2.5	4,908	1.4
Production workers, transport equipment operators, laborers	21,098	25.1	47,412	30.9	79,337	32.1	120,337	35.1
Other workers	110	0.2	441	0.3	1,136	0.5	562	0.2
All groups	84,210	100.0	153,612	100.0	246,993	100.0	342,584	100.0

SOURCES: See Table 13.1.

TABLE 13.4
Female Economic Activity Rates by Marital Status

Marital Status	Economic Activity Rates			
	1957 (%)	1970 (%)	1975 (%)	1979 (%)
Single	24.8	35.6	39.1	66.5
Married	14.0	14.7	22.1	26.8
Widowed	25.8	15.5	14.8	21.4
Divorced	46.5	47.6	50.0	68.5

SOURCES: See table 13.1.

the manufacturing sector are the most prominent. In 1979, manufacturing accounted for 38.4 percent; commerce, 24.2 percent; and the services, 20.8 percent of the total female labor force (table 13.2). These changes in women's economic roles are reflected in the occupational structure itself. In 1979, 35.1 percent of the female labor force was engaged in production work, operation of transport equipment, and general labor. Clerical workers made up the next largest occupational category (26.3 percent), while 14.0 percent of the female labor force did service work (table 13.3).

As a result of the postwar baby boom, Singapore's population is young; thus the majority of new entrants into the labor market are young and single women. On the other hand, there has also been an increasing proportion of married women seeking employment. In 1957, the economic activity rate among married women was only 14.0 percent, but it rose to 26.8 percent by 1979 (table 13.4).

Female Labor-Force Participation

The rates and patterns of economic activity among women no doubt reflect the expanding employment opportunities of a rapidly growing economy. Three other factors for female employment, however, must be noted. First, female economic participation is inextricably bound to the pattern of foreign investment in Singapore. Second, the recent increase in employment of married women is a result of the rising cost of living in Singapore as the economy goes multinational, leaving Singapore wide open to the inflationary tendencies of the world market economy. Third, employment for some married women represents a return to the labor market after an initial loss of independent economic status; many were previously engaged in self-employment, agricultural work, and service jobs. All of these factors have important implications for understanding the role of women in Singapore's economic development, and they indicate as well some adverse effects of development on the women themselves.

Singapore's industrial success, then, has depended heavily on foreign investment. The interrelationship between women's employment and Singapore's economic dependence on the industrial West is clear; the majority of female industrial workers are engaged in light manufacturing financed by foreign capital, particularly in the electronics, textile, and garment industries. These labor-intensive industries have traditionally been characterized by a predominance of female labor, even in advanced capitalist economies. Recently established branches of such industries in developing countries actually represent a last stage in the constant search for cheap labor, made possible by the increasing fragmentation of the labor process and the international free flow of capital (see ch. 4). The semiconductor branch of the electronics industry, in particular, has literally built a global assembly line encompassing almost all the countries of Southeast Asia (Grossman 1979:2–17).

In Singapore, as elsewhere in the developing world, foreign corporate managers consider women workers to have special qualities—docility, diligence, and the "swift fingers" and tolerance necessary for repetitive tasks—that make them especially suitable for unskilled work in the export-processing industries. In spite of keen competition among the firms for female workers, wages are low and employment is unstable, fluctuating with world market demands for the products. Thus, when economic recession came in the wake of the world oil crisis, female workers felt the impact first. In 1974 alone, out of the 16,900 workers who were retrenched, 79 percent were women. Singapore weathered the crisis and recovery was quick. But the long-expected American recession in 1980 again brought about massive layoffs of female electronics workers in large U.S. firms (*Straits Times* 10 Oct. 1980).

Age and Marital Status

The light-manufacturing industries generally prefer to hire young, single women. Young workers are more easily trained and can be paid less because of their lack of seniority. Older, married workers, then, are easily displaced, even during periods of full employment. This displacement has occurred, although the expanding economy has been able to absorb more married women into the commerce and the service sectors. Married workers, however, encounter discriminatory practices in recruitment as well as promotion. Whether working in the industrial or service sector, married women are generally regarded as less productive and less committed to their work because of their family responsibilities. Yet married women have to seek outside employment because of the rising costs of living, a fact made clear in recent surveys (A. K. Wong, 1979).

The age-specific rates of female economic participation and the historical distribution of the female labor force by industry indicate that it was easier for married women in the past to combine work and family responsibilities. The present pattern of age-specific activity appears to be unimodal (table 13.5). The highest participation rate is found among young single women between

TABLE 13.5
Age-Specific Female Economic Activity Rates

Age Group (Years)	1957 %	1970 %	1979 %
15–19	23.4	43.0	43.1
20–24	22.9	53.6	76.6
25–29	16.5	30.8	55.3
30–34	17.3	22.7	40.8
35–39	20.8	19.3	37.7
40–44	26.3	17.8	31.7
45–49	30.1	17.5	25.6
50–54	28.8	17.5	19.2
55–59	24.7	16.2	16.2
60–64	17.1	13.4	12.5
65 and over	5.8	6.5	7.5
All age groups	21.6	29.5	41.9

SOURCES: See Table 13.1.

the ages of twenty and twenty-four. The rate steadily declines for every older age group, with no resurgence among women in their early forties, as is typical of developed countries, where women with older children return to the work force. In 1957, the activity rates were much more evenly distributed throughout the various age groups, even though the overall rate of participation was much lower than the present. This implies that older women and married women with children were able to find some kind of paid employment in the past. The jobs they held, however, were quite different then. Nearly 50 percent of women workers in 1957 were in community, social, and personal services, with another 16 percent in commerce and 12 percent in agricultural activities (table 13.2). These occupations did not discriminate against older, married women.

The Informal Sector

Women who worked on family farms and in small businesses, as domestic servants, or as hawkers and traders were engaged in the informal sector of the economy which, some researchers estimate, provided employment for 23 percent of the 1970 labor force (Lin-Sien & Siow-Yue 1978). Although earnings were small and working hours long, women could derive some measure of economic independence from these activities. In most developing economies, the informal sector has persisted and has remained important, especially in providing employment for the urban poor. Development economists used to view the informal sector as backward or marginal—an anomaly caused by the slow growth of the formal sector. Now the more dominant view is that the informal sector serves some very useful functions for the developing economy, and is attractive to the workers themselves, when compared with wage employment in the formal sector. The boundaries of this informal sector are difficult to draw, but there is evidence that its size in Singapore has declined considerably for several reasons: the rapid expansion of the formal sector; the increasing emphasis placed on educational training requirements for entry into industrial and commercial jobs; urban renewal and relocation programs, which disrupt traditional trading and marketing activities; and increasing government regulation of formerly unregulated activities, such as hawking. The shrinkage of the informal sector has important implications for the economic activity of women since informal-sector activities typically require little capital outlay and minimal training or skills and are characterized by ease of entry, flexible working hours, and opportunity for self-employment. The shrinkage of this sector may mean that women who could not find jobs in the formal sector because of age, education, or family responsibilities will have fewer opportunities to find employment in what remains of the informal sector. More definite observations on the shrinkage of this sector await further research.

Because of a tight labor supply and rising wages, the Singapore government realized late in 1978 that its strategy for industrial development had to take a new twist if Singapore was to survive competition from neighboring countries that still offered very cheap labor and equally attractive incentives to foreign capital. Hence, Singapore is embarking on a third stage in its industrialization, one which emphasizes capital-intensive, high-technology, and high-value-added industries in place of the former emphasis on labor-intensive processing industries (Chee-Meow 1980:144–54). This strategy calls for the development of indigenous industrial technology and skills, but it does not necessarily reduce Singapore's dependence on the industrial West for continued economic development, at least not in the short run. Singapore will still seek the overseas markets of the industrial West for its industrial products. Foreign expertise will still be required to help upgrade the skills of the Singapore workers. Although the government has set up an industrial skills development fund for retraining workers and upgrading their skills, it is by no means clear how women workers will benefit from such government assistance. In fact, a recently published guideline for applications to use the fund indicates that women workers, most of whom are unskilled, cannot apply, since the fund is earmarked for higher skills development rather than for basic training (*Straits Times* 9/26 1980). It is also easy to predict that women will bear the brunt of Singapore's industrial transformation, as they will be the first victims of industrial layoffs resulting from the structural transformation of industries and the withdrawal of multinational firms to neighboring countries in search of lower wage costs.

The tight labor supply has had another consequence for female labor-force participation. Because of the local labor shortage, the government has been admitting large numbers of migrant workers from neighboring countries, primarily Malaysia, on a work-permit basis. A sizable proportion of the work force in Singapore, then, is of foreign citizenship—8.8 percent in 1979 (Ministry of Labour 1979).[2] The majority of the migrant workers are men who work in the production and construction industries, but female migrant workers have come to constitute a substantial proportion of the women working in manufacturing and in personal services. In 1979, 9.3 percent of the total number of female workers in manufacturing were not citizens of Singapore. Most of these migrant workers were concentrated in the textile, garment, electrical, and electronics industries. As many as 13.0 percent of the female workers in personal and household services were also of foreign citizenship. Recently, the government has been issuing work permits to foreign workers other than Malaysians—to Thai women working in the textile and electronics industries, and to Filipino women working in domestic service.[3] Migrant workers are not necessarily discriminated against in pay, but they are subject in greater degrees to unstable employment and low unionization, and are restricted in geographical and job mobility and even in their options regarding marriage and family.[4]

Although the international migration of labor has long been researched by social scientists, the focus on female migrant workers is a recent phenomenon. Apart from a small number of studies, this important area of research has yet to be developed in Singapore and Malaysia (Lim 1978; Heyzer 1983; Chee-Hoe 1981).

CLASS, STATUS, AND WOMEN'S EDUCATION

In Singapore, educational development has been deliberately geared toward the economy's changing labor-force requirements. The educational reforms of the 1960s and those of more recent years have brought both the structure and content of education in line with the government's industrialization strategies. Emphasis on technical training and science is introduced at the junior-high-school level and, for some students, right after primary education (Keng-Swee 1978).[5] Under the colonial regime, education in the English language and in the arts and humanities was the prerequisite for entering secure jobs in civil service and the professions. Now education in science and technology provides the certificates to industrial jobs and professional training in management to top positions in business. English proficiency is a basic requirement for most types of occupations in Singapore's open economy.

There is little question that girls and young women have been able to benefit from the expanding educational opportunities. In 1978 they constituted 47.1 percent of the primary-school enrollment, 51.6 percent of the secondary-school enrollment, and 43.0 percent of the university enrollment (Dept. of

Statistics 1978–79). But in spite of the almost equal split in the student population between girls and boys, sex-role segregation is very evident in the educational system. Young women tend to elect the academic and vocational streams, rather than the technical stream. In 1978, for example, only 8.3 percent of the students enrolled in technical and vocational institutes were female. At the postsecondary level, while 84.2 percent of the students training at the Institute of Education were women, only 20.1 percent of those at technical colleges were. This lack of technical training means that women with a high-school education or less generally become semiskilled or unskilled workers when they enter industry. Women also tend to concentrate in other low-pay, low-status jobs in commerce and the services; they form the majority of the domestic-service workers, stenographers and typists, clerks and cashiers, tailors and dressmakers.

In the universities the difference in the subjects chosen by women and men is also obvious. As in many countries, young women in Singapore tend to study the arts, the social sciences, and other science subjects, all of which prepare them primarily for the teaching profession. Although more women have taken up law, accounting, and business administration in recent years, other professions such as medicine, engineering, and architecture remain largely male dominated. Medicine, a field of study that assures the graduate lifelong high income and social status, is restrictive for female students. By explicit policy, the Minister of Health recently declared a 30 percent quota for female entrants into the field beginning in 1979. Among all women workers that year, 9.6 percent were working in professional, technical, or related occupations, and many of them were in the lower-status professions traditionally assigned to women: teaching, nursing, and social work. Only 0.5 percent were administrative and managerial workers, compared with 3.9 percent of the male work force.

As in other developing countries, education is an important avenue for upward social mobility in the emerging class structure. In Singapore, however, formal education is the most important determinant of initial occupational placement, subsequent career advancement, and lifelong income and social status (Clark & Eng-Fong 1979: 83–100; Eng-Fong 1975). A recent survey on the social values and attitudes of young people in Singapore also shows that an education and material wealth are considered the two most important symbols of success in life, and that working hard and getting an education are the two most important ways of achieving success in the local society (Ching-Ling 1980). Thus, the differing types of education received by women and men take on added significance; the differences tend to widen the income gap between males and females and increase sex inequality in other aspects of socioeconomic life.

ETHNIC STRATIFICATION AND WOMEN'S ECONOMIC PARTICIPATION.

The population of Singapore is heterogeneous: 76 percent are Chinese, 15 percent Malay, 7 percent Indian, and 2 percent Eurasian or other ethnicity. Each of the major groups is also divided by dialect, region, and caste. There is no definitive study on social stratification in Singapore, but the available evidence suggests that all the major ethnic groups have achieved a substantial degree of upward mobility as the social structure itself continues to open up into a middle-class society. Development in Singapore has not been accompanied by the widening income disparities that often characterize the initial stages of development in other countries (Eng-Fong 1975:15–28). But though all the ethnic groups are represented in the different social classes, a slight majority of the Chinese and the Indians are middle class, while the great majority of the Malays are lower- and working-class people (Chen 1973:15).

The economic participation of women from the major ethnic groups has been altered as a consequence of industrialization. In 1957, Chinese women had the highest economic activity rate, 21.8 percent, compared with a rate of 6.3 percent among the Malays and 7.1 percent among the Indians. By 1979, the economic activity rates of the three major groups had leveled out to approximately 42 percent each. Malay and Indian women became economically active later than the Chinese, but at a faster rate (table 13.6). In the past only the highly educated Malay and Indian women worked as professionals, usually teaching school, while those with little education took jobs in the personal services, working mainly as domestics. The largest proportion of both Malay and Indian women workers in 1979 were engaged in manufacturing; they have entered industrial jobs at a much faster rate than Chinese women. In 1970 the proportions of Malay and Indian female workers in manufacturing were 31.2 percent and 18.9 percent, respectively, compared with 32.2 percent for the Chinese. By 1979 the proportions of Malay and Indian women jumped to 55.3 percent and 41.1 percent, respectively, while the proportion of Chinese women rose only slightly, to 35.3 percent (table 13.7). Malay and Indian women have

TABLE 13.6
Female Economic Activity Rates by Ethnic Group

Ethnic Group	1957 %	1970 %	1975 %	1979 %
Chinese	21.8	27.0	31.5	42.2
Malays	6.3	14.3	22.4	42.0
Indians	7.1	16.0	25.6	42.4

SOURCES: See Table 13.1.

TABLE 13.7
Distribution of Female Labor Force by Industry and Ethnic Group

Industry	1957 %			1970 %			1979 (%)		
	Chinese (N=76,217)	Malays (N=3,438)	Indians (N=1,441)	Chinese (N=136,489)	Malays (N=9,737)	Indians (N=4,375)	Chinese (N=268,064)	Malays (N=49,977)	Indians (N=20,424)
Agriculture, forestry, fishing	12.5	8.1	2.8	3.4	1.0	0.3	1.5	0.2	0.5
Mining, quarrying	0.2	—	—	0.1	—	0.1	0.1	—	—
Manufacturing	21.0	3.7	2.1	32.2	31.2	18.9	35.3	55.3	41.1
Electricity, gas, water utilities	0.1	0.1	0.6	0.4	0.2	0.6	0.3	0.3	0.6
Construction	2.2	0.3	1.2	2.0	0.2	0.8	1.5	0.5	1.2
Commerce	16.0	10.9	8.5	19.6	11.8	12.8	27.3	12.4	13.9
Transport, communication	1.0	0.5	2.3	2.4	3.1	3.2	4.8	5.9	6.7
Finance, insurance, business services	2.3	0.6	1.7	3.6	0.9	2.3	9.1	5.9	6.7
Community, social, personal services	44.5	75.7	80.4	36.2	51.6	60.9	20.1	19.5	30.5
Other	0.2	0.1	0.4	0.1	—	0.1	—	—	—
All industries	100.0	100.0	100.0	100.0	100.0	100.0	100.0	100.0	100.0

SOURCES: See Table 13.1.

experienced a corresponding decline in the proportion of their ranks involved in community, social, and personal services. The large-scale entry of young Malay and Indian women into the manufacturing sector has come about not only as a consequence of expansion in industrial employment but also because older Chinese women are now often seeking the better-paying white-collar jobs in commerce and the services.

As long as social scientists continue to measure social class based on men's occupations, education, and other indices of household socioeconomic characteristics, the effects of women's increased economic participation on social stratification will not be evident. On one hand, women's gainful employment brings additional income to the household, perhaps enhancing its resources for upward social mobility. On the other hand, women's employment among both the working and the middle classes may be necessary for such families simply to maintain their present social class positions. In any case, it is not likely that women's employment has great potential for changing the relative class status of ethnic groups in the near future.

Among the Malays and the Indians in particular, recent rapid entry into the industrial labor force may have serious repercussions for individuals and families, as industrial work brings drastic changes in work routines and lifestyles. Periodic press reports of outbreaks of mass hysteria among young Malay women workers in electronics assembly plants bear witness to the psychological adjustment problems faced by such workers in a dehumanized work setting. Furthermore, industrial employment may change women's family roles, reproductive behavior, and self-perceptions.

REPRODUCTION AND WOMEN'S STATUS

The traditional religiocultural systems of Confucianism, Hinduism, and Islam prescribed a subordinate status to women within the household. Whether born Chinese, Indian, or Malay, a woman was socialized from a young age both to play the roles of wife, mother, and daughter-in-law, and to lead a secluded life. Not much is known about the status of women in premodern Singapore, but there is evidence that immigrant women had a higher social standing than in their native countries due to Singapore's customs and the experience of immigration (A. K. Wong 1975). Before independence, Singapore was a commercial port. The status of women did not depend only on their cultural background; it also varied according to the social status of their fathers and husbands—whether they were merchants, civil bureaucrats, and skilled artisans, or laborers and farmers. And like so many other stratified societies, women in the lower classes seemed to enjoy more effective control over their own and household activities. Among upper-class women, seclusion was an unavoidable fact of life. It was uncommon for women to be educated; on the other hand many women helped run family businesses, engaged in the sale of farm and fishery products, or controlled the family purses. These were not the fabled manipulative Asian women who were said to wield influence but not power within the household; they were women who, under certain circumstances and by customary practice, had actual control over their households.

As Singapore's economy becomes increasingly urban based and industrialized, the separation of the private and public domains becomes more apparent. Men entered wage-earning occupations, while women forfeit their previous income-earning activities that arose from home production. Women also lose material support from their kin as the individual family unit is disengaged from kin-based economic production. The issue of whether a married woman can successfully combine home and a career arouses a strong emotional reaction from the public, which demonstrates that women's work is now defined as work outside the home and is therefore considered incompatible with family responsibilities.

Over time, the age of marriage in Singapore has risen to an average of twenty-eight years for men and twenty-four years for women. Marriages are now primarily a matter of individual choice, and young couples generally form independent households right after marriage. Furthermore, small families with two or three children have become the norm. Education and economic employment have had definite effects on the age of marriage for women. Young women now have ample opportunities for paid work. Many postpone marriage in order to enjoy personal freedom, friendship and social activities with other workers, and the release from household chores, as well as to help support their parents and younger siblings. Because young women do not expect to continue working very long after marriage, especially after childbirth, they are motivated to postpone marriage as long as possible. But marriage remains the single most important life goal.

Among young people in Singapore, the ideal husband-and-wife relationship is identified as the companionship type common in modern Western societies. There is, however, a strong emphasis on the husband being the main provider and the wife being a good mother. A clear-cut conception of separate sex roles is evident (Swee-Hock & Wong 1981). Although some recent studies have shown that husbands and wives share decision making over a large number of family matters, especially when the wives work, housework and child care have remained the wives' main responsibilities even when they work outside the home (A. K. Wong 1980).

It is difficult to conclude that women in Singapore have made indisputable gains in family status. Education and employment have served to increase role strain and psychological pressure for working women. Well-educated professional women have held their ground and continued their pursuit of independent careers, generally with the help of paid domestic servants and some willing relatives. Lower-class women have little choice but to work in order to augment meager household incomes. They do so by alternating household duties and working shifts and by calling on relatives or child-care workers to watch their children.

Because of the shortage of part-time jobs for women, many have had to do shift work in the manufacturing industries,[6] especially in the electrical and electronics industry, which also hires predominantly female workers. A recent National Productivity Board survey of production workers reveals that 58 percent of a total of 16,017 shift workers in 419 manufacturing firms were women. The survey also shows that Singapore women take up permanent night work nearly three times more than men (*Sunday Times* 1980). A study of the child-care problems of low-income mothers with preschool children living in public flats found that 43 percent of the working mothers were shift workers. In order to work shifts, many women have had to send their children to relatives, or to professional child-care workers when relatives are unavailable. But even with child-care help, shift workers tire more easily and more often than other working mothers (A. K. Wong 1980).

Among working mothers as a whole, 23 percent send their preschool children to relatives or child-care workers, and of this 23 percent, as many as 10 percent leave their children with the caretaker for the entire work week or more. In some cases, then, children do not get to see their mothers except on weekends or on even less frequent visits. Work may mean a measure of economic independence for women and give them some say in family matters, but it also means a double day for women who carry the major responsibility for housework and child care.

CONCLUSION

Development has hardly altered the sexual division of labor in Singapore. Women are now better educated and have expanded economic opportunities; they bear fewer children and enjoy more personal freedom. But they have not benefited fully from the development process. Most of the female workers earn very low wages and are engaged in low-status, dead-end jobs.[7] In all occupational categories women are earning much less than their male counterparts, even when education is held constant. The income differential is the greatest at the upper end of the educational scale (Ministry of Labour 1978). Homemakers and women who work outside the home continue to bear the major burden of reproductive activities—household chores, child care, and family-status maintenance. Even if economic employment has brought personal independence to single or married women, their family status has not been translated into public status.[8]

Many argue that integrating women in development will raise their status. This argument is usually accompanied by a call for expanded educational and employment opportunities for women. But in Singapore, and in other developing countries as well, it is clear that expanded opportunities have not necessarily altered the sexual division of labor. As long as sexual segregation characterizes the occupational world and women are bound by domestic responsibilities, they will remain a peripheral work force. Singapore's dependent economic development also tends to transform women into a type of reserve labor force. An official comment on a labor force survey made the government's attitude toward female workers very clear. The survey found that nearly half a million married women in 1979 were staying home, and that only 7.6 percent of them would consider taking a job. Government officials responded: "This figure, low as it is, can still go a long way towards relieving the current labour shortage." Those women, the government knew, could fill at least twenty thousand full-time vacancies.

Notes

1. In 1977, the per capita GNP for Singapore was U.S. $2,880 (World Bank 1979).

2. Figures on foreign workers in the survey are typically underestimated due to inadequate coverage of workers in the construction industry, which employs large numbers of foreign men. Official figures on the numbers of work-permit holders are not available, but there are unofficial estimates of 100,000–120,000 foreign workers in Singapore.

3. In 1979 there were about one thousand Thai female factory workers in Singapore (Chee-Hoe 1981). The estimate for Filipinos working as domestics is also around one thousand (*Straits Times* 3 Nov. 1980).

4. Foreign workers are categorized according to whether they hold professional passes or work permits. Work permits are periodically renewed and can be withdrawn if the holders "job hop." Some foreign workers have only one- or two-day work permits. Permit holders are also required to apply to the Commissioner of Labour for permission to register their marriages to Singapore citizens. If permission is granted, they must sign an agreement to be voluntarily sterilized after having two children.

5. Popularly known as the Goh Report, this document summarized past developments in education and suggests new reforms.

6. In 1979, only 6.5 percent of the women workers were engaged in part-time work, defined as less than forty hours per week (Ministry of Labour 1979).

7. The median gross monthly income for female workers in 1979 was $290 (U.S. currency) (Ministry of Labour 1979).

8. Space permits neither a discussion of women's lack of involvement in politics and mass organizations nor an overview of the sociocultural effects of Singapore's westernization, particularly the influences of multinational firms. Both have significant implications for the roles and status of women. It should be noted that feminine values are becoming more bourgeois; many women are adopting a family-centered life-style and are increasingly emphasizing beauty care, leisure-time activities, and consumerism. Multinational firms also tend to promote Western tastes in consumption and Western social activities among their female workers.

14

Rural Production and Reproduction: Socialist Development Experiences

ELISABETH J. CROLL

In this chapter* I examine the degree to which alterations in the relations of production that may be part of socialist development strategies affect the productive and reproductive activities of peasant women.[1] I am concerned with the extent to which the productive structures determine the interplay between women's reproductive activities (those related to childbearing, child care, and family maintenance) and their role in social production (or in waged employment outside the household). How far has women's role in reproduction influenced the extent and form of women's participation in social production and the sexual division of labor within employment? How far has women's participation in social production affected their role in reproduction and the sexual division of labor within the domestic sphere?

I have based my discussion of these questions on the experience of four societies—the Soviet Union, China, Cuba, and Tanzania—each of which has undergone some form of planned economic and social change as part of a socialist strategy of development.[2] In examining the implications of these strategies for the position of women, the Soviet Union and China form the primary case studies. They have each attempted on a large scale and over a period of time to redefine the position of women. Their policies in this area have been based on the premises of Marx and Engels, and they have been modified over time to resolve certain problems arising out of both the policy

*An earlier version of this chapter appeared in *Signs,* vol. 7, no. 2 Winter 1981. © 1981 by The University of Chicago.

assumptions themselves and their implementation. Moreover, their example has influenced other countries embarking on socialist strategies of development, and from this category, Cuba and Tanzania have been chosen for examination. Naturally the four have varied in their attempts to meet certain criteria basic to socialist development, but their rural development policies have included some alteration in the relations of production as part of a collectivization program. (Collectivization programs here refer to one of a number of broad processes whereby state farms, cooperatives, or communes are established as productive units and separate some production from that of individual small-producer households.) At the same time, there have been in each of these societies some explicit but variable attempts to draw women into the waged agricultural labor force[3] and, to a lesser extent, to reduce the domestic labor required of women. In this chapter I will look at each of these areas in turn—the relations of production, the position of women in the waged agricultural labor force, and the content of domestic labor in rural areas—before assessing the degree to which the sexual division of labor in production and reproduction has been subjected to change as a result of alterations in the relations of production.

RELATIONS OF PRODUCTION

The Soviet Union, China, Cuba, and Tanzania have all embarked on programs of collectivization with the aims of establishing an agricultural sector independent of individual smallholdings; reducing private property; and socializing the means of production in order to establish the state farm, the cooperative, or the commune as the unit of production. In theory, policies to collectivize fully the means of production should directly affect the position of peasant women by removing the economic foundations for the patriarch's authority to arrange and supervise production and to control property and labor. Because women would be registered individually as members of the collective, their labor should become visible, individually remunerated, and a source of economic independence. Moreover, the surplus could be collectively dispensed in establishing community services, which would help to relieve peasant women of the onerous domestic tasks that have traditionally been their lot.

Although all four societies have attempted to alter the relations of production and to establish some form of collective as a unit of production, their productive structures show a considerable degree of diversity. They vary in the extent to which the collectives have come to dominate the agricultural economy and in the amount of land still owned privately. For instance, in the Soviet Union and China, the collective is the main productive unit, and only the small private or household plot remains outside collective production; in Cuba, despite recent increases in the number of state farms and cooperatives in the rural areas, approximately 20 percent of the land is still privately owned. In Tanzania, on the other hand, although 70 percent of the rural population has been "villagized," the number of ujamaa villages (in which all but the individual plot is farmed communally) is small, and may be decreasing. Some villages have communal plots, but the lands farmed communally still constitute only a very small proportion of the total, and the individual smallholding continues to dominate the agricultural economy.

The collectives themselves also take very different forms in the four societies. In the Soviet Union and China they have evolved as the result of a collectivization process beginning with the redistribution of land, and the establishment of mutual labor or marketing cooperatives preceded the establishment of the collective as the unit of production, distribution, and accounting. In Cuba many of the large plantations and reserve lands have been converted into state farms, small farmers have been organized into supply and marketing cooperatives, and recently some small-scale peasant producers have taken steps to pool their land and cultivate it in common. In contrast, there has been no land reform in Tanzania and very little land redistribution. Although the process of villagization has concentrated producers in one settlement, the individual smallholder peasant producers who comprise these settlements cooperate only to the extent that they may collectively receive inputs and market the produce, and in some cases provide labor for the small communal plots set aside for common cultivation.

The Soviet Union

One of the most striking features of the Soviet economy is the number of women in waged labor and their central position not only in the industrial and professional work force but in agriculture as well. The high proportion of agricultural workers in the civilian labor force, the high proportion of those workers who are women, and the high proportion of women workers who are in agriculture were revealed in the 1959 census (Dodge 1966; Dodge & Feshbach 1967; Dodge 1971). This situation evolved because all but a very small proportion of the working population in pre-Revolutionary Russia were engaged in agricultural pursuits, and planting, cultivating, and harvesting were as much part of a woman's as a man's tasks. Moreover, the main impetus for the incorporation of women into waged agricultural employment in the twentieth century has been the imbalance of the sexes produced by civil war, the Second World War, collectivization, and the demands of industrial growth. The very production of the nation's food stocks to feed an increasingly urbanized and industrialized work force required an increase in peasant women's labor input. Women thus made up a substantial proportion of workers in all four sectors of the agricultural labor force: on collective farms (56.7 percent), state farms (41 percent), individual peasant farms (65.2 percent), and private subsidiary farms (90.7 percent) (Dodge 1966; Dodge & Feshbach 1967; Dodge 1971).

Typically, although there is some variation from region to region, the number of days per year that women must work is considerably lower, perhaps by fifty to a hundred, than the number required of men (Dunn & Dunn 1967; Dunn 1977). If women work fewer labor days than men on the collective farms, they more than make up for it in their contribution to the private subsidiary sector, raising livestock and cultivating garden plots to produce vegetables and fruit for household consumption and the local market. Although there has been much debate about the value of this sector to the economy as a whole, estimates show that private plots provide 80 percent of the meat products, 84 percent of milk, 90 percent of eggs and potatoes, and 75 percent of vegetables for the rural collective family's consumption (Anokhina et al. 1973; Dunn & Dunn 1967; Dunn 1977). It is women, and especially women of the older generation, who supply more than 90 percent of the labor for this sector; they may spend up to a third of their time on an average summer day tending to the livestock and vegetables (Dodge 1966; Dodge & Feshbach 1967; Dodge 1971; Ostapenko 1971).

The majority of women agricultural workers provide what is termed "physical labor": the heavier, less skilled, and nonspecialist types of work. And although in the economy as a whole women have formed an increasing proportion of the administrative, managerial, and specialized personnel, in agriculture this proportion has remained low (Dodge 1966; Dodge & Feshbach 1967; Dodge 1971). Women form just 20 percent of the agricultural administrators and 40 percent of the agricultural specialists (Dodge 1966). In his speech at the 1968 Plenum of the Central Committee of the Communist Party, Brezhnev commented on this discrepancy when he noted that women in the rural villages were still a minority among the heads of farms, brigades, dairy departments, and farm divisions. He stressed the need to train women to operate farm machinery and generally to create better employment conditions in the countryside (Ostapenko 1974).

It is estimated that, on average, about 35 percent of the members of political organizations at the national level are women, and present female membership in the Party (23 percent), the Supreme Soviet (31 percent), and local soviets (40 percent) represents some improvement over the levels for past decades (St. George 1973; Gruzdeva & Chertikhina 1975; M. G. Field 1978). This improvement is also reflected in local studies of a state farm, a collective farm, and a lumber mill carried out in the 1920s and again in 1967–68. In the 1920s it was reported that women were likely to be persuaded to spend only three to four hours per year attending meetings and villages gatherings. In the 1960s, however, 70 percent were reported to spend one to two hours per week, and 30 percent as much as two to three hours, in political work (Ostapenko 1971). On the whole, those who participate are more likely to be younger women not yet burdened with family responsibilities, and they are more likely to be active in typical women's fields of interest such as health, education, and the family. Furthermore, they are concentrated at the local and lower administrative levels. All reports suggest that women were, and still are, handicapped by their burden of household responsibilities and simply unable to match men's resources of time, commitment, training, and physical mobility. In one village study 40 percent of the women expressed a desire to be more active politically, but said that their daily routines prevented them (Ostapenko 1971). The problem was succinctly stated by the Secretary of the Soviet Women's Committee in Moscow, who suggested that because unpaid and time-consuming political work in the Soviet Union is undertaken as additional *ngruzka,* or work on top of a person's usual occupation, women just cannot compete with men (St. George 1973).

Almost as soon as the new government was established in 1917 it introduced programs to give women more control over their own fertility, granted substantial freedoms in marriage and divorce, and provided for the economic support of wives, widows, and divorcees. Measures were established to protect the health of childbearing women, and there were marked improvements in the mortality rates of women in this age group. The rearing of children was to be shared by crèches, nurseries, and boarding schools, not only because women could then be released for production outside the home, but also because children could benefit from early conditioning to collective and socialist norms (Geiger 1968). The state also established services such as canteens and laundries to reduce the domestic labor required of women.

Although much effort was expended in the calculation of the number of hours of labor required by the household, and in publicizing the uneconomic nature of the small isolated family unit, the few dining rooms that have been established are in the cities, and the quantity and quality of their service, have been the subject of constant complaint (Geiger 1968). In both rural and urban areas finding alternative forms of child care is still the main difficulty for working women. In rural areas only 6–7 percent of preschool children, compared to 37 percent of urban children, can be accommodated in permanent nurseries, although more are looked after in seasonal nurseries during periods of peak labor demand (Dodge 1966; Dodge & Feshbach 1967; Dodge 1971). Only 40 percent of the collective farms are equipped with nurseries or kindergartens, and half of these are seasonal (Dodge and Feshbach 1967).

The limited development of the service sector and the inadequacy of community facilities means that each household must continue to produce, transform, and consume most of its food and to provide its own child care. Servicing the household is very time-consuming when there is an inadequate supply of consumer goods and retail facilities, a low level of electrification, and an absence of modern plumbing, and when the production of services and appliances lags behind the country's general technological level. Time budget studies have noted that women still perform most of these unremunerated tasks and thus sleep shorter hours and enjoy less leisure than their menfolk (Field 1968; St. George 1973). There has been little effort to alter the sexual division of labor and the relations of exchange within the household through the introduction of a new ideology of sexual equality. Even the constant changes in legislative codes and procedures have not been publicized in rural areas as much as they might have been, and although there has been some suggestion in the media that what is needed to alter the sexual division of labor fundamentally in the Soviet Union is a change in the attitudes and beliefs of both sexes, there has been no real or sustained effort to achieve this (M. G. Field 1968; St. George 1973; Ostapenko 1974).

The conflict between women's productive and reproductive roles has been particularly sharpened in the Soviet Union by the government's pressure on women to bear children in order to halt the downward trend in the birthrate. The decline from 44.3 births per thousand in 1928 to 24.9 per thousand in 1960 is one of the most rapid ever recorded (Dodge 1966; Geiger 1968). Demographers and economists have warned of the adverse impact upon demographic structures, political and military power, ethnic balance, and economic development, and the government has set about creating conditions to counter the trend (Belova 1972). Several amendments to the Codes of Marriage and Family Law have protected the rights of women and offered new financial incentives to married, and for a time unmarried, women to bear more children (Schlesinger 1949). Motherhood has been extolled as a patriotic duty, and those who have had many children have been honored accordingly. Yet despite promises to the contrary, mothers are still expected to take primary responsibility for the bearing and rearing of children and for servicing the members of the household.

Women have resolved this conflict by resisting the pressures to bear more children. Several surveys in the Soviet Union reveal that there is a definite discrepancy between ideal and actual family sizes, and that one of the principal reasons for this discrepancy is women's difficulty in combining the demands of employment and of the home, and especially in finding satisfactory substitute child care (Belova 1972). This latter has been a particularly strong motive for restricting family size. There is some evidence that this tension between production and reproduction is not quite as marked in the rural areas. Certainly the birthrate for 1962 was still slightly higher in the countryside (24.9 per thousand) than in urban areas (20.0 per thousand) (Dodge 1966). Possibly the seasonality of agricultural production work may allow rural women to combine the demands of production and reproduction more easily for much of the year. Although they have to produce much of the food for their families, this may not amount to much more than the elaborate demands of shopping for food and consumer goods in urban areas. Moreover, the lack of physical mobility and the proximity of several generations of kin means that domestic labor is much more likely to be shared.

However, in both rural and urban areas, the great problem of reconciling conflicting demands and roles has particularly concerned women and formed the subject of complaints in the Soviet media (M. G. Field 1968; St. George 1973; Geiger 1968). One women doctor interviewed by a foreign observer said the main problem was that all proposals to improve women's position had so far come from the men in government and, though she appreciated their efforts on her behalf, they just could not identify with the needs of her reproductive roles. Despite all the achievements of socialism, these still remained to be satisfied; although men could advance the theories, it was women who were involved in that much-neglected area of government policy, reproduction (St. George 1973).

The People's Republic of China

In the 1950s the government of the People's Republic of China introduced a number of policies and measures to encourage women to take part in agricultural production. Although peasant women had always labored hard and for long hours within the household, they were less likely to have performed work in the fields. According to one comprehensive survey of the 1930s, men performed 80 percent of all the farm labor, women 13 percent, and children 7 percent. The major exceptions to this pattern were in the southern rice cultivation regions where women planted, transplanted, and harvested, and during the busy harvesting seasons when women in all areas probably contributed some labor (J. L. Buck 1937). A combination of government policies was introduced to overcome the many obstacles to women's laboring outside the home and to encourage them to enter social production: separate women's work teams were to be given their share of new inputs and training in technical skills; women were to be individually remunerated on the principle of equal pay for equal work; safeguards were to be established to protect their health; and facilities were planned to reduce their traditional domestic responsibilities (Croll 1979).

The Communist Party had made its first concerted effort to mobilize women for agricultural production during the Second World War when men were being recruited into the armies. Women in the northern provinces on the Communist Party bases were encouraged to take up agricultural pursuits and sideline occupations such as spinning and weaving, and 1949 estimates indicated that an average of 40–50 percent of all able-bodied women on the bases had done so (All-China Democratic Women's Federation 1949). There is no evidence that land reforms in the late 1940s and early 1950s that theoretically allocated women a share of the land especially increased the number of women entering production. In quantitative terms, the greatest increase in both the numbers of women in agricultural production and their contribution to total labor came with the establishment of collectives.

The establishment of cooperatives and communes expanded the scope of productive and service occupations available to women. Most of the reports published during the Great Leap Forward suggest that by 1958, 90 percent of all women capable of labor were working in the waged labor force. There was also a rise in the number of days worked by women, although women in the collective sphere worked less than their male counterparts, especially in the southern rice regions (Kuo-chun 1960; Schran 1969).

However, piecemeal and local reports, in the absence of national statistics, suggest that the number of women in the collective work force declined during the 1960s and 70s (*Zhongguo Funu*, 1 August 1965, 1 October 1965; *Honggi*, 30 Sept. 1969; *Renmin Ribao*, 13 May 1973). Yet it seems that women, especially older women, may take a major share in private household production—raising domestic animals such as chickens and pigs, and tending the vegetables on the private plot. Apart from the collective grain allocation, rural households are required to be largely self-sufficient in these meat and vegetable foodstuffs.

Within the rural labor force women have entered occupations that were hitherto male preserves; there are now women tractor drivers, women's fishing teams, and women agricultural engineers. At the same time, the majority of women are still to be found in certain of the least mechanized, less skilled, and lower-paid occupations. This has had the effect of reinforcing the notion that there is a natural sexual division of labor between heavy and skilled on the one hand and light and unskilled on the other (*Honggi*, 1 Feb. 1972). Media reports would also suggest that in rural areas where there is a demand for men to take part in nonagricultural occupations, a new division of labor between agricultural and nonagricultural work may have been established (*New China News Analysis*, 4 Dec. 1958, 1 Jan. 1959). These divisions of labor, both within agriculture and between agriculture and other activities, have affected the rates of remuneration to women, although there has been a consistent advance of the policy of equal pay for equal work. Wage scales continue to reflect the division of labor between lighter, less skilled and heavier, more skilled tasks as well as women's inability to contribute equal labor to the collective because of the demands of domestic labor. Agricultural tasks themselves are evaluated according to degrees of strength, skill, and experience required, and on all three counts, women or the jobs assigned to women normally are ranked lowest on the pay scale (Davin 1976; Croll 1979).

Women's increasing contribution in agricultural production was also expected to give them a greater share in controlling productive processes and allocating social and economic resources. One measure of such female participation is the number of women cadres or women who are in positions of responsibility in the Communist Party, government organs, and production units. Figures indicate that although the number of women participating in decision making has increased over the years, it still remained disproportionately low in the 1970s. Women generally represent one-third to two-fifths of the members of the Party and committees of production management. Of the 6 million new members admitted to the Communist Party between 1966 and 1973, 27 percent were women (*Renmin Ribao*, 1 July 1973, 6 March 1972). Several newspaper reports have expressed some government dissatisfaction at the continuing low proportions of women in political decision making (*Renmin Ribao*, 8 March 1973). In the many commentaries on the subject published in China, women's domestic responsibilities have been identified as the source of this discrepancy, which is compounded both by the prejudice of male leaders who want to involve women in production but not in politics and by discrimination against women in elections and appointments to positions of responsibility (*Honggi,* 1 Dec. 1973). As in the Soviet Union, many of the positions of political responsibility are part-time and unpaid, and the meetings tend to be held in the lunch hours and evenings during the peak domestic demands on women's labor.

An important component of the policies designed to encourage women to enter social production were programs to support the reproductive role of women and to reduce individual household responsibilities and chores. Marriage reforms introduced the right of free choice marriage, and contraception was made freely and readily available (Davin 1976; Croll 1980). Over the years women have increasingly benefited from the measures taken to improve and protect their health. After a significant rise in gynecological disorders following women's initial entry into agricultural production, collective management committees and women have been constantly reminded of labor protection measures to safeguard physical well-being and of special health care required before and after childbirth (*Renmin Ribao,* 16 May 1956; 12 Aug. 1956; *Zhongguo Funu,* 1 Aug. 1961). The government and women's movement have given much attention to improving hygiene and methods of childbirth and the health of mothers and infants during pre- and postnatal periods. By 1960 it was estimated that trained health workers supervised 60 percent of rural births, thus greatly reducing infant and maternal mortality (Salaff 1972). Paramedical personnel, or barefoot doctors, and a full network of local clinics have served to provide treatment and ongoing health protection to peasant women.

Domestic labor was traditionally time-consuming and onerous in rural China, where in addition to the daily washing, cooking, and child care, water had to be fetched and carried, grain stone-ground by hand, fuel gathered from the hills, clothes and shoes sewn, and vegetables pickled or dried for the long winter months. The new policies recognized that in conditions like these, most women would find it impossible to take part in regular production or political activities (*Renmin Ribao,* 13 July 1958). During the Great Leap Forward in the late 1950s, there was a concerted effort to make "all round arrangements for the people's livelihood" in order to free women for other activities. As a result, the majority of the newly created rural communes boasted a range of services available to women: community dining rooms, nurseries, kindergartens, grain-processing plants, and sewing centers. By 1959 it was estimated that in rural areas there were 4,980,000 nurseries and kindergartens and more than 3,600,000 public dining rooms (*Renmin Ribao,* 8 March 1959). One collective calculated that whereas in the past 105 persons were required for preparing meals in 105 households, now eight persons were sufficient, thereby making it possible to save over 6,000 labor days over the whole year. According to a survey in Honan province, the use of sewing machines and hand-operated mills alone helped reduce women's household labor by 40–50 percent (*Renmin Ribao,* 2 June 1958).

Initially these collective services were praised as a successful resolution of the age-old contradiction between women's participation in social production and in domestic labor. However, although an impressive array of these services was established in the late 1950s, many were closed shortly afterward, often as suddenly as they had been opened. Child-care facilities failed for several reasons: shortage of trained personnel, dissatisfaction with the levels of care, and widespread availability of grandmothers willing to look after children. Community dining rooms proved to be very expensive when unpaid domestic labor became paid labor in the public sector. Many complained about the quality of their service, and because individual stoves still had to be fueled for heat in many regions, the reduction in labor was not judged to be significant (Crook & Crook 1966). Since this large-scale experiment in the late 1950s, the distribution of community services has been very uneven in the rural areas. Corn-grinding operations are widespread, but most community dining rooms did not survive the Great Leap Forward—though many collectives still organize canteens during the very busy agricultural seasons (Sidal 1972).

Subsequent policies have led to a very gradual increase in community services, especially child care, but instead of pushing the socialization of housework, most new measures have promoted the redistribution of domestic tasks within the household. If women were to enter into the public sphere, then the corollary surely was that men should move into the domestic sphere (*Honggi*, 1 Dec. 1973). There has been much education and encouragement of men to undertake an equal share of the housework. At the time of my first trip to China, the most recent meeting of men and women called by the local women's association in several villages concerned the sharing of domestic labor. The media have published accounts of men who, as role models, no longer dismiss housework as women's work and now undertake their share (Croll 1978). This policy may have had some results among the younger generation and has certainly shaped new attitudes, although how far it has influenced action has yet to be determined. Even in the 1970s, however, policy statements have been marked by a certain ambiguity. As one article stated, "Domestic work should be shared by men and women. But some household chores should generally be done by women. . . . After a certain phase of farm work is completed during very busy seasons or on rainy days or in winter, women should be given some time off to attend to essential domestic chores" (*Honggi*, 3 March 1973). At the end of 1973, articles in the media admitted that the question of domestic labor is a continuing problem in China because of both limited material conditions and services and persisting attitudes of male supremacy (*Honggi*, 1 Dec. 1973).

Under these conditions it is the peasant women who largely continue to maintain and service the household. Without the outside agencies that provide urban women with labor-saving devices and household services, rural women must continue to transform much of what the household consumes. They participate in all three sectors of the rural economy: the individually remunerated collective sector, the private sphere, and the nonremunerated domestic sphere of the individual household. Again, one way women resolve the combined demands is by sharing the burdens of domestic labor among themselves. Women within the extended household usually do this, and older women often retire from collective labor to undertake many of the sideline activities, the domestic chores, and the care of young children (Croll 1977). There may also be some sharing between neighboring households during busy agricultural seasons. Yet women's limited participation in social production and political activities is largely due to their continued responsibility for the essential task of maintaining and rearing workers for production.

Cuba

Prior to 1959 in Cuba, in an economy characterized by underemployment and unemployment, only 17 percent of all wage labor was performed by women. They were concentrated in the professions; in textile, food, and tobacco industries; and in domestic service. Fewer than 2 percent of these women were employed in agriculture, a figure that reflected women's exclusion from physically demanding work in the predominant sugarcane industry (S. K. Purcell 1973). On the small family farms that produced rice, potatoes, peanuts, corn, coffee, tobacco, and fruits, men performed virtually all the field work and livestock care, though it does seem likely that, given the seasonal labor demands of crops such as coffee, women in poor peasant households participated in the harvesting (Nelson 1970).

Since the revolution, a number of agricultural reforms have transferred private lands to the state, and state farms have been built on the foundations of the previously extensive sugar plantations and cattle ranches. About 20 percent of the land is still farmed by small peasant producers incorporated into the National Association of Small Farmers (ANAP) (Seers 1964). In the last year or two there has been some move by small producers to form agricultural production societies that pool most of their members' land and cultivate it on a common basis; in 1977 there were approximately 275 of these societies, each having about twenty-five members.

By the early 1960s most of the underemployed and unemployed male labor in the rural areas had been mobilized, and because of the continuing shortage of labor—exaggerated during the peak seasons—women have been encouraged to enter waged agricultural production. But given the extremes in demand for labor caused by the seasonal requirements of the main crops in Cuba, women have tended to form the reserve labor force in both collective and private sectors. On the smallholding, the hiring of labor has been actively discouraged, and the family remains the primary source especially at harvest times. This means that the head of a household usually controls the allocation of a woman's labor, and she is not normally assigned independent returns. The women's organization in cooperation with ANAP has attempted to benefit peasant women individually by organizing large numbers of women from the smallholdings into Work or Mutual Aid Brigades which aim to increase women's labor input. In 1973, for example, they trained 107,247 peasant women to raise livestock and vegetables on their smallholdings which could be sold to state agencies and also organized them into a seasonal labor force for the state farms and cooperatives (Federation of Cuban Women 1974; Ruiz 1977; Murray 1978). These brigades of women participate in the harvests of sugar, coffee, tobacco, and fruits. It was estimated that almost five thousand women took part in the sugar harvest of 1976–77, thus meeting the goals of the national harvest support plan (*Granma,* 4 Sept. 1977). Voluntary work by the brigades was rationalized on the grounds that this was a first step to incorporating the women into a salaried labor force; now in fact much of their labor is remunerated (Bengelsdorf & Hageman 1978).

Women in civilian state jobs, which include the majority of productive activities, services, and administration, represent 590,000 out of a total of 2,331,000 workers, that is, 25.3 percent (Castro 1974). Apparently, women have not entered the permanent waged agricultural labor force in the collectivized sector in large numbers. The continuing concentration of production within the small family farm and the informal or the voluntary nature of much of women's work both on the smallholdings and in the brigades of the collectivized sector means that most women receive no remuneration for their own labor. They neither exercise control over the allocation of their labor inputs nor receive an income independent of their husbands'. The limitations inherent in these policies may of course characterize a necessary stage dictated by the underdevelopment of the Cuban economy.

The distribution of agricultural work is based on the assumption that there is a natural sexual division of labor largely grounded in differences of physical strength. Although much publicity was given to women who had taken up the physically demanding job of sugarcane cutting and who had acquired a strong male-oriented ethos, the sexual division of labor was sanctioned by law in the Ministry of Labour's Resolutions 47 and 48, which reserved some categories of employment for women and prohibited them from entering others (Rowbotham 1972; Murray 1978). Nevertheless there has been some attempt to educate women generally and in agricultural skills. The campaign against illiteracy in 1961 reduced the rate of illiteracy from 23 percent to 3.6 percent, and of the 707,000 persons made literate, 56 percent were women (Seers 1964; Purcell 1973). There were special schools for peasant women in Havana where they stayed for a few months to acquire literacy as well as domestic and agricultural skills. By 1968, when these special schools were being phased out, 55,000 women between fifteen and nineteen years of age had graduated from them (Murray 1978). By the mid-1960s the goal of providing basic education was said to be nearly accomplished, and the expansion of educational facilities in rural areas meant that the newly literate could now be encouraged to continue their studies within the formal education system or in training programs especially designed for women. By 1970 women composed 49 percent of Cuba's elementary school students, 55 percent of the high school students, and 40 percent of the students in higher education (Bengelsdorf and Hageman 1978). One school for agricultural technicians, however, was made up almost entirely of sons of small farmers or agricultural workers (Murray 1978). The need for maximum productivity coupled with firmly held beliefs about women's capabilities tended to confine women to highly seasonal, informal, and voluntary labor and to the support tasks in the production of the main crops.

If women are not involved in large numbers in production, then they are automatically excluded from exercising control over production. Women hold 15 percent of all leadership posts in production enterprises, the services, and administration (Castro 1974). In the country as a whole, women are 12.8 percent of the membership of the Communist Party, and 6 percent of Party officials; out of 112 members of the Central Committee only five are women (Castro 1974). In the Youth League, where the proportion of young female members is generally higher, they comprise 29 percent of the membership and 10 percent of the national leadership (Bengelsdorf & Hageman 1978). Women are also in the minority in the elections to the administrative bodies through which government is decentralized; in 1967, of the 23,000 delegates, only 10.9 percent were women. In the same elections held in 1974 in the province of Matanzas, only 7.6 percent of the candidates proposed by the people and only 3 percent of those elected were women (Murray 1978). Although this example was used to publicize the need for more women candidates, in the 1976 nationwide elections they represented only 22.2 percent of those elected, and only 8 percent of the deputies selected to be delegates to the National Assembly (Murray 1978). The most common reason women themselves gave for these low proportions was the lack of social facilities and the persistence of the double day. Married women especially found it difficult to make the commitment to the traveling, training, and extra time required by the voluntary political positions. In 1975, when a number of persons were interviewed to find out why women were so underrepresented in the elections, the major factors cited as inhibiting greater female participation were women's domestic obligations (87 percent) and their low cultural levels (51 percent). When women were asked if they would be willing to stand if proposed, 54.3 percent said that they would not because of "domestic tasks and care of children and husband" (Bengelsdorf & Hageman 1978).

In his speeches Fidel Castro has always emphasized that women merit special consideration since, besides their special obligations and on top of their employment, they also carry the weight of reproduction and childbearing (Castro 1974). And in Cuba, as in the Soviet Union and China, women have benefited from policies to improve their general health and provide the means of birth control. A nationwide public health program established a network of hospitals and Sanitary Brigades. These latter were subdivided into groups of three hundred or so families, and a member who had received elementary training in a variety of subjects including vaccination, hygiene, pediatrics, and obstetrics was assigned to each. Special attention has been given by local clinics to women's health and hygiene, and especially to pregnancy and childbirth; in 1973 the death rates for babies and women in childbirth were reduced to twenty-six per thousand births and fewer than six per ten thousand births, respectively (Adoum 1975). Contraception and abortion were made widely and freely available to women, and there has probably been more more discussion in Cuba of what constitutes the ideal relation between men and women than in any other socialist society. Observers have recorded a wide variety of views on the subject, ranging from the older peasant women, who still believe in segregation of the sexes and the protection of virginity, to the progressive young students, who talk as if they have overthrown traditional sexual norms (Sutherland 1969; Larguia & Dumoulin 1973). However, there is still considerable opposition to the dissemination of birth control information and facilities. It is widely feared that contraception will promote an undesireable sexual freedom among women, and it is widely believed that many and frequent births are proof of a man's virility. There is also a latent distrust of the type of population policies that "developed" countries dictate to the "developing" countries. Though clinics provide advice and contraception to all those who seek them, the government has not yet felt able to implement a visible campaign actively propagating birth control (Rowbotham 1972; Murray 1978).

To enable women to participate in new economic and political activities, the government has committed itself to socializing household tasks. As Vilma Espin, the chair of the women's organization, has said, the provision of day nurseries, workers' dining rooms, student dining rooms, semi-boarding schools, laundries, and other social services would overcome the numerous obstacles of a material nature that make it difficult for the housewife to enter employment (Rowbotham 1972). Day-care centers providing daily or weekly care for children from six weeks to six years of age have steadily increased from 109 in 1962 to 658 in 1975, and provide care for 55,000 children (Murray 1978). However, this number is still insufficient, especially in rural areas; priority is given to the children of employed women, and it is often a question of which comes first, the job or child care. Other examples of socialized services include communal eating facilities in factories, in schools, and on cooperative and state farms, shopping priorities for employed women, laundry services, and the availability of labor-saving devices such as refrigerators. But because of cost, the provision of these services is slow and biased toward the urban working women. This situation caused women's organizations in 1974 to call for expansion and improvements in the availability of clothes and prepared foods and reduction in work shifts and also caused the government to popularize the equitable distribution of household chores between the sexes (Bengelsdorf & Hageman 1978).

The government has recently incorporated the equalization of domestic labor into legislation. As well as redefining marriage and divorce procedures, the Family Code of 1974 states unequivocally that in homes where both partners have entered employment, both must share equally in household tasks and the raising of children, whatever their social responsibilities or the nature of their employment. The force of law was thereby applied to the notion of shared responsibility, and theoretically at least a woman may now take her husband to the People's Court or ultimately divorce him on the grounds that his behavior and nonparticipation in domestic labor prevented her from either studying or entering employment (Adoum 1975; Murray 1978). The appropriate sections of the highly publicized, much-discussed law are read at all marriage services and in one recent survey almost 80 percent of a sample comprising both sexes thought that men and women should share housework. However, there is no evidence yet that any widespread sharing has actually occurred or greatly reconciled the conflicting demands of production and reproduction on the time and energies of women (Murray 1978).

As in the other societies, peasant women have been, and still are, largely responsible for servicing and maintaining their households, and they have practically resolved the dual demands of production and reproduction by informally cooperating among themselves or abstaining from entering waged employment. During an intensive campaign to mobilize women to enter employment, large numbers of women—maybe as many as three out of four—refused to take on paid labor primarily because of the domestic demands on their time, the lack of servicing facilities, and the conservative attitudes of their husbands (S.K. Purcell 1973). The double day was also responsible for high dropout rates among those who did enter the labor force. For the period from 1969 to 1974, it has been estimated that over seven hundred thousand women had to be recruited into the work force in order to achieve a net gain of just under two hundred thousand women workers (Bengelsdorf & Hageman 1978).

Tanzania

Agriculture is the backbone of the Tanzanian economy, and women have traditionally been the chief producers of agricultural products. In the patrilineal societies that made up most of what is now Tanzania, land rights were vested in the men who either owned or controlled its use; women were usually given land by their husbands to use for the production of food. Women were expected to provide for nearly all the subsistence needs of the household and to raise or to help raise the cash crops: coffee, sisal, cashew, and cotton. The intensification of labor required by the expansion of cash cropping in the colonial era had largely been met by increasing women's labor inputs. The penetration of capital and the introduction of a dual economy during the colonial period led to a situation in which the women were left in the rural areas to bear the burden of agricultural production while men who may have migrated continued to control land, labor, and other resources.

Since Tanzania has become independent, Nyerere has acknowledged women's contribution to agriculture and the strains the recent colonial period had placed upon women's labor. In his *Socialism and Rural Development* he thought it was "impossible to deny that the women did, and still do, more than their fair share of the work in the fields and in the home" (Nyerere 1967). In recognition of this contribution, the government has aimed to introduce measures to change the relations of production so as to benefit women. The *ujamaa** village policy of relocating dispersed peasant households in concentrated village settlements was particularly intended to be a positive influence on women's position in the productive process. The Arusha Declaration of 1967 anticipated that these villages would come to dominate the rural economy and set the social pattern for the country as a whole. Most of the farming would thus be undertaken by groups of farmers who produce and market as collectives and provide their own local services out of their common surplus. Village concentrations would also allow for a more efficient provision of agricultural inputs, extension advice, credit and banking facilities, and marketing infrastructures, as well as medical, water, and educational facilities. Above all, their establishment as a production unit allows for the collectivization of the means of production and a change in the relations of production. In an *ujamaa* village all but the individual household plot is farmed communally. At the present time 70 percent of the population of Tanzania can be said to be "villagized," but while a number of villages have *ujamaa,* or communal plots, the overwhelming majority have maintained a combination of individual and vestigial communal plots (Blue & Weaver 1977).

In present-day Tanzania, therefore, most of the agricultural products continue to be produced by small farms, and most agricultural workers are smallholder peasant producers. Within the household women tend subsistence crops, and men and women, or primarily women, tend the cash crops depending on whether the male heads of household are present. But all the allocation of labor and control of the products remains in the hands of the men (*Sunday News,* 30 July 1972). Even when a married woman farms her own cash crops, she usually sells her harvest to the local cooperative society through her husband or the male head of her household. As long as the smallholder peasant household has been the site of the labor process, the size of women's labor input in production has been camouflaged by their lack of direct relationship to the market. Women remain dependent upon and dominated by men due to the primary place men have in relation to production (as controllers of commodity production) and the peasant women's position as laborer for her husband (manager and owner of land) (Mblinyi 1977).

Ujamaa means "freedom"—hence used for the development program of newly independent Tanzania.

Relations of exchange between men and women in the household remain asymmetrical. Although the Mariage Law allowed for a wife's right to ownership over all properties acquired since the time of marriage, many women have pointed out that a wife's ownership rights extend only to material goods or "products" that she had acquired, ignoring her present contribution to peasant subsistence production—which leaves no tangible products (*Daily News*, 20 July 1976). When the proceeds of individual household produce are distributed, the producer wife is not assured of just returns for her labor or of a substantial source of income independent of her husband (*Daily News*, 5 July 1976). One of the major difficulties facing rural women derives from their continuing weak position based on their restricted access to land (*Sunday News*; 17 Aug. 1975) For example, because women cultivate their spouses' land, divorced women with no alternative source of economic support are often forced temporarily to turn to prostitution in the towns in order to earn the cash necessary to purchase their own land and form independent female-headed households (Bader 1975).

Although relatively few *ujamaa* villages have so far been established in Tanzania, they form the major component of rural development programs and therefore have important implications for productive structures and the position of women. In theory, the introduction of communal production could mean that each adult member of a household could have his or her own relation to production by virtue of village membership. Indeed, to implement a policy of equal opportunities in the rural sector, the government has stipulated that all men and women workers over the age of eighteen must be registered as individual members of the production brigade and rewarded according to their individual labor inputs. It is the receipt of tangible and equal rewards for women's labor and the provision of communal facilities and services to reduce the time and effort in domestic work that form the major innovations for peasant women (*Sunday News*, 20 Aug. 1972, 10 Aug. 1975, 14 Sept. 1975). In practice, however, there has as yet been no radical change in the relations of production in most *ujamaa* villages. The lands farmed communally still constitute only a small proportion of the total land, and each household continues to have its own individual farms under the control of the male household head. Women perform most of the work on the *ujamaa* communal plots, and because the small family unit of production has been maintained, communal farming frequently places an additional demand on women's time and energies (*Sunday News*, 14 Sept. 1975). But the individual cash returns for communal work may also provide women with a measure of independence and, for many, their first cash remuneration on a regular basis. However, the regulations that women be registered as individuals and receive rewards commensurate with inputs have not always been observed; male heads of households are often the only registered members, and they frequently send their wives to do their share of the work on the communal plots unless they can afford to hire labor (Bader 1975). In one *ujamaa* village the women were initially registered as members of a male-headed household, and they watched their husbands receive and spend the proceeds at the end of the year; the next year these same women decided to register independently rather than come under their husband's registration (*Sunday News,* 3 Nov. 1975). Unfortunately, however, even where women are registered as individual members, there are not automatically cash returns to be had, especially where poor leadership, disorganization, and absenteeism contribute to low crop yields (Bader 1975).

Most changes brought about by *ujamaa* policies have principally benefited independent women or female heads of households. Research data suggest that where women have been able to purchase land, or where they have been allocated their own plots in *ujamaa* villages, their tenure of the individual plots has been recognized by virtue of their membership in the village and their labor inputs in the communal sector (*Sunday News,* 12 Oct. 1975; Bader 1975). Female heads of households are often the most active participants in communal work even though they also have sole responsibility for their private field work and child care. As independent women, they are able to organize their labor as they wish and to control the proceeds; often they cooperate with other female heads of household in organizing and sharing household tasks. Independent women were more assured than married women of receiving just returns for their labor (Bader 1975). The predominance of smallholder and individualized production in rural Tanzania has meant that married women have seen little change in the distribution of proceeds within their households (*Sunday News,* 14 Sept. 1975, 21 Sept. 1975). The incomplete implementation of the *ujamaa* policies in rural areas means that although women's labor inputs have increased, men continue to control the resources and market the products of their labor both at the household and the village levels.

Within agriculture, women performed the more continuous routine chores of weeding, planting, and harvesting, while men provided the more infrequent but heavier labor. There have been no apparent substantial changes in the sexual division of labor, and in addition to work on the private farms and on *ujamaa* plots, women are also expected to process, prepare, and preserve food; to collect firewood and fresh water; and to provide child care. Although there are many child-care centers in the towns, there are relatively few in rural areas. The Ministry of Labour and Social Welfare has recently made plans to open one in every rural village with regional coordinating centers to provide training and supervision (*Daily News,* 26 Nov. 1974. At present it is not uncommon to observe women with their children on their backs working in the fields or traveling the substantial distances to and from the fields, the market, and the well (*Sunday News,* 17 Sept. 1972)

Intensive efforts to raise the educational level of women through literacy campaigns and formal educational reforms aim to equip women for a larger role in economic and political development programs. Whereas the illiteracy rates were high for all persons before 1970, those for women were consistently higher. In the age groups extending from twenty to thirty years of age, for example, the percentage of illiterate women ranged from 79.3 percent to 91.9 percent, as compared to the equivalent range for men from 46.2 percent to 61.1 percent (Mblinyi 1970). In the early 1970s, after a number of literacy campaigns, the number of women who took part in adult education programs designed to introduce new concepts in nutrition, health education, and agriculture rose thirteen times from 174,864 to 2,334,506, which was a little more than half of the total number of participants (McLaro 1977). Despite an increase in literacy rates and the increase in the number of girls entering formal education, there is still a significant disparity between the educational levels of boys and girls.

Preliminary census figures for rural Tanzania show that 65 percent of the girls in the fifteen- to nineteen-year age group have no schooling whatsoever, compared to 38 percent of the boys (Mblinyi 1972). The proportion of girls in the education system drops with each successive level of education after the primary years, and this affects their employment opportunities (*Sunday News*, 14 Jan. 1973). Peasant women are commonly thought of as less intelligent, interested, and reliable than men, and therefore unable to assume major economic and political responsibilities (Mblinyi 1970, 1977).

Despite their contribution to labor and the official policies encouraging women to take up management and positions in decision making, few have done so. At national levels, leadership of the government and Party rests largely in the hands of men; at village levels women share in the leadership, but only to a small degree (*Sunday News*, 30 July 1972). In a survey of ujamaa villages, less than 10 percent of the committee members were women in more than half of the villages sampled, although in one village women held 44 percent of the committee positions (Mblinyi 1976). As in other societies, women were most frequently to be found on the village committees related to health, education, culture, or shopping—traditionally defined as female concerns.

In Tanzania the government has constantly emphasized that health clinics, birth control, maternity leave, and day-care centers are necessary to enable women to combine their roles as producers and reproducers and thus participate in rural development (*Sunday News*, 14 May 1972, 4 April 1976). There has been some progress in general health care in Tanzania, and the establishment of rural health centers and public health campaigns has led to some improvement in the health of women and a decrease in the maternal and infant mortality rates (McLaro 1977). It is generally admitted by the government and in the media that the introduction of birth control is necessary for both the health of women and their contribution to village and rural development activities. Nevertheless these policies have met with much opposition and the average Tanzanian woman bears seven children (Mblinyi 1972; *Sunday News*, 14 May 1972; 29 June 1975). In both the patrilineal and matrilineal societies of rural Tanzania, the most important of women's functions was to reproduce children in order to maintain the lineage. A sterile wife was liable to be repudiated. In the subsistence rural economy children were valued as important labor resources on the farm and in the household. Sons were relied upon as support for parents in old age and daughters brought in wealth in the form of the bride price. Because of the high child-mortality rates in the past, it was necessary to have as many children as possible. Even now most Tanzanians argue that their country is sparsely populated and that there is no need to limit the number of children born (Mblinyi 1974). Most of the education in family planning is thus directed at spacing births rather than limiting their numbers. The women themselves, however, have argued that they should have the facilities that would allow them to exercise the right to decide if and when to have children (*Sunday News*, 28 May 1972). As one woman argued, "Tanzanian women have shown their loyalty to their menfolk and the nation. It is now the nation's duty to provide them with the opportunity to have a say in the one question which concerns them most deeply" (*Sunday News*, 11 Feb. 1973). Although legislation has introduced three-month maternity leave with full pay for both married and single mothers, in practice the benefit does not extend to peasant women. They return to the fields soon after childbirth, and in the absence of child-care centers, very often they have to take their children with them (*Sunday News*, 18 March 1973, 17 Sept. 1972).

Since independence the government has promulgated some progressive legislation and introduced new educational, economic, and political reforms to benefit women. Many reforms have failed to take hold because they have been introduced in a hostile environment where male dominance is an assumed and admired heritage and where each step aimed at its demise has been interpreted as a decline in female morals, even by those in government circles. The government has also been accused in the media of concentrating too much on the political and economic equality of women and not enough on women's reproductive functions (*Daily News*, 8 March 1976).

Discussion

In the development programs of each of these nations, the emphasis on attracting women into the collective waged labor force has outweighed the concern for redefining women's reproductive and domestic roles. The limited development of the service sector, the existence of a large private subsistence sector of the economy, and the persistence of a traditional sexual division of labor within the household have meant that the burden of subsistence and domestic responsibilities continues to devolve upon peasant women, who in effect subsidize the rural development programs with their intensified labor. In order to reduce this burden, each society must provide a new material base for subsistence and domestic activities, and must reallocate resources and investments at both national and local levels. Yet in the absence of well-defined long-term policies concerning the reproductive sphere, the demands of production and economic development take priority. The question is, Are the present

inequalities in the sexual division of labor, which may be justified by the
scarcity of social funds, caused by an inadequate implementation of socialist
policies, or are they inherent in the definition and underlying theory of the
policies themselves? We must begin to search for an answer as we examine the
important achievements and the very considerable problems in socialist development experiences.

The governments of three of these societies have not only assumed that
women's involvement in agricultural production is necessary for the success
of their rural development programs, but have also emphasized, after the
example of Marx and Engels, that women's entry into the waged labor force is
an important precondition for improving women's position in society. Not only
was paid labor seen to benefit women economically, but a direct correlation
was also predicted between women's entry into the labor force and the degree
of their participation in its controls and in the distribution of the fruits of
production. In the Soviet Union, China, and Cuba, policies of collectivization
required and provided for the incorporation of large numbers of peasant
women into the waged agricultural labor force on a full-time, part-time, or
seasonal basis. Peasant women had traditionally undertaken some agricultural
work in these societies, but their productive activities were rarely separated
from the transformation of materials for consumption and the onerous domestic chores performed within the household. Tanzania was an exception, for
there women had always performed most of the field labor. In the other
societies they were less likely to have undertaken agricultural work in the
fields except during the busy harvesting seasons. In all four—even in Tanzania—their contribution to agricultural labor often went unrecognized. There
was little differentiation between it and their domestic labor, they were not
directly related to production, and their remuneration was normally paid to
the household head. In all cases the initial collectivization policy included
some measures to encourage women to take part in the newly organized teams
of waged agricultural workers. These might include registering women as
individual members of the collective work teams; establishing the principle of
equal pay for equal work; and providing facilities to expand women's skills, to
improve their health, and to reduce their traditional domestic tasks.

Women now make up a substantial proportion of the collective and private
agricultural work force in all four societies. In the Soviet Union where women
have traditionally participated in agricultural work, collectives have been
forced to rely on large inputs of female agricultural labor because of the
demographic imbalance between the sexes resulting from the World Wars, the
Revolution, collectivization, and industrialization programs that draw male
laborers from the rural areas. There have consistently been more female than
male laborers, although men perform a higher number of labor days than
women. However, it is estimated that women also contribute 90 percent of the
labor required to cultivate the private plots and rear private livestock. In
China, where the majority of women did not work in the fields except in some

very specific regions, the largest increase in the number of women laborers in the agricultural work force coincided with the peak of collectivization or establishment of communes. At that time approximately 90 percent of all able peasant women entered the work force. Since this period the number of peasant women engaged in full-time agricultural production has fluctuated a great deal, but it is probable that most women do contribute labor to the collectives at the very least during the peak harvest season. Variations in the amount of female labor are probably tied to cropping patterns, their type and intensity, and the availability of nearby nonagricultural occupations for men. In addition to collective labor, women still do much of the vegetable cultivating and livestock rearing in the private sector. In Cuba, the systematic incorporation of peasant women into the waged agricultural labor force has taken place largely in the 1970s as a result of an increasing labor shortage. Many peasant women provide family labor on the rural smallholdings or within the rural household on the state farm, cultivating crops and vegetables and rearing private livestock. They also join teams that work on the state sugar and coffee farms during the busy harvesting season. In Tanzania, women continue to form the mainstay of the agricultural labor force, cultivating both subsistence and some cash crops on the smallholdings. Since the Arusha Declaration in 1967, which collectivized ownership of land and production of agricultural products, and the establishment of small communal plots in some villages, women have also largely undertaken the planting, weeding, and harvesting of the communal crops.

The remuneration accorded to peasant women in the four societies suggests that there may be some correlation between the extent of collectivization and the degree of women's visibility, and the scale of rewards distributed directly to them. However, despite policies based on the principle of equal pay for equal work, women still receive less than male laborers and are found predominantly among the lower-paid agricultural workers on the collectives. Whether the jobs accorded to women were rated according to physical strength, skills, or experience required, they tend to be evaluated toward the lower end of the remuneration scales. Any alteration in the relations of production has thus left the sexual division of labor largely untouched. Although some women may have moved into occupations that were hitherto male preserves, the majority of peasant women in all four societies tend to be confined to the lower-skilled occupations, the "lighter" but no less physically demanding jobs, and the least specialized and mechanized sectors of the agricultural economy. If men are recruited into any nonagricultural occupations in the locality, peasant women may well undertake a wider variety of jobs, but then a new division of labor seems to be established; the distinction between skilled and unskilled or lighter and heavier jobs within agriculture is replaced by one between agricultural and nonagricultural jobs.

The establishment of the collective as the unit of production may allow the payment of wages to individuals, but does not necessarily mean that women

will receive an individual wage. Although governments nearly always allow
women to register as individual members of collectives, actual payments may
continue to be made to the heads of households. Nonetheless, in all four
societies where women are registered as individual members and where the
collective lands are more than small appendages to groups of individual
smallholdings, women normally receive a cash sum in return for their labor,
and this may provide them with a source of economic independence or at least
increase their bargaining position within the household.

REPRODUCTION

A second social change that might proceed from some alteration in the
relations of production and that would directly affect peasant women is the
allocation of a portion of the collective surplus for the establishment of self-
financing community and service facilities.[4] Policies that would reduce the
time and energy peasant women expend in domestic labor were introduced in
these four societies. Their formulation was based on the assumptions of
Engels and Lenin that the redefinition of women's roles could come about
only through the "transformation of sundry household chores into the great
socialist economy" (Lenin 1938). On this basis each government has in principle made a long-term commitment to improving the health of mothers and
children and to establishing household services for child care, food supply and
preparation, washing, and sewing so that women may be released from exclusive responsibility for the tasks involved in maintaining a small individual
household.

    In the Soviet Union, China, and Cuba, the intention of the government was
to socialize domestic tasks by establishing public and community services
such as crèches, nurseries, food-processing plants, and public dining rooms.
Their success in this area has varied. The most extensive effort to substitute
collective services for individual and scattered household tasks occurred in
China in the late 1950s during the Great Leap Forward when the rural
communes were developed. Unfortunately these services soon declined,
largely due to the costs involved in substituting collective waged labor for
women's individual nonremunerated domestic labor. In the Soviet Union,
China, and Cuba today, community services available to women are far from
sufficient to meet the demand and are unevenly distributed in favor of the
cities. In Tanzania, although the Ministry of Labour and Social Welfare has
publicly committed itself to establishing day-care centers in rural areas and
especially in ujamaa villages, the socialization of domestic services has been
of less concern. What is common to the four societies, despite the contrary
implications of some programs, is the degree to which the rural economy still
requires the individual household to function as a unit of production and
consumption and to provide for itself a large share of necessary goods and

services. This has determined the content of domestic labor in rural areas, where the maintenance of the household requires more than the "sundry household chores" that Lenin and Engels had in mind.

The continuing requirements of domestic labor have forced the Chinese and Cuban governments to make other attempts to redistribute and equalize the amount of housework performed by both sexes within each household. The ideology of sharing has been stressed, and in Cuba the Family Code of 1974 stated unequivocally that household tasks must be shared if partners are employed. By contrast, there has been little or no attempt in the Soviet Union and Tanzania to alter the sexual division of labor within the household through the introduction of a new ideology of sharing. However, in all four societies, even where collectivization has been extensive, it seems that peasant women continue to undertake the considerable amount of domestic labor still required to maintain and service the household.

Production and Reproduction

In each of these societies, then, peasant women have been expected to enter the waged labor force and at the same time to continue to service and maintain the household, thereby intensifying rather than reducing the demands on women's labor. Women shoulder a "double burden" and experience evident tensions in combining conflicting demands that productive and reproductive activities place on their times and energies. This conflict is perhaps sharpest in the Soviet Union where women have been exhorted both to enter into production on a full-time basis and to have more children to counter the declining birthrate.

To mitigate this conflict, the governments of the Soviet Union, China, and Cuba have frequently taken steps to reduce slightly the demands made on women in the collective labor force (for example, requiring fewer labor days per month or year or fewer hours per day), but in each case these policies have ultimately discriminated against and financially penalized women in the productive sector. Peasant women have themselves reduced the conflict in a number of ways, sometimes by withdrawing their labor from either the productive or reproductive sphere. In the Soviet Union they have so far resisted the pressures to have more children, and in Cuba they have proved reluctant to enter the waged labor force in larger numbers or for long periods. The most common solution for peasant women in all four societies though, and a means particularly suited to rural conditions, is the informal sharing of domestic responsibilities with other women of the same household, kin group, or village. It is common for such women to rotate or share cooking, child care, and other tasks, and thus reduce each individual's burden. However, whether tasks are shared or not, peasant women have not found it easy to combine their productive and reproductive activities, except by working longer hours.

The emphasis on women's entry into the labor force has caused an imbalance—a lack of attention to women's reproductive and domestic roles versus concerted efforts to attract women into social production. In each society the limited development of the service sector in rural areas and the persistence of the traditional division of labor within the household have meant that the burden of household responsibilities continues to fall on women's shoulders.

Although government leaders may have estimated that the gains from the provision of nurseries and social services in theory offset the costs, the fact remains that the inadequate resources have been set aside for reducing the reproductive and domestic responsibilities of individual peasant women in these countries. The important point that emerges from a study of the development experience of these societies is that the conditions for reducing women's domestic responsibilities require a material base of their own and the allocation of resources at both national and local levels.

In all these societies the concentration of investment and resources on increasing industrial production in urban areas and the demands made on the agricultural surplus for capital formation and accumulation have meant that low priority is inevitably given to precisely those economic sectors and activities that might have lightened the burden for women in employment. The limited development of the service sector and the inadequate provision for consumption in the public sector, aggravated in the countryside by the diversion of resources away from rural development, has meant that female unpaid labor has to a certain extent subsidized development programs. Of course, it can be argued that the partial financing of development by the intensification of all and not just female, labor may be a necessary phase and one which in the long term may not be to women's ultimate disadvantage. But the danger is that priorities set in the interest of short-term goals may become long-term policies. The experience of these four societies suggests that the intensity of female labor and the subsidy it provides for rural development will be reduced only when the sexual division of labor is thoroughly redefined in favor of agriculture and the service sectors of the economy.

None of these societies has achieved a total alteration in the relations of production; in each a substantial private sector has survived. This means that a good deal of a woman's labor—the considerable portion of her time and energies devoted to the private sector—continues to be invisible, unpaid, and indistinguishable from domestic labor. Changes in the relations of production may in fact have little effect on asymmetric relations of exchange within the household.

In each of these societies, the content of domestic labor has been defined by the production and transformation of materials for consumption required of each household. This raises the question of how to conceptualize domestic labor within socialist strategies of development and make it a visible and recognizable sector of the economy or a constituent of the labor of both sexes. Underlying all policies related to the sexual division of labor has been a set of conflicting assumptions: that women can perform exactly the same labor as men and that women have certain biological and physical characteristics that determine the type of work they can and should do.

When the problem has been addressed, the continuing extra demands on women's labor have been explained by the persistence of beliefs and customs that underpin the traditional division of labor within the household. Both China and Cuba have looked primarily to the ideological origins of the discrimination against women and introduced programs criticizing and attempting to eradicate these beliefs and customs. They have popularized the idea of an equitable distribution of household labor. Although the programs have been aimed at raising the consciousness of both men and women, the acquisition of men's roles by women has received the most attention. In these two countries, then, the problems of tackling or accommodating domestic labor have been conceived in ideological rather than material terms.

The experience of the Soviet Union, China, and Cuba demonstrates that ideological beliefs based on women's supposed inferiority and the sexual division of labor can survive quite radical changes in the relations of production and in the material circumstances of women. It appears from the examples of China and Cuba that struggle for reform at this level is not only necessary but also destined to be very long and arduous. However, their experiences also suggest that an emphasis on ideological constraints may obscure the need to change certain material practices that sustain discriminatory beliefs against women. Although it may be very convenient to define the problem ideologically, this may only sidestep more radical solutions (Diamond 1975; Croll 1976). Policies regarding consciousness raising may be necessary, but they are no substitute for the reallocation of material resources and the further reorganization of the relations of production to include the production and consumption activities of the household.

Political Intervention

One of the crucial questions that arises in assessing socialist development processes in relation to women is the degree to which women have been able to define their own needs and interests and to intervene in the political process to represent these interests. Does the separation of production from the individual household and the incorporation of women into collective production provide women with the opportunity to participate in political decision making? In each of the four societies women clearly have not entered into formal positions of collective decision making in proportion to their representation either in production or in the population as a whole. When productive and political structures coincide or overlap and when women have been incorporated into productive structures, men continue to dominate the leadership committees and positions of authority. Women have been unable to compete for any number of reasons, one of the most prominent being that many local political positions are part-time unpaid positions that require attendance at meetings held outside work hours when the demands on women's labor are greatest.

The establishment of local women's organizations under the nation-wide organizations of the Zhenotdel in the Soviet Union, the All-Democratic Women's Federation in China, the Federation of Cuban Women (FMC), and the Umoja Wa Wanawake (UWT) in Tanzania might have given women the opportunity to intervene collectively at local levels and influence policies. However, in each case, there is evidence to suggest that women's organizations have not always intervened to protect or further their own interests, especially where these may seem to conflict with the overall priorities of development. They have not been able to equalize the relations of exchange within the productive structures, and the very conflict between production and reproduction evident to a greater or lesser degree in all four societies reflects this fact.

Government statements in all four societies have suggested that while the establishment of separate women's organizations is a matter of practical revolutionary expediency, they should eventually become unnecessary in any socialist society where levels of consciousness are such that policies affecting women's position are not a separate but an integral part of development strategies. The "temporary" legitimacy accorded to women's organizations seems to have affected their position within the political structure and increased the tension surrounding their dual tasks: to act as a mechanism of the Party, extending its influence among a female constituency, and to act as a separate pressure group encouraging women to take an active part in defining and asserting their own needs and demands. This sometimes implicit and sometimes explicit controversy over appropriate activities and methods of work has affected the ability of women's organizations to intervene in political processes.

Fears of separatism and women's isolation from class struggle led to the Soviet Union's abolition of the Zhenotdel in 1930. Although this move was defended on the grounds that women should be encouraged to work through regular political organs such as the Communist Party and trade unions, the abolition of a functionally distinct body has effectively undermined recognition of gender-specific questions as a distinct subject of ideological and political concern (Lapidus 1975, 1977). In China and Cuba, the women's organizations have played an impressive and active part in explaining and implementing government policies to the benefit of women. In China the ambiguities in the definition and priorities of the All-Democratic Women's Federation have affected the organization's ability to intervene in the political process and to further women's interests in a society where class consciousness takes precedence (Croll 1976, 1978). These same conflicts also led to its temporary demise during the Cultural Revolution in the mid-1960s, a period of acute class struggle; but interestingly the resulting neglect of women's interests by class associations and the government spurred women to organize once again and to intervene actively on their own behalf. The women's organizations have consequently been rebuilt during the late 1960s and early 1970s, although whether the competition between class- and gender-specific demands can again be resolved during times of conflict remains to be seen. In Cuba and Tanzania the tension surrounding the women's organizations has not been so acute, largely because class struggle has been a less explicit matter of government policy. In these two societies, and especially in Tanzania, the organizations continue to reflect the interests of certain urban-based ruling classes, which are less likely to introduce conflict between the women's organizations and the government. Several analyses indicate that as mass organizations created by the government, women's organizations in all four countries have so far been more effective in soliciting women's support for official policies than in getting policies changed to meet women's needs, especially when those policies do not contribute to, or actually conflict with, the priority goals of increasing production and promoting economic development.

A Basic Dilemma

The main problem confronting women in societies undergoing planned socialist development programs is that policies concerning women are frequently perceived as derivative from the broader socioeconomic and political strategies for change. Ultimately theirs is conceived as a revolution within a revolution, and the priorities of the other revolution have frequently conflicted with women's needs and interests. Indeed, many women in these societies see a large gap between the theory of equality and their own experience as producers and reproducers. In each of these societies the initial problem of acquiring a new and secure material base have been severe, and their resolution has tended to take priority. The degree of attention accorded to women has depended on their contribution to this overall goal. For instance, a certain congruence characterized the economic and ideological motives for incorporating women into the waged labor force: it is necessary to counter the overall shortage of labor power, and it benefits the women themselves. Collectivization raised new standards in the basic necessities of food, health care, housing, education, and clothing, and provided women specifically with visibility and remuneration as laborers. On the other hand, less attention has been directed to decreasing women's household responsibilities, a goal that would have much less direct benefit for the economy and might even be of some cost. Although relations of exchange within the household have not been targeted for change, the separation of most agricultural production from the individual household has definitely benefited women to some extent, and there is some correlation between the extent of collectivization, the degree of women's visibility, and the scale of their reward. Yet there have

been far fewer benefits for women than there might have been, perhaps
because the sexual division of labor and the relations of exchange within the
household have not formed sufficiently coherent and well-defined areas of
practical and theoretical concern to counter the priority accorded to economic
development during periods of intensive socialist reconstruction.

Women in these societies repeatedly assert that socialist development
programs will not of their own accord bring about changes in gender relations,
and it seems apparent that in the absence of well-defined policy, female labor
has intensified, which to a certain extent has subsidized economic development. The danger is that without foresight, careful planning, and a high degree
of consciousness, short-term priorities decided in the interests of economic
development may become long-term policies to the detriment of women.

Notes

1. The research underlying this chapter was undertaken while I was a Visiting Fellow at the
Institute of Development Studies (IDS), Brighton, during the academic year 1977–78. I would like
to express my appreciation to members of the Subordination of Women Workshop and especially
to Maxine Molyneux, whose ongoing discussions have greatly stimulated me in working on this
subject. I am grateful to Christine White, Kate Young, Maxine Molyneux, Ann Segrave, and Jim
Croll for their comments on an earlier draft of this chapter, which was originally published as a
discussion paper by IDS.

2. For a discussion of socialist criteria of development, see Elisabeth Croll and Maxine
Molyneux, "Women and Socialist Development: An Initial Discussion" (paper present at Conference 133, Continuing Subordination of Women in the Development Process, Institute of Development Studies, Brighton 1978).

3. Women were to be incorporated into the agricultural labor force as required. The "labor
force" here refers to all those engaged in wage work, even though the work may be only on a part-
time or temporary basis during harvesting seasons.

4. Physical reproduction—not only activities related to children, but also household maintenance—is distinguished from social reproduction, or maintenance of a social system. For a
discussion of three different aspects of reproduction that correspond to different levels of abstrac-
tion, see Edholm, Harris, and Young (1977).

Postcript: Implications for Organization

ELEANOR LEACOCK

The United Nations Decade for Women brought with it many declarations of
formal support for the legal, economic, and social equality of women.* It also
brought some scattered gains, particularly in education. However, despite
formal commitment to women's equality and a plenitude of proposals and
programs supposedly designed to bring it about, the institutionalization of
women's unrecompensed household and farm labor, combined with male
supremacist attitudes and practices, made it easy for both national economies
and multinational corporations to continue taking advantage of women's unpaid services while also using them as a source of grossly underpaid labor.
Despite openings for a few women in well-paid, high-status occupations, there
has been little or no improvement for the vast majority of women. Instead the
situation for many has deteriorated further.

Given this situation, one might well ask what can be accomplished by
conducting research on the gender division of labor. And why bring in
history? In the face of women's evident needs, is it not almost trivial to spend
time probing the origins and development of their oppression? Why not
simply focus on women's work conditions, family problems, and social dis-
abilities and determine how to fight for what women clearly need: an end to
job discrimination, equal pay, equal educational opportunity (including training for high-paying and prestigious occupations), adequate child care for
working mothers, health services, a good diet, equal access to political
positions, and the full legal rights of adults.

To state the question is to answer it, for changes of any magnitude will not
come about without organized pressure from the women most concerned, and

*An earlier version of this Postscript appeared in *Signs*, vol. 7, no. 2, Winter 1981. © 1981 by The
University of Chicago.

effective organization requires a full analysis of the basis for women's oppression, and of its relation to the present world crisis and military buildup.

Through the decade there has been a growing understanding that a major
obstacle to the advancement of women is the structure of world capitalism,
whereby relatively high standards of living in developed countries depend in
large part on profits derived from developing countries. Midway in the decade
a United Nations Division for Economic and Social Information bulletin
(1980: 4–8) referred to "the unequal world economic structure" and its adverse
effect on women. The bulletin stressed that a "new international economic
order was needed in order to reduce the gap between the labour input of
women and their socioeconomic returns." Instead of "strategies for the advancement of women . . . based on the premise that the existing socioeconomic and political structures could operate in a sufficiently different way to
achieve full equality for women in society," alternative strategies were needed
that "would envisage the integration of women in national life as part of the
larger process of social transformation."

The "pattern of relationships between developed and developing countries" referred to in the UN bulletin has not, of course, changed. Instead, the
second half of the decade has seen a worsened situation, leading to the food
crisis in Africa, the debt crisis in Latin America, and the terrifying buildup of
nuclear weaponry. The decade has not been altogether without advances,
however. The importance of women's work has had to be at least partially
recognized, and women have certainly become more conscious of the organizational role they must play both on their own behalf and that of society
generally.

As I see it, information and analysis in four areas can be especially helpful
in helping women formulate organizational goals and strategies at local, national, and international levels. Needed first is material to counter widely held
assumptions that male dominance and female subservience are inevitable as
outcomes of a natural division of labor by gender. Feminist research has
effectively challenged ideologies that define women's service role as natural,
and has revealed the vast ramifications that stem from women's internalization
of this belief. Predictably, however, as soon as one argument for innate female
subservience is refuted, new ones appear and must be dealt with. Also
predictably, arguments that assert biological bases for female subservience
(such as those put forward in the well-funded field of sociobiology, with its
argument that the double standard for sexual behavior is biologically based
[Barash 1977: 301])[1] or inferiority (such as the recent "discovery" that women
are biologically less able than men in mathematics) receive far greater attention from the media than their refutations. Thus, in the course of their other
activities, women's organizations and networks have a responsibility to disseminate the results of feminist research that counters such arguments.

The three other research areas that are particularly germane to the formulation of organizational strategies for the world-wide improvement of
women's lives are: analyses of women's work and family life during the period

of modernization and industrialization in Europe; analyses of historical changes in the sexual division of labor and the effects of that division on women's position in Third-World nations; and analyses of the interconnections linking the sexual division of labor, patriarchal gender relations, and capitalist exploration. It is not my intention to summarize or recapitulate the rich materials that feminist scholars have been producing along these lines. Anyone familiar with recent work on women's labor will see the influence of this scholarship in the bulletin cited earlier. Instead, my purpose is to draw on the chapters in this book to illustrate the relevance that historical and cross-cultural analyses of the sexual division of labor have for understanding the sources of women's oppression and creating strategies for organization.

The chapters by Wande Minge (ch. 1) and Louise Tilly draw on their research and that of others on European industrialization, which shows the superexploitation of women—and children—to have been central to the development process in Europe. Such data underscore the point made by Lourdes Benería and Gita Sen (ch. 9) and documented in other chapters in Part III as true for different parts of the world: development in capitalist terms relies on the exploitation of women both in public production and in the private domain of reproduction. The human cost of European industrialization was not only the enslavement of labor and looting of resources around the world but the severe exploitation of women and children, even harsher than that of men, in the home countries as well.

THEORIES OF EXPLOITATION

That European development was dependent on profits from colonized areas has been repeatedly shown, first by Karl Marx and later by W. E. B. DuBois (1946), Eric Williams (1944), A. Gunder Frank (1967), and Walter Rodney (1972). Furthermore, the grinding exploitation of women and children as well was well documented by nineteenth-century writers, including Friedrich Engels (1950). Nonetheless, a certain image of development in Europe as governed by the rational and scientific attitudes embodied in the Protestant ethic has been widely promulgated, along with the essentially racist inference that the central problem in a nation's development lies in achieving Western standards of scientific and technical knowledge and skill.[2] In this context, feminist research on the condition of women in the industrializing West reveals anew the severe exploitation required by development in the capitalist European framework, even when countries exerted full control over the profits from production—as Third-World nations today do not.

Attempts to build socialism are strongly committed to women's equality and do eliminate the direct and brutal forms of personal tyranny to which women have often been subjected. However, although they open up many areas previously closed to women, they have as yet fallen far short of achieving gender equality. As Elisabeth Croll's chapter (ch. 14) shows, it is not simply the persistence of male chauvinist habits and attitudes that creates difficulties, but the fact that a real contradiction exists between women's liberation as a goal and the enormous expense entailed by the socializing of domestic labor.[3] The contradiction is seriously exacerbated—indeed, in part created—by the fact that new socialist nations are developing nations. Economic sanctions, indirect forms of economic control, and the threat or open use of military intervention exert heavy drains on their economies. The nations may also have to cope with popular desire for a way of life based on conspicuous consumption and planned waste, a desire assiduously promoted by capitalist interests. In contrast, industrialized countries already have forms for socializing domestic labor and child care. All manner of food preparation and dispensing services, cleaning services, and formal and informal child-care arrangements are at hand. All that is required is to make them more healthy, accessible, and cheap by removing them from a profit-making structure and making them responsive to the needs of the people using them.

Data on both European and contemporary development, then, show how central the gender division of labor and women's privatized service in the reproductive sphere have been to the process of industrialization. However, the structure of reproduction and its relation to production are often obscured by reference to Engels's statement that "the first condition for the liberation of the wife is to bring the whole female sex back into public industry," without including the follow-up: "this in turn demands that the characteristic of the monogamous family as the economic unit of society be abolished" (1972: 137–38). Engels was arguing that with the development of commodity production and the privatization of property, the individual family became separated from the kin-based collective as an economic unit privately responsible for care of the young, the aged, and the infirm. Women and children became dependent on the productive work of men in a newly defined public sphere, and socially necessary household labor became transmuted into private service—the "open or concealed domestic slavery" of women.[4]

The abolition of the family as an economic unit, Engels argued, requires that "women can take part in production on a large, social scale." This in turn demands that "domestic work no longer claims anything but an insignificant amount of her time," a development that becomes possible with modern large-scale industry, which "tends toward ending private domestic labor by changing it more and more into a public industry (Ibid. 221)."[5] However, although industrialization makes women's freedom from domestic chores possible, the last hundred years have made it clear that capitalism is not about to abandon the increased profits derived from women's servitude by discarding the family as an economic unit or by ending the gender division of labor it requires. As Benería and Sen stress, a fundamental transformation of society is required to effect such a change. I would add the suggestion that its final realization is part of the transition from intermediate socialist forms to full communism.

The economic importance of women's domestic labor for capitalism, and for class society generally, was forcefully raised several years ago by Mariarosa Dalla Costa and Selma James (1972), who stressed that the family in capitalist society is not only a center for socialization, consumption, and reserve labor, but also a center for production. Dalla Costa's argument, tied as it was to the wages-for-housework movement in Italy and England, became central in the intense debates of the 1970s over the relation between women's domestic labor and the production of surplus value and the corollary relation between patriarchal family structure and the capitalist system[6]: The counterpoint to Dalla Costa's position was stated in Heleieth Saffioti's (1978) influential analysis of women in capitalist society with special reference to Brazil. Saffioti showed that capitalism drew women out of production and marginalized them in the family as reserve labor, to be drawn upon or discarded according to economic exigencies, to hold down wages and divide the working class, and to mystify for both women and men the structure of capitalist exploitation. Subsequent research on women's domestic labor and public labor in different times and places has shown how inseparably linked the two are in capitalist society. In the present book, Mona Hammam for the Middle East (ch. 10), Lourdes Arizpe and Josefina Aranda for Mexico (ch. 11), Elizabeth Eviota for the Philippines (ch. 12), Aline Wong for Singapore (ch. 13), and Helen Safa for contemporary capitalism (ch. 4) all document ways in which the sexual division of labor and patriarchal relations in peasant and other precapitalist societies are manipulated in order to draw women into industry as cheap labor. In spite of such studies, however, the question of whether women's unpaid domestic labor or underpaid public labor holds ultimate priority in the maintenance of women's oppression continues to figure importantly in discussions of feminist organizational perspectives.

A major form of debate over the primary source of women's oppression addresses the question, Who are the main beneficiaries of the sexual division of labor, the bourgeoisie or men? Recently, Heidi Hartmann and Ann Markusen (1980:90) have restated in strong terms Hartmann's proposition—that men are the main beneficiaries. Defining patriarchal gender relations as "a system of social relations between men and women, governing the production and reproduction of people and their gender identities," they state: "Just as the division of labor between workers and capitalists connotes exploitation of surplus labor from workers by capitalists, so does the division of labor between women and men connote the exploitation of surplus labor from women for the benefit of men." Men are clearly the immediate, short-term beneficiaries, and in their desire to maintain their petty dominance, they are subject to self-destructive co-option in the service of capitalism, as Hartmann (1976) has elsewhere forcefully described. However, to create a formal separation between a capitalist division of labor serving the bourgeoisie and a patriarchal division of labor serving men makes it easy to underestimate the centrality of women's oppression to capitalism. To do so is to miss a potential source of unity that women's organizations can call upon to bring together diverse struggles in the building of a revolutionary movement.

Given women's isolation in the home, "at the point of exploitation," Hartmann and Markusen define the "organizational strategy for smashing patriarchy" as a "bedroom-to-bedroom" struggle, "one-to-one with the patriarch." The purpose of women's political organization to them "is to build a consensus strategy, provide support for all women in their home struggle, and raise demands on the private and state sectors to remove their supports for patriarchy" (1980: 91–92). With respect to struggles concerning work, they state:

> Whether or not capitalists have benefited from such practice . . . the fundamental meaning for feminist workplace demands—equal pay for equal work, an end to occupational discrimination, change in the work process to accommodate women—is the attack on the role of work discrimination in the past in reinforcing men's control over women. The restriction of women to low-wage jobs has forced women's labor-power to be confined primarily to production in the home, where women have been subjugated to men in marriage simply because they could not for the most part support themselves otherwise. Thus, these struggles have to be seen as directed primarily not at capitalism but at patriarchy [1970: 91–92].

Hartmann and Markusen point out that women also struggle against capitalism: "As wage workers, of course, women share the same or worse conditions as men workers and they too have an interest in destroying capitalism." However, in their justifiable anger at political programs that treat the special exploitation of women, like that of blacks, as secondary to the exploitation of workers (typically conceived of as white and male), Hartmann and Markusen set up a false dichotomy that narrows the field of women's struggles. Taking issue with analyses that "postulate the domination of class relations over gender relations and support class-first political strategies" (ibid.: 88), Hartmann and Markusen in effect opt for "gender-first" strategies. In closing, they state in overly dramatic terms the potential of what they have defined as a fight against patriarchy: "Feminist demands . . . remain a leading force for social transformation. Although aimed at patriarchy, they are probably capable of pulling capitalism down along with it" (ibid.: 93).

Hartmann and Markusen's criticism is primarily directed at treatments of the working-class family as a source of unity rather than divisiveness. However, within working-class families, women work with as well as against men, as Tilly's (ch. 2) and Mullings's (ch. 3) chapters document, and as Hartmann (1981) has elsewhere agreed. In a reasoned appraisal of arguments concerning women in the working-class family, Sen has pointed out that "the claim that the working-class family has beneficial aspects for women does not contradict the view that women are indeed subordinate to men within that same family. What is contradictory is not the analysis, but rather the position of women itself (1980: 84–85). Within the Third World, particularly, the fact cannot be ignored that families are often bases for building "cultures of resistance" against an imperialist and racist oppression that is often very severe (Caulfield 1974). How to link rather than separate women in these families and women from middle-class backgrounds in order to strengthen the fight against all forms of oppression is a central issue for socialist feminists.

Rayna Rapp has pointed out that some of the problems involved in effecting unity among women of different classes, at least in the United States, are caused by reifying "the family." When women disagree over the issue of family relations, Rapp writes, one stating that "the nuclear family ought to be abolished because it is degrading and constraining to women," and another rebutting that "the attack on the family represents a white middle-class position, and that other women need their families for support and survival, . . . both speakers are, in some senses, right." However, she continues, it is evident that "they aren't talking about the same families" (1978:278). When one distinguishes between households as functioning residential units, usually called families, and "the family" as an ideological concept referring either to coresident father–mother–child units or to wider networks of kin, class differences become clear. While middle-class families are closer to the ideologically defined norm, working-class and black communities build on ties of coresidence and fictive kinship "to cement and patch tenuous relations to survival." Firmly committed to a belief in "the family," Rapp states, the very poor "have invented networks capable of making next-to-nothing go a long way" (1978:294). Sen makes a similar point. In relation to the support networks to be found in working-class communities, she writes: "The most basic unit of the network is the working-class household. Within the household, one finds resource pooling and reciprocity over time, the sharing of work and consumption, and the support of those with weaker social claims of subsistence. This is the meaning of the working-class family *to the working class*. It is the reason why attacks on the family strike few resonant chords among the working class" (1980:85). Leith Mullings's chapter offers poignant illustration of why this is so, for the contrast in life experiences for women of different classes and races she documents for the nineteenth-century United States has worldwide counterparts, and has not fundamentally changed.

Many battles of working-class women for survival—for child-care centers and decent schools, for decent housing, for health care, and for welfare programs—are typically phrased in terms of goals for family life, particularly with respect to children. Furthermore, these women generally try not to confront their menfolk, but to win their political support.[7] Nonetheless, most of their struggles in effect are demands that society at large, not individual wage earners, take responsibility for children as well as for the aged, the sick, and the incapacitated. Although seemingly distinct from overt feminist demands, the reforms they seek would in effect undercut the structural basis for their oppression, since the family as an economic unit creates the fundamental link between capitalism and patriarchy.

The position of women who head and support their households sharply illustrates that the privatized labor of women in the family as an economic unit benefits the bourgeoisie by absolving society at large—meaning in effect that section of society that owns and controls the major resources—from taking responsibility for the young and other nonproducers.[8] Some female household heads are well-trained women from middle economic classes who are able to command salaries that support child-care assistance; in some working-class settings, women household heads who are free to negotiate their relations with men fare better than married women, or at least as well (Brown 1975; Sutton and Makiesky-Barrow 1977). In most cases, however, female household heads experience extreme poverty. Raising their children with minimal support from the state, these women are pitted against men on the labor market and are considered a ready pool for low-paying and undesirable jobs. As pointed out by Safa, many such women are migrants; others may have supported themselves reasonably weil by marketing garden produce and home manufactures before full capitalization of the economy pushed them into a low-paid industrial labor pool.[9]

Clearly, then, patriarchy and capitalism are so inseparably related through the institution of the family as an economic unit that to make the greatest headway, women must find ways of uniting struggles against both. Yet someone taking Hartmann and Markusen's position might understandably respond that it is necessary to single out patriarchy, because when the fight against it has been linked to other issues, the overthrow of patriarchy has been accorded low priority and sooner or later has lost out. Certainly efforts to link feminist goals with other demands should not imply giving up separate women's organizations. They are essential. Organizations within which women wage a constant battle with men for full integration of women's issues into political programs make a travesty of unity as a goal. Past experience shows that only on the basis of strength in their own organizations—when these organizations are oriented toward united actions—can women unify the struggle against patriarchy with those against class, race, and colonial oppression.[10]

BUILDING UNITY AMONG WOMEN

Necessary to such an effort, however, is building broader unity among women themselves. This in turn requires women's understanding of and respect for the diversity of their situations. Western academic women in particular have to overcome a tendency to project their own experience upon other women (Sutton 1976). As Felicity Eldholm, Olivia Harris, and Kate Young have written: "While at first sight it seems absurd to suggest that women's role is often presented as unchanging, the gender categories founded in the ideas of biological reproduction and the sexual division of labour have a magnetic power of attraction; even as we recognize the important differences between women's roles in differing cultures, classes, and historical periods, we are drawn back to universals" (1977:127).

Differences between the ways Western, middle-class people, on one hand, and working-class and colonized peoples on the other, interpret and use family and kin ties are a major case in point. Another is offered by differences between the sexual division of labor and gender relations in industrialized societies and in societies that retain something of a peasant base, where families are the loci of production and the sexual division of labor is not fully dichotomized in terms of public and private spheres. However, in peasant as in industrial economies, patriarchy and class stratification are linked by the family (whether extended, polygynous, or nuclear) as the basic economic unit. Though the category "peasant" is a loose one that subsumes great variations, it generally refers to societies in which the conditions of women's labor in and around the household are defined by economic, political, and religious institutions that assign household authority to men. For a sharp contrast that reveals how variable gender relations can be, it is necessary to consider, not peasant or nonindustrial stratified societies, but nonstratified societies.

Diane Bell's chapter (ch. 5) in the present volume describes the Kaititj, a nonstratified Aboriginal society of north-central Australia, which is characterized by a high degree of female–male reciprocity—economically, socially, and ritually. Kaititj gender relations offer a contrast with patriarchally structured gender systems, one made all the more sharp by the female dependency that has been brought about as colonization and usurpation of their lands have transformed a formerly independent people into virtually outcaste dependents of the Australian state.

Bell (1980) conducted her research in the *jilimi*, the women's section of an Aboriginal camp—an economic, social, and ritual center taboo to all men. Widows who choose not to remarry (but may take lovers), wives who have left their husbands (usually because of the violence associated with drinking that now plagues Aboriginal towns), women who are sick, and visiting women live in the *jilimi*, share food with one another, and support their children. Married women spend much of the day there. Like other researchers, Bell noted women's economic independence among the Kaititj, in a sexual division of labor according to which men procure large game and women procure small game and vegetable food (though among some Aborigines women hunt large game as well). However, she did not find the pattern of male authority, ritual superiority, and control over women's marriages often reported in ethnographic accounts of Aboriginal Australian cultures. Instead, looking at Aboriginal life from a woman's point of view, Bell found that a reciprocal structure of female–male participation in decision making and ritual life accompanied the reciprocal structure of the subsistence economy among both the Kaititj and other north-central Aboriginal Australians.[11] Both separately as women, and together with men, women participated in the decision-making discussions and the sacred rituals that maintained the social well-being of the camp. This was particularly the case in the east side of Warribri, the settlement where Bell worked. There people were not removed from ready access to their ancestral lands, they were less disrupted by drinking, and "the maintenance of law and order . . . is still a co-operative venture between men and women who turn to each other for assistance on some issues and assert their independent rights on others" (Bell & Ditton 1980:42–43, 51).

Bell points out that women at Warribri fear men's challenge to their independence and autonomy; they have a strong feminist consciousness when it comes to awareness of their needs and interests as women. Most relevant for the present discussion, however, is the difference between the content of their consciousness and that of women in Western society. In part the difference lies in the awareness of Aboriginal women that their problems as women are now inseparably bound to their problems as a people who have been robbed of economic and political independence. The more cogent difference, however, is that they are not fighting to achieve a status they have never held by breaking into areas defined as male. Instead they are fighting to protect and enhance the domain that once assured their security and independence. They are trying to maintain their position as economically independent individuals, who shoul-dered responsibilities toward their society as a public constituency vis-à-vis that of men, and who were recognized and respected as such by themselves, by young people, and by their menfolk (ibid.: 4–5, 16–20).[12] In sum, they are resisting the erosion of their political base as women.

A similar point is made by Annette Weiner for the Trobriand Islands (ch. 6). In this case, women use their production and distribution of traditional valuables to maintain the kinship organization that affords them the social basis for independent action. Through continuing to involve men in traditional mortuary exchanges of these valuables, they counteract the men's drive for individual entrepreneurship encouraged by new wage labor and market rela-tions—relations that inevitably lock women into the status of dependent wives. For Samoa as well, Weiner demonstrates the publicly recognized importance of women's work producing valuables—in this case, fine mats. Exchanges of these mats were at the core of ritual, economic, and political concerns in precolonial Samoan society and they continue to be important. Thus, although Samoa is a highly rank-oriented society, the gender division of labor accorded women a publicly recognized status that characterizes non-stratified societies and stands in marked contrast to Western culture.

Soheila Shashahani's chapter on the Mamasani of southwestern Iran (ch. 7) demonstrates that one cannot too quickly assume the privatization of women's work in a pastoral economy. Sedentarization and "modernization" did not improve women's status vis-à-vis that of men, Shashahani argues, but instead undercut their participation in the "public" economy, making them more dependent upon men.

Among the Yoruba of southwest Nigeria, women are actively engaged in public production and are expected to order their own affairs and protect their interests as women (Afonja 1975; Awe 1977). Simi Afonja (ch. 8) warns against a simplistic view of Yoruba society, and indicates that many changes have taken place during the course of history as the Yoruba shifted from a largely subsistence economy to a more commercial and then a capitalist economy. The Yoruba have long been characterized by strong status differences and by a measure of inequality between the sexes; as Afonja has written elsewhere: "One can hardly expect a high degree of egalitarianism between the sexes in a socially stratified society with some degree of political centralization and an exchange economy based on the division of labour" (Afonja 1985). The development of capitalism as well as the antiwoman bias of colonialism have further undermined these women's position; I would suggest that capitalism has encouraged the institutionalization of the individual family as an economic unit, or, as María Patricia Fernández Kelly notes, it has sharpened the contradiction between production and reproduction. Afonja points out that capitalist production was not simply imposed by Europeans on African society. Entrepreneurial Yoruba men were active in developing cash-crop production and in controlling trade, and, as local enterprises grew, women's marketing activities were reduced to a secondary place in Yoruba economy.

The traditional principle that women should be represented at all levels of Yoruba society was institutionalized through the presence of women chiefs, cult leaders, members of royal councils, market officials, heads of craft guilds, and occasionally, women rulers (Afonja 1985). Despite the development of capitalism, the gender division of labor apart from actual factory production still entails the public activity of both women and men in every domain of life: economic, ritual, associational, political, and familial (Sutton n.d.). This high degree of gender parallelism is similar to that described for many African societies. Each sex is expected to play important roles in both "public" and "domestic" spheres, or, to put it another way, public influence on the part of both women and men is built on family and lineage ties rather than set apart from them (Lebeuf 1971; Okonjo 1976: Sudarkassa 1976).

Within the Yoruba gender system, feminist consciousness is not separated from concern with and a feeling of responsibility for the totality of social issues. Achola Pala (1977:10) has written that where African women's organizations take up the cry for equal opportunities and launch social protest on behalf of women, they are invariably motivated by the totality of economic and political problems which result in great part from their neocolonial status; they are not motivated by "feminism per se." Indeed, such women have often enough chided Western women for, in effect, defining feminist consciousness in terms of hostility to men, rather than in terms of the respect they hold for themselves as women.

In a study of Nigerian women's political action between 1900 and 1965, Nina Mba (1977:589, 594, 599) has documented the activities carried on by women who were organized at the local, regional, and national levels. "Motivated by ideological and civic concerns as well as their own political and economic interests," women struggled to achieve the franchise and protested as well against the colonial appointment of chiefs, against taxes and market controls, and against school fees. They took for granted the necessity of having their own organizations and formed their own associations when they entered political parties. Furthermore, with a base in their common interests as women, they were often able to achieve greater national unity than men. Organizations such as the National Women's Union and the National Council of Women's Societies "were genuine attempts at forming nationwide organisations at a time when political parties were already regionalized." In 1976, when a draft constitution threatened to exclude women from executive and administrative bodies, the National Council of Women's Societies and the Women of the State of Oyo protested, pointing out that in Nigeria, "women were always represented as a group and as individuals, participating in the decision-making activities of their communities, whether these were villages, towns, or kingdoms." Indeed, they stated, "The International Women's Year is not introducing an alien concept into Nigeria but only drawing attention to the traditional female powers and participation which were eroded by colonialism."

It behooves Western feminists to listen to such women and learn from them, rather than prejudging or delimiting the many forms that struggle for women's liberation can take. Women are experiencing severe exploitation in much of the world, and their oppression is inseparably related to the threat of nuclear war and annihilation that the world confronts. There has never been a more pressing need for an international movement of women committed to pursuing the struggle for their liberation by uniting it with fights against oppression by class and by race. It is counterproductive, in working toward this goal, to separate the battle against patriarchal oppression from that against capitalist exploitation.

Notes

1. Along with other biological arguments for male dominance, sociobiological theorizing ignores the fact that patriarchal structuring of gender relations did not characterize gathering–hunting societies where relations between humans and the rest of nature were the most direct, but emerged as technological innovations increasingly mediated human relations with nature (Leacock 1980).

2. I was struck by the force of this myth when studying schooling in Zambia. At that time, in 1970, I could not find clear rebuttals to statements that school difficulties for African children were caused by "the presence of conservative, traditional, and primitive cultures often antagonistic to both the modern literary-humanistic and the scientific–rationalistic value system" (De Witt, 1969:125), or by "basic intellectual hindrances to national development" in cultures that provide "little in the way of scientific concepts" to children (Poole 1968:57–62). Later, when attending the 1973 African Regional Conference of the International Association for Cross-Cultural Psychology that met at the University of Ibadan, I was dismayed at how many African psychologists and educators were applying this type of formulation to working-class African children. My own research, in part, documented the skills that Zambian children were developing in their out-of-school experiences and their play, where they engaged in the same kinds of activities that leading educational circles in Great Britain and the United States encourage as the cognitive foundation for learning scientific concepts (Leacock 1972; 1980b).

3. Although not stated in these terms, Bee-Lan Chan Wang's (1980) comparison of women in China, Taiwan, and Malaysia illustrates this point well. Even so, recent reports on the USSR, such

as William Mandel's (1975), and on Cuba, such as Margaret Randall's (1981), show considerable further progress in equalizing women's work and social participation; and, in evaluating Tanzania, it is important to remember that, although it is committed to socialist goals, only a small part of the land is farmed communally.

4. For elaboration and documentation of this process, see references in Leacock 1981:193, 156–61; also Leacock 1977 and Sacks 1979.

5. Today one would, of course, insist that however significant the time involved, household tasks must be shared by all members of a household.

6. For an appraisal of theoretical and practical issues involved in the debate, see Holstrom 1981.

7. This point has been made for Latin America by Helen Safa 1983 and Marianne Schmink 1984.

8. The Grey Panther movement insists that care for the aged should be a social, not an individual, responsibility. They are, of course, not talking about segregated homes for the aged, but about the assurance of economic support through various services.

9. Not that this process was automatic or obvious. The greater availability of cash provided by industrial work in economies that depend in good part on subsistence farming temporarily masks the deterioration in diet caused by a decrease in farming. Furthermore, generalizing statements about women's exploitation tend to make them appear helpless victims. Hence Gail Omvedt's (1977) stress on studying sources of resistance rather than forms of oppression alone. An example of women's resourcefulness when their public labor is displaced by commercialism is afforded by Jamaican higglers, who use a network of assistants to buy out a desired item from a local supermarket in order to sell it at a marked-up price on the street (Gonzales 1980).

10. The parallel with respect to racism is close. Colonization and slavery associated with the rise of capitalism welded it firmly to racist institutions. It is useless to debate whether race or class has priority in the oppression of black workers in the United States. Further, racism has effectively divided the working class, and white workers trade in possibilities for making any real gains by succumbing to maneuvers that focus instead on saving their advantages over black workers. Black activists work either in separatist organizations committed to "going it alone," or in organizations that devote little more than lip service to the fight against racism. Unfortunately, as yet all too few seek the third alternative—strong, independent organization conceived as the basis for effecting working-class unity.

11. Other accounts of Aboriginal life from women's viewpoints are given in Gale 1974, Rohrlich-Leavitt, Sykes, and Weatherford 1975 and C. Berndt 1981.

12. Two ethnographic accounts of women's economic independence and personal autonomy and gender complementarity among economically similar peoples are Estioko-Griffin and Griffin (1981) and Wiessner (1982). The Agta of the Philippines and the !Kung San of Botswana differ from Aboriginal Australians in that female–male complementarity is not highly formalized. All three are similar in that, to borrow a formulation from Kelly's introduction, the contradiction between production and reproduction brought about by colonization did not exist previously.

References

Adoum, Jorge E. 1975. "In the Name of the Law, Hubby, Wash the Dishes." *Courier* 18–23.

Afonja, Simi. 1975. "Nigerian Women in Traditional Public Affairs." La Civilisation de la femme dans la tradition Africaine, *Présence Africaine*. 367–375.

———. 1976. "Barriers to the Supply and Demand of Women in the Nigerian Labour Force." Paper presented at the National Conference on Nigerian Women and Development in Relation to Changing Family Structure, University of Ibadan, Nigeria.

———. 1985. "Women, Power and Authority in Traditional Yoruba Society." In Leela Dube, Eleanor Leacock, and Shirley Ardener, eds., *Visibility and Power: Essays on Women in Society and Development*. Delhi: Oxford University Press.

All-China Democratic Women's Federation. 1949. *Documents of the Women's Movement in China*. Peking: Foreign Language Press.

Amin, Samir. 1977. *Unequal Development*. New York: Monthly Review Press.

Anokhina, L. A., et al. 1973. Review of Stephen and Ethel Dunn, *Peasants of Central Russia*, *Current Anthropology* 14:143–57.

Aptheker, Herbert. 1984. "We Will be Free: Advertisements for Runaways and the Reality of American Slavery." Occasional Paper No. 1, Ethnic Studies Program, University of California, Santa Clara.

Archives Nationales de France. Prefect of the Nord to Paris. 30 March 1867. F12 4562, Paris.

———. 10 July 1867, F12 4652, Paris.

———. Report. 5 May 1880, F12 4660, Paris.

———. 22 Dec. 1880, F12 4660, piece 719. Paris.

———. Report of the Conseiller de Prefecture Delegue to Paris. 28 Jan. 1886, F12 4661, Paris.

Archives Departementales du Nord. Police report to Prefect, Roubaix, 23 Nov. 1899, France.

———. Police report, Wattrelos. 4 Dec. 1899, M 625/106, France.

———. Song. M 625/106, France.

Arensberg, Conrad, 1937. *The Irish Countryman*. Garden City, N.Y.: Natural History Press.

Ariès, Phillippe. 1962. *Centuries of Childhood: A Social History of Family Life*. London: Jonathan Cape.

Arizpe, Lourdes, and Josefina Aranda. 1978. *Migracion, etnicismo y cambio economico*. Mexico City: Colegio de Mexico.

Atanda, J. A. 1973. *The New Oyo Empire: Indirect Rule and Change in West Nigeria 1893–1934*. London: Longmans Green.

Audiganne, Armaud. 1860. *Les Populations ouvrières et les industries de la France: Etudes comparatives*. Paris: Capelle.

Austen, Leo. 1940. "Botabalu: A Trobriand Chieftainess." *Mankind* 2: 270–73.

Awe, Bolanle. 1977. "The Iyalode in the Traditional Yoruba Political System." In Alice Schlegel, ed., *Sexual Stratification: A Cross-Cultural View*. New York: Columbia University Press.

Bader, Zimmat. 1975. "Private Property and Production in Bukoba District." M.A. thesis, Dar es Salaam.

Banks, J. A. 1954. *A Study of Family Planning among the Victorian Middle Classes.* London: Routledge & Kegan Paul.

Baran, Paul. 1959. *The Political Economy of Growth.* New York: Monthly Review Press.

Barash, David P. 1977. *Sociobiology and Behavior.* New York: Elsevier-North Holland.

Bautista, Germelino. 1977. "Socio-economic Conditions of the Landless Rice Workers in the Philippines: The Landless of Barrio Sta. Lucia as a Case in Point." In S. Hirashima, ed., *Hired Labor in Rural Asia.* Tokyo: Institute of Developing Economies.

Baxandall, Rosalyn, Linda Gordon, and Susan Reverby, eds. 1976. *America's Working Women.* New York: Vintage.

Beck, L., and N. Keddie, eds. 1978. *Women in the Muslim World.* Cambridge, Mass.: Harvard University Press.

Beechey, Veronica. 1977. "Some Notes on Female Wage Labor in Capitalist Production." *Capital and Class* 3:45–66.

Bell, Diane. 1980. "Desert Politics: Choices in the 'Marriage Market.'" In Mona Etienne and Eleanor Leacock, eds. *Women and Colonization: Anthropological Perspectives.* New York: Praeger.

———. 1983. *Daughters of the Dreaming.* Melbourne/Sydney: McPhee & Gribble/Allen & Unwin.

Bell, Diane, and Pam Ditton. 1980. *Law: The Old and the New: Aboriginal Women in Central Australia Speak Out.* Canberra: Aboriginal History.

Belova, U. A. 1972. "Family Size and Public Opinion." *Soviet Sociology* 11:126–44.

Benería, Lourdes. 1979. "Reproduction, Production and the Sexual Division of Labor." *Cambridge Journal of Economics* 3, 3:203–25.

———. 1983. "Accounting for Women's Work." In Lourdes Benería, ed., *Women and Development: The Sexual Division of Labor in Rural Economies.* Geneva: International Labor Organization.

Benería, Lourdes, and Gita Sen. 1981. "Accumulation, Reproduction, and Women's Role in Economic Development: Boserup Revisited." *Signs: Journal of Women in Culture and Society* 7:279–99.

Bengelsdorf, Carollee, and Alice Hageman. 1978. "Emerging from Underdevelopment: Women and Work in Cuba." *Race and Class* 14, 4:345–60.

Berndt, Catherine. 1950. "Women's Changing Ceremonies in Northern Australia." *L'Homme.* Paris: Hermann.

———. 1965. "Women and the 'Secret Life.'" In Ronald M. Berndt and C. H. Berndt, eds., *Aboriginal Man in Australia.* Sydney: Angus & Robertson.

———. 1981. "Interpretations and 'Facts' in Aboriginal Australia." In Frances Dahlberg, ed., *Woman the Gatherer.* New Haven, Conn.: Yale University Press.

Berndt, R. M. and C. H. Berndt. 1951. *Sexual Behavior in Western Arnhem Land.* New York: Viking Fund.

Bernstein, Henry. 1979. "African Peasantries: A Theoretical Framework." *Journal of Peasant Studies* 6:421–43.

Berry, Sarah. 1975. *Cocoa, Custom and Socio-Economic Change in Rural Western Nigeria.* Oxford: Clarendon Press.

Binder, L. 1976. "Area Studies: A Critical Reassessment." In L. Binder, ed., *The Study of the Middle East: Research and Scholarship in the Humanities and Social Sciences.* New York: Wiley.

Birks., S., and C. Sinclair. 1979. "Aspects of International Migration in the Arab Near East: Implications for USAID Policy." USAID. Mimeographed.

———. 1978. International Migration Project, Country Case Studies, University of Durham, England.

Blaise, Charles. 1899. *Le Tissage à la main du Cambresis: Etude d'industrie à domicile.* Lille: Bigot.

Blau, Francine. 1978. "Data on Women Workers: Past, Present and Future." In A. Stromberg and S. Harkess, eds., *Women Working.* Palo Alto, Calif.: Mayfield.

Blau, Francine, and Carol Jusenius. 1976. "Economists' Approaches to Sex Segregation in the Labor Market." In Martha Blaxall and Barbara Reagan, eds., *Women and the Workplace*. Chicago: University of Chicago Press.

Bloomberg, Susan E., et al. 1971. "A Census Probe into Nineteenth-Century Family History: Southern Michigan, 1850–80." *Journal of Social History* 5:26–45.

Blue, Richard N., and James H. Weaver. 1977. *A Critical Assessment of the Tanzanian Model of Development*. Agricultural Development Council Reprint, no. 39. New York: Agricultural Development Council.

Bolles, Lynn. 1979. "From Slavery to Factory: Women, Family Structures and Development in Jamaica." Paper presented at the American Anthropological Association Meeting, Cincinnati, Ohio.

Bonte, Pierre. 1977. "La Guerre dans les sociétés d'éleveurs nomades." *Etudes sur les sociétés de Pasteurs Nomades*. Les Cahiers du Centre d'Etudes et de Récherches Marxistes, no. 133. Paris.

Boserup, Ester. 1965. *The Conditions of Agricultural Growth*. London: Allen & Unwin.

———. 1970. *Woman's Role in Economic Development*. London: Allen & Unwin.

Bossen, L. 1975. "Women in Modernizing Societies." *American Ethnologist* 7:587–601.

Braun, Rudolf. 1966. "The Impact of Cottage Industry on an Agricultural Population." In David Landes, ed., *The Rise of Capitalism*. New York: Macmillan.

Braverman, Harry. 1974. *Labor and Monopoly Capital: The Degradation of Work in the Twentieth Century*. New York: Monthly Review Press.

Bridenthal, Renate, and Claudia Koonz, eds. 1977. "Women in Egalitarian Societies." *Becoming Visible: Women in European History*. Boston: Houghton Mifflin.

Brown, Susan E. 1975. "Love Unites Them and Hunger Separates Them: Poor Women in the Dominican Republic." In Rayna R. Reiter, ed., *Toward an Anthropology of Women*. New York: Monthly Review Press.

Buck, John L. 1937. *Land Utilization in China*. Nanking: University of Nanking.

Buck, P. H. (Te Rangi Hiroa). 1930. *Samoan Material Culture*. Honolulu: B. P. Bishop Museum Bulletin, no. 75.

Bukh, Jette. 1979. *The Village Woman in Ghana*. Uppsala: Scandinavian Institute of African Studies.

Burawoy, Michael. 1979. "The Anthropology of Industrial Work." *Annual Review of Anthropology* 8:231–66.

Burbach, R., and P. Flynn. 1978. "Agribusiness Targets Latin America." *NACLA Report on the Americas* 12:5.

Buttner, Thea. 1970. "The Economic and Social Character of Pre-Colonial States in Tropical Africa." *Journal of the Historical Society of Nigeria* 5.

Butts, R. Freeman, and Lawrence Cremin. 1953. *A History of Education in American Culture*. New York: Henry Holt & Co.

Buvinic, M., and N. Youssef. 1978. "Women-Headed Households: The Ignored Factor in Development Planning," International Center for Research on Women (ICRW), Report submitted to USAID/WID, March 1978.

Campbell, Shirley. 1981. "A Vacutan Mortuary Cycle." Paper presented at the Second Kula Conference, University of Virginia, Charlottesville.

Carapico, S., and Hart, S. 1977. "The Sexual Division of Labor and Prospects for Integrated Development: Report on Women's Economic Activities in Mahweet, Tawhile and Jihana Regions (Yemen Arab Republic), USAID/Yemen mimeo, June 1977.

Carner, George. 1980. "Survival, Interdependence and Competition among the Rural Poor." Paper presented at the Philippine Sociological Society National Convention, Manila.

Carr, Lois, and Lorena Walsh. 1979. "The Planter's Wife." In N. Cott and E. Pleck, eds., *A Heritage of Her Own*. New York: Simon & Schuster.

Castillo, Gelia T. 1979. *Beyond Manila: Philippine Rural Problems in Perspective*. Ottawa: International Development Research Centre.

Castro, Fidel. 1974. "The Revolution Has in Cuban Women an Impressive Political Force." Address delivered at the Second Conference of Cuban Women, Havana.

Caulfield, Mina Davis. 1974. "Imperialism, the Family, and Cultures of Resistance." *Socialist Revolution* 20:67–85.

Chee-Hoe, Chan. 1981. "A Study on Thai Female Factory Workers" Honors thesis, Department of Sociology, National University of Singapore.

Chee-Meow, Seah. 1980. "Singapore 1979: The Dialectics of Survival." *Asian Survey* 20:144–54.

Chen, Peter S. J. 1973. "Social Stratification in Singapore." Department of Sociology Working Paper, no. 12. Singapore: University of Singapore.

Ching-Ling, Tai. 1980. *Survey on Youth Attitudes in Singapore.* Singapore: Nanyang University.

Ciancanelli, Penelope. 1980. "Exchange, Reproduction, and Sex-Subordination among the Kikuyu of East Africa." *Review of Radical Political Economics* 12(2):25–36.

Cipolla, Carlo. 1969. *Literacy and Development in the West.* Baltimore: Penguin.

Circel, David, and Thomas Collins. 1980. "The Segmented Labor Market: A Perspective in Industrial Anthropology." Paper presented at the 15th Annual Meeting of the Southern Anthropological Society, Louisville, Ky.

Clark, David H., and Pang Eng-Fong. 1979. "Returns to Schooling and Training in Singapore." *Malayan Economic Review* 15:83–100.

Clark, Alice. 1968. *Working Life of Women in the Seventeenth Century.* London: Frank Cass.

Cliffe, Lionel. 1976. "Rural Political Economy in Africa." In Peter C. W. Gutkind and Emmanuel Wallerstein, eds., *The Political Economy of Contemporary Africa.* Beverly Hills, Calif.: Sage.

Codrington, R. H. 1891. *The Melanesians: Studies in Their Anthropology and Folklore.* Oxford: Clarendon Press.

Coote, W. 1883. *The Western Pacific.* London: Sampson, Low, Marston, Searle & Rivington.

Coquery-Vidrovitch, Catherine. 1975. "The African Mode of Production." *Critique of Anthropology,* nos.4/5.

Coveney, Peter. 1957. *Poor Monkey: The Child in Literature.* London: Dufour.

Croll, Elisabeth J. 1976. "Social Production and Female Status: Women in China." *Race and Class* 18:39–52.

———. 1977. "Jiang Village: A Household Survey." *China Quarterly* 72:786–814.

———. 1978. *Feminism and Socialism in China.* London: Routledge & Kegan Paul.

———. 1979. *Women and Rural Development: The Case of the People's Republic of China.* Geneva: International Labor Organization.

———. 1980. *The Politics of Marriage in Contemporary China.* Cambridge: Cambridge University Press.

———. 1981. "Women in Rural Production and Reproduction in the Soviet Union, China, Cuba, and Tanzania: Socialist Development Experiences." *Signs: Journal of Women in Culture and Society* 7:361–75.

Crook, Isabel, and David Crook. 1966. *The First Years of Yangyi Commune.* London: Routledge & Kegan Paul.

Daaku, Kwame Y. 1971. "Trade and Trading Patterns of the Akan in the Seventeenth and Eighteenth Centuries." In Claude Meillassoux, ed., *The Development of Indigenous Trade and Markets in West Africa.* London: Oxford University Press.

Daily News (Dar es Salaam).

Dalla Costa, Mariarosa, and Selma James. 1972. *Women and the Subversion of the Community.* Bristol: Falling Wall Press.

Damon, F. 1983. "What Moves the Kula: Opening and Closing Gifts on Woodlark Island." In E. R. Leach and J. W. Leach, eds., *New Perspectives on the Kula.* Cambridge: Cambridge University Press.

Davenport, William. 1959. "Nonunilineal Descent and Descent Groups." *American Anthropologist* 61:552–72.

David, Karina Constantino. 1978. "Slums and Underdevelopment." *Philippine Labor Review* 3:29–38.

David, Randolf, et al. 1980. "Transnational Corporations and the Phillippine Banana Export Industry." *Third World Papers*. Commodity Series, no. 2. Manila: Third World Center, University of the Philippines.

Davin, Delia. 1976. *Woman-Work: Women and the Party in Revolutionary China*. Oxford: Clarendon Press.

Davis, Angela Y. 1981. *Women, Race and Class*. New York: Random House.

Deere, Carmen Diana. 1977. "Changing Relations of Production and Peruvian Peasant Women's Work." *Latin American Perspectives* 4:48–69.

Deere, Carmen Diana, and Magdalena León de Leal. 1981. "Peasant Production, Proletarianization, and the Sexual Division of Labor in the Andes." *Signs: Journal of Women in Culture and Society* 7:338–360.

Degler, Carl. 1980. *At Odds: Women and the Family in America from the Revolution to the Present*. New York: Oxford University Press.

Delano, I. I. 1963. *L'ojo ojo un*. New York: Thomas Nelson.

Demos, John, and Virginia Demos. 1969. "Adolescence in Historical Perspective." *Journal of Marriage and the Family* 31:632–38.

Department of Statistics. 1978. *Report on the Census of Industrial Production*. Singapore.

———. 1978–79. *Yearbook of Statistics*. Singapore.

DeWitt, Nicholas. 1969. "Some Problems of Science Education in the Developing Countries of Africa." *The Social Reality of Scientific Myth, Science and Social Change*. New York: American Universities Field Staff.

Diamond, Norma. 1975. "Collectivisation, Kinship and the Status of Women in Rural China." *Bulletin of Concerned Asian Scholars* 25–32.

Dill, Bonnie Thornton. 1979. "The Dialectics of Black Womanhood." *Signs* 4:543–55.

———. 1983. "Racial Ethnic Families in the 19th Century." Presented at the Summer Institute on Women, Color, Center for Research on Women (June). Memphis State University, Memphis Tenn.

Dixon, R. 1979a. "Jobs for Women in Rural Industry and Services," University of California, Davis. Report submitted to USAID/WID, September 1979.

———. 1979b. "Women's Employment in the Context of Agrarian Reform and Rural Development: Review of Programs and Policies." Draft paper submitted to USAID/WID, May 1979.

Dodge, Norton T., and Murray Feshbach. 1967. "The Role of Women in Soviet Agriculture." In Jerzy Fl Korez, ed., *Soviet and East European Agriculture*. Berkeley and Los Angeles: University of California Press.

Dodge, Norton T. 1966. *Women in the Soviet Economy: Their Role in Economic, Scientific and Technical Development*. Baltimore: Johns Hopkins University Press.

———. 1971. "Recruitment and the Quality of the Soviet Agricultural Labor Force." In James R. Millar, ed., *The Soviet Rural Community: A Symposium*. Urbana: University of Illinois Press.

Dublin, Thomas. 1979. *Women at Work*. New York: Columbia University Press.

Dubois, W. E. B. 1946. *The World and Africa*. New York: Viking Press.

Dunn, Ethel. 1977. "Russian Rural Women." In Dorothy Atkinson, Alexander Dallin, and Gail Warshofsky Lapidus, eds., *Women in Russia*. Stanford, Calif.: Stanford University Press.

Dunn, Stephen P., and Ethel Dunn. 1967. *The Peasants of Central Russia*. New York: Holt, Rinehart & Winston.

Ecevit, Z. 1979. "International Labour Migration in the Middle East and North Africa: Trends, Effects and Policies." Paper presented at the Rockefeller Foundation Conference on International Migration, Bellagio, Italy, June.

Edholm, Felicity, Olivia Harris, and Kate Young. 1977. "Conceptualizing Women." *Critique of Anthropology* 3:101–30.

Einzig, P. 1949. *Primitive Money*. Oxford: Pergamon Press.

Elson, Dorothy, and Ruth Pearson. 1981. "Nimble Fingers Make Cheap Workers: An Analysis of Women's Employment in Third World Export Manufacturing." *Feminist Review* 87–107.

Ember, Melvin. 1959. "The Nonunilineal Descent Groups of Samoa." *American Anthropologist* 61:573–77.

Engels, Frederick. 1950. *The Condition of the Working Classes in England in 1844.* London: Allen & Unwin.

———. 1972. *The Origin of the Family, Private Property and the State.* New York: International Publishers.

Eng-Fong, Pang. 1975. "Growth, Inequality and Race in Singapore." *International Labor Review* 3:15–28.

Esman, Milton J., et al. 1978. *The Landless and Near-Landless in Developing Countries.* Ithaca, N.Y.: Cornell University, Center for International Studies.

Espenshade, Thomas J. 1977. *The Value and Cost of Children.* Population Bulletin, vol. 32, no. 1. Washington, D.C.: Population Reference Bureau.

Espiritu, Rafael. 1978. "Access and Participation of Landless Rural Workers in Government Programs." In *Proceedings of the Workshop on Landless Rural Workers (Laguna, Philippines).*

Estioko-Griffin, Agnes, and P. Bion Griffin. 1981. "Woman the Hunter: The Agta." In Frances Dahlberg, ed., *Woman the Gatherer.* New Haven, Conn.: Yale University Press.

Etienne, Mona. 1980. "Women and Men, Cloth and Colonization: The Transformation of Production–Distribution Relations among the Baule (Ivory Coast)." In M. Etienne and E. Leacock, eds., *Women and Colonization.* New York: Praeger.

Eviota, Elizabeth U. 1980. "Women Workers in the Electronics Industry: Case Studies From the Philippines." Paper prepared for the Project on the Effects of Transnational Corporations on Women Workers. Honolulu: East-West Culture Learning Institute.

Eviota, Elizabeth U., and Peter C. Smith. 1983. "The Migration of Women in the Philippines." In James T. Fawcett, et al., *Women in the Cities of Asia: Female Migration and Urban Adaptation.* Colorado: Westview Press.

Fage, J. 1962. "Some Remarks on Beads and Trade in Lower Guinea in the 16th and 17th Century." *Journal of African History* 6:342–47.

Farber, Bernard. 1973. "Family and Community Structure: Salem in 1880." In M. Gordon, ed., *The American Family in Social-Historical Perspective.* New York: St. Martin's Press.

Fasâ'i, Hasan, and Farsname-ye Naseri. 1972. *History of Persia under Qajar Rule,* tr. Heribert Busse. New York: Columbia University Press.

Feder, Ernst. 1977. *El Imperialismo Fresca.* Mexico: Ed. Campesina.

Federation of Cuban Women. 1974. *Statement of Fundamental Concepts.* Theses of Second Congress of Cuban Women. Havana: Second Congress of Cuban Women.

Fee, Terry. 1976. "Domestic Labor: An Analysis of Housework and Its Relation to the Production Process." *Review of Radical Political Economics* 8:1–8.

Field, Alexander J. 1976. "Education in Mid-Nineteenth Century Massachusetts: Human Capital Formation or Structural Reinforcement?" *Harvard Education Review* 46:521–552.

Field, Mark G. 1968. "Workers (and Mothers): Soviet Women Today." In Donald R. Brown et al., ed., *Role and Status of Women in the Soviet Union.* New York: Teachers College Press.

Flonneau, Jean-Marie. 1970. "Crise de vie chère et Mouvement Syndical, 1910–1914." *Le Mouvement Social* 72:49–81.

Fohlen, Claude. 1973. "The Industrial Revolution in France, 1700–1914." In Carlo Cippola, ed., *The Emergence of Industrial Societies.* London: Fontana.

Folbre, Nancy. 1979. "Patriarchy and Capitalism in New England, 1650–1900." Ph.D. diss., University of Massachusetts.

———. 1980. "Patriarch in Colonial New England." *Review of Radical Political Economics* 12:4–13.

Foner, Philip. 1974. *Organized Labor and the Black Worker.* New York: International Press.

———. 1980. *Women and the American Labor Movement,* vol. 1. New York: Free Press.

Frank, A. Gunder. 1967. *Capitalism and Underdevelopment in Latin America.* New York: Monthly Review Press.

———. 1978. "Superexploitation in Third World Countries." *Two Thirds: A Journal of Development Studies* 1:2.

Franklin, S. H. 1969. *The European Peasantry: The Final Phase*. London: Methuen.

Freeman, Derek. 1964. "Some Observations on Kinship and Political Authority in Samoa." *American Anthropologist* 66:553–68.

Freeman, Richard. 1975. "Overinvestment in College Training." *Journal of Human Resources*.

———. 1976. *The Over-Educated American*. New York: Academic Press.

Frobel, Folker, Jurgen Heinrichs, and Otto Kreye. 1980. *The New International Division of Labour*. Cambridge: Cambridge University Press.

Gailey, Christine W. 1980. "Putting Down Sisters and Wives: Tongan Women and Colonialization." In Mona Etienne and Eleanor Leacock, eds., *Women and Colonialization*. New York: Praeger.

Gale, Fay, ed. 1974. *Women's Role in Aboriginal Society*. Canberra: Australian Institute of Aboriginal Studies.

Geiger, H. Kent. 1968. *The Family in Soviet Russia*. Cambridge, Mass.: Harvard University Press.

George, Susan. 1977. *How the Other Half Dies*. Montclair, N.J.: Allanheld, Osmun.

Gimenez, Martha. 1977. "Population and Capitalism." *Latin American Perspectives* 4:5–40.

Glass, D. V. 1967. *Population: Policies and Movements in Europe*. London: Frank Cass.

Goldin, Claudia. 1977. "Female Labor Force Participation: The Origin of Black and White Differences, 1870–1880." *Journal of Economic History* 37:87–92.

Goldman, Irving. 1970. *Ancient Polynesian Society*. Chicago: University of Chicago Press.

Gonzales, Victoria. 1980. "Rural and Urban Employment Patterns of Women." Paper presented at the Conference on the Impact of "Development" on Women in the Caribbean, University of Minnesota, Minneapolis. February.

Goody, Jack, and Joan Buckley. 1973. "Inheritance and Women's Labour in Africa." *Africa* 43:108–121.

Grafteaux, Serge. 1975. *Meme Santerre: Une Vie*. Verviers: Marabout.

Granma (Havana). 1977.

Griffen, Sally, and Clyde Griffen. 1977. "Family and Business in a Small City: Poughkeepsie, N.Y., 1850–1880." In Tamara A. Hareven, ed., *Family and Kin in Urban Communities, 1700–1930*. New York: New Viewpoints.

Groneman, Carol. 1977. "She Earns as a Child; She Pays as a Man: Women Workers in a Mid-Nineteenth-Century New York City Community." In M. Canto and B. Laurie, eds., *Class, Sex, and the Woman Worker*. Westport, Conn.: Greenwood Press.

Grossman, Rachel. 1979. "Women's Place in the Integrated Circuit." *Southeast Asia Chronicle* 66:2–17.

Gruzdeva, E., and E. Chertikhina. 1975. "Women's Role in Social Production in Advanced Socialist Society." *Working Class and Contemporary World* 6:1–3.

Guerrero, Sylvia H. 1975. *Hawkers and Vendors in Manila and Baguio*. Manila: Institute of Social Work and Community Development, University of the Philippines.

Guilbert, Madeleine. 1966. *Les Femmes et l'Organisation Syndicale avant 1914*. Paris: Editions de CNRS.

Gutman, Herbert. 1976. *The Black Family in Slavery and Freedom*. New York: Pantheon.

Hammam, S. 1979. "Financing in the Informal Sector." Paper presented at the Sixth Africa Housing Conference, Rabat, Morocco, October.

Hammond, J. L., and B. Hammond. 1925. *The Rise of Modern Industry*. London: Methuen.

Hammond, Joyce D. 1981. *Tifaifai of Eastern Polynesia: Meaning and Communication in a Women's Reintegrated Art Form*. Ph.D. diss., University of Illinois at Urbana-Champaign.

Hamont, P. 1843. *L'Egypte sous Mehmet Ali*. Paris.

Hanagan, Michael. 1976. *Artisans and Industrial Workers: Work Structure, Technological Change and Worker Militancy in Three French Towns: 1870–1914*. Ph.D. diss., University of Michigan.

Hanson, Paul R. 1976. "The 'Vie Chère' Protests in France, 1911." University of California, Berkeley. Photocopy.

Harik, E. 1979. "Socioeconomic Profile of Rural Egypt." Research paper, International Islamic Centre for Population Studies and the Rural Development Committee, Cornell University, Cairo, March.

Harris, Barbara. 1978. *Beyond Her Sphere: Women and the Professions in American History.* Westport, Conn.: Greenwood Press.

Hartmann, Heidi. 1976. "Capitalism, Patriarchy and Job Segregation by Sex." In M. Blaxall and B. Reagen, eds., *Women and the Workplace.* Chicago: University of Chicago Press.

———. 1981. "The Family as the Locus of Gender, Class, and Political Struggle: The Example of Housework." *Signs: Journal of Women in Culture and Society* 6:366–94.

Hartmann, Heidi I., and Ann R. Markusen. 1980. "Contemporary Marxist Theory and Practice: A Feminist Critique." *Review of Political Economics* 12:87–94.

Helleiner, G. K. 1973. "Manufactured Exports from Less Developed Countries and Multinational Firms." *Economic Journal* 83:21–47.

Heng-Chee, Chan. 1975. "Politics in an Administrative State: Where Has the Politics Gone?" In Seah Chee-Meow, ed., *Trends in Singapore.* Singapore: Singapore University Press.

———. 1976. *The Dynamics of One Party Dominance: The PAP at the Grass-Roots.* Singapore: Singapore University Press.

Hershberg, Theodore. 1972. "Free Blacks in Antebellum Philadelphia: A Study of Ex-Slaves, Freeborn, and Socioeconomic Decline." *Journal of Social History* 5:183–209.

Hewitt de Alcantara, Cynthia. 1978. *La Modernizacion de la agricultura Mexicana.* Mexico: Siglo XXI Editores, S.A.

Heyzer, Noeleen. 1983. "From Rural Subsistence to an Industrial Peripheral Workforce: Female Malaysian Migrants in Singapore." In Lourdes Benería, ed., *Women and Development: The Sexual Division of Labor in Rural Economies.* Geneva: International Labor Organization.

Himmelweit, Susan, and Simon Mohun. 1977. "Domestic Labour and Capital." *Cambridge Journal of Economics* 1:15–31.

Hjarno, Jan. 1979–80. "Social Reproduction: Towards an Understanding of Aboriginal Samoa." *Folk* 21/22:73–123.

Hodder, B. W. 1962. "The Yoruba Rural Market." In Paul Bohannan and George Dalton, eds., *Markets in Africa.* Evanston, Ill.: Northwestern University Press.

Holstrom, Nancy. 1981. "Women's Work, the Family and Capitalism." *Science and Society* 45:186–211.

Hopkins, A. G. 1973. *An Economic History of West Africa.* London: Longman.

Huntington, Suellen. 1975. "Issues in Woman's Role in Economic Development: Critique and Alternatives." *Journal of Marriage and the Family* 37:1001–12.

IRCW. See International Center for Research on Women.

ILO. See International Labor Organization.

India, Committee on the Status of Women in India. 1974. *Towards Equality.* New Delhi: Committee on the Status of Women in India.

International Center for Research on Women. 1980. "Keeping Women Out: A Structural Analysis of Women's Employment in Developing Countries." ICRW.

International Labor Organization. 1967. *Household Income and Expenditure Statistics.* Geneva: International Labor Organization.

———. 1970. *Conditions of Work of Women and Young Workers in Plantations. Geneva: International Labor Organization.*

———. 1974. *Sharing in Development: A Programme of Employment, Equity and Growth for the Philippines.* National Economic and Development Authority.

———. 1976. *Employment, Growth and Basic Needs: A One-World Problem.* New York: Praeger.

———. 1980. *Women in the Economic Activities of the World: A Statistical Analysis.* Geneva: International Labor Organization.

Johnson, Samuel. 1921. *The History of the Yorubas.* Lagos, Nigeria: Church Missionary Society.

Joint Housing Team. 1977. "Low Income Housing and Community Upgrading for Low Income Egyptians." Federation for Cooperative Housing, report submitted to USAID.

Jurado, Gonzalo P., and Rosalinda Tidalgo. 1978. *The Informal Services Sector in the Greater*

Manila Area, 1976. Manila: University of the Philippines, Institute of Economic Development and Research, no. 7805.

Kaberry, Phyllis M. 1939. *Aboriginal Women: Sacred and Profane.* London: Routledge & Kegan Paul.

Kaeppler, Adrienne L. 1978. "Exchange Patterns in Goods and Spouses: Fiji, Tonga and Samoa." *Mankind* 11:246–52.

Kellenbenz, Herman. 1974. "Rural Industries in the West from the End of the Middle Ages to the Eighteenth Century," tr. K. E. M. George. In Peter Earle, ed., *Essays in European History 1500–1800.* Oxford: Clarendon Press.

Kelly, María Patricia Fernández. 1980. "'Maquiladoras' and Women in Cuidad Juarez: The Paradoxes of Industrialization under Global Capitalism." Department of Sociology, University of California, Berkeley. Mimeographed. Published in abridged version as "The 'Maquila' Women," *NACLA Report on the Americas* 14, no. 5.

———. (Introduction to this book!)

———. 1983. "Mexican Border Industrialization: Female Labour Force Participation and Migration." *International Migration Review.*

Keng-Swee, Goh. 1972. *The Economics of Modernization and Other Essays.* Singapore: Asia Pacific Press.

———. 1978. *Report on the Ministry of Education.* Singapore: Ministry of Education.

Kennedy, Susan. 1979. *If All We Did Was to Weep at Home.* Bloomington: Indiana University Press.

Kessler-Harris, Alice. 1975. "Stratifying by Sex: Understanding the History of Working Women." In Richard E. Edwards, Michael Reich II, and David M. Gordon, eds., *Labor Market Segmentation.* Lexington, Mass.: D. C. Heath.

Kleinberg, Susan. 1977. "The Systematic Study of Urban Women." In M. Cantor and B. Laurie, eds., *Class, Sex and the Women Worker.* Westport, Conn.: Greenwood Press.

Krämer, A. 1930. *The Samoan Islands,* trans. D. H. and M. DeBeer. 2 vols. Stuttgart: E. Naegele.

———. 1958. *Salamasina: Scenes from Ancient Samoan Culture and History, 1923,* tr. Association of the Marist Brothers. Pago Pago: Marist Brothers.

Kuo-Chun, Chao. 1960. *Agrarian Policy of the Communist Party, 1921–1959.* New Delhi: Asia Publishing House.

Labour Force Survey. 1975. Amman, Jordan: Department of Statistics.

Lambton, A. K. S. 1953. *Landlord and Peasant in Persia.* Oxford: Oxford University Press.

Lammermeir, Paul. 1973. "The Urban Black Family of the Nineteenth Century: A Study of Black Family Structure in the Ohio Valley, 1850–1880." *Journal of Marriage and the Family* 35:440–56.

Landes, David. 1965. "Technological Change and Development in West Europe 1750–1914." *The Cambridge History of Europe,* vol. 6. Cambridge: Cambridge University Press.

Langdon, S. 1974. "The Political Economy of Dependence: Note toward Analysis of Multinational Corporations in Kenya." *Journal of East African Research and Development,* vol. 4, no. 2.

Lapidus, Gail Warshofsky. 1975. "Political Mobilization, Participation and Leadership: Women in Soviet Politics." *Comparative Politics* 8:90–118.

———. 1977. "Sexual Equality in Soviet Policy: A Developmental Perspective." In Dorothy Atkinson, Alexander Dallin, and Gail Warshofsky Lapidus, eds., *Women in Russia.* Stanford, Calif.: Stanford University Press.

Lappe, Francis Morre et al. 1977. *Food First: Beyond the Myth of Scarcity.* Boston: Houghton Mifflin.

Laquian, Aprodicio. In press. *The Political Integration of Urban Squatters and Slum Dwellers in the Philippines.* Mimeographed.

Larguia, Isabel, and John Dumoulin. 1973. "Towards a Science of Women's Liberation." *Casa de las Americas* (March-June 1971): Reprinted as *Red Rag Pamphlet,* no. 11. London: Red Rag Collective.

Laslett, Peter, ed. 1971. *The World We Have Lost.* New York: Scribner.

Layard, J. 1924. *Stone Men of Malekula.* London.

Lazonick, William. 1978. "The Subjection of Labor to Capital: The Rise of the Capitalist System." *Review of Radical Political Economy* 10:1–31.

Leacock, Eleanor. 1972a. "At Play in African Villages." *Natural History Magazine* 80:60–65.

———. 1972b. "Introduction." In Frederick Engels, *The Origin of the Family, Private Property and the State*. New York: International Publshers.

———. 1977. "Women in Egalitarian Society." In Bridenthal and Koonz, eds., *Becoming Visible*. Boston: Houghton Mifflin.

———. 1979. "Class, Commodity and the Status of Women." In S. Diamond, ed., *Toward a Marxist Anthropology*. The Hague: Mouton.

———. 1980a. "Social Behavior, Biology and the Double Standard." In George W. Barlow and James Silverberg, eds., *Sociobiology: Beyond Nature/Nuture? Reports, Definitions and Debate*. Boulder, Colo.: Westview Press.

———. 1980b. "Politics, Theory and Racism in the Study of Black Children." in S. Diamond, ed., *Theory & Practice*. The Hague: Mouton.

———. 1981. *Myths of Male Dominance: Collected Articles on Women Cross-Culturally*. New York: Monthly Review Press.

Lebeuf, Annie M. D. 1971. "The Role of Women in the Political Organization of African Societies." In Denise Paulme, ed., *Women of Tropical Africa*. London: Routledge & Kegan Paul.

Ledesma, Antonio J. 1979. Socioeconomic Aspects of Filipino Sugar Farm Workers: Three Views from the Cane Field. *Philippine Studies* 27:231–46.

Lee, Soo Ann. 1973. *Industrialization in Singapore*. Victoria, Australia: Longman Australia.

Lenin, Vladimir Ilyich Ulyanov. 1952. *Women and Society*. Reprint ed. New York: International Publishers.

Lepowksi, Maria. 1981. "Death and Mortuary Ritual on Vanatinai (Sudest Island), Papua New Guinea." Paper presented at the Second Kula Conference, University of Virginia, Charlottesville.

Lerner, Gerda. 1979. "The Lady and the Mill Girl." In N. Cott and E. Pleck, eds., *A Heritage of Her Own*. New York: Simon & Schuster.

LeRoy-Beaulieu. 1873. *Le Travail des femmes au XIXe Siècle*. Paris: Charpentier.

Lim, Linda. 1978. *Women Workers in Multinational Corporations: The Case of the Electronics Industry in Malaysia and Singapore*. Michigan Occasional Papers, no. 9. Ann Arbor: University of Michigan.

Lin-Sien, Chia, and Chia Siow-Yue. 1978. "The Informal Sector in Singapore." Paper presented at the Seminar on the Informal Sector, Indonesian Human Resources Development Foundation, Jakarta.

Lloyd, Peter C. 1955. "The Yoruba Lineage." *Africa* 25:235–51.

Longhurst, Richard. In press. "Resource Allocation and the Sexual Division of Labor: A Case Study of a Moslem Hausa Village in Northern Nigeria." In Lourdes Benería, ed., *Women and Development: The Sexual Division of Labor in Rural Economies*. Geneva: International Labor Organization.

Lopez, Maria Elena, and Mary Racelis Hollnsteiner. 1976. "People on the Move: Migrant Adaptations to Manila Residence." In Rodolfo A. Bulatao, ed., *Philippine Population Research*. Makati, Philippines: Population Center Foundation.

Lowenberg, Bert, and Ruth Bogin, eds. *Black Women in Nineteenth-Century American Life*. University Park, Pa., and London: The Pennsylvania State University Press.

MacIntyre, Martha. 1981. Personal Communication.

Mackintosh, Maureen. 1979. "Domestic Labour and the Household." In Sheila Burman, ed., *Fit Work for Women*. London: Croom Helm.

Malinowski, Bronislaw. 1922. *Argonauts of the Western Pacific*. New York: E. P. Dutton.

———. 1926. *Crime and Custom in Savage Society*. London: Kegan Paul, Trench & Trubner.

Mamdani, Mahmood. 1972. *The Myth of Population Control*. New York: Monthly Review Press.

Mandel, William. 1975. *Soviet Women*. New York: Doubleday.

Mannheim, Charles. 1902. *De la Condition des ouvriers dans les manufactures de l'état (tabacs-allumettes)*. Paris: Giard & Eriere.

Maritch, Srefen. 1930. *Histoire de Mouvement Social sous le Second Empire à Lyon*. Paris: Rousseau.

Marshall, Gloria. 1964. *Women, Trade and the Yoruba Family*. Ph.D. diss., Columbia University.

Marx, Karl. 1974. *Capital*, vol. I, tr. Eden and Cedar Paul. New York: Dutton.

Mass, Bonnie. 1977. "Puerto Rico: A Case Study of Population Control." *Latin American Perspectives* 4:66–81.

Massiah, Jocelyn. 1980. "Family Structure and the Status of Women in the Carribean, with Particular Reference to Women Who Head Households." UNESCO. SS-80/Conf. 627/COL. 34. Paper delivered at the Conference on Women, Development and Population Trends, Paris.

Mauss, Marcel. 1979. *Sociology and Psychology*, tr. B. Brewster. London: Routledge & Kegan Paul.

Mba, Nina Emma. 1977. "Women in Southern Nigerian Political History: 1900–1965." Ph.D. diss., University of Ibadan, Nigeria.

———. 1974. "Barriers to the Full Participation of Women in the Socialist Transformation of Tanzania." Paper presented at Conference on the Role of Rural Women in Development, Princeton University, Princeton, N.J.

———. 1972. "The 'New Woman' and Traditional Norms in Tanzania." *Journal of Modern African Studies* 10:57–72.

———. 1977. "The Status of African Women." Paper presented at Conference on Women and Development, Maseru, Lesotho.

———. 1976. "Women as Labour in Underdevelopment." Paper presented at Conference on Women and Development, June. Wellesley College, Wellesley, Mass.

Mblinyi, Marjorie. 1970. "Traditional Attitudes towards Women: A Major Constraint on Rural Development." Paper presented at East African Social Sciences Conference, Dar es Salaam.

McClelland, C. 1978. "Yemeni Worker Migration and Remittances." USAID mimeograph, June 1978.

McDougall, Mary Lynn. 1977. "Working Class Women during the Industrial Revolution, 1780–1914." In Renate Bridenthal and Claudia Koonz, eds., *Becoming Visible: Women in European History*. Boston: Houghton Mifflin.

McLaro, N. E. 1977. *Literacy: A Tool for the Development of Rural Women in Tanzania*. Studies of Adult Education, Research Paper, no. 27. Dar es Salaam: University of Dar es Salaam.

McLaughlin, V. 1977. "Italian Women and Work." In M. Camptr and B. Laurie, eds., *Class, Sex and the Woman Worker*. Westport, Conn.: Greenwood Press.

McManus, Edgar. 1973. *Black Bondage in the North*. New York: Syracuse University Press.

Mead, Margaret. 1930. *Social Organization of Manu'a*. Honolulu: B. P. Bishop Museum Bulletin, no. 76.

Medrano, Diana. 1980. "El caso de las obreras de los cultivos de flores de los municipios de Chia, Cajica, y Tabio en la sabana de Bogota, Columbia." Research paper, Rural Employment Policies Branch, ILO, Geneva.

Meehan, Betty Hiatt. 1970. "Woman the Gatherer." In Fay Gale, ed., *Women's Role in Aboriginal Society*. Canberra: Australian Institute of Aboriginal Studies.

Meggitt, Mervyn J. 1962. *Desert People*. Sydney: Angus & Robertson.

Meillassoux, Claude. 1964. *Anthropologie économiques des Gouro de Côte d'Ivoire*. Paris: Mouton.

———. 1975. "From Production to Reproduction: A Marxist Approach to Economic Anthropology. *Economy and Society* 1. 93-104.

Mendras, Henri. 1970. *The Vanishing Peasant: Innovation and Change in French Agriculture*. Cambridge, Mass.: MIT Press.

Metge, Joan. 1967. *The Maoris of New Zealand*. London: Routledge & Kegan Paul.

Mies, Maria. In press. "The Dynamics of the Sexual Division of Labor and the Integration of Women into the World Market." In Lourdes Benería, ed., *Women and Development: The Sexual Division of Labor in Rural Economies*. Geneva: International Labor Organization.

Minge, Wanda. 1978. "A Theory of the European Household Economy during the Peasant to Worker Transition." *Ethnology* 17: 183–196.

Ministry of Labour. 1978. *Report on the Labour Force Survey of Singapore*. Singapore.

———. 1979. *Report on the Labour Force Survey of Singapore*. Singapore.

Mitch, David. 1979. "The Causes and Spread of Literacy in 19th Century England." Paper presented at Workshop on Social History, Harvard, Dec. 1977.

Moissonier, Maurice. 1972. *La Première Internationale et la commune a Lyon (1865–1871)*. Paris: Editions Sociales

Mullings, Leith. 1978. "Ethnicity and Stratification in the Urban United States." *Annals NY Acad. Sci.*, vol. 318.

Munn, Nancy D. 1973. *Walbiri Iconography*. London: Cornell University Press.

Murra, John V. 1962. "Cloth and Its Functions in the Inca State." *American Anthropologist* 64:710–28.

Murray, Nicola. 1978. "Changes in the Position of Women in Cuban Society." B. Lit. thesis, Cambridge University.

Musgrave, P. W. 1967. *Technical Change, the Labour Force and Education: A Study of the British and German Iron and Steel Industries 1860–1964*. New York: Pergamon Press.

Myntti, C. 1971. *Women and Development in the Yemen Arab Republic*. Eschborn: German Agency for Technical Cooperation, Ltd.

NACLA. *See* North American Conference on Latin America.

Nayyar, Deepak. 1978. "Transnational Corporations and Manufactured Exports from Poor Countries." *Economic Journal* 88:59–84.

Nelson, Lowry. 1970. *Rural Cuba*. New York: Octagon.

Newbury, C. W. 1969. "Trade and Authority in West Africa, 1850–1880." In L. H. Gann and Peter Guignan, eds., *History and Politics of Colonialism, 1870–1914*. Cambridge: Cambridge University Press.

North American Congress on Latin America (NACLA). 1978. "Capital's Flight: The Apparel Industry Moves South." *NACLA Report on the Americas* 11, no. 3.

Nyerere, Julius. 1967. *Socialism and Rural Development*. Dar es Salaam: Government Printers.

Nzula, A. T., I. I. Potekhin, and A. Z. Zusmanovich. 1979. In Robin Cohen, ed., *Forced Labour in Colonial Africa*, tr. Hugh Jenkins. London: Zed Press.

Ofreneo, Rene E. 1980a. *Capitalism in Philippine Agriculture*. Quezon City: Foundation for Nationalist Studies.

———. 1980b. "Monopoly Expansion in Philippine Agriculture." Paper presented at the Philippine Sociological Society Convention.

Ogunbiyi, I. A. 1969. "The Position of Muslim Women as Stated by Uthman B. Fudi." *Odu: A Journal of West African Studies*, n.s. 2.

Oguntuyi, A. 1952. *A Short History of Ado Ekiti, Part II*. Akure, Nigeria: Aduralere Press.

Okonjo, Kamene. 1976. "The Dual-Sex Political System in Operation: Igbo Women and Community Politics in Midwestern Nigeria." In Nancy J. Hafkin and Edna G. Bay, eds., *Women in Africa*. Stanford, Calif.: Stanford University Press.

Olomola, I. 1977. *Pre-Colonial Patterns of Inter-State Relations in Eastern Yorubaland*. Ph.D. diss., University of Ife, Ile-Ife, Nigeria.

Omvedt, Gail. 1977. "On the Participant Study of Women's Movements: Methodological, Definitional, and Action Considerations." In Gerrit Huizer and Bruce Mannheim, eds., *The Politics of Anthropology*. The Hague: Mouton.

Ortner, Sherry. 1981. "Gender and Sexuality in Hierarchical Societies: The Case of Polynesia and Some Comparative Implications." In Sherry Ortner and Harriet Whitehead, eds., *The Cultural Construction of Gender and Sexuality*. Cambridge: Cambridge University Press.

Oshuntogun, A. 1976. "Rural Women in Agricultural Development." Paper presented at the National Conference on Nigerian Women and Development in Relation to Changing Family Structure, University of Ibadan, Nigeria.

Ostapenko, I. V. 1971. "The Village of Cadyshi Today." *Soviet Sociology* 10:47–71.

———. 1974. "The Effect of Woman's New Production Role on Her Position in the Family." *Soviet Sociology* 12:85–99.

Owens, Leslie. 1976. *This Species of Property.* New York: Oxford University Press.

Pala, Achola O. 1977. "Definitions of Women and Development: An African Perspective." *Signs: Journal of Women in Culture and Society* 3:9–13.

Palmer, Robert, and Neil Parsons, eds., 1977. *The Roots of Rural Poverty in Central and Southern Africa.* Berkeley and Los Angeles: University of California Press.

Palmer, Ingrid. 1977. "Rural Poverty in Indonesia." *Poverty and Landlessness in Rural Asia.* Geneva: International Office.

Palmer, Robert, and Neil Parsons, eds., 1977. *The Roots of Rural Poverty in Central and Southern Africa.* Berkeley: University of California Press.

Pedler, J. 1955. *Economic Geography of West Africa.* London: Longmans Green.

People's Daily. (13 May 1973; 1 July 1973; 6 March 1972; 8 March 1973; 16 May 1956; 12 Aug. 1956; 13 July 1958; 8 March 1959; 2 June 1958). *Renmin Ribao.* Peking.

Perrot, Michelle. 1974. *Les Ouvriers en grève: France, 1871–1890.* Paris: Mouton.

———. ed. 1978. "Document: Le Témoignage de Lucie Baud, ouvrière en soie." *Le Mouvement Social* 105:139–46.

Petersen, Glenn. 1982. "Ponapean Matriliny: Production, Exchange, and the Ties that Bind." *American Ethnologist* 9:129–44.

Pleck, Elizabeth. 1972. "The Two Parent Household: Black Family Structure in Late Nineteenth-Century Boston." *Journal of Social History* 6:3–31.

———. 1979. "A Mother's Wages." In N. Cott and E. Pleck, eds., *A Heritage of Her Own.* New York: Simon & Schuster.

Polanyi, Karl. 1944. *The Great Transformation.* New York: Holt, Rinehart & Winston.

Poole, H. E. 1968. "The Effect of Urbanization upon Scientific Concept Attainment among Hausa Children of Northern Nigeria." *British Journal of Educational Psychology* 38:57–65.

Powell, H. A. 1980. Review of *Women of Value, Men of Renown,* by Annette Weiner. *American Anthropologist* 82:700–702.

Purcell, Kate. 1979. "Militancy and Acquiscence among Women Workers." In Sandra Burman, ed., *Fit Work for Women.* New York: St. Martin's Press.

Purcell, Susan Kaufman. 1973. "Modernizing Women for a Modern Society: The Cuban Case." In Ann Pescatello, ed., *Female and Male in Latin America.* Pittsburgh: University of Pittsburgh Press.

Quick, Patricia. 1974. "Education and Industrialization: Elementary Education in Nineteenth Century England and Wales." Ph.D. diss., Harvard University.

Quiggan, A. H. 1949. *A Survey of Primitive Money.* London: Methuen.

Radwan, S. 1978. *Agrarian Reform and Rural Poverty in Egypt: 1952–1975.* Geneva.

Randall, Margaret. 1981. *Women in Cuba: Twenty Years Later.* New York: Smyrna Press.

Raphael, D., ed. 1975. "Introduction." In *Being Female, Reproduction, Power and Change.* The Hague: P. L. Mouton.

Rapp, Rayna. 1978. "Family and Class in Contemporary America: Notes toward an Understanding of Ideology." *Science and Society* 43: 278–300.

Red Flag. 30 Sept. 1969; 1 Feb. 1972; 11 Dec. 1973. *Honggi.* Peking.

Reddy, William. 1979. "Some Comments on the History of the Family." Paper presented at the Conference on Social History and Social Theory, Institute on Western Europe, Columbia University, New York.

Reed, Ritchie H., and Susan McIntosh. 1972. "Costs of Children." In *Research Reports,* vol. 2. Commission on Population Growth and the American Future. Washington, D.C.: U.S. Government Printing Office.

Richards, A. 1980. "Egyptian Agriculture in Trouble." *MERIP* No. 84 (January).

Rivers, W. H. R. 1914. *The History of Melanesian Society.* Cambridge: Cambridge University Press.

Rodman, Margaret. 1981. "Border-Crossing between Spheres of Exchange in East Aoba." In M.

Allen and M. Patterson, eds., *Vanualu: Politics and Ritual in Island Melanesia.* New York: Academic Press.

Rodney, Walter. 1972. *How Europe Underdeveloped Africa.* London: Bogle-L'Ouverture.

Roheim, Geza. 1933. "Women and Their Life in Central Australia." *Journal of the Royal Anthropological Institute,* vol. 63.

Rohrlich-Leavitt, Ruby, Barbara Sykes, and Elizabeth Weatherford. 1975. "Aboriginal Woman: Male and Female Anthropological Perspectives." In Rayna R. Reiter, Ed., *Toward an Anthropology of Women.* New York: Monthly Review Press.

Roldan, Marta. 1980. "Trabajo asalariado y condiction de la mujer rural en un cultivo de exportacion: El caso de las trabajadoras del tomate en el estado de Sinaloa, Mexico." Research paper, Rural Employment Policies Branch, ILO, Geneva.

Ronner, Lucila Diza, and Maria Elena Muñoz. 1978. "La Mujer asalariada en el sector agricola." *America Indigena* 38: 327–34.

Rosenzweig, Mark. 1977. "The Demand for Children in Farm Households." *Journal of Political Economy* 85:123–46.

Rowbotham, Sheila. 1972. *Women, Resistance and Revolution.* London: Allen Lane.

Ruiz, Nancy, 1977. "Cuban Women's Federation." Paper presented at the Workshop on Women's Development, Institute of Social Studies, The Hague.

Ryan, Mary. 1983. *Womanhood in America.* New York: Franklin Watts.

Sacks, Karen. 1979. *Sisters and Wives.* Westport, Conn.: Greenwood Press.

Safa, Helen I. 1980. "Class Consciousness among Working-Class Women in Latin America: Puerto Rico." In June Nash and Helen I. Safa, eds., *Sex and Class in Latin America: Women's Perspectives on Politics, Economics and the Third World.* New York: Bergin & Garvey.

———. In press. "The Differential Incorporation of Hispanic Women Migrants into the U.S. Labor Force.: In Delores Mortiner and R. S. Bryce-Laporte, eds., *Caribbean and Latin Immigrants to the United States: The Female Experience.* Washington, D.C.: Smithsonian Institution.

———. In press. "Work and Women's Liberation: A Case Study of Garment Workers." In Leith Mullings, ed., *The Anthropology of Urban America.* New York: Columbia University Press.

———. 1983. "Women, Production and Reproduction in Industrial Capitalism: A Comparison of Brazilian and U.S. Factory Workers." In June Nash and M. Patricia Fernández Kelly, eds., *Women, Men, and the International Division of Labor.* Albany: State University of New York Press.

Saffioti, Heleieth I. E. 1978. *Women in Class Society,* tr. Michael Vale. New York: Monthly Review Press.

Safi-Nejâd, J. 1355. "Qarat" (Raiding), "daramadhaye qeir-e mostamer-e xan dar do re-ye xan xani." Majale-ye danesga, somare 6, sal 2, nasriye-ye markazi-ye danesgah-e tehran, safhe 42: 10–54.

Sahlins, Marshall. 1958. *Social Stratification in Polynesia.* Seattle: University of Washington Press.

St. George, George. 1973. *Our Soviet Sister.* Washington, D.C.: Robert B. Luce.

St. John, J. 1841. *Egypt and Mohamed Ali,* vol. 2. London.

Salaff, Janet. 1972. "The Role of the Family in Health Care." In *Medicine and Health Care in China.* Washington, D.C.: U.S. Department of Health.

———. 1981. *Working Daughters of Hong Kong.* New York: Cambridge University Press.

Sanderson, Michel. 1972. *The Universities and British Industry, 1850–1970.* London: Routledge.

Santa Cruz Collective on Labor Migration. 1978. "The Global Migration of Labor and Capital." In *U.S. Capitalism in Crisis.* New York: Union for Radical Economics.

Schaar, Stuart. 1979. "Orientalism at the Service of Fascism." *Journal of Race and Class* 73–79.

Schlesinger, Rudolf. 1949. *The Family in the USSR.* London: Routledge & Kegan Paul.

Schmink, Marianne. 1985. "Women in Brazilian 'Aberture' Politics." In Leela Dube, Eleanor Leacock, and Shirley Ardener, eds., *Visibility and Power: Essays on Women in Society and Development.* Delhi: Oxford University Press.

Schoeffel, Penelope. 1977. "The Origin and Development of Contemporary Women's Associations in Western Samoa." *Journal of Pacific Studies* 3:1–22.

———. 1981. *Daughters of Sina: A Study of Gender, Status and Power in Western Samoa*. Ph.D. diss., Australia National University.

Schran, Peter. 1969. *The Development of Chinese Agriculture, 1950–1959*. Chicago: University of Chicago Press.

Seers, Dudley, ed. 1964. *Cuba: The Economic and Social Revolution*. Chapel Hill: University of North Carolina Press.

Seligman, C. G. 1910. *The Melanesians of British New Guinea*. Cambridge: Cambridge University Press.

Sen, Gita. 1980. "The Sexual Division of Labor and the Working-Class Family: Toward a Conceptual Synthesis of Class Relations and the Subordination of Women." *Review of Radical Political Economics* 12:76–86.

———. In press. "Women Workers and the Green Revolution." In Lourdes Beneriá, ed., *Women and Development: The Sexual Division of Labor in Rural Economies*. Geneva: International Labor Organization.

Shanin, Teodor, ed. 1971. *Peasants and Peasant Societies*. Baltimore, Md.: Penguin.

Shashahani, Soheila. 1981. *The Four Seasons of the Sun*. Ph.D. thesis, New School for Social Research.

Sheridan, George J., Jr. 1979. "Household and Craft in an Industrializing Economy: The Case of the Silk Weavers of Lyon." In John M. Merriman, ed., *Consciousness and Class Experience in Nineteenth-Century Europe*. New York: Holmes & Meier.

Shore, Brad. 1983. *Sala'i Lua: A Samoan Mystery*. New York: Columbia University Press.

Shorter, Edward. 1975. *The Making of the Modern Family*. New York: Basic Books.

Sidal, Ruthy. 1972. *Women and Child Care in China*. London: Penguin Books.

Silva de Rojas, Alicia E., and Consuelo Corredor de Prieto. 1980. "La explotacion de la mano de obra femenina en la industria de las flores: Un estudio de caso en Columbia." Research paper, Rural Employment Policies Branch, ILO, Geneva.

Simon, Brian. 1960. *Studies in the History of Education 1780–1870*. London: Lawrence & Wishart.

Smith, Daniel. 1979. "Family Limitation, Sexual Control and Domestic Feminism in Victorian America. in N. Cott and E. Pleck, eds., *A Heritage of Her Own*. New York: Simon & Schuster.

Smith, Peter, and Paul Cheung. 1981. "Social Origins and Sex Differential Schooling in the Philippines." *Comparative Education Review* 29:1.

Snow, Robert T. 1980. "The New International Division of Labor and the U.S. Workforce: The Case of the Electronics Industry." Honolulu: Culture Learning Institute, East-West Center. Mimeographed.

Socknat, J., and C. Sinclair. 1978. "Migration for Employment Abroad and Its Impacts on Development in the Yemen Arab Republic." July 1978.

Speiser, Felix. 1923. *Ethnographische Materialen aus den Neuen Hebriden und den Banks Inselin*. Berlin.

Spindel, Cheywa. 1980. "Capital Oligopolico e producao rural de base familiar papel socioeconomico de mulher." Research paper, Rural Employment Policies Branch, ILO, Geneva.

Spruill, Julia. 1938. *Women's Life and Work in the Southern Colonies*. Chapel Hill: University of North Carolina Press.

Stair, J. B. 1897. *Old Samoa; or, Flotsam and Jetsam from the Pacific Ocean*. London: Religious Tract Society.

Starobin, Robert S. 1970. *Industrial Slavery in the Old South*. New York: Oxford University Press.

Stoler, Ann. 1977. "Class Structure and Female Autonomy in Rural Java." *Signs: Journal of Women in Culture and Society* 3:74–89.

Stone, Lawrence. 1977. *The Family, Sex and Marriage in England 1500–1800*. New York: Harper & Row.

Stowe, Charles Edward. 1889. *Life of Harriet Beecher Stowe*. Boston & New York: Houghton Mifflin; Cambridge: Riverside Press.

Straffa, P. 1972. *Production of Commodities by Means of Commodities*. Cambridge: Cambridge University Press.

Straits Times (Singapore). 25 Sept. 1980; 26 Sept. 1980; 21 Oct. 1980; 3 Nov. 1980.

Strehlow, Theodor G. H. 1971. *Love Songs of Central Australia.* Sydney: Angus & Robertson.

Strumingher, Laura S. 1979. *Women and the Making of the Working Class: Lyon, 1830–1870.* Montreal: Eden Press Women's Publications.

Sudarkasa, Niara. 1976. "Female Employment and Family Organization in West Africa." In Dorothy G. McGuigan, ed., *New Research on Women and Sex Roles.* Ann Arbor: University of Michigan Center for Continuing Education of Women.

Sunday News (Dar es Salaam)

Sunday Times (Singapore). 4 May 1980.

Sutherland, Elizabeth. 1969. *The Youngest Revolution: A Personal Report on Cuba.* New York: Dial Press.

Sutton, Constance, and Susan Makiesky-Barrow. 1977. "Social Inequality and Sexual Status in Barbados." In Alice Schlegel, ed., *Sexual Stratification: A Cross-Cultural View.* New York: Columbia University Press.

Sutton, Constance. 1976. "The Power to Define: Women, Culture, and Consciousness." In R. S. Bryce-Laporte and C. R. Thomas, eds., *Alienation in Contemporary Society.* New York: Praeger.

———. In press. "Female Hierarchies in Yoruba Kingdoms." In Christine Gailey and Mona Etienne, eds., *Women and State Formation in Pre-industrial Societies.* New York: J. F. Bergin.

Swee-Hock, Saw, and A. K. Wong. 1981. *Adolescents in Singapore: Sexuality, Courtship and Family Values.* Singapore: Singapore University Press.

Sweet, L. 1974. "In Reality, the Middle Eastern Woman." In C. J. Mathiasson, ed., *Many Sisters: Women in Cross-Cultural Perspectives.* New York: Free Press.

Szalai, Alexander, ed. 1972. *The Use of Time: Daily Activities of Urban and Suburban Populations in Twelve Countries.* Paris: Mouton.

Szymanski, Al. 1976. "The Socialization of Women's Oppression: A Marxist Theory of the Changing Position of Women in Advanced Capitalist Society." *Insurgent Sociologist* 6:31–58.

Takahashi, Akira. 1977. "Rural Labor and Agrarian Changes in the Philippines." In S. Hirashima, ed., *Hired Labor in Rural Asia.* Tokyo: Institute of Developing Economies.

Tejada, Ed. 1978. "Socioeconomic Study of Landless Rural Workers in Sugar Cane Plantations in Negros Occidental." Proceedings of the Workshop on Landless Rural Workers, Laguna, Philippines.

Terray, Emmanuel. 1972. *Marxism and Primitive Societies.* New York: Monthly Review Press.

Thaubault, Roger. 1971. *Education and Change in a Village Community: Mazieres-en-Gatine 1848–1914.* New York: Schocken.

Thompson, E. P. 1966. *The Making of the English Working Class.* New York: Vintage.

Tilly, Charles. 1978. *From Mobilization to Revolution.* Reading, Mass.: Addison-Wesley.

———. 1979. "Did the Cake of Custom Break?" In John M. Merriman, ed., *Consciousness and Class Experience in Nineteenth-Century Europe.* New York: Holmes & Meier.

Tilly, Louise, A. 1977. "Production and Reproduction: Economic Links of Work and Family in Early Industrialization." Paper presented at the Conference on Social History and Social Theory, Institute on Western Europe, Columbia University.

———. 1979. "The Family Wage Economy of a French Textile City, Roubaix, 1872–1906." *Journal of Family history* 4:381–94.

———. 1980. "Linen Was Their Life: Family Survival Strategies and Parent–Child Relations in a French Handloom Weaving Village." Paper prepared for Round Table II: History and Anthropology. Sponsored by the Max Planck Institute für Geschichte, Göttingen, and the Maison des Sciences de l'Homme, Paris.

———. 1981. "Paths to Proletarianization: Organization of Production, Sexual Division of Labor, and Women's Collective Action." *Signs: Journal of Women in Culture and Society* 7:400–18.

Tilly, Louise A., and Joan W. Scott. 1978. *Women, Work and Family.* New York: Holt, Rinehart & Winston.

Tinker, I. 1976. "The Adverse Impact of Development on Women." In I. Tinker, M. B. Bransen, and M. Buvinic, eds., *Women and World Development*. New York: Praeger.

Tinker, Irene, and Michele Bo Bramsen, eds. 1976. *Women and World Development*. Washington, D.C.: Overseas Development Council.

Todaro, Michael. 1977. *Economics for a Developing World*. London: Longman.

Tomiche, N. 1968. "Le hierarchie sociale en Egypt à l'èpoque de Mehemet Ali." In *Political and Social Change in Modern Egypt*, P. M. Holt, ed. London.

Trajtenberg, Raul, and Jean-Paul Sajhau. 1976. "Las empresas transnacionales y el bajo costa de la fuerza de trabajo en los paises subdesarrollados." Working Paper, no. 15, World Employment Programme, ILO, Geneva.

UNDP. See United Nations Development Program.

United Nations Development Program. 1980. "Rural Women's Participation in Development." UNDP Evaluation Study, no. 3. Geneva: United Nations.

United Nations Division for Economic and Social Information, Department of Public Information. 1980. "48 Resolutions Adopted by World Conference of the United Nations Decade for Women (Vienna)." Note, no. 28, *International Women's Decade*.

———. 1980. "Worsening Situation of Women Will Be Main Issue Confronting Commission on the Status of Women." Note, no. 22, *International Women's Decade*.

———. 1981. *Women 1980*. Newsletter, no. 5:4–5.

United Nations Industrial Development Office. 1980. "Women in the Redeployment of Manufacturing Industry to Developing Countries." UNIDO Working Paper No. 3.

U.S. Department of Labor. 1975a. *Handbook on Women Workers*. Women's Bureau Bulletin, no. 197. Washington, D.C.: Government Printing Office.

———. Bureau of Labor Statistics. 1975b. *A Socio-Economic Profile of Puerto Rican New Yorkers*. New York: USDL, Middle Atlantic Regional Office.

Utrecht, Ernst. 1978. "Corporate Agriculture versus Subsistence Agriculture in the Southern Philippines." Paper presented at the Seminar on Underdevelopment and Subsistence in Southeast Asia, University of Bielefeld.

Van Vallen, Judith. 1972. "Sitting on a Man: Colonialism and the Lost Political Institutions if Igbo Women." *Canadian Journal of African Studies* 6:165–82.

van Bath, Slicher. 1963. *The Agrarian History of Western Europe 500–1800*, tr. Olive Ordish. New York: St. Martin's Press.

Vanoli, Dominique. 1976. "Les Ouvrières enfermées: Les Couvents soyeux." *Révoltes Logiques*, vol. 2.

Wallerstein, Immanuel. 1976. "Three Stages of African Involvement in the World Economy." In Peter C. W. Gutkind and Immanuel Wallerstein, eds., *The Political Economy of Contemporary Africa*. Beverly Hills, Calif.: Sage.

Wang, Bee-Lan Chan. 1980. "Chinese Women: The Relative Influences of Ideological Revolution, Economic Growth, and Cultural Change." In Beverly Lindsay, ed., *Comparative Perspectives of Third World Women*. New York: Praeger.

Ware, Caroline. 1936. *The Early New England Cotton Manufacturers: A Study in Industrial Beginnings*. Boston: Houghton Mifflin.

Washington, D.C., Council on Hemispheric Affairs. 1983. "U.S. Labor Challenges CBI Trade Incentives." *Washington Report on the Hemisphere*, vol. 3, no. 9.

Weiner, Annette. 1976. *Women of Value, Men of Renown: New Perspectives in Trobriand Exchange*. Austin: University of Texas Press.

———. 1980. "Stability in Banana Leaves: Colonialism, Economics, and Trobriand Women." In Mona Etienne and Eleanor Leacock, eds., *Women and Colonization*. New York: Praeger.

———. 1980. "Reproduction: A Replacement for Reciprocity." *American Ethnologist* 7:71–85.

———. 1983b. "Sexuality among the Anthropologists, Reproduction among the Informants." *Social Analysis* 12.

———. 1983a. "A World of Made Is not a World of Born—Doing Kula in Kiriwina." In E. R.

Leach and J. W. Leach, eds., *New Perspectives on the Kula*. Cambridge: Cambridge University Press.

Weston, Sharon W. 1972. *Samoan Social Organization: Structural Implications of an Ambilineal Descent System*. Ph.D. diss., University of California, Los Angeles.

Wiessner, Polly. 1982. "Risk, Reciprocity, and Social Influences on Kung San Economics." In Eleanor Leacock and Richard Lee, eds., *Politics and History in Band Society*. Cambridge: Cambridge University Press.

Williams, Eric. 1944. *Capitalism and Slavery*. Chapel Hill: University of North Carolina Press.

Women of China (Peking). 1 Aug. 1961; 1 Aug. 1965; 1 Oct. 1965. *Zhonogguo Funu.*

Wong, Aline K. 1975. *Women in Modern Singapore*. Singapore: University Education Press.

———. 1979. "Women's Status and Changing Family Values." In Kua & Wong, eds., *The Contemporary Family in Singapore*. Singapore: Singapore University Press.

———. 1980. "Working Mothers and the Care of Preschool Children in Singapore—A Research Report." Singapore: Singapore Girl Guides Association.

Wong, John. 1979. *Asian Economies in Perspective: A Comparative Study of Indonesia, Malaysia, the Philippines, Singapore and Thailand*. London: Macmillan.

Wool, Harold. 1976. "Future Labor Supply for Lower Level Occupations. *Monthly Labor Review* 99.

World Bank. *World Development Report, 1979*. Washington, D.C.: World Bank.

———. 1980. *Aspects of Poverty in the Philippines: A Review and Assessment*. Washington, D.C.: World Bank.

Wynn, Margaret. 1967. "Time, Work-Discipline, and Industrial Capitalism." *Past and Present* 38:56–97.

———. 1972. *Family Policy: A Study of the Economic Cost of Rearing Children and Their Social and Political Consequences*. Middlesex, England: Penguin.

Yans-McLaughlin, Virginia. 1977. "Italian Women and Work." In M. Cantor and B. Laurie, eds., *Class, Sex and the Woman Worker*. Westport, Conn.: Greenwood Press.

Yetman, Norman R. 1970. *Life Under the 'Peculiar Institution.'* New York: Holt, Rinehart & Winston.

Yoshihara, Kunio. 1976. *Foreign Investment and Domestic Response*. Singapore: Eastern Universities Press.

Young, Kate. In press. "Sex Specificity in Migration: A Case Study from Mexico." In Lourdes Benería, ed., *Women and Development: The Sexual Division of Labor in Rural Economies*. Geneva: International Labor Organization.

Youssef, N., et al. 1979. "Women in Migration: A Third World Focus." Int. Ctr. for Research on Women (ICRW). Submitted to USAID/WID, June 1979.

Zylberberg-Hocquard, Marie-Hélène. 1978. "Les Ouvrières d'état (tabacs-allumettes) dans les dernières années du XIXe siécle." *Le Mouvement Social* 105:87–107.

Index

Index

Aborigines. *See* Kaititj

Afonja, Simi, 6, 122–34

Africa, economics of polygamy, 142

Africa, women as food providers, 142, 143

Afro-American women: access to employment, 3, 52; double responsibility, 54; freed, 52; networks, reciprocity, fictive kinship, 4; unfeminine, 43, 148; wage differentials, 55

Agriculture: cash crop, 129, 131–32; China, 230; double responsibility, 251; Egypt, 171; gender discrimination, 245; Latin America, 176; Mexico, 174–93; Philippines, 197, 198; plow cultivation, 146, 147; share croppers, 52–3; share tenants, 197, 198; slave labor, 45, 47, 48, 52; socialist, 225; Soviet Union, 226, 227; subsistence 2, 111, 127–28, 131, 152; Tanzania, 238, 239. *See also* Informal sector occupations

Agroindustry: chemical hazards, 199; colonial expansion of, 147–50; Mamasani, 119; Mexico, 174–93; patriarchy, 192. *See also* Subminimal wages and conditions

Aguascalientes, 190

About the Authors

Simi Afonja, reader in the Department of Sociology/Anthropology at the University of Ife, Ile-Ife, Nigeria, has conducted a study financed by the Ford Foundation on the impact of precolonial, colonial, and post-colonial institutions on sex roles and inequality among the Yoruba. Her publications include "Barriers to Female Supply and Demand in the Nigerian Labor Force," in *Nigerian Women and Development,* and "Women, Power and Authority in Traditional Yoruba Society," in *Visibility and Power: Essays on Women in Society and Development.*

Josefina Aranda, with a degree from the Escuela Nacional de Antropologia, Mexico City, has conducted research on the organization of women workers in Mexico City and on market systems in peasant areas of Mexico.

Lourdes Arizpe, professor at El Colegio de Mexico, Mexico City, has done research on peasant social organization, Mexican Indian cultures, women in rural communities and in the urban informal sector, and women migrants. She is currently on leave from El Colegio as Acting Director of the Museo de Arte Popular in Mexico City.

Diane Bell, Research Fellow in the Research School of Social Science, Australian National University, has had extensive field work experience in Northern Australia. She has acted as consultant to the Aboriginal Land Commission, the Australian Law Reform Commission, Aboriginal Land Councils, and Legal Aid Societies. Her publications include *Daughters of the Dreaming* (1983) on the ritual life of Aboriginal women of Warrabri, and *Law: the Old and The New* (1980) on women's role in the maintenance of customary law.

Lourdes Benería teaches economics at Rutgers University. She has edited the book, *Women and Development: The Sexual Division of Labour in Rural Societies* (Praeger, 1982) and published articles on the subject of labor markets, women and development. She is currently finishing, with Martha Roldan, a study on home work and subcontracting in Mexico City to be published by the University of Chicago under the title *The Crossroads of Class and Gender.*

Elisabeth J. Croll is a sociologist and a Fellow of Wolfson College; she is a Member of the Faculty of Social Studies at Oxford University. She has spent over a decade studying China, where she has visited many times. Her books include *Feminism and Socialism in China; Women in Rural Development; The Case of the People's Republic of China; The Politics of Marriage in Contemporary China; The Family Rice Bowl: Food and the Domestic Economy in China;* and *Chinese Women since Mao.* She is now engaged in a study of children's welfare in China funded by UNICEF.

Elizabeth U. Eviota is from the Philippines. She received her M.A. from the New School for Social Research in New York City and her Ph.D. in Sociology from Rutgers. She is now continuing research on gender relations, the sexual division of labor, and social and economic development in the Philippines.

Mona Hammam is from Egypt and received her Ph.D. from the University of Kansas. She has taught sociology at the University of Kansas and at the American University, and is now working as a consultant for the Food and Agriculture Organization of the United Nations in Rome. She has published a number of articles on Egyptian and other Arab women and development.

María Patricia Fernańdez Kelly, now in the Program in United States–Mexican Studies, University of California, San Diego, has conducted extensive research on working women in Cuidad Juarez's multinational assembly plants. Her published works include *For We are Sold: I and My People* (1983), and, with June Nash, *Women, Men and the International Division of Labor* (1983).

Eleanor Leacock is professor in the Department of Anthropology at the City College, CUNY, in New York City. In addition to her cross-cultural research on women, she has conducted field work in Samoa, on Canadian Indians, and has studied elementary schooling in New York City and Zambia. Her publications on women include *Women and Colonization* (coedited with Mona Etienne), *Myths of Male Dominance: Collected Articles on Women Cross-Culturally,* and introductions to Engels's *The Origin of the Family, Private Property, and the State* and Morgan's *Ancient Society.*

Wanda Minge has conducted field work on the family in England and Switzerland. Formerly a lecturer on Anthropology at Harvard University, she is now working in Washington D.C. as a congressional consultant. Her published works include "Household Economy During the Peasant-to-Worker Transition in the Swiss Alps," (*Ethnology* 17:1978) and "Does Labor Time Decrease with Industrialization? A Survey of Time-Allocation Studies" (*Current Anthropology* 21:1980).

Leith Mullings is Associate Professor of Anthropology at the Sophie Davis School of Bio-Medical Education, the City College, and at the Graduate School and University Center, CUNY. She has published articles on ethnicity, stratification, and gender, in addition to *Therapy, Ideology and Social Change: Mental Healing in Urban Ghana* (1984); she is the Editor of *The Anthropology of Urban America* (in press). She is a founding member of the Harlem branch of *Women for Racial and Economic Equality* (WREE).

Helen I. Safa is the author of *The Urban Poor of Puerto Rico* and the editor of *Migration and Development, Sex and Class in Latin America, Toward a Political Economy of Urbanization in Third World Countries,* and other books. Her articles and reviews on migration, urbanization, and women and development have appeared in a variety of scholarly journals and periodicals. She participated in both the 1980 NGO Mid-Decade Conference on Women in Copenhagen and the 1985 NGO Conference in Nairobi ending the decade. She is currently Professor of Anthropology at the University of Florida and was Director of the Center for Latin American Studies from 1980 to 1985. She is Past President of the Latin American Studies Association and Chair of the Advisory Committee for the American Republics, Council for International Exchange of Scholars (Fulbright).

Gita Sen currently divides her time between the Department of Economics at the New School for Social Research in New York City and the Center for Development Studies in Trivandrum, India. She has worked on the interaction of class and gender both in India and in working class families in the United States and has published in the *Review of Radical Political Economics* and other journals.

Soheila Shashahani received her Ph.D. in anthropology in 1981 from the New School for Social Research in New York, and taught for a year at the University of Tehran. She now lives mostly in France where she is collaborator on *Abstracts Iranica* since its first issue in 1978. She is also associated with a research group called l'Iran Contemporain, the International Women's Anthropology Conference IWAC, and is a core member of the IUAES Commission on Women. Her research has focussed on tribal women and development and she has written extensively on this in both Persian and English, including her forthcoming book *The Four Seasons of the Sun*. Currently, she is working on understanding the indigenous and philosophic basis of anthropology in Iran.

Louise A. Tilly is Professor of History and Sociology in the Graduate Faculty, New School for Social Research, and Chair of its Committee on Historical Studies. Her current research includes a comparative historical study of the state, class, and family in French cities; she is completing a monograph on labor force and working class in late nineteenth century Milan. She is co-author of *The Rebellious Century: 1830–1930* and *Women, Work and Family*.

Annette B. Weiner, David B. Kriser Professor of Anthropology and Chair of the Anthropology Department, New York University, has done extensive field research in the Trobriand Islands, Papua New Guinea. She also has conducted field work in Western Samoa. She is the author of *Women of Value, Men of Renown: New Perspectives in Trobriand Exchange*. Her present research is on the relation between gender roles, material culture, and systems of exchange in Oceania.

Aline K. Wong is an Associate Professor of Sociology at the National University of Singapore. She obtained her Ph.D. in sociology from the University of California, Berkeley, in 1970. She has published extensively in the areas of family sociology, population, women, and development. Among her major publications are: *Women in Modern Singapore* (Singapore: University Education Press, 1975); *The Contemporary Family in Singapore,* co-edited with Eddie C.Y. Kuo (Singapore: Singapore University Press, 1979); *Youths in Singapore: Sexuality, Courtship and Family Values,* co-authored with Saw Swee Hock (Singapore: Singapore University Press, 1981); and *Ethnicity and Fertility in Southeast Asia,* co-authored with Ng Shui Meng (Singapore: Institute of Southeast Asian Studies, 5 vol., forthcoming, 1986).

Other Books of Interest from *Bergin & Garvey*

Women & Change in Latin America
New Directions in Sex and Class
JUNE NASH, HELEN I. SAFA, & CONTRIBUTORS
"When women's issues are made paramount then we must question development goals that emphasize production for profit rather than concern for quality of life."

— FROM THE INTRODUCTION

384 Pages   Illustrations

In Her Prime
A New View of Middle-Aged Women
JUDITH BROWN, VIRGINIA KERNS, & CONTRIBUTORS
"These ethnographies are fascinating, heartening, and provocative."
— WOMEN'S REVIEW OF BOOKS

240 Pages   Illustration

Nicaragua — *The People Speak*
ALVIN LEVIE
Introduction by Richard Streb
"Outstanding . . . For everyone questioning Nicaraguan self-determination."

— ED ASNER, ACTOR

224 Pages   Illustrations

The Politics of Education
Culture, Power & Liberation
PAULO FREIRE
"Here speaks a teacher who lives life, a revolutionary with hope."
— CHANGE

240 Pages   Illustrations

Applied Anthropology
An Introduction
JOHN VAN WILLIGEN
320 Pages   Illustrations

The Nicaraguan Revolution in Health
From Somoza to the Sandinistas
JOHN DONAHUE
188 Pages   Illustrations

Women & Nutrition in Third World Countries
SAHNI HAMILTON & CONTRIBUTORS
160 Pages

Now in Paper!
Transnationals & the Third World
The Struggle for Culture
ARMAND MATTELART
192 Pages